HARBRACE COLLEGE HANDBOOK   6TH EDITION

JOHN C. HODGES
The University of Tennessee

and MARY E. WHITTEN
North Texas State University

6th

edition

HARBRACE
COLLEGE
HANDBOOK

HARCOURT, BRACE & WORLD, INC.

New York / Chicago / San Francisco / Atlanta

To the Instructor

The *Harbrace College Handbook* is both a guide for the individual writer and a text for use in class. It presents its subject matter in a readily usable form and thus lightens the instructor's task of reading student papers. Although the rhetoric sections of the Sixth Edition have been strengthened, other sections have been carefully shortened to keep the book compact and convenient to use.

Numbers. The book contains only thirty-five major sections, or numbers, referring to the principles of effective writing. These include (as has been shown by a comprehensive examination of student writing) everything to which instructors normally refer in marking papers. But the principles less frequently needed have not been overlooked. They are subordinated logically to the thirty-five primary numbers and may be found readily by reference to the back endpapers or to the detailed index. If an instructor wishes to have any of these subordinate principles conveniently before his students, he can have them added in the blanks provided on the chart inside the front cover. Some college students may need Sections 1-18 only for review or for occasional reference.

Symbols. Instead of the simplified list of numbers, the instructor may, if he prefers, use the corresponding symbols. Most of these symbols are well known to English teachers; they are entered on both front and back charts.

General Plan. The sections on **Sentence Sense (1)** and **Grammatical Terms (35)** are general sections. The former may be used, whenever needed, as an introduction to the other sections; the latter should be used throughout as a glossary of terms. For corrections of specific errors, students will normally be referred to Sections **2-34**. Some instructors may wish to begin with Section **32**, **Planning and Writing the Whole Composition**. Others may prefer beginning with Section **31**, **The Paragraph**, or with Sections **19-30**. Emphasis from the start on good subject matter, clarity of organization, and effective style will help the student keep in mind the primary objectives of his writing.

Sentence Patterns. The Sixth Edition makes extensive use of sentence patterns, which many students find more helpful than diagrams. For those who prefer diagrams, a brief explanation is given in Section **35**, **Grammatical Terms**.

Drill Materials. Exercises are provided both for the major sections and for many of the subsections. Many of these exercises consist of lively paragraphs instead of conventional lists of unrelated sentences. Many of the exercises are of a positive type, in which the student is asked not to correct errors but to give reasons why sentences are correct, to drill orally so that correct forms will sound right, or to compose good sentences to illustrate the principle being studied. Some classes may need very little of the drill materials; others may need all of them, or even additional exercises such as those in the *Harbrace College Workbook*, Form 6A (keyed to the *Harbrace College Handbook*, Sixth Edition).

Recent Language Studies. Any English handbook such as this owes a great debt to all scholars, past and present, who have increased our understanding of the language. The authors of this handbook have endeavored to make full use of those linguistic principles—both new and old—

that have definite practical value in college composition courses. These selected principles have been thoroughly tested in freshman English classes.

Acknowledgments. Among the many individuals who have generously offered suggestions for making this handbook more usable are Professors Ben H. Adelson (Los Angeles Pierce College), Donald L. Cross (Upsala College), David F. Finnigan (Oregon State University), George D. Hendricks (North Texas State University), John McKiernan (College of St. Thomas), John W. Morris (Wisconsin State University), and Bain Tate Stewart and others on the Freshman Staff (University of Tennessee). For important contributions to Section **33, Library Paper,** the authors are grateful to Miss Eleanor Goehring, of the Library Staff (University of Tennessee), and to Miss Barbara J. Reid (University of Tennessee). To Professor Roy F. Montgomery (Spring Hill College) is due continuing appreciation for his help with the exercises.

Sections **19-32** still owe a great deal to the genius of the late Francis X. Connolly, whose untimely death is a great loss to the teaching profession.

The authors are especially indebted to Miss Audrey Ann Welch of Denton, Texas, who assisted in revising the manuscript and who wrote new exercise materials.

To the Student

Contemporary Usage; Authority.   This Sixth Edition of the *Harbrace College Handbook* attempts to describe the usual practice of good contemporary writers and to state that practice as simply as possible. The "rules" in boldface are to be interpreted as descriptions derived from usage, and they have authority only to the extent that they describe usage. In your reading you should observe the practice of good writers so that you may eventually gain the confidence that comes from first-hand knowledge of what good writing is.

Numbers or Symbols.   A number or a symbol written in the margin of your paper indicates a need for correction or improvement and calls for revision. If a number is used, turn directly to the corresponding number at the top of the page in the handbook. If a symbol is used, first consult the alphabetical list of symbols inside the front cover to find the number to which you should turn.

Ordinary References.   The ordinary reference will be to the number or symbol (**2** or **frag, 9** or **cap, 18** or **sp, 28** or **ref**) standing at the head of one of the thirty-five sections of the handbook. The statement in large boldface at the beginning of each section covers the section as a whole. One of the statements in smaller boldface within the section will usually be needed to solve your problem. Study the section to which you have been referred—the whole of the section if necessary—and master the specific part of the section that explains your difficulty.

Specific References.   Whenever your instructor wishes to refer you to a specific part of a section, he will add the appropriate letter to the number or symbol.

EXAMPLES   **2c** (OR **frag-c**), **9a** (OR **cap-a**), **18b** (OR **sp-b**), **28d** (OR **ref-d**). A still more specific reference might be **9a(4)** or **cap-a(4)**.

General References.   At times your instructor may give you a very general reference from which you are to determine and correct your error. For example, the symbol **gr** will refer you to the whole division on GRAMMAR, including Sections 1–7; the symbol **m** to the division on MECHANICS, including Sections 8–11; the symbol **p** to the division on PUNCTUATION, Sections 12–17; and so forth. An obvious error may be called to your attention by the symbol **x**, and general awkwardness by the symbol **k**.

Additional Help.   Some of the principles treated in English handbooks can be mastered only by students who understand the fundamentals of the sentence. A well-developed "sentence sense" is especially helpful in the mastery of Sections 2 (**Sentence Fragment**), 3 (**Comma Splice**), 5 (**Case**), 6 (**Agreement**), 12 (**The Comma**), 14 (**The Semicolon**), 21 (**Wordiness**), 23 (**Unity**), 24 (**Subordination**), 25 (**Coherence**), 26 (**Parallelism**), and 30 (**Variety**). If you have difficulty in understanding these sections, you should first master the fundamentals of the sentence treated in Section 1 (**Sentence Sense**) and then turn again to the principle immediately involved. If you fail to understand any grammatical term used in the handbook, consult the alphabetical list in Section 35 (**Grammatical Terms**).

Correction and Revision.   After you have mastered the principle underlying the correction of each error called to your attention, you should make careful revision of your paper in the manner recommended by your instructor. One method of revision is explained and illustrated in

Section 8 (**Manuscript Form and Revision**), pages 87–90. To prove that you have found the specific principle needed for the revision, your instructor may ask you to write the appropriate letter (**a, b, c,** etc.) after the number or symbol he has supplied. An **x** written by the instructor after a number or symbol calls for the writing out of the appropriate exercise.

Contents

GRAMMAR

6 Agreement   54

7 Tense and Mood   66

MECHANICS

PUNCTUATION

13 Superfluous Commas 129

DICTION

LARGER ELEMENTS

GRAMMAR

Sentence Sense

1

Master the essentials of the sentence as an aid to clear thinking and effective writing.

Acquiring sentence sense means developing the ability to recognize what *makes* a sentence. An understanding of the grammar of English sentences is prerequisite to good writing.

As you study grammar, you should always be aware of the fact that English is a living, changing language. It has been evolving for some fifteen centuries. What we now call Old English prevailed in England from about 450 A.D. to about 1100 A.D. This Old English, derived from West Germanic, contained many inflections.

OLD ENGLISH

Sē þe wǣs ǣrur rīce cyng and maniges landes
He that was before powerful king and of many lands

hlāford, hē næfde þā ealles landes būton seofon fōt mǣl.
lord, he had not then of all land but seven foot space.

—FROM THE *Anglo-Saxon Chronicle*

Middle English dates from about the twelfth century to the end of the fifteenth century.

MIDDLE ENGLISH

Thenne within two yeres king Uther felle seke of a grete maladye. And in the meane whyle hys enemyes usurpped upon hym, and dyd a grete bataylle upon his men, and slewe many of his peple. —FROM MALORY'S *Morte d'Arthur*

The English in use from 1500 to the present is called Modern English. As it has emerged, nearly all the old inflections have been lost, and the order of words in the sentence has become more fixed. See also **19a (4)**.

A study of Sections **1** through **7** of this textbook should help you understand how words are related to one another, why their forms change, and what order they take in sentence patterns of Modern English.

1a
Learn to recognize verbs.

Words such as *drank, organizes, falsify,* and *reoccurred* function as verbs. The verb is the heart of the sentence; without a verb no group of words is grammatically a sentence. You can recognize a verb by (1) its form and (2) its meaning.

Form   When converted from the present to the past tense, nearly all verbs change form (*eat-ate*). In the present tense, all verbs change form to indicate a singular subject in the third person (I *eat*-he *eats*); all verbs in the progressive tense end in *-ing* (*is eating*).

PRESENT	I *play.* It *plays.*	We *eat* early. He *eats* early.
PAST	Leonard *played* well.	All of them *ate* here today.
PROGRESSIVE	He *is playing.*	They *were eating* breakfast.

Meaning   Often defined as a predicator or as a word expressing action or a state of being, a verb is used to make a statement, to ask a question, or to give a command or direction.

Charles *slept* well.	*Leave* the computer alone!
Was it necessary?	*Turn* left at Akard Street.

Verb phrases   A verb consisting of more than one word is often referred to as a verb phrase (or cluster). A verb phrase comprises the verb together with the auxiliary words.

will endanger, may be studying, ought to rest

Words commonly used as auxiliaries are *has, have, had, am, is, are, was, were, be, been, do, does, did, used to, may, might, must, have to, has to, had to, shall, will, am (is, are, etc.) going to, am (is, are, etc.) about to, would, should, ought to, can,* and *could.*

The words that make up a verb phrase are often separated.

A gentleman *may,* of course, *become* angry at times.
He *does* not often *show* his anger.

Note: A verb may be combined with the adverb *not* or with a contraction of *not.*

He *can*not *leave* now.   *Doesn't* it *matter?*

▶ **EXERCISE 1**   Write sentences using the first five words below as verbs. Then write sentences using the second five words in verb phrases.

1. up   3. long   5. yellow   7. record   9. question
2. tree   4. bone   6. down   8. signal   10. experiment

▶ **EXERCISE 2**   Underline the fifteen verbs and seven verb phrases in the following sentences.

¹ Jim angrily called himself a fool, as he had been doing all the way through the woods.   ² Why had he listened to Fred's mad idea?   ³ What were ghosts and family legends to him, in this year of grace and nuclear fission?   ⁴ He had mysteries enough of his own, of a highly complex electronic sort, which would occupy him through the rest of a lifetime.   ⁵ But now he was plodding along here, like the Mississippi schoolboy that he had been a dozen years before; this ghost chase in the middle of the night was

preposterous. ⁶ It was an outrage to all that he represented; it was lunacy. ⁷ It was—he swallowed the truth like
a bitter pill—frightful! ⁸ The legend and the ghost had
been a horror to him as a child; and they were a horror
still. ⁹ As he stood at the edge of the weed-choked, briar-
tangled slope, on the top of which the decayed mansion
waited evilly, he felt almost sick. ¹⁰ The safe, sure things
of every day had become distant, childish fantasies.
¹¹ This grotesque night and whatever, ghoulish and mon-
strous, inhabited it were clammily and horribly real.

1b

Learn to recognize subjects and objects of verbs.

Nearly every grammatically complete sentence has a
verb and a subject; the only exception is the command,
or imperative, which omits the subject, often considered as
implied. In the following sentences the subjects are in
boldface and the verbs are in *italics*.

The **ambassador** *arrived* shortly before noon.
There *will be* a formal **reception** tonight.
Fasten your safety belt. [Imperative]

The subject of a sentence that asks a question (an interrogative sentence) is more readily located when the
sentence is recast in the form of a statement.

Has the **last** of the deserters *surrendered?*
The **last** of the deserters *has surrendered.*

The *complete subject* is the subject and words associated
with it; the *complete predicate* is the verb and words associated with it.

Complete subject	*Complete predicate*
The stewardess on Flight 118	often smiled during the storm.

Many sentences require objects of the verb to complete

their meaning. In the following sentences the objects are in SMALL CAPITALS.

> **Frank** *has met* HELEN.
> I *laid* the PLIERS on that shelf.
> One **man** in the crowd *raised* his VOICE in protest.

One test for an object is that it can be made the subject of a passive verb: "Helen was met by Frank."

You can learn to recognize subjects and objects by observing (1) their form, (2) their meaning, and (3) their position.

Form   Nouns and noun substitutes (sometimes called *substantives* or *nominals*) are used as subjects and objects of verbs. The most frequently used subject or object of the verb is the noun or pronoun.

Forms of pronouns (*I, you, he,* etc.) are easy to recognize; see the list on page 47. Most nouns (words used to name persons, places, things, ideas, or actions) change their form to indicate number (*movement, movements; city, cities; woman, women*) and the possessive case (*John's* car, the *boys'* dogs, the *men's* job). Such suffixes as *-ance, -ation, -ence, -ment, -ness,* and *-ship* frequently indicate that a word is a noun: *appearance, atonement, boldness, determination, hardship, reference.* The articles *a, an,* and *the* are sometimes called "noun indicators" or "noun determiners" because they regularly point to a following noun: "a *chair*," "an *activity*," "the last *race*."

Meaning   In order to find the subject, simply ask, in connection with the verb, "Who or what?"

> The **actor,** after a long flight from South America, happily *greets* the REPORTERS at the Miami airport. [*Who* or *what* greets? The *actor* greets.][1]

Ordinarily an object receives, or is in some way affected

---

[1]It is sometimes helpful to make a diagram, or to form a mental picture, of the subject and its verb; see **Diagraming,** Section 35.

by, the action of the verb. To find the object, ask, in connection with the subject and verb, "Whom or what?" For example, in the sentence about the actor, "The actor greets *whom?*" *Reporters,* the answer, is the direct object.

Some verbs (such as *give, offer, bring, take, lend, send, buy,* and *sell*) may have both an indirect object and a direct object. To find the indirect object, ask, *"To whom* or *for whom* is something done?"

> **Dad** *gave* HARRY a BOAT. [Dad gave a boat (direct object) *to whom?* Harry is the indirect object.]

Position　A third way to recognize subjects and objects is to become thoroughly aware of the meaningfulness of English word order, normally SUBJECT—VERB—OBJECT. As you study carefully the following commonly used sentence patterns, observe the importance of word order (especially in Pattern 2) in determining meaning.

1. **SUBJECT—VERB.**

   Coyotes howl in the distance.
   Diseases of the blood *are* often *caused* by bacteria.

2. **SUBJECT—VERB—OBJECT.**

   Elephants frighten mice.
   Mice frighten elephants.
   Sparrows in our yard *eat* all the *seed* in the feeder.

3. **SUBJECT—VERB—INDIRECT OBJECT—DIRECT OBJECT.**

   Mary baked Fred a *cake.*
   Candidates often rashly *promise voters* lower *taxes.*

4. **There[2]—VERB—SUBJECT.**

   There have been no *objections.*
   There are nearly forty national *parks* in America.

---

[2]*There* used as an introductory word or filler is an expletive, which is never the subject.

For patterns with subject complements, see **4b.**

The preceding patterns are patterns of statements, or declarative sentences. Notice the changes that take place when these patterns are transformed into questions:

5. **AUXILIARY—SUBJECT—VERB?**

   Do coyotes howl in the distance?
   Are diseases of the blood *caused* by bacteria?

6. **AUXILIARY—SUBJECT—VERB—OBJECT?**

   Have mice ever *frightened elephants?*
   Would sparrows eat all the *seed* in the feeder?

7. **AUXILIARY—SUBJECT—VERB—INDIRECT OBJECT— DIRECT OBJECT?**

   Will Mary bake Fred a *cake?*
   Had the *candidates promised voters* lower *taxes?*

8. **OBJECT—AUXILIARY—SUBJECT—VERB?**

   What did the *mice frighten?*
   Which *seeds* in the feeder *will* the *sparrows eat?*

9. **VERB—there—SUBJECT?**

   Were there any *objections?*
   Are there forty national *parks* in America?

10. **AUXILIARY—there—VERB—SUBJECT?**

    Has there been any *objection?*
    Should there be only forty national *parks* in America?

The common patterns of commands, or imperative sentences, are derived from the first three patterns of statements. Notice, however, that the imperative sentences in the examples below have no expressed subjects.

Sell now.   Sell the car now.   Sell him the car now.

Many exclamatory sentences are also derived from patterns of statements:

There have been a hundred objections!
Mary baked Fred a cake!

Such sentences as the following, however, usually take an exclamation point because the word order is not that of an ordinary statement, question, or command:

How many objections there were!
What a cake Mary baked Fred!

Depending upon the writer's intention, a sentence pattern such as the following may be a statement, a question, or an exclamation:

Mice frighten elephants.
Mice frighten elephants?
Mice frighten elephants!

For other sentence patterns, see **1d, 3a, 4b, 5f, 12a, 12b, 14a,** and **30b.**

Note: Subjects, verbs, and objects may be compound.

The high *wheeler* and the safety *bicycle* were popular in the late nineteenth century. [Compound subject]
A capable student *can face* and *solve* his *problems* or *difficulties.* [Compound verb and compound object]

▶ EXERCISE 3   Make a list of the twelve verbs, the nine subjects, and the nine objects, direct and indirect, in the paragraph below. Be prepared for a class discussion of the sentence patterns used.

¹ On New Year's Eve, I joined the happy throng at Times Square.   ² Between eleven and twelve o'clock, the noisy mob celebrated the death of the old year.   ³ Many people leaned against boarded-up store windows, milled in the streets, or blew ear-splitting horns.   ⁴ Others formed snake lines and whipped their way through the crowd. ⁵ A few fighting ragamuffins gave the police trouble. ⁶ Confetti filled the air.   ⁷ Airplanes roared overhead.

⁸ Subways thundered.   ⁹ Television cameras flashed the spectacular hubbub across the nation.

▶ EXERCISE 4   Write two sentences of your own to illustrate each one of the ten patterns on pages 7–8.

1c
Learn to recognize all the parts of speech.

Words are usually grouped into eight classes or "parts of speech": *verbs, nouns, pronouns, adjectives, adverbs, prepositions, conjunctions,* and *interjections.* Verbs, nouns, adjectives, and adverbs are sometimes called *vocabulary words* because they make up more than ninety-nine percent of all words listed in the dictionary. But pronouns, prepositions, and conjunctions—though small in number— are important because they are used over and over in our speaking and writing. Prepositions and conjunctions, often called *function words,* connect and relate vocabulary words and pronouns. Of the eight word classes, only three —prepositions, conjunctions, and interjections—do not change their form.

For a summary of the form changes of verbs, nouns, pronouns, adjectives, and adverbs, see Section **35,** under **Inflection.**

Carefully study the forms, meanings, and functions of each of the eight parts of speech listed below.

VERBS   *notify, notifies, notified, are notifying*
       write, writes, wrote, has written, is writing

Verbs function as predicators in sentences:

The dean *notified* Brad's parents.

NOUNS   *neighbor, neighbors (neighbor's, neighbors')*
          kindness, kindnesses, prudence, the *money,* an
          understanding

In sentences, nouns function as subjects, complements, objects, appositives; they are also used in direct address and absolute phrases. Nouns may name persons, places, things, ideas, animals, qualities, actions.

Edward paid the *men* for the *work.*

PRONOUNS   *I, me, my, mine, myself, they, you, him, it*
          one, ones (one's), both, everybody, anyone
          who, whose, whom, which, that, these, this

Pronouns take the positions of nouns in sentences.

He paid *them* for *it. Everyone* knows *this.*

ADJECTIVES   *young, younger, youngest, a, an, the, this* day
          three men, *a sturdy* chair, *the only* one

Adjectives modify or qualify nouns and pronouns. Generally adjectives are placed near the words they modify. A *predicate adjective,* however, is nearly always separated from the word modified. A predicate adjective helps to complete the meaning of a linking verb (*am, is, are, was, were, be, been, taste, smell,* etc.) and modifies the subject. See **4b.**

The poems of E. E. Cummings look *different.*

Adjectives may precede or follow the words they modify.

The weary driver, *alone* and *sleepy,* was *glad* to see *the familiar* streets of home.

ADVERBS   *slowly* walking, *very* short, *almost never* wins
          too, not, sometimes, soon, sooner, soonest

Adverbs usually modify verbs, adjectives, or other adverbs.

They may also modify a verbal, a whole phrase or clause, or the rest of the sentence in which they appear.

Honestly, she *nearly always* lies about her age.

PREPOSITIONS *at* times, *between* us, *because of* rain
to the door, *by* them, *before* class

Other words commonly used as prepositions are *across, after, as, for, from, in, in front of, in regard to, like, of, on, over, through, together with, under, until, up, with.* A preposition, a function word, always has an object, which is usually a noun or a pronoun; the preposition with its object (and any modifiers) is called a *prepositional phrase.*

These poems express *with* great force the poet's love *of* liberty.

The preposition may follow, rather than precede, the noun or noun substitute, and be placed at the end of the sentence. At times a sentence is most idiomatic or emphatic with the preposition at the end.

UNNATURAL	*For* what are you waiting?
NATURAL	What are you waiting *for?*
NATURAL	We live *by* faith.
NATURAL *(and more emphatic)*	Faith is what we live *by.*

Note: Words like *up, off, on, out, in, over* may be used as prepositions, as adverbs, or as parts of verb-adverb combinations (verb equivalents).

Prepositions	Adverbs	Verb-adverb combinations
up the ladder	Look *up.*	*Look up* (Find) George.
a mile *off* shore	He marched *off.*	I *put off* (delayed) the work.

CONJUNCTIONS eat *and* sleep, Carl *or* Helen, long *but* witty, rested *while* it rained, a spot *where* we meet

Conjunctions function as connectors. They fall into two classes: (1) the coordinating conjunctions (*and, but, or, nor, for,* and sometimes *so* and *yet*), used to connect words or phrases, or clauses that are of equal rank; and (2) the subordinating conjunctions (such as *after, because, if, since, till, when, where, while*), used to connect subordinate clauses with main clauses.

> According to one biographer, Bacon did not look at friends *when* he talked with them, *for* he was concerned chiefly with ideas, not people.

INTERJECTIONS *Ouch! Oh,* pardon me.

Interjections are exclamations, which may be followed by an exclamation point or a comma.

The dictionary shows the word class (often the several word classes) in which a given word may be used, but the actual classification of any word is dependent upon its use in the sentence. Notice how the classification of *round* varies in accordance with its use in the following sentences:

> The second *round* was tiring. [Noun]
> Any *round* table will do. [Adjective]
> Some drivers *round* corners too rapidly. [Verb]
> The sound goes *round* and *round.* [Adverb]
> He lives *round* the corner. [Preposition]

▶ **EXERCISE 5** As you fill in the blanks below with appropriate parts of speech to make logical sentences, note how word order, inflectional endings, and function words determine your choices. Above each word you add, write its part of speech.

1. The _____ have _____ed a _____.
2. _____ were _____ing in the _____.
3. _____ly the _____ are not _____.
4. A very _____ _____ may _____.
5. _____ of the _____ on the _____ looked _____.
6. Did _____ and _____ _____ their _____?

7. A _____ boy was _____ing _____ly on the _____.
8. Either _____ or _____ ought to _____ the _____.
9. _____ _____ not _____ a _____ or a _____.
10. During the _____ _____, _____ _____ed for _____.

▶ **EXERCISE 6**   Give the part of speech of each of the italicized words below.

The sea, of course, is never [1] *silent*. I have [2] *often* thought that if our ear [3] *were* finer, [4] *it* would catch the soft, smooth friction [5] *between* the glassy wave top and the resisting air. [6] *Even* far out, [7] *when* a still day lies like [8] *metal* [9] *on* the oily surface, and the lazy [10] *patches* of the sun dilate between imperceptible [11] *rises*, a little wave will suddenly [12] *raise* its head out of nothingness with a [13] *plop* and subside into [14] *nothingness* again: and yet when [15] *those* days have fulfilled [16] *us* with their long, empty hours, and in spite of the interrupted [17] *but* fairly [18] *continuous* rap of canvas against a mast, the feeling we take home is [19] *that* of silence, the thing we have [20] *never* known.   —FREYA STARK[3]

1d

Learn to recognize phrases and subordinate clauses.

Phrases

A phrase is a group of related words, without subject and predicate, functioning as a verb, a noun, an adjective, or an adverb. Phrases are generally classified as:

[3] From "On Silence," *Holiday*, December, 1965. By permission of the author.

VERB PHRASES   The rose *has wilted. Did* you *see* it? Mr. Kelly *may run up* the bill. The roof *used to leak.*

PREPOSITIONAL PHRASES   A special program *on the growth of flowers* fascinated audiences everywhere. *In fact,* the timed photography was spectacular.

PARTICIPIAL PHRASES   A person *seeing an accident* should stay on the scene. *Seeing the accident,* a man stopped. *Seen by three men,* the accident was reported at once.

GERUND PHRASES   *Riding a horse* takes skill. I prefer *riding a bicycle.*

INFINITIVE PHRASES   Does James like *to swim in the ocean?* That is the problem *to be solved now.*

Notice in the examples above that the gerund *riding,* like the present participle *seeing,* ends in -*ing* and that the two are to be distinguished only by their use in the sentence: the participle is the adjective and the gerund is the noun.

Participles, gerunds, and infinitives are derived from verbs and are therefore called *verbals.* (See also Section **35.**) They are much like verbs in that they have different tenses, can take subjects and objects, and can be modified by adverbs. But they are not verbs, for they cannot serve as the heart of a sentence: they cannot make a statement, ask a question, or give a command.

(1) **Phrases used as nouns**

Gerund phrases are always used as nouns. Infinitive phrases are often used as nouns (though they may also function as modifiers). Occasionally a prepositional phrase functions as a noun.

NOUNS	PHRASES USED AS NOUNS
The *decision* is important.	*Choosing a major* is important. [Gerund phrase—subject]
Sandra likes the *job.*	Sandra likes *to do the work.* [Infinitive phrase—object]

NOUNS	PHRASES USED AS NOUNS
His *action* prompted the *change*.	*His leaving the farm* caused *her to seek a job in town.* [Gerund phrase—subject; infinitive phrase—object]
That *hour* is too late.	*After supper* is too late. [Prepositional phrase—subject]

▶ **EXERCISE 7** Make a list of the five gerund phrases and five infinitive phrases used as nouns in the following sentences (selected from *Time*).

1. Successfully merchandising a product is creative.
2. Great wealth seems to produce a security and mobility that usually enable the rich to grow richer.
3. They prefer instead to hear counterpoint, to hear the architecture of the music.
4. "We just want to take some of the blindness out of blind dates," explains the founder of Operation Match.
5. He insisted on calling every play from the bench; he tried installing a radio receiver in his quarterback's helmet, and when other teams started tuning in on his broadcast, he switched to shuttling "messenger guards" back and forth with his orders.

(2) Phrases used as modifiers

Prepositional phrases nearly always function as adjectives or adverbs. Infinitive phrases are also used as adjectives or adverbs. Participial phrases are used as adjectives.

ADJECTIVES	PHRASES USED AS ADJECTIVES
It is a *significant* discovery.	It is a discovery *of significance.* [Prepositional phrase]
Appropriate language is important.	Language *to suit the occasion* is important. [Infinitive phrase]

ADJECTIVES	PHRASES USED AS ADJECTIVES
Destructive storms lashed the Midwest.	Storms, *destroying many crops of corn and oats,* lashed the Midwest. [Participial phrase containing prepositional phrase used as adjective]
The *icy* bridge was dangerous.	*Covered with ice,* the bridge was dangerous. [Participial phrase modified by prepositional phrase]

ADVERBS	PHRASES USED AS ADVERBS
Drive *carefully.*	Drive *with care on slick streets.* [Prepositional phrases]
Certainly Mary Ann lacks self-confidence.	*To be sure,* Mary Ann lacks self-confidence. [Infinitive phrase]

The examples on pages 15–17 show how phrases function in the same way as single-word modifiers. Remember, however, that phrases are not merely substitutes for single words. Many times phrases express more than can be packed into a single word.

> The gas gauge fluttered *from empty to full.*
> He telephoned his wife *to tell her of his arrival.*
> *Walking down Third Avenue,* I noticed many new buildings.

▶ **EXERCISE 8** Each italicized phrase below is used as a modifier. First classify each phrase as prepositional, participial, or infinitive; then state whether the phrase functions as an adjective or as an adverb. (These sentences were selected from *Life.*)

The open road, the freedom [1] *to move on,* these are among the most treasured American traditions.
[2] *Reading the piece and looking at the pictures,* I was overwhelmed [3] *by conscience.*

⁴ *On the mist-shrouded moors* ⁵ *of northern England,* men poked sticks ⁶ *into the mushy peat* and then held the stick ends ⁷ *to their noses,* ⁸ *seeking—and fearing—the smell* ⁹ *of death.*

She is too shy ¹⁰ *to employ the hustle and muscle necessary* ¹¹ *to win the honor.*

¹² *Working like a sculptor,* José Limon molds large groups ¹³ *of dancers* ¹⁴ *into heroic units,* ¹⁵ *telling intensely dramatic stories* ¹⁶ *like* <u>Othello</u> *and* <u>The Emperor Jones.</u>

¹⁷ *Cradled in his mother's arms,* a skinny monkey baby ¹⁸ *with a forlorn face* made his debut ¹⁹ *at the San Diego Zoo.* The infant is a rare proboscis monkey, the first of its kind ²⁰ *born in captivity.*

Subordinate Clauses

A clause is a group of related words which contains both a verb and its subject. Unlike a *main clause* (which can either stand alone as a sentence or function with other clauses in complex and compound sentences—see **1e**), a *subordinate clause* functions as a noun, an adjective, or an adverb and is therefore only part of a sentence. Subordinating conjunctions (such as *after, although, as, because, before, if, since, until, when, while*) and relative pronouns (such as *who, which, that*) are called "subordinate clause markers" because they introduce subordinate clauses and make them dependent.

MAIN CLAUSES   *Money had been stolen,* and *I called the police.*
[Two main clauses in a compound sentence]

SUBORDINATE CLAUSES   The police knew *that the money had been stolen.* [Noun clause, object of the verb *knew*] The money *which had been stolen* was found. [Adjective clause modifying *money*] *Because money had been stolen,* I called the police. [Adverb clause preceding main clause]

(1) Subordinate clauses used as nouns

NOUNS	NOUN CLAUSES
The newspaper *accounts* may be false.	*What the newspapers say* may be false. [Subject]
I do not remember his *name*.	I do not remember *what his name is*. [Object]
Give the tools to *Paul*.	Give the tools to *whoever can use them*. [Object of the preposition *to*]

▶ **EXERCISE 9** Bracket the noun clauses in the following sentences and explain the use of each clause.

¹ The repairman said that he would have to take the typewriter into the shop. ² What it needed most of all was to be junked. ³ But he remembered that his customer had a sentimental fondness for this old machine. ⁴ And he had long ago learned that a battered, used-up piece of machinery could be to some people what politics, wife, or religion was to others. ⁵ What one man loved, other men had to pretend to respect. ⁶ The repairman wondered whether that saying was in the Bible. ⁷ He thought that it might well be.

(2) Subordinate clauses used as modifiers

Two types of subordinate clauses, the adjective clause and the adverb clause, are used as modifiers.

ADJECTIVE	ADJECTIVE CLAUSE
The *golden* window reflects the sun.	The window, *which looks like solid gold*, reflects the sun.

ADVERB	ADVERB CLAUSE
The work stops *then*.	The work stops *when it rains*.

Adjective clauses   Any clause that modifies a noun or a pronoun is an adjective clause. An adjective clause may also modify a gerund. Adjective clauses, which nearly always follow the words modified, are most frequently introduced by a relative pronoun, which often is the subject or object in the subordinate clause.

> A man *who knows the truth* is fortunate. [The relative pronoun *who* is the subject of *knows* in the adjective clause.]
> He is a man *whom I have always admired.* [The relative pronoun *whom* is the object of *have admired.*]

Other words (for example, conjunctions and adverbs) may introduce adjective clauses: "a time *when all things went well for him,*" "the reason *why I changed my mind.*"

Note: If not used as a subject, the word introducing an adjective or a noun clause may sometimes be omitted. (See also **22a.**)

> He is a man [*whom* or *that*] I have always admired.
> I know [*that*] she is right.

Adverb clauses An adverb clause may modify a verb, an adjective, an adverb, a verbal, a prepositional phrase, or even a whole clause.

An adverb clause often precedes or follows the main clause:

ADVERB CLAUSE, MAIN CLAUSE.

> When Bill decided to leave, everyone expressed regret. [An adverb clause in this position is usually followed by a comma. See **12b.**]

MAIN CLAUSE ADVERB CLAUSE.

> Everyone expressed regret when Bill decided to leave. [An adverb clause in this position is usually not set off by a comma. See **12b.**]

An adverb clause may also interrupt a main clause.

> I can, *if you wish,* help you paint the woodwork. [A parenthetical adverb clause set off by commas. See **12d.**]

The position of the adverb clause depends on its relative importance in the sentence. See **29a–b**.

▶ **EXERCISE 10** Bracket the five adjective clauses in the following sentences.

¹ William was not at the corner where he usually took the bus. ² The bus driver, who knew all his regular passengers, commented about it to one of those getting on. ³ The passenger remembered something that William had said one day about beginning his vacation in the middle of the week. ⁴ That sounded reasonable to the driver, who after all had a schedule to maintain. ⁵ Edging the big bus back into the traffic that was streaming by, he mentally put William on his "absent with leave" list for the next two weeks.

▶ **EXERCISE 11** Bracket the eleven adverb clauses in the following paragraph.

¹ While Mr. Baker was shaving, he thought of the day ahead. ² He always began his day's work before he arrived at the office. ³ After he got on the train, he nearly always started planning his day. ⁴ Sometimes he began before the train arrived if it was a minute or two late. ⁵ But this morning, as he was shaving the tender place under his chin, details of the day's work clicked through his mind. ⁶ Since he had first been made head accountant, he couldn't remember having brought the job home with him. ⁷ Whenever anything was not the usual routine with him, he naturally wondered. ⁸ Suddenly he remembered; while he was rinsing his razor under the hot water, he smiled cheerfully. ⁹ Today, unless the state auditors broke a long habit, they would show up. ¹⁰ And because this time he had worked extra carefully to have the books ready for them, he could look forward happily to their coming.

1e

Learn to recognize main clauses and the various types of sentences.

As we have already noted in **1d,** a main clause has both a subject and a verb and can stand alone as a sentence. And as we observed in **1b,** nearly every grammatically complete sentence (all except commands or imperatives) has a subject and verb expressed.

A sentence is a unit of expression that can stand alone grammatically, though it may require other sentences to complete its meaning. It is followed in speaking by a full stop and in writing by a period, a question mark, or an exclamation point.

He refused the offer. [Statement—followed by a period]
Refuse the offer. [Command—followed by a period]
Did he refuse the offer? [Question—followed by a question mark]
How absurd the offer was! [Exclamation—followed by an exclamation point]

Sentences are classified, according to the number and kind of clauses they contain, as (1) simple, (2) compound, (3) complex, or (4) compound-complex.

A simple sentence (with the exception of the imperative) is made up of one main clause; see various patterns of the simple sentence on pages 7–8.

SIMPLE SENTENCES   One part of the TV screen carried the football game. The other part showed the launching countdown.

A **compound sentence** has two or more main clauses.

COMPOUND SENTENCE   One part of the TV screen carried the football game, and the other part showed the launching countdown.

Except when joined by one of the coordinating conjunctions (*and, but, or, nor, for*), main clauses are separated by a semicolon. See Section 14.

One part of the TV screen carried the football game; the other part showed the launching countdown.

A **complex sentence** has one main clause and at least one subordinate clause.

COMPLEX SENTENCE   While one part of the TV screen carried the football game, the other part showed the launching countdown.

A **compound-complex sentence** is made up of two or more main clauses and at least one subordinate clause.

COMPOUND-COMPLEX SENTENCE   The Saturday afternoon program was like a two-ring circus; while one part of the TV screen carried the football game, the other part showed the launching countdown.

▶ EXERCISE 12   Classify each of the following sentences (selected from the *New Yorker*) as (1) simple, (2) compound, (3) complex, or (4) compound-complex. Be prepared to justify your classification by analysis of the sentence.

1. On distant hillsides, whole stands of trees lay pointing in the same direction, like combed hair.
2. She was a chameleon, a restless, untrammeled creature dappled with sunlight and shadow.
3. Just why Bruckner's Sixth Symphony has always been the most neglected of his works has always been a puzzle to me.
4. I was happy in my own world of snow, as if I were living inside one of those glass paperweights that snow when you shake them, and I went back to sleep easily.
5. Time and again we are led through one or another of Conrad's works, detail by detail, to reach the startling conclusion that what Conrad put into the story is still there and that the story means what he said it meant.

6. Once, the stone floor of the portico must have rung with the sound of iron wheels and shod hoofs; now it is silent and the doors of the stables are shut.

7. The harvests are scanty, for the clay sheds the rain, and, with no trees to hold it, the water rushes to the valley, carrying seeds with it and carving great, gray, gutterlike channels.

8. As part of our program to promote clean and efficient business methods, we spent many years developing a copying paper that would eliminate the need for carbons.

9. His face faintly suggested mumps, and he once tipped the theatre-ticket girl in the lobby of the Hotel New Yorker three cents for getting him four tickets to a show that was sold out for a month in advance.

10. The crowd moved through the two anterooms into the Great Hall, where, from their portraits on the wall, mayors, presidents, and justices looked down with the complacent rosiness of those who have dined and died.

▶ EXERCISE 13   Compose ten sentences and classify each sentence as (1) simple, (2) complex, (3) compound, or (4) compound-complex. Write at least two sentences of each type.

▶ EXERCISE 14   Analyze the following sentences of the Gettysburg Address as directed by the instructor.

1. Fourscore and seven years ago our fathers brought forth on this continent a new nation, conceived in liberty, and dedicated to the proposition that all men are created equal.

2. Now we are engaged in a great civil war, testing whether that nation, or any nation so conceived and so dedicated, can long endure.

3. We are met on a great battlefield of that war.

4. We have come to dedicate a portion of that field as a final resting place for those who here gave their lives that that nation might live.

5. It is altogether fitting and proper that we should do this.

6. But in a larger sense we cannot dedicate, we cannot consecrate, we cannot hallow this ground.

7. The brave men, living and dead, who struggled here, have consecrated it far above our power to add or detract.

8. The world will little note, nor long remember, what we say here, but it can never forget what they did here.

9. It is for us, the living, rather to be dedicated here to the unfinished work which they who fought here have thus far so nobly advanced.

10. It is rather for us to be here dedicated to the great task remaining before us, that from these honored dead we take increased devotion to that cause for which they gave the last full measure of devotion; that we here highly resolve that these dead shall not have died in vain; that this nation, under God, shall have a new birth of freedom, and that government of the people, by the people, for the people shall not perish from the earth.

Sentence Fragment

2

Do not carelessly write a sentence fragment —a phrase or a subordinate clause—as if it were a complete sentence.

Both sentences and nonsentences begin with capitals and end with periods in such writing as the following:

> He wasn't a gorilla. *Just the cutest little baboon.* And the garbage wasn't garbage. It was ice cream. *A genuine strawberry and fish-guts sundae.*   —ALDOUS HUXLEY

Fragments (nonsentences) such as those italicized above are sometimes used intentionally and effectively by professional writers, especially in fiction. Even in formal exposition, grammatically incomplete sentences such as those in the left column below are considered standard.

NONSENTENCES	SENTENCES
How undemocratic!	How undemocratic it is!
By raising prices? No.	No, do not raise prices.

College students are usually advised, however, to learn the fundamentals of English composition before permitting themselves to take liberties with the accepted patterns of the complete sentence. (See pages 7–8.) Make it a practice, therefore, to avoid fragments; do not set off a phrase or a subordinate clause as if it were a complete sentence. The fragment should be either (1) included in the preceding or following sentence—that is, attached to the main clause—or (2) rewritten to form a sentence by itself.

FRAGMENT He registered for the summer session. Hoping thus to graduate ahead of his class. [We have here one sentence and one fragment, a participial phrase.]

REVISED He registered for the summer session, hoping thus to graduate ahead of his class. [Participial phrase included in the sentence]

He registered for the summer session. By this means he hoped to graduate ahead of his class. [Participial phrase made into a sentence]

FRAGMENT He registered for the summer session. Because he hoped thus to graduate ahead of his class. [We have here one sentence and one fragment, a subordinate clause.]

REVISED He registered for the summer session because he hoped thus to graduate ahead of his class. [Subordinate clause included in the sentence]

TESTS FOR SENTENCE COMPLETENESS

A sentence fragment may be obvious to the student who reads it aloud in context. If he reads the fragment properly, he will find that either it is not preceded by a full stop or else it is not followed by one. That is, the fragment belongs with the preceding sentence or with the following one.

Sentence completeness may also be tested (1) by searching for the verb and its subject and (2) by determining whether this verb and subject are introduced by a subordinating conjunction or relative pronoun. If the supposed sentence does not have a verb and its subject, it may be identified at once as a phrase. *Hoping thus to graduate ahead of his class,* for example, has neither verb nor subject. *Hoping* is a participle and *to graduate* is an infinitive. Even when both verb and subject are present, they may be introduced by a subordinating conjunction or relative pronoun and thus constitute a subordinate clause. *Because he hoped to graduate ahead of his class* has the verb *hoped* and the subject *he*. But since these words are introduced by the subordinating conjunction *because,* the group of words is a subordinate clause—still a sentence fragment.

If you unintentionally write fragments, carefully proofread your compositions. Form a mental picture of the core of each of your sentences after you have reviewed the sentence patterns on pages 7–8.

▶ EXERCISE 1   Find the seven fragments in the following paragraphs. Revise each fragment by attaching it logically to a main clause or by rewriting the fragment so that it will stand by itself as a sentence.

¹ As a weather watcher, I am often amused by official forecasts.   ² Or, rather, by occasional prophecies made by weather men who seldom bother to glance out the window. ³ For example, one day last spring when heavy rain and large hail lashed the city.   ⁴ I promptly telephoned the weather bureau.   ⁵ To ask about the possibility of a tornado.   ⁶ A confident voice replied glibly, "Oh, don't worry about a tornado; we're not even in an alert area."

⁷ Relieved, I turned on the radio, found a chair near a window, and watched the angry clouds.   ⁸ Amazingly enough, I soon saw a swirling funnel emerge from a black cloud and reach for the ground.   ⁹ Just north of the city, about five miles away.   ¹⁰ Of course, I immediately notified the weather bureau.

¹¹ A short time later.   ¹² An important message interrupted the jazz on the radio: "The weather bureau has issued a warning that a tornado may strike north of here." ¹³ I smiled as I repeated the words "may strike."   ¹⁴ Knowing that the official prophets were vigilant.   ¹⁵ As they busily observed falling barometers and erratic wind gauges instead of paying attention to the turbulent weather itself.

2a

Do not carelessly write a phrase (participial, prepositional, or infinitive) as a complete sentence.

FRAGMENT   I made little progress. *Finally giving up all my efforts.* [Participial phrase]

REVISED   I made so little progress that I finally gave up all my efforts. [Fragment included in the sentence]

I made little progress. Finally I gave up all my efforts. [Fragment made into a sentence]

FRAGMENT   Soon I began to work for the company. *First in the rock pit and later on the highway.* [Prepositional phrases]

REVISED   Soon I began to work for the company, first in the rock pit and later on the highway. [Fragment included in the sentence]

FRAGMENT   He will have an opportunity to visit his home town. *And to talk with many of his old friends.* [Infinitive phrase]

REVISED   He will have an opportunity to visit his home town and to talk with many of his old friends. [Fragment included in the sentence]

▶ EXERCISE 2   Eliminate each fragment below by including it in a sentence or by making it into a sentence.

1. We had a wonderful time at the lake. Swimming near the dock and fishing on the barge.
2. I spray the shrubbery twice a year. Once in the late spring and again in the early fall.
3. The pampered Dennis finally left home. Earnestly seeking to become an individual in his own right.
4. He was once a beautiful child. With curly black hair and bright blue eyes.
5. I want to make high grades. To succeed not only as an athlete but also as a scholar.
6. In high school I was a "discipline problem." In more ways than one.

7. My grandmother is a delightful conversationalist. Often speaking of the "days of her youth," during what she calls the "Renaissance period."
8. I think that it is wise to ignore his sarcasm. Or to make a quick exit.
9. Squinting her eyes, the gossip leaned forward. To whisper this question in my ear: "Have you seen that mangy little thug she dates?"
10. Bill smiled self-consciously. Like a politician posing before a television camera.

2b

Do not carelessly write a subordinate clause as a complete sentence.

FRAGMENT   A railway control board should be constructed with care. *Because from this board trains are moved through a system of tracks and switches.* [Subordinate clause]

REVISED   A railway control board should be constructed with care because from this board trains are moved through a system of tracks and switches. [Fragment included in the sentence]

FRAGMENT   I was trying to read the directions. *Which were confusing and absurd.* [Subordinate clause]

REVISED   I was trying to read the directions, which were confusing and absurd. [Fragment included in the sentence]

   I was trying to read the directions. They were confusing and absurd. [Fragment made into a sentence]

▶ EXERCISE 3   Some of the following numbered word groups contain fragments; others do not. Write *F* after each fragment; write *S* after each sentence.

1. I stopped trying to read my assignment. As soon as he

started imitating my favorite comedian by doing the tango with a lamp shade on his head.

2. The little thief was almost sick from fright. And the sheriff believed that he could handle his prisoner alone.

3. My hobby is oil painting. In fact, that is my pride, my joy, and my dependable moneymaker.

4. Mr. Adams did not insist on my buying insurance. Which is more than I can say for the last agent we had here.

5. Then she would fail. This was the nightmare that haunted her, the dread of the inevitable surrender to defeat.

6. Grandmother was proud of her Indian pudding. Especially when several of the guests asked for second helpings.

7. I do not believe the printed label. As a rule, it takes all night for the paint to harden.

8. The adjuster had no trouble last time. Although I know, of course, that this is an entirely different situation.

9. Mrs. Gayle never speaks about her travels abroad. As if she knew everything and we were all ignoramuses.

10. The *Titanic* rammed into an iceberg. Which took place on April 15, 1912.

2c
Do not carelessly write as a complete sentence any other fragment, such as an appositive (noun or noun substitute) or a member of a compound predicate.

FRAGMENT   My father was born in Cartersville. *A little country town where everyone knows everyone else.* [Appositive modified by a subordinate clause]

REVISED   My father was born in Cartersville, a little country town where everyone knows everyone else.

FRAGMENT	William was elected president of his class. *And was made a member of the National Honor Society.* [Detached member of a compound predicate]
REVISED	William was elected president of his class and was made a member of the National Honor Society.

▶ EXERCISE 4   Attach each fragment below to the preceding sentence or make the fragment into an independent sentence.

1. Fred received an invitation to my wedding. And acknowledged it by sending me a sympathy card.
2. You should work when you are young and enthusiastic. And should leave dreams to old men.
3. I am often told to do things I do not like. Such as getting out of bed.
4. The hydraulic lift raises the plows out of the ground. And lowers them again.
5. I had a feeling that some sinister spirit of evil brooded over the place. A feeling that I could not analyze.

▶ EXERCISE 5   Identify each fragment; determine whether it falls under the rule for **2a**, **2b**, or **2c**; then make the appropriate correction. Write *C* after each numbered item which contains no fragment.

1. I knew that he was asking for trouble. As soon as I heard of his buying that motorcycle.
2. He let me believe that I had first chance at the job. But without definitely committing himself.
3. He was still angry with me. His eyes glaring fiercely.
4. He killed three ducks with one shot. Against the law of averages but possible.
5. She dressed exactly like the Hollywood starlets. Since she wanted to become one of them herself.
6. To watch Dempsey in the ring was to watch a perfectly engineered machine operated with exact precision.
7. To anyone who knew him in 1840, it would have seemed ridiculous beyond belief. To predict that one

day this rawboned frontier lawyer would be President of the United States.

8. The festival beginning on the twentieth of June and continuing through the month of July.

9. Early in life he decided upon a simple philosophy. From which grew all his subsequent opinions.

10. Doc Potter is exactly what you said he would be. A thoroughly profane and entertaining old reprobate.

▶ EXERCISE 6   Attach each fragment below to an existing sentence or make it into an independent sentence.

¹ Very late in *The Merry Wives of Windsor,* Shakespeare introduces an incident which is altogether extraneous to either of the plot lines in the play.   ² And which advances the action in no way whatsoever.   ³ Bardolph in a very brief scene with the Host announces that "the Germans" desire three of the Host's horses.   ⁴ So that they may go to meet "the Duke," who is to be at court on the next day.   ⁵ The Host seems to know so little of these Germans that he must ask if they speak English.   ⁶ A highly improbable ignorance on his part, for in his next lines he states that they have been already a week at his tavern.   ⁷ But he lets them have the horses.   ⁸ Insisting, however, that they must pay for them.   ⁹ Two scenes later Bardolph returns to the tavern with the report that the villainous Germans have handled him roughly on the road.   ¹⁰ Thrown him into a puddle, and run off with the horses.   ¹¹ Immediately on his heels, in come first Sir Hugh and then Dr. Caius.   ¹² With rumors confirming Bardolph's assurance of the evil character of the Germans.   ¹³ So that the Host is at last alarmed.   ¹⁴ He is convinced now that the Germans have indeed cozened him of a week's board bill.   ¹⁵ And stolen his horses in the bargain.

Comma Splice
and Fused Sentence

3

Do not carelessly link two main clauses with only a comma between them (comma splice) or run main clauses together without any punctuation (fused sentence).

COMMA SPLICE   The current was swift, he could not swim to shore. [Two main clauses linked only by a comma]
FUSED SENTENCE   The current was swift he could not swim to shore. [Omission of all punctuation between main clauses]

If you cannot recognize main clauses and distinguish them from subordinate clauses, study Section 1, **Sentence Sense,** as you apply the following instructions to your writing.

3a

Correct either comma splices or fused sentences by one of the following methods:

(1) By subordinating one of the main clauses—usually the best method. (See also Section 24.)

COMMA SPLICE   The current was swift, he could not swim to shore.
REVISED   Since the current was swift, he could not swim to shore. [First main clause changed to a subordinate clause]

PATTERN SUBORDINATE CLAUSE, MAIN CLAUSE.

(2) By making each main clause into a sentence.

FUSED   The current was swift he could not swim to shore.
REVISED   The current was swift. He could not swim to shore.

(3) By joining main clauses with a semicolon.

REVISED   The current was swift; he could not swim to shore.

PATTERN   **MAIN CLAUSE; MAIN CLAUSE.**

(4) By joining the main clauses with a comma plus a coordinating conjunction.

REVISED   The current was swift, and he could not swim to shore.

PATTERN

MAIN CLAUSE, *and* (or *but, or, nor, for*) **MAIN CLAUSE.**

Some exceptions: Short coordinate clauses in series, parallel in form and unified in thought, may be separated by commas.

I came, I saw, I conquered.

The comma is also used to separate a statement from an echo question.

You can come, can't you? [Statement echoed by question]

Main clauses separated only by commas are fairly common in some informal types of writing. Occasionally examples are found in more formal writing, chiefly when there is a balance or contrast between the clauses.

They trundle mobile baskets at the A&P, they sit under driers at the hairdressers, they sweep their porches and set out bulbs and stitch up slip covers.   —PHYLLIS MC GINLEY

The student learning to write formal papers in college will do well, however, to make sure that main clauses in his sentences are separated (1) by a comma plus a coordinate conjunction or (2) by a semicolon.

3b

Caution: Do not let a conjunctive adverb, a transitional phrase, or a divided quotation trick you into making a comma splice. (See also 14a.)

Unlike coordinating conjunctions, which have a fixed position when they link main clauses, conjunctive adverbs and transitional phrases do not have a fixed position: they may join main clauses or be used parenthetically. A semicolon or a comma before a conjunctive adverb or transitional phrase is therefore an important signal to the reader, telling him whether or not to expect a main clause to follow.

> I do not like ice cream, *but* I sometimes eat it at parties.
> [Coordinating conjunction with fixed position]
> I do not like ice cream; *however,* I sometimes eat it at parties.
> [Conjunctive adverb with semicolon introducing a main clause]
> I do not like ice cream; I sometimes eat it, *however,* at parties.
> [Parenthetical *however* set off by commas]

Remember that **conjunctive adverbs** (such as *accordingly, also, anyhow, besides, consequently, furthermore, hence, henceforth, however, indeed, instead, likewise, meanwhile, moreover, nevertheless, otherwise, still, then, therefore, thus*) and **transitional phrases** (such as *for example, in fact, on the contrary, on the other hand, that is*) connecting main clauses are always preceded by a semicolon.

Divided quotations

COMMA SPLICE	"Your answer is wrong," he said, "correct it."
REVISED	"Your answer is wrong," he said. "Correct it."
COMMA SPLICE	"What are you looking for?" she asked, "may I help you?"
REVISED	"What are you looking for?" she asked. "May I help you?"

EXERCISES ON BUILDING SENTENCES
AND OBSERVING SENTENCE PATTERNS
(TO AVOID THE COMMA SPLICE)

▶ EXERCISE 1   Write two sentences to illustrate each construction specified below.

1. Main clause; main clause.
2. Main clause, *coordinating conjunction* main clause.
3. Main clause; *conjunctive adverb* (,) main clause.

▶ EXERCISE 2   All of the following sentences (selected from *Harper's Magazine*) are correctly punctuated. Identify the pattern or construction of each sentence.

1. The forest became a dancing pattern of light and shade, and a pathway of light fell before me on the ground.
2. The other day a police car shot past me at about 150 miles an hour, and I did not even crunch my toes.
3. He may haggle fiercely over details, but he also has a magnificent detachment and an almost saintly freedom from any sense of grievance toward his detractors.
4. In ancient times, fats were the hallmark of affluence; they still are in some cultures.
5. Chris thinks scholarship is a matter for the young, and he's ravenous for it as a sort of intellectual hamburger.
6. But policemen are scarce in the country districts; besides, the Moustheni Explorers planned to work at night.
7. The first cars are very long; hence there are correspondingly long intervals between the flashes of daylight you see between them.
8. She wore her hair in a bun to seem mature, but the blue jeans necessary for climbing among the rafters took ten years off her age.
9. Both James and Dreiser had a profound feeling for the femininity of cities, but they had revealingly different attitudes toward it.

10. The villas drip with wooden fringe; they support cornices that are sunbursts of frilly lattice and balconies that seem to be squeezed from pastry tubes.

▶ **EXERCISE 3** Determine which of the following sentences contain comma splices. (As an aid to your analysis, you may wish to bracket each subordinate clause and to underline the subject and verb of each main clause.) Write *C* after each sentence that needs no revision. Correct each comma splice in the most appropriate way.

1. Mary Queen of Scots' death warrant was written on a playing card, the nine of diamonds, therefore this card is sometimes called "the curse of Scotland."
2. If Jay's batting average had been better, for example, he would have been the best baseball player in the league.
3. "Rate the entries," he said, "Interview the applicants, and study their recommendations."
4. Irving exploited local legends, he helped to start American folklore by writing "Rip Van Winkle."
5. Typhus used to kill more soldiers than actual warfare did, however the disease is rarely heard of now.
6. Fred was lucky in his choice of rooms, although they were small, they were close to his work.
7. Liechtenstein postage stamps are especially beautiful, stamp collectors eagerly buy special issues.
8. To be a baby sitter, one should know something of child care, for example, one should know how to warm a bottle and to burp a baby.
9. The western world is indebted to the Saracens for paper. It was the Saracens, moreover, who built Europe's first paper mill.
10. Frogs swallow moving objects, as a matter of fact, they will die of hunger rather than strike a motionless insect.

▶ EXERCISE 4   Revise each comma splice (or fused sentence) by some method of subordination. Write *C* after any sentence that needs no revision.

1. Frantically I wound and jerked the starting cord a tow of gravel barges was bearing directly down upon me.
2. Sheila has her mind made up, nothing you can say will change it.
3. We have enough bricks we can build a barbecue pit.
4. I spoke of the Rufus Kane matter to Chief Kelly, he recalled the case quite clearly.
5. The plaster hardens rapidly it should not be mixed in large quantities.
6. When you come to a red brick church across from a filling station, turn left and go exactly one block.
7. There is a roadside market on the Maryville highway you can buy all the berries you want there.
8. At farrowing, her pigs weighed slightly over three pounds apiece, this is a little above average weight.
9. We do not plan to come back in the fall, therefore we are giving up our apartment.
10. One man was digging at the bottom of the well, and the other stayed at the top to haul up the loose dirt.

Adjectives and Adverbs

4

Distinguish between adjectives and adverbs and use the appropriate forms.

Adjectives and adverbs are modifiers. That is, they qualify or limit, make clearer or more specific, other words in the sentence. Any word modifying a noun or a pronoun functions as an adjective; an adjective may also modify a gerund or a noun phrase. Any word modifying a verb, an adjective, or another adverb functions as an adverb; an adverb may also modify verbals (gerunds, infinitives, participles) or even whole clauses. In the following examples, arrows indicate modification; brackets enclose modified groups of words.

NO MODIFIERS	Lobbyists advocated laws. (Noun—verb—noun.)
ADJECTIVES	*Many* lobbyists advocated *severe* [*blue* laws].
ADVERBS	*Honestly,* [*too* many lobbyists *very deceitfully* advocated *unduly* severe blue laws].

Forms of Adjectives and Adverbs

As a rule, suffixes such as *-al, -ish, -ive, -ly, -like,* and *-ous* make adjectives out of nouns:

NOUNS	a *nation,* my *friend,* a *boy,* the *danger*
ADJECTIVES	*national* bank, *friendly* cat, *boyish* prank, *dangerous* work

The *-ly* ending nearly always converts adjectives to adverbs:

ADJECTIVES   *formal* dress, a *quick* turn, a *real* gem, *sure* thing
ADVERBS   *formally* dressed, *quickly* turning, *really* valuable, *surely* is

Note: A few words ending in *-ly* (such as *only, early, cowardly*) may be either adjectives or adverbs, and the same is true for a considerable number of common words not ending in *-ly* (such as *far, fast, late, little, near, right, straight, well*). For the comparative and superlative forms of adjectives and adverbs, see **4c**.

A good dictionary shows the appropriate form for adjective or adverb, but only the use to which the word is put in the sentence determines whether the adjective or the adverb form is required.

▶ EXERCISE 1   Identify each italicized word below as an adjective or an adverb and explain why it is appropriately used.

1. We took a *leisurely* drive. We drove *leisurely*.
2. He is *sure* of victory. He will *surely* win.
3. The Boy Scouts did *good* work. The Boy Scouts did the work *well*.
4. The silence in the catacombs was *awful*. It was *awfully* silent in the catacombs.
5. The patient expressed *real* gratitude. He was *really* grateful.

4a

Use the adverb form for modifiers of verbs, adjectives, and other adverbs.

(1) Modifiers of verbs

NONSTANDARD   His clothes fit him perfect. [The adjective *perfect* misused to modify the verb *fit*]

STANDARD	His clothes fit him *perfectly*.
NONSTANDARD	He ran good for the first half mile. [The adjective *good* misused to modify the verb *ran*]
STANDARD	He ran *well* for the first half mile.

(2) Modifiers of adjectives

NONSTANDARD	The farmer has a reasonable secure future. [The adjective *reasonable* misused to modify the adjective *secure*]
STANDARD	The farmer has a *reasonably* secure future.
NONSTANDARD	The plane was a special built fighter.
STANDARD	The plane was a *specially* built fighter.

(3) Modifiers of adverbs

INFORMAL	Only by working real hard can I pass the course.
FORMAL	Only by working *really* hard can I pass the course.

▶ EXERCISE 2   Choose the standard form of the modifier within parentheses appropriate to formal writing. If necessary, use your dictionary to distinguish between formal and informal usage.

1. If you study (consistent, consistently) and (regular, regularly), you should overcome (most, almost) any handicap.
2. The wind blew (fierce, fiercely), and the snow fell (continuous, continuously) all the long night.
3. The next few weeks passed very (rapid, rapidly).
4. I am afraid that the good woman is (some, somewhat) confused.
5. Dave is (uncommon, uncommonly) light on his feet for such a (heavy, heavily) built man.
6. It was a (fair, fairly), warm day in April.
7. It was a (fair, fairly) warm day in April.
8. Mr. Porter was so excited that he could not play his part (good, well).
9. I want someone who can do the work (prompt and

efficient, promptly and efficiently) and still behave (courteous, courteously) toward the customers.
10. Do you realize how (bad, badly) your grades may suffer if you do not work (steady, steadily) or (serious, seriously) enough?

4b

Use adjectives rather than adverbs as subject complements.

As subject complements, adjectives always modify the subject. Subject complements usually follow but sometimes precede linking verbs. *Be, am, are, is, was, were, been, seem, become,* and their equivalents, as well as such verbs as *feel, look, smell, sound,* and *taste* are commonly used to link subjects and complements.

SUBJECT—LINKING VERB—SUBJECT COMPLEMENT.
The name sounds *familiar.* [*Familiar* name]
Still waters run (or are) *deep.* [*Deep* waters]
This cake does not taste very *fresh.* [*Fresh* cake]

Apparent exception: The modifier should be an adverb when it refers to the action of the verb. In that case the verb is not used as a linking verb.

The blind beggar felt *cautiously* along the wall. [The adverb *cautiously* qualifies the verb *felt.*]
The woman looked *angrily* at him. [The adverb *angrily* qualifies the verb *looked.*]

Note: A modifier following a verb and its direct object is an adjective when it refers to the object rather than to the action of the verb.

PATTERN   SUBJECT—VERB—OBJECT—COMPLEMENT.
The boy dug the hole *deep.* [*Deep* hole]

▶ EXERCISE 3   Using adjectives as subject complements, write five sentences that illustrate the following
pattern:

   SUBJECT—LINKING VERB—SUBJECT COMPLEMENT.

4c

**Use the appropriate forms for the comparative and the
superlative.**

   In general the shorter adjectives (and a few adverbs)
form the comparative degree by adding *-er* and the superlative by adding *-est;* the longer adjectives and most
adverbs form the comparative by the use of *more* (*less*) and
the superlative by the use of *most* (*least*). A few modifiers
have an irregular comparison.

Positive	*Comparative*	*Superlative*
warm	warmer	warmest
warmly	more warmly	most warmly
helpful	less helpful	least helpful
good, well	better	best
bad, badly	worse	worst

(1) **Use the comparative degree for two persons or things.**

   Was Monday or Tuesday *warmer?*
   James was the *taller* of the two boys. [The superlative is
      occasionally used in such sentences, especially in informal
      speaking and writing.]

(2) **Use the superlative degree for three or more persons or
things.**

   Today is the *warmest* day of the year.
   William was the *tallest* of the three boys.

4d

Avoid any awkward or ambiguous use of a noun form as an adjective.

Although many noun forms (*boat* race, *show* business, *opera* tickets, etc.) are used effectively as adjectives, especially when appropriate adjectives are not available, such forms should be avoided when they are either awkward or ambiguous.

AWKWARD   I sometimes forget basic mathematics principles.
BETTER   I sometimes forget basic mathematical principles. OR:
               I sometimes forget principles of basic mathematics.

▶ EXERCISE 4   Revise the following sentences to provide the proper adjectives or adverbs in accordance with formal English usage. Write *C* after each sentence that needs no revision.

1. Don's explanation, the clearest of the two, indicates that he will do good at teaching.
2. Mr. Hawkins takes life entirely too serious.
3. If you want to catch him, you had better be quick about it.
4. We felt certain that we had walked long enough.
5. If Edna expects a passing grade, she had better study a reasonably amount of time.
6. So vivid does the author picture the meeting that the reader sure feels as if he is present.
7. Karen gets along with her professors, but she is not real smart.
8. When the truck stopped so sudden, Herb's car rammed into it.
9. Although this desk is probably some cheaper than that, it is not so well built.
10. I sure hope I can pronounce that French title correctly.

▶ EXERCISE 5   Compose sentences containing these constructions:

1. *good* as a subject complement
2. *well* modifying a verb
3. *surely* modifying a verb
4. an adjective used as subject complement after *looked*
5. an adverb modifying *looked*
6. an adjective following and modifying a direct object
7. an adverb following a direct object and modifying the verb
8. the superlative form of *bad*
9. the comparative form of *good*
10. a clear, effective noun form used as an adjective

Case

5

Use the proper case form to show the function of pronouns or nouns in sentences.

The pronouns *I*, *me*, *my*, and *mine* all refer to the one who is speaking or writing. The change in form to indicate function is called *case*. *I* is in the subjective or nominative case; *me*, in the objective case; and *my* and *mine*, in the possessive case. Nouns and some indefinite pronouns (*anyone*, *someone*, *everyone*, etc.) have a distinctive case form only for the possessive (the *boy's* book, the *boys'* mother; see **15a**), but six of our common pronouns have distinctive forms in all three cases and must be used with care.

FORMS

SUBJECTIVE	I	we	he, she	they	who
POSSESSIVE	my	our	his, her	their	whose
	(mine)	(ours)	(hers)	(theirs)	
OBJECTIVE	me	us	him, her	them	whom

Note: The personal pronouns *it* and *you* change form only to indicate the possessive—*its*, *your* (*yours*).

USES

SUBJECTIVE	*He* and *I* traveled together in France. [Subjects]
	It was *she who* paid the bill. [*She* used as subject complement, and *who* as subject of *paid*]
POSSESSIVE	That is *your* gift, not *mine*. [Possessors]
	Carl approved of *his* amending the motion. [Before the gerund]

OBJECTIVE Frances has already met *him.* [Direct object]
Give *them* our best regards. [Indirect object]
The task was hard for *us.* [Object of preposition]
Our guest did not expect *us* to entertain *him.* [*Us* is
subject of the infinitive; *him,* the object. See also **5e.**]

5a

Take special care with pronouns in apposition and in compound constructions.

(1) Appositives

An appositive takes the same case as the noun or pronoun with which it is in apposition.

We—John and *I* (not *me*)—are responsible for the damage.
[*I* is in the subjective case since it is in apposition with the
subject *we.*]
Let's you and *me* (not *I*) go together. Let us—you and *me*—
go together. [*Me* and *us* are in the same case]
Two boys—John and *I* (not *me*)—represented our class. [*I*
is in the subjective case since it is in apposition with the
subject *boys.*]
Our class was represented by two boys, John and *me* (not *I*).
[*Me* is in the objective case since it is in apposition with *boys,*
object of the preposition *by.*]

Note: Do not let an appositive following a pronoun trick you into making a mistake with case.

We boys often study together. [*We* is the subject of *study: We
study.* No one would say *Us often study.*]
He would not let *us* girls do any of the hard work. [Since *us*
is the subject of the infinitive (*to*) *do,* it is in the objective
case. See **5e.**]

(2) Compound constructions

My brother and *I* (not *me*) share expenses. [*I* is a subject
of the verb *share.*]

Everyone but Hazel and *her* (not *she*) signed the petition. [*Her* is an object of the preposition *but*.]

Last summer my father hired Tom and *me* (not *I*). [*Me* is an object of the verb *hired*.]

Note: In formal writing, *myself* is usually avoided as a substitute for *I* or *me*. See **19i**. The *-self* pronouns (such as *myself, himself, ourselves, themselves*) are ordinarily used either as reflexive or intensive pronouns.

REFLEXIVE James hurt *himself*.
INTENSIVE James *himself* was hurt.

▶ **EXERCISE 1** Compose brief sentences correctly using five of the following compound elements as appositives and five as subjects or objects.

1. Bill and he
2. Bill and him
3. you or I
4. you or me
5. her sister and her
6. her sister and she
7. Ann and she
8. her and Ann
9. they or we
10. them or us

5b

Determine the case of each pronoun by its use in its own clause.

(1) Pronoun as subject of a clause.

The subject of a clause always takes the subjective case, even when the whole clause is the object of a verb or a preposition.

He will employ *whoever* is willing to work. [*Whoever* is the subject of *is willing*. The whole clause *whoever is willing to work* is the object of *will employ*.]

He has respect for *whoever* is in power. [The complete clause *whoever is in power*, not merely the pronoun *whoever*, is the object of the preposition *for*.]

(2) Pronoun followed by a parenthetical *I think, he says,* etc.

Such parenthetical expressions as *I think, he says, we know* often cause the subjective *who* (*whoever, whosoever*) to be incorrectly changed to *whom* (*whomever, whomsoever*).

> Henry is a person *who* (not *whom*) I think will prove worthy of every trust. [*Who* is the subject of *will prove.*]
> Jones is a man *who* (not *whom*) we know is dependable.

(3) Pronoun following *than* or *as*.

A pronoun following *than* or *as* takes the subjective or objective case according to whether the pronoun is subject or object of an implied verb.

> He is older than *I* [am].
> He is as wise as *they* [are].
> He likes you better than *I* [like you].
> He likes you as much as *I* [like you].
> He likes you better than [he likes] *me*.
> He likes you as much as [he likes] *me*.

5c

In formal writing use *whom* for all objects.

EXAMPLES   For *whom* did you vote? [Good usage, formal or informal, calls for the objective *whom* when the pronoun immediately follows a preposition.]
                   The artist *whom* she loved has gone away. [*Whom* is the object of *loved.*]

Informal English tends to avoid the use of the objective *whom* unless it comes immediately after a preposition.

FORMAL   *Whom* did you vote for?
INFORMAL   Who did you vote for? [*Who* may be used in an informal situation to begin any question.]

Both informal and formal English may avoid *whom* by omitting it in sentences such as the following:

The artist she loved has gone away.

▶ EXERCISE 2   First underline each subordinate clause below and determine the use of the relative pronoun in its own clause; then choose the correct pronoun within the parentheses.

1. Mary Todd, (who, whom) historians say was socially ambitious, married a country lawyer.
2. Daniel Boone is the hero (who, whom) I most admire.
3. The author is a local woman to (who, whom) a Pulitzer prize was awarded.
4. (Whoever, Whomever) designed the August cover is a clever cartoonist.
5. Do you know the name of the Frenchman (who, whom) it is said made a helicopter as long ago as 1784?
6. Fran, (who, whom) the boys think is a poor dancer, won the figure skating championship.
7. He is an orator (who, whom), I believe, has a golden tongue.
8. Are these the astronauts (who, whom) your father talked about?
9. (Who, Whom) will be his opponent is not yet known.
10. (Who, Whom) he will fight is not yet known.

5d

A pronoun immediately before the gerund (verbal noun) is usually in the possessive case.

EXAMPLES   *His* leaving the farm was a surprise.
           Mother approved of *my* (*our, his, her, your, their*) going to the fair.

Note: Since the gerund (verbal noun) and the present participle (verbal adjective) both end in *-ing*, they are sometimes difficult to distinguish. See **Verbals**, Section 35. When the emphasis is on the noun or pronoun preceding the verbal, the verbal may be interpreted as a participle modifying the noun or pronoun. Then the noun or pronoun is not used in the possessive case.

PARTICIPLE (VERBAL ADJECTIVE)	GERUND (VERBAL NOUN)
We caught *John* running away.	*John's* running away was unexpected.
We could not think of *him* acting the part.	*His* acting was surprisingly good.

5e

Use the objective case for subject, object, or complement of an infinitive.

EXAMPLES He asked *me* to help *him*. [*Me* is the subject and *him* is the object of the infinitive *to help*. *Me to help him* is the object of the verb *asked*.]
We expected *him* to be *her*. [*Him* is the subject and *her* is the complement of the infinitive *to be*.]

Note: In formal writing the complement of the infinitive *to be* is in the subjective case when the infinitive *to be* has no subject.

I would like to be *he*.

5f

Use the subjective case for the complement of the verb *be*.

PATTERN SUBJECT—LINKING VERB *BE*—COMPLEMENT.

| That | may be | she. |
| It | was | they. |

Note: Informal usage accepts *It is me (It's me)*.

▶ EXERCISE 3 Give the reason why each italicized noun or pronoun below is correct by pointing out its function. If any sentence sounds wrong to you, read it aloud several times so that you will become accustomed to saying and hearing correct case forms.

1. Just between you and *me*, both her sister and *she* are in love with the same man.
2. The losers, you and *he*, deserve this booby prize.
3. It is Doris and *she whom* he blames.
4. He blames Doris and *her*, not you and *me*.
5. *Jack's* teasing did not annoy Tom or *me*.
6. Since Marian eats a great deal more than *I*, I do not weigh as much as *she*.
7. Let's you and *me* send an invitation to Kate and *him*.
8. The professor asked *us* students to write a composition about someone *whom* we particularly admired.
9. He introduced me to Ruth and *her*, *who* I think are his sisters.
10. *We* boys always cooperate with our coach, *whom* we respect and *who* respects us.

▶ EXERCISE 4   Find and correct all case errors in the following sentences. Write *C* after each sentence that needs no revision.

1. Van objected to me buying Hogarth's *The Shrimp Girl.*
2. He wanted us—Luke, you, and I—to choose *Calais Gate* instead.
3. Whom do you think is the best pitcher in the league?
4. Between you and I, I prefer Japanese wood-block prints.
5. It was I who made the mistake.
6. My sister, who I have told you of, collects Grant Wood paintings.
7. Us boys all landed at Kennedy Airport yesterday.
8. Jorge can do the trimming and spraying as well as me.
9. Sheriff Comstock, to who I had introduced myself, had records of three men who he believed were capable of committing a burglary such as that in East Dover Heights.
10. Whom does your professor consider is the best modern composer?

Agreement

6

Make a verb agree in number with its subject; make a pronoun agree in number with its antecedent.

Singular subjects require singular verbs; plural subjects require plural verbs.[1] Pronouns agree with their antecedents (the words to which they refer) in the same way. Note that in the subject the -*s* ending is the sign of the plural, that in the verb it is the sign of the third person singular.

The *risk* of the workers *seems* great. [Singular subject—singular verb]

The *risks* of the workers *seem* great. [Plural subject—plural verb]

The *woman* washes *her* own clothes. [Singular antecedent—singular pronoun]

The *women* wash *their* own clothes. [Plural antecedent—plural pronoun]

Single out each subject and its verb and connect them mentally (*risk seems, risks seem*). Do the same with each antecedent and its pronoun (*woman ← her, women ← their*). This practice will make it easy to avoid errors in agreement. If you find it difficult to distinguish verbs and relate them to their subjects, review **1a** and **1b**.

---

[1] Although verbs have no number, it is customary to use the terms *singular verbs* for verb forms used with singular subjects and *plural verbs* for those used with plural subjects.

6a

Make a verb agree in number with its subject.

(1) Do not be misled (a) by nouns or pronouns intervening between the subject and the verb or (b) by subjects and verbs with endings difficult to pronounce.

> The *recurrence* of like sounds *helps* (not *help*) to stir the emotions.
> Every *one* of you *is* (not *are*) invited to the panel discussion.
> The *scientist asks* (not *ask*) pertinent questions.

The number of the subject is not changed by the addition of parenthetical expressions introduced by such words as *with, together with, as well as, no less than, including, accompanied by.*

> *John*, together with James and William, *was drafted* into the Army.
> *Thomas*, like his two brothers, *was* often in debt.

(2) Subjects joined by *and* are usually plural.

> A hammer and a saw *are* useful tools.
> Mary, Jane, and I *were* tired after our morning's work.

Exceptions: A compound subject referring to a single person, or to two or more things considered as a unit, is singular.

> My best friend and adviser *has gone.* [A single individual was both friend and adviser.]
> The tumult and the shouting *dies.*—KIPLING. [Two nouns considered a single entity]

Each or *every* preceding singular subjects joined by *and* calls for a singular verb.

> Each boy and each girl *is* to work independently.
> Every boy and girl *has been urged* to attend the play.

(3) Singular subjects joined by *or, nor, either . . . or, neither . . . nor* usually take a singular verb.

> Neither the boy nor the girl *is* to blame for the accident.
> Either the man or his wife *knows* the exact truth of the matter.

When the meaning is felt to be plural, informal English occasionally uses the plural verb: "Neither she nor I *were* dancing, for we felt tired."

If one subject is singular and one plural, the verb usually agrees with the nearer.

> Neither teacher nor pupils *are* invited.
> Neither pupils nor teacher *is* invited.
> Either you or I *am* mistaken.

Many writers prefer to recast such sentences and thus avoid the problem:

> The invitation included neither teacher nor pupils.
> Either you are mistaken or I am. OR One of us is mistaken.

(4) When the subject follows the verb (as in sentences beginning with *there is, there are*) special care is needed to determine the subject and to make sure that it agrees with the verb.

> According to the rules, there *are* to be at least three *contestants* for each prize. [Contestants—are]
> There *are* many possible *candidates*.
> There *is* only one good *candidate*.

Before a compound subject the first member of which is singular, a singular verb is sometimes used: "In the basement there *is* a restaurant, which serves delicious food, and a poolroom and two barber shops."

Note: The expletive *it* is always followed by a singular verb: "It *is* the *woman* who suffers." "It *is* the *women* who suffer."

(5) A relative pronoun used as a subject takes a plural or singular verb to accord with its antecedent.

Boys who *work* .... A *boy* who *works* ....

Mary is among the *students* who *have done* honor to the college. [*Students* is the antecedent of *who.*]

Mary is the only *one* of our students who *has achieved* national recognition. [*One,* not *students,* is the antecedent of *who.* The sentence means, "Of all our students Mary is the only *one* who *has achieved* national recognition."]

(6) When used as subjects, *each, either, neither, another, anyone, anybody, anything, someone, somebody, something, one, everyone, everybody, everything, nobody, nothing* regularly take singular verbs.

Each *takes* his turn at rowing.
Neither *likes* the friends of the other.
Someone *is* likely to hear the signal.
Everyone *has* his prejudices.
Nobody *cares* to listen to worries.

None is plural or singular, depending upon the other words in the sentence or in the immediately surrounding sentences (the context) which condition its meaning.

None *are* so blind as those who will not see.
None *is* so blind as he who will not see.

(*Any, all, more, most,* and *some* are used with plural or singular verbs in much the same way as *none.*)

(7) Collective nouns (and numbers denoting fixed quantity) usually take singular verbs because the group or quantity is usually regarded as a unit.

The whole family *is* concerned. [The common use: *family* regarded as a unit]

The family *have gone* about their several duties. [Less common: individuals of the family regarded separately]

A thousand bushels *is* a good yield. [A unit]
A thousand bushels *were crated.* [Individual bushels]

The number of students *was* small. [*The number* is regularly taken as a unit.]

A number of students *were* sick. [*A number* refers to individuals.]

(8) **A verb agrees with its subject, not with its predicate noun.**

His chief support *is* his brother and sister.
His brother and sister *are* his chief support.

But such sentences are often better recast so as to avoid the disagreement in number between subject and predicate noun.

BETTER　His support came chiefly from his brother and sister.

(9) **Nouns plural in form but singular in meaning usually take singular verbs. In all doubtful cases a good dictionary should be consulted.**

Regularly singular: aesthetics, civics, economics, genetics, linguistics, mathematics, measles, mumps, news, physics, semantics

Regularly plural: environs, trousers

Some nouns ending in *-ics* (such as *athletics, acoustics,* and *statistics*) are considered singular when referring to an organized body of knowledge and plural when referring to activities, qualities, or individual facts.

Athletics [activity in games] *is required* of every student.
Athletics [various games] *provide* good recreation.

Acoustics *is* an interesting study.
The acoustics of the hall *are* good.

Statistics *is* a science.
The statistics *were* easily *assembled.*

(10) A title of a single work or a word spoken of as a word, even when plural in form, takes a singular verb.

> *Twice-Told Tales was written* by Hawthorne.
> The New York *Times has* a wide circulation.
> *They is* a pronoun.

▶ **EXERCISE 1**   Read the following correct sentences aloud, stressing the italicized words. If any sentence sounds wrong to you, read it aloud as many times as necessary for the verb form to sound right.

1. After the lecture, *everybody* in the group *is* invited to meet the speaker.
2. The *farmer,* as well as his sons, *grows* wheat.
3. *Each* of those lawyers *has* won many suits.
4. One of the *men who were* fishing on the pier caught a stingaree.
5. He was the *only one* in the group *who was* bored.
6. A *dictionary* and a *thesaurus are* lying on my desk.
7. Doyle's *"The Five Orange Pips" is* a fascinating story.
8. There *are* a few *cookies* and potato *chips* left.
9. Here *come* the *clowns!*
10. Every *one* of the *boys who belong* to the organization *is* planning to help build and decorate the float.

▶ **EXERCISE 2**   Choose the correct form of the verb within parentheses in each of the following sentences.

1. Taste in magazines (differ, differs) greatly.
2. There (is, are) ever so many men needed to fill the quota.
3. Each of the awards (carries, carry) several guarantees.
4. (Is, Are) either of the novels likely to become a best seller?
5. The cat or her kittens (are, is) to blame for turning over the Christmas tree.
6. Those buttermilk clouds (presage, presages) a storm.
7. Everyone in the stands (were, was) unusually quiet.

8. Almost every illustration in these folios (has, have) been done by an amateur.
9. (Is, Are) neither of those clever floats to be awarded a prize?
10. A rustic lodge with tall pines and fishing waters close by (was, were) what we wanted.

▶ EXERCISE 3   In the following sentences, find each verb and relate it to its subject. If subject and verb do not agree, change the verb to secure agreement. Justify every change. Write *C* after each sentence that needs no revision.

1. Neither rain nor sleet stop our postman.
2. Do either of you really understand the extent of your obligations?
3. Neither of you appreciates my sense of humor.
4. Everybody we met in town were excitedly talking about Mr. Zello's speech.
5. A simple majority are sufficient to elect Gene class secretary.
6. His aging parents and the provision he might make for them were his one principal concern.
7. There comes to my mind now the two or three men who were most influential in my life.
8. The significance of words is learned by breaking them up into suffixes, prefixes, and roots.
9. A study of the many contrasts in the poetry of Browning and Tennyson seem a good research topic.
10. Has each and every one of the figures been checked on that account sheet?

▶ EXERCISE 4   Rewrite the following *correct* sentences as directed. Change verbs to secure agreement and make any additional changes required for good sentence sense.

¹ Certain portions of our collection are kept in an underground, air-conditioned vault and are never placed on exhibit. [Insert *One* before *Certain.*]   ² Each piece in

the exhibit has to be carefully dusted and polished once a day and then put back in place. [Change *Each piece* to *The pieces*.]   ³ I might mention that this particular specimen has a distinguished place in history. [Change *this* to *these*.]   ⁴ Our staff takes great pride in the efficient cataloging system which we have developed here. [Insert *members* after *staff*.]   ⁵ In this room is my assistant, who is cataloging a newly arrived shipment. [Change *assistant* to *assistants*.]   ⁶ One of our research parties has just returned from the field and is to be meeting with the directors during the remainder of the week. [Change *One* to *Two*.]   ⁷ A detachment of four men has been left behind to maintain a permanent camp at the excavation site. [Omit *A detachment of*.]   ⁸ Eaton Murray, the leader of the expedition and an especially capable man, is among the four. [Insert *John Wade* after *and*.]   ⁹ Neither of the others is known to us here. [Change *is known* to *are unknown*.]   ¹⁰ Both, however, were selected for particular abilities which they have shown. [Change *they* to *he*.]

6b

Make a pronoun agree in number with its antecedent.

A singular antecedent (one which would take a singular verb) is referred to by a singular pronoun; a plural antecedent (one which would take a plural verb) is referred to by a plural pronoun.

(1) **In formal English, use a singular pronoun to refer to such antecedents as** *man, woman, person, one, anyone, anybody, someone, somebody, everyone, everybody, each, kind, sort, either, neither, no one, nobody.* **See also 6a(6).**

An outstanding trait of primitive *man* was *his* (NOT *their*) belief in superstitions.

In informal English, plural pronouns are sometimes used after such antecedents when the sense is clearly plural.

> Each of the boys had planned to follow *his* father's occupation. [Formal]
> Each of the boys had planned to follow *their* father's occupation. [Informal]

Note: Avoid illogical sentences that may result from strict adherence to this rule.

ILLOGICAL	Since every one of the patients seemed discouraged, I told a joke to cheer him up.
LOGICAL	Since all the patients seemed discouraged, I told a joke to cheer *them* up.

(2) **Two or more antecedents joined by *and* are referred to by a plural pronoun; two or more singular antecedents joined by *or* or *nor* are referred to by a singular pronoun. If one of two antecedents joined by *or* is singular and one plural, the pronoun usually agrees with the nearer. See also 6a(2),(3).**

> *Henry and James* have completed *their* work.
> Neither *Henry nor James* has completed *his* work.

> Neither the *master* nor the *servants* were aware of *their* danger. [The plural *servants* is the nearer antecedent.]
> Neither the *servants* nor the *master* was aware of *his* danger. [If the danger is to the master rather than the servants, the subjects can be reversed.]

Note: Avoid clumsy sentences that may result from strict adherence to the rule.

CLUMSY	When a *boy or girl* enters college, *he or she* finds it different from high school.
BETTER	When *boys and girls* enter college, *they* find it different from high school.

(3) **Collective nouns are referred to by singular or plural pronouns depending on whether the collective noun is considered singular or plural. See also 6a(7).**

Special care should be taken to avoid making a collective noun *both* singular and plural within the same sentence.

INCONSISTENT   The group is writing their own music. [The *group* is first considered singular because of the choice of *is* and then plural because of *their*.]

CONSISTENT   The *group is* writing *its* own music. [Singular]

CONSISTENT   The *group are* writing *their* own music. [Plural]

▶ **EXERCISE 5**   Compose brief sentences using each antecedent and pronoun listed below.

EXAMPLE   type ← its
That *type* of battery soon loses *its* power.

1. everybody ← he
2. neither ← she
3. each ← his
4. a person ← him
5. committee ← they
6. committee ← its
7. none ← those
8. none ← he
9. boy or his sisters ← they
10. girls or their brother ← he

▶ **EXERCISE 6**   Write *C* after each correct sentence below. If a sentence contains a pronoun that does not agree with its antecedent in number, eliminate the error by substituting a correct pronoun form.

1. According to G. B. Shaw, a woman delights in wounding a man's ego, though a man takes most pleasure in gratifying hers.
2. An author like Shaw, however, seldom captures the whole truth with their generalizations.
3. A generalization is frequently only partially true, though a person may quote it and think they wholly believe it.
4. For example, nearly everyone, to express their appreciation, has said with great conviction, "A friend in need is a friend indeed."
5. At the same time, probably no one will deny that far too often a successful man avoids the very shoulders

that they have climbed upon or despises the hands that once fed them.

6. Each of these quotations contains its grain of truth, but not the whole truth: (1) "As a rule man is a fool." (2) "What a piece of work is a man! how noble in reason!"

7. That these quotations are contradictory anyone in their right mind can see.

8. Though contradictory, each of the quotations may be true if they are applied to specific persons in particular circumstances.

9. A great satirist like Swift or Mark Twain in their works may often depict man as a fool.

10. Yet every reader who thinks for himself knows that the satirist—by pointing out man's foibles and follies—strives to reform man by showing him the value of making good use of his reason for lofty purposes.

▶ EXERCISE 7   In the following sentences select the pronoun in parentheses that agrees with its antecedent in accordance with formal English usage. Note any pronouns that would be acceptable in conversation or familiar writing but not in formal writing.

¹ The foreman unlocked the shed and everybody went in and got (his, their) tools.   ² Each man, and Charlie too, left (his, their) lunch pail inside.   ³ Roy and Dave were tearing out concrete forms, and (he, each, they) took a section apiece and went to work.   ⁴ One or another would yell for help to clear away the salvage lumber (he was, they were) tearing out.   ⁵ The helpers were supposed to pile the lumber outside the foundation, where Andy was cleaning (it, them) up and stacking (it, them) for re-use.   ⁶ Every few minutes someone would call out for the water boy to bring (him, them) a drink.   ⁷ The crew was small, but (its, their) thirst was large.   ⁸ Charlie, the water boy, had all he could do to keep (it, them) satisfied.   ⁹ "If anybody here ever drank water when (he was, they were)

off the job," he grumbled, "I'd be proud to shake (him, them) by the hand." ¹⁰ But nobody volunteered (his, their) hand to be shaken. ¹¹ Every minute, instead, somebody new would be yelling for water, and Charlie would trudge off toward (him, them). ¹² It was either Roy or Dave who was whooping for (his, their) ninetieth drink when the noon whistle blew. ¹³ Nobody was so ready to stop where (he was, they were) as Charlie. ¹⁴ "Whoever wants a drink knows where (he, they) can get it," he let it be known, and emptied his bucket out on the ground.

▶ **EXERCISE 8** In Exercise 7 make each change as directed below and then complete the sentence so as to secure agreement of pronoun with its antecedent. In Sentence 1, change *everybody* to *the workmen*. In 4, change *One or another* to *Both*. In 9, change *anybody here* to *these men*. In 11, change *somebody new* to *two or three more*.

Tense and Mood

7

Use the appropriate form of the verb.

Verbs have more inflections than any other part of speech. All verbs have at least three forms: the form in the dictionary, the *-s* form, and the *-ing* form.

set, sets, setting   hurt, hurts, hurting

Most verbs have four forms. All regular verbs (those which take the endings *-d*, *-ed*, or *-t*) have four forms.

REGULAR VERBS   believe, believes, believing, believed
repeat, repeats, repeating, repeated
sweep, sweeps, sweeping, swept

Some irregular verbs (those not taking the endings *-d*, *-ed*, or *-t*) have four forms; others have five; a few, three. *Be*, the most irregular verb in the language, has eight forms.

IRREGULAR VERBS   become, becomes, becoming, became
choose, chooses, choosing, chose, chosen
burst, bursts, bursting
be, am, is, are, was, were, being, been

It is very important that you learn not only how to recognize verbs but also how to use appropriate verb forms in your speaking and writing.

Tense relates to *time*. Verb forms indicate time and therefore have tense. Actually, there are three main divisions of time: past, present, and future. But actual time and grammatical tense do not always agree. Some grammarians (basing their classification upon form changes of single-word verbs) designate only two tenses: present and past. Other grammarians (considering both auxiliaries and single-word form changes) describe the following six tenses. Notice that the six tenses in the following examples are built on three forms of the verb *see,* called the *principal parts.* (See the list of principal parts of verbs on pages 71–72.)

PRESENT TENSE   *see*—used with all subjects except third-person singular ones
                 sees—used only with third-person singular subjects

He *sees* me daily. [Habitual action]
Tomorrow I *see* my lawyer. [Used for future]
The Spaniards *see* their Armada defeated. [Historical present]
Men *see* that death is inevitable. [Universal truth]

PAST TENSE   *saw*

He *saw* me yesterday. [Past action at a specific time stated or implied]

FUTURE TENSE   *will see, shall see*

Tomorrow he *will see* his lawyer.

PRESENT PERFECT   *have seen*—used with all subjects except third-person singular
                   has seen—used with third-person singular subjects

Have you ever *seen* a mermaid? [Past action at any time before now]
Myra *has seen* the fair. [Before now]

PAST PERFECT   *had seen*

I *had seen* him before the game started. [Past action completed before another past action]

FUTURE PERFECT (rarely used)   *shall have seen, will have seen*

By tomorrow evening I *will have seen* the report. [Action completed before a set future time]

Other auxiliaries (in addition to *will, shall, has, have,* and *had*) also express time:

I *used to* see him every day. [Past]
We *are going to* see much progress. [Future]
He *is about to* see defeat. [Immediate future]

In the indicative mood, both active and passive verbs have all these six tense forms. (See the conjugation of the verb *see* under **Conjugation** in Section **35.** See this section also for definitions of such terms as **Mood** and **Voice.**)

In addition to the simple verb forms illustrated by the conjugation, English uses a progressive form (the *-ing* form—*is seeing*) to show action in progress and a *do* form (*do see, does see, did see*) for (1) emphatic statements, (2) questions, or (3) negations. The *do* form is used only in the present and the past.

EMPHATIC   I *did see* a mirage.
QUESTION   *Did* you *see* that picture?
NEGATION   He *does* not *see* her often.

Below is a summary of the forms of *see*—the simple forms and the progressive forms, both active and passive voice.

PRESENT	he sees, is seen, is seeing, is being seen
PAST	he saw, was seen, was seeing, was being seen
FUTURE	he will see, will be seen, will be seeing, will be being seen
PRESENT PERFECT	he has seen, has been seen, has been seeing, has been being seen
PAST PERFECT	he had seen, had been seen, had been seeing, had been being seen
FUTURE PERFECT	he will have seen, will have been seen, will have been seeing, will have been being seen

In the imperative mood, verbs have only present tense: *See. Be seen.* For forms of the subjunctive, see **7c.** See also **Conjugation** in Section **35.**

Verbals also have tense, but not all six tenses:

INFINITIVES	to see, to be seen, to be seeing [Present tense]
	to have seen, to have been seen, to have been seeing [Present perfect]
PARTICIPLES	seeing, being seen [Present tense]
	seen [Past tense]
	having seen, having been seen [Present perfect]
GERUNDS	seeing, being seen [Present tense]
	having seen, having been seen [Present perfect]

7a

Avoid confusing similar verbs or misusing principal parts of verbs.

Confused Verbs

The forms of transitive verbs such as *lay* and *set* are sometimes confused with intransitive verbs such as *lie* and *sit.* A verb with an object is a *transitive* verb; the object can ordinarily be made into the subject of the same verb made passive. Master the principal parts of the following verbs, observing in the examples that (1) forms of the intransitive verbs *lie* and *sit* do not have objects and are not passive, and (2) forms of the transitive verbs *lay* and *set* either have an object or are in the passive. Also observe the meanings of these verbs.

Present stem (infinitive)	Past tense	Past participle	Present participle
lie (to recline)	lay	lain	lying
lay (to cause to lie)	laid	laid	laying
sit (to be seated)	sat	sat	sitting
set (to place or put)	set	set	setting

Lie down. Yesterday he *lay* asleep in Ward 20. *Has* it *lain* there long? Papers *are lying* on the porch.

Lay it down. Yesterday he *laid* bricks. They *are laying* plans now. A foundation *was laid* last week.

Sit down. Helen *sat* up straight. *Have* you *sat* here long? A flowerpot *was sitting* on the window ledge.

Set that down. *Will* you *set* the time? They *were setting* the table. A date *has been set.*

▶ EXERCISE 1   Oral Drill. Respond to each of the following commands (1) in the present progressive tense, (2) in the past tense, and (3) in the present perfect tense. For example, the responses to *Sit down* would be: *I am sitting down; I sat down; I have sat down.*

1. Sit in the rocking chair.
2. Lay the facts in front of him.
3. Set that vase on the mantelpiece.
4. Lie down for a few minutes.
5. Set the tray where he can reach it.
6. Lay a little money aside each pay day.
7. Sit where you can see well.
8. Set a bowl of fruit in the middle of the table.
9. Lie in wait for him.
10. Lay your coat over a chair.

Misused Principal Parts

If you do not know the verb form needed to express a given tense, you can determine the correct form by consulting your dictionary for the principal parts of the verb. In the dictionary every irregular verb is listed by its infinitive or present stem—for example, *see*. Then follow the past tense (*saw*), the past participle (*seen*), and the present participle (*seeing*). *See, saw,* and *seen* are the principal parts from which you can readily derive the proper form for any of the six tenses. For regular verbs (such as *use*) the past tense and the past participle, when not given, are understood to be formed by adding *-d* or *-ed*.

NONSTANDARD	The boy seen where the bullet had entered. [Past tense needed; the dictionary gives *saw* as the correct form.]
STANDARD	The boy *saw* where the bullet had entered.
NONSTANDARD	I use to live in the country. [Past tense needed]
STANDARD	I *used* to live in the country.

▶ **EXERCISE 2**   Make your own SPECIAL LIST OF PRINCIPAL PARTS of verbs which you need to study and review. Include from the following list any verbs whose principal parts are not thoroughly familiar to you, and add all verbs that you have used incorrectly in your writing. Master your SPECIAL LIST and compose sentences to illustrate the correct use of each principal part.

Present stem	*Past tense*	*Past participle*
bear	bore	borne
begin	began	begun
bite	bit	bitten, bit
blow	blew	blown
break	broke	broken
bring	brought	brought
burst	burst	burst
catch	caught	caught
choose	chose	chosen
come	came	come
dive	dived, dove	dived
do	did	done
drag	dragged	dragged
draw	drew	drawn
drink	drank	drunk
drive	drove	driven
eat	ate	eaten
fall	fell	fallen
fly	flew	flown
forbid	forbade, forbad	forbidden
freeze	froze	frozen
get	got	got, gotten
give	gave	given
go	went	gone

Present stem	Past tense	Past participle
grow	grew	grown
know	knew	known
lead	led	led
lose	lost	lost
raise	raised	raised
ride	rode	ridden
ring	rang	rung
rise	rose	risen
run	ran	run
shake	shook	shaken
shrink	shrank, shrunk	shrunk, shrunken
sing	sang, sung	sung
sink	sank, sunk	sunk
speak	spoke	spoken
spring	sprang, sprung	sprung
steal	stole	stolen
swear	swore	sworn
swim	swam	swum
swing	swung	swung
take	took	taken
tear	tore	torn
throw	threw	thrown
wear	wore	worn
wring	wrung	wrung
write	wrote	written

7b

Use logical tense forms in sequence, focusing upon the tense of the main or governing verb.

(1) Verbs in clauses

Make the tense of a verb in a subordinate clause relate logically and naturally to the tense of the verb in the main clause.

> The audience *rose* as the speaker *entered.* [The past *entered* follows the past *rose.*]
>
> I *have ceased* worrying because I *have heard* no more rumors. [The present perfect follows the present perfect.]

When I *had been* at camp four weeks, I *received* word that my father *had died*. [The past perfect *had been* or *had died* indicates a time prior to that of the main verb *received*.]

If Bill *had attended* (NOT *attended*) classes regularly, he *could have passed* the final examination.

(2) Infinitives

Use the present infinitive to express action contemporaneous with, or later than, that of the governing verb; use the perfect infinitive for action prior to that of the governing verb.

I hoped *to go* (NOT *to have gone*). I hope *to go.* [Present infinitives. At the time indicated by the verbs I was still hoping *to go,* not *to have gone.*]

I would like *to have lived* in Shakespeare's time. [Perfect infinitive—expressing time prior to that of the governing verb. *Simpler:* I wish I had lived in Shakespeare's time.]

I would have liked *to live* (NOT *to have lived*) in Shakespeare's time. [Present infinitive—for time contemporaneous with that of the governing verb]

(3) Participles

Use the present participle to express action contemporaneous with that of the governing verb; use the perfect participle for action prior to that of the governing verb.

Walking along the streets, he met many old friends. [The walking and the meeting were contemporaneous.]

Having walked all the way home, he found himself tired. [The walking was prior to the finding.]

▶ **EXERCISE 3**   Choose the verb form inside parentheses that is the logical tense form in sequence.

1. When the fire sale (ended, had ended), the store displayed new merchandise.
2. Fans cheered as the touchdown (had been made, was made).

3. The freshmen hope (to celebrate, to have celebrated) tomorrow.

4. We should have agreed (to have chartered, to charter) a bus.

5. (Having finished his test, Finishing his test), James left the room.

6. (Having bought the tickets, Buying the tickets), Mr. Selby took the children to the circus.

7. The chairman had left the meeting before it (had adjourned, adjourned).

8. It is customary for ranchers (to brand, to have branded) their cattle.

9. Phoebe had not expected (to see, to have seen) her cousin in the shop.

10. The pond has begun freezing because the temperature (dropped, has dropped).

7c

Use the subjunctive mood in the few types of expressions in which it is still regularly used.

Distinctive forms for the subjunctive occur only (1) in the present and past tenses of *be* and (2) in the present tense of other verbs used with third-person singular subjects.

INDICATIVE   I *am,* you *are,* he *is,* others *are* [Present]
                 I *was,* you *were,* he *was,* others *were* [Past]

SUBJUNCTIVE (with all subjects): *be* [Present], *were* [Past]

INDICATIVE   he sees, others see [Present]

SUBJUNCTIVE (that) he see, (that) others see [Present]

See also **Conjugation,** Section **35.**

Although the subjunctive mood has been largely displaced by the indicative, the subjunctive is still used in a few structures, such as the following:

> As Steinberg once remarked, it was as if he *were* guided by an ouija board.   —OLIVER LA FARGE

> Such a school demands from the teacher that he *be* a kind of artist in his province.   —ALBERT EINSTEIN

The subjunctive is required (1) in *that* clauses of motions, resolutions, recommendations, orders, or demands and (2) in a few idiomatic expressions.

> I move that the report *be* approved.
> Resolved, that dues for the coming year *be* doubled.
> I recommend (order, demand) that the prisoner *see* his lawyer.
> I demand (request, insist) that the messenger *go* alone.
> If need *be* . . . . *Suffice* it to say . . . . *Come* what may . . . .
> [Fixed subjunctive in idiomatic expressions]

Many writers prefer the subjunctive in contrary-to-fact conditions.

INFORMAL   If the apple was ripe, it would be good. [Indicative form]

PREFERRED   If the apple *were* ripe, it would be good. [Subjunctive]

INFORMAL   I wish that he was here now. [Indicative form]

PREFERRED   I wish that he *were* here now. [Subjunctive]

▶ EXERCISE 4   Underline all subjunctive verb forms used in the following sentences. Write *R* after those sentences containing *required* subjunctives; write *P* after those containing subjunctives preferred by many writers. Write *I* after sentences with verb forms that would be labeled *informal*.

1. If Lena was here, she'd explain everything.
2. We insist that he be punished.
3. I wish that peace were possible.
4. Americans now speak of Spain as though it were just across the river.

5. Present-day problems demand that we be ready for any emergency.
6. If there was time, I could finish my report.
7. Come what may, we will never choose anarchy.
8. I demand that he make amends.
9. If I were you, I would apply tomorrow.
10. The man acts as though he were the owner.

▶ EXERCISE 5 Compose five sentences in which the subjunctive is required. Compose three other sentences in which either the subjunctive or the indicative may be used, giving the indicative (informal) form in parentheses.

7d

Avoid needless shifts in tense or mood.

SHIFT He came to the river and pays a man to ferry him across. [Inconsistent use of tenses within one sentence]

IMPROVED He *came* to the river and *paid* a man to ferry him across.

INCONSISTENT It is necessary to restrain an occasional foolhardy park visitor lest a mother bear *mistake* his friendly intentions and *supposes* him a menace to her cubs. [Mood shifts improperly from subjunctive to indicative within the compound predicate.] But females with cubs *were* only one of the dangers. [A correct enough sentence if standing alone, but here inconsistent with present tense of preceding one, and therefore misleading] One *has* to remember that all bears *were* wild animals and not domesticated pets. [Inconsistent and misleading shift of tense from present in main clause to past in subordinate clause] Though a bear *may* seem altogether peaceable and harmless, he *might* not remain peaceable, and he is never harmless. [Tense shifts improperly from present in introductory clause to past in main clause.] It *is* therefore an important part of the park ranger's duty *to watch* the tourists, and above all *don't* let anybody try to feed the bears. [Inconsistent. Mood shifts needlessly from indicative to imperative.]

IMPROVED It is necessary to restrain an occasional foolhardy park visitor lest a mother bear *mistake* his friendly intentions and *suppose* him a menace to her cubs. But females with cubs *are* only one of the dangers. One *has* to remember that all bears *are* wild animals and not domesticated pets. Though a bear *may* seem altogether peaceable and harmless, he *may* not remain peaceable, and he is never harmless. It *is* therefore an important part of the park ranger's duty *to watch* the tourists and above all not *to let* anybody try to feed the bears.

See also **27a** and **27b**.

▶ EXERCISE 6   In the following passage correct all errors and inconsistencies in tense and mood and any other errors in verb usage. Write *C* after any sentence which is satisfactory as it stands.

¹ Across the Thames from Shakespeare's London lay the area known as the Bankside, probably as rough and unsavory a neighborhood as ever laid across the river from any city.   ² And yet it was to such a place that Shakespeare and his company had to have gone to build their new theater.   ³ For the Puritan government of the City had set up all sorts of prohibitions against theatrical entertainment within the city walls.   ⁴ When it became necessary, therefore, for the Company to have moved their playhouse from its old location north of the city, they obtain a lease to a tract on the Bankside.   ⁵ Other theatrical companies had went there before them, and it seemed reasonable to have supposed that Shakespeare and his partners would prosper in the new location. ⁶ Apparently the Puritans of the City had no law against anyone's moving cartloads of lumber through the public streets.   ⁷ There is no record that the Company met with difficulty while the timbers of the dismantled playhouse are being hauled to the new site.   ⁸ One difficulty the partners had foresaw and forestalled, and that is the effort that their old landlord might make to have stopped their removing the building.   ⁹ Lest his presence complicate their task and would perhaps defeat its working altogether, they waited until he had gone out of town.

10 And when he came back, his lot was bare; the building's timbers were all in stacks on the far side of the river; and the theater is waiting only to be put together. 11 It is a matter of general knowledge that on the Bankside Shakespeare continued his successful career as a showman and went on to enjoy even greater prosperity after he had made the move than before.

7e

Observe such distinctions as exist among *should, would, shall,* and *will*.

(1) Use *should* in all persons to express an obligation (in the sense "ought to") or a condition.

> I (You, He, We, They) *should* (*ought to*) help the needy.
> If I (you, he, we, they) *should* resign, the program would not be continued.

(2) Use *would* in all persons to express a wish or a customary action.

> *Would* that I (you, he, we, they) had received the message!
> I (You, He, We, They) *would* spend hours by the seashore during the summer months.

Caution: Do not use *would have* as a substitute for *had*.

> If you *had* (not *would have*) arrived earlier, you would have seen the President.

Shall is generally used for the first person in asking questions (*Shall* I go first?), and it is often used in all persons for special emphasis. Except for these uses of *shall*, and for the use of *should* to express an obligation or condition, informal English tends to use *will* and *would* in all persons.

A few writers still distinguish between *shall* and *will*:

(a) By using *shall* in the first person and *will* in the second and third to express the simple future or expectation (I *shall* plan to stay; he *will* probably stay).

(b) By using *will* in the first person and *shall* in the second and third to express determination, threat, command, prophecy, promise, or willingness (I *will* stay; you and he *shall* stay).

▶ **EXERCISE 7**   Revise those sentences below which contain any incorrect verb form; write *C* after those needing no revision. Be prepared to justify each revision.

1. Has spring training began yet?
2. If he would have registered later, he would have had Saturday classes.
3. Start the engine, and then you should release the brake.
4. If you set up too late, you may wish to lay in bed till noon next day.
5. If Mary enrolled in the class at the beginning, she could have made good grades.
6. It has been said that a rolling stone gathers no moss.
7. A stone lying in one position for a long time may gather moss.
8. The members recommended that all delinquents be fined.
9. It was reported that there use to be very few delinquents.
10. After Mr. Norwood entered the room, he sat down at the desk and begins to write rapidly.
11. Until I received your letter, I was hoping to have had a visit from you.
12. We attend religious services to learn how we would conduct ourselves toward our fellows.
13. Follow the main road for a mile; then you need to take the next road on the left.
14. The beggar could not deny that he had stole the purse.
15. I should have liked to have been with the team on the trip to New Orleans.

MECHANICS

Manuscript Form and Revision; Syllabication

8

Put your manuscript in acceptable form. Make revisions with care.

8a
Use the proper materials.

(1) **Paper.**   Unless you are given other instructions, use standard theme paper, size 8½ by 11 inches, with lines about half an inch apart, and write only on the ruled side of the paper. (The usual notebook paper, even if it is the standard size, should not be used because the narrow spaces between lines make for hard reading and allow insufficient space for corrections.) For type-written manuscripts use the unruled side of theme paper; or, if you prefer, regular weight typewriter paper (not onion skin), size 8½ by 11 inches.

(2) **Ink.**   Use black or blue-black ink.

(3) **Typewriter.**   Unless otherwise instructed, submit type-written papers only if you do your own typewriting. Use a black ribbon and make sure that the type is clean.

8b

Arrange your writing in clear and orderly fashion on the page. Divide a word at the end of a line only between syllables.

(1) **Margins.**   Leave sufficient margins—about an inch and a half at the left and top, an inch at the right and bottom—to prevent a crowded appearance. The ruled lines on theme paper indicate the proper margins at the left and top.

(2) **Indention.**   Indent the first lines of paragraphs uniformly, about an inch in longhand and five spaces in typewritten copy.

(3) **Paging.**   Use Arabic numerals—without parentheses or period—in the upper right-hand corner to mark all pages after the first.

(4) **Title.**   *Do not put quotation marks around the title or underline it* (unless it is a quotation or the title of a book), and use no period after the title. Center the title on the page about an inch and a half from the top or on the first ruled line. Leave the next line blank and begin the first paragraph on the third line. In this way the title will stand off from the text. Capitalize the first and last word of the title and all other words except articles, short conjunctions, and short prepositions.

(5) **Poetry.**   Quoted lines of poetry should be arranged and indented as in the original. (See also **16a.**)

(6) **Punctuation.**   Never begin a line with a comma, a colon, a semicolon, or a terminal mark of punctuation; never end a line with opening quotation marks, bracket, or parenthesis.

(7) **Endorsement.**   Papers are endorsed in the way prescribed by the instructor to facilitate handling. Usually

papers carry the name of the student and the course, the date, and the number of the assignment.

(8) **Word Division at End of Line.**   You will seldom need to divide words, especially short ones, if you leave a reasonably wide right-hand margin. The reader will object less to an uneven margin than to a number of broken words. When division is necessary, remember to divide words carefully between syllables. Whenever you are uncertain about the proper syllabication of a word, consult a good dictionary.

> ig-ni-tion, sen-ti-nel, te-na-cious, in-con-gru-ous

Double consonants are usually divided except when they come at the end of a simple word.

> can-ning, com-mit-ting, *but* kill-ing

Do not divide a word so that a single letter is on either line (*e-vade, man-y*); a single letter on the first line is too small a saving of space to justify the break, and a single letter on the second line is no saving at all, for it could use the space on the first line needed for the hyphen. Do not confuse the reader by setting off an *-ed* pronounced as part of the preceding syllable (*enjoy-ed, gleam-ed*). Divide hyphenated words only where the hyphen comes in the regular spelling (*mass-produced* or *Pre-Raphaelite*).

▶ EXERCISE   With the aid of your dictionary write out the following words by syllables, grouping (1) those that may properly be divided at the end of a line, and (2) those that may not be divided:

affection	levy	through	veiled
against	looked	tolerate	walked
alone	nature	transient	weary
combed	omit	treaty	willing
decadent	rainy	troller	willow

8c

Write legibly, so that your writing may be read easily and accurately.

(1) Spacing for Legibility. Adequate space between lines and between the words in the line is essential to easy reading. In typewritten copy use double space between lines. Single-spaced copy is difficult for the instructor to read and even more difficult for the student to revise. Leave one space after a comma or semicolon, one or two after a colon, and two or three after a period, a question mark, or an exclamation point. In longhand make each word a distinct unit: join all the letters of a word and leave adequate space in the line before beginning the next word.

(2) Shaping for Legibility. Shape each letter distinctly. Avoid flourishes. Many pages of manuscript, though artistic and attractive to the eye, are almost illegible. Dot the *i*, not some other letter nearby. Cross the *t*, not the adjoining *h* or some other letter. Make dots and periods real dots, not small circles. Let all capitals stand out distinctly as capitals and keep all small letters down to the average of other small letters. Remember that you will not be present to tell the reader which letters you intend for capitals, which for small letters.

8d

Revise the manuscript with care.[1]

(1) Revise the paper before submitting it to the instructor.

If time permits, the writer should put the paper aside for a day or more after completing his first draft. Then

---

[1]For marks used in correcting proofs for the printer see *Standard College Dictionary*, pp. 1604–06; *Webster's Seventh New Collegiate Dictionary*, pp. 1051–52; or *The American College Dictionary*, p. xxxv.

he will be able to read the paper more objectively, to see what parts need to be expanded, what to be excised. After he has revised his paper, he should make a completely new copy to submit to the instructor. If slight revisions are needed in this final copy or if the student is writing in class, the paper may be handed in—after corrections have been made—without re-writing. The changes should be made as follows:

(a) Draw one line horizontally through any word to be deleted. Do not put it in parentheses or make an unsightly erasure.

(b) In case of a short addition of one line or less, place a caret ($_\wedge$) in the line where the addition comes and write just above the caret the word or words to be added.

CHECK LIST FOR REVISION

1. Have I stated my central idea clearly, and have I developed it adequately in effective paragraphs? (See Sections **31–32.**)
2. Is the paper correct in
    (a) manuscript form? (See Section **8.**)
    (b) grammar and mechanics? (See Sections **1–7, 9–11.**)
    (c) punctuation? (See Sections **12–17.**)
    (d) spelling? (See Section **18.**)
3. Is the diction standard, exact, concise? (See Sections **19–22.**)
4. Are the sentences as effective as possible? (See Sections **23–30.**)
5. What do my answers to the foregoing questions show my chief difficulties to be? (Review intensively the sections of this book which deal with your defects. Later, after the paper has been read and returned by the instructor, observe the same procedure for additional defects noted by your instructor.)

(2) Revise the paper after the instructor has criticized it.

The best way to learn the mechanics of writing is by correcting one's own errors. Corrections made by another are of comparatively little value. Therefore the instructor points out the errors but *allows the student to make the actual revision for himself.*

The instructor usually indicates a necessary correction by a number or a symbol from the handbook marked in the margin of the paper opposite the error. For example, if he finds a fragmentary sentence, he will write either the number **2** or the symbol **frag.** The student should then find in the text the specific part (**a**, **b**, or **c**) of Section **2** that deals with his error, correct the error in red (or as the instructor directs), and write the appropriate letter after the instructor's number or symbol in the margin. (See the example paragraph marked by the instructor and then corrected by the student on pages 88–89.)

The comma   After the number **12** in the margin the student should take special care to supply the appropriate letter (**a**, **b**, **c**, or **d**) to show why the comma is needed. The act of inserting a comma teaches little; understanding why it is required in a particular situation is a definite step toward mastery of the comma.

The following pages reproduce a paragraph from a student paper and show, on the first page, the instructor's markings (for grammar and other details) and, on the second page, the same paragraph after it has been corrected by the student. These corrections should be in a different color to make them stand out distinctly from the original paragraph and the markings of the instructor.

Give special attention to the instructor's comments on content and organization, which are even more important than details of grammar and mechanics.

Marked by the Instructor—with Numbers

3 Making photographs for newspapers is hard work,

12 it is not the romantic carefree adventure glorified

in motion pictures and fiction books. For every

18 great moment recorded by the stareing eye of the

camera, there are twenty routine assignments that

28 must be handled in the same efficient manner. He

must often overcome great hardships. The work con-

24 tinues for long hours. It must meet the deadline.

At times he is called upon to risk his own life to

2 secure a picture. To the newspaper photographer,

getting his picture being the most important thing.

Marked by the Instructor—with Symbols

cs Making photographs for newspapers is hard work,

⁹/ it is not the romantic carefree adventure glorified

in motion pictures and fiction books. For every

sp great moment recorded by the stareing eye of the

camera, there are twenty routine assignments that

ref must be handled in the same efficient manner. He

must often overcome great hardships. The work con-

sub tinues for long hours. It must meet the deadline.

At times he is called upon to risk his own life to

secure a picture. To the newspaper photographer,

frag getting his picture being the most important thing.

Corrected by the Student

3a   Making photographs for newspapers is hard work*/;*

12c   it is not the romantic*,* carefree adventure glorified

in motion pictures and fiction books. For every

18d   great moment recorded by the ~~staring~~ *staring* eye of the

camera, there are twenty routine assignments that

28c   must be handled in the same efficient manner. ~~He~~ *The*

newspaper photographer must often overcome great
~~must often overcome great hardships. The work con-~~

24a   *hardships and work long hours to meet the deadline.*
~~tinues for long hours. It must meet the deadline.~~

At times he is called upon to risk his own life to

2a   secure a picture. To the newspaper photographer,

is
getting his picture ~~being~~ the most important thing.

Corrected by the Student

cs a   Making photographs for newspapers is hard work*/;*

¶/c   it is not the romantic*,* carefree adventure glorified

in motion pictures and fiction books. For every

sp d   great moment recorded by the ~~staring~~ *staring* eye of the

camera, there are twenty routine assignments that

ref c   must be handled in the same efficient manner. ~~He~~ *The*

newspaper photographer must often overcome great
~~must often overcome great hardships. The work con-~~

sub a   *hardships and work long hours to meet the deadline.*
~~tinues for long hours. It must meet the deadline.~~

At times he is called upon to risk his own life to

frag a   secure a picture. To the newspaper photographer,

is
getting his picture ~~being~~ the most important thing.

8e

Keep a record to check the improvement in your writing.

A clear record on a single notebook page will show at a glance the progress you are making from paper to paper. As you write each paper, try to avoid mistakes already pointed out. Master the correct spelling of each word you have misspelled. *Be sure that you have made every correction and have considered every comment on your last paper before you write the next.* If you follow this plan consistently throughout the year, your writing will show marked improvement.

One simple but useful way to record your errors is to write them down in the order in which they occur in each paper, grouping them in columns according to the seven major divisions of the handbook as illustrated below. In the spaces for Paper Number 1 are recorded the errors from the student paragraph on the preceding page. In the spelling column appears the correct spelling of the mis-spelled word, and in other columns the section number with the letter to indicate the specific error made. You may wish to add on your record sheet other columns for date, grade, and instructor's comments.

RECORD OF ERRORS

Paper No.	Grammar 1-7	Mechanics 8-11	Punctuation 12-17	Words Misspelled 18	Diction 19-22	Effective-ness 23-30	Larger Elements 31-34
1	3 b 2 a			staring		28 c 24 a	
2							

Capitals

9

Capitalize words in accordance with standard conventions. Avoid unnecessary capitals.[1]

Capitalization of individual words may be checked in a good dictionary, such as *The American College Dictionary, Standard College Dictionary, Webster's New World Dictionary,* or *Webster's Seventh New Collegiate Dictionary.* Words regularly capitalized begin with capital letters in dictionary entries.

9a

Capitalize proper names, words used as an essential part of proper names, and usually derivatives of proper names and abbreviations of them.

Proper names begin with capitals, but not names of classes of persons, places, or things: *Churchill, England, Broadway—man, country, street.*

(1) Proper Names

Capitalize names of specific persons, places, and things; organizations and institutions; historical periods and events; members of national, political, racial, and religious groups;

[1]For a more detailed discussion of capitalization of words and abbreviations see the *Style Manual* of the United States Government Printing Office, 1959, pp. 21–56, or *A Manual of Style,* University of Chicago Press, 1949, pp. 23–45.

calendar items; and words pertaining to the Deity and Holy Scripture.

> Milton, Abraham Lincoln, Mary, George the First, America, Arabia, Texas, London, Mount McKinley, the Statue of Liberty, a Winchester, Young Men's Christian Association, Federal Bureau of Investigation, the Second World War, the Middle Ages, the Alamo, Negro, Episcopalian, Memorial Day, the Lord, Christ and His followers, the Old Testament.

(2) Words Used as Essential Parts of Proper Names

Such words as *college, high school, club, lake, river, park, building, street, pike, county, railroad,* and *society* are (except in newspapers) usually capitalized when they are an essential part of a proper name, but not when used alone as a substitute for the name: *the Statue of Liberty, a statue; Central High School, the high school; Madison Street, the street; the Pennsylvania Railroad, the railroad.*

(3) Derivatives

Words derived from proper names are usually capitalized: *Miltonic, Marian, Georgian, American, Arabian, Texan, Londoner, Southerner.*

(4) Abbreviations

In general, abbreviations are capitalized or not according to the capitalization of the word abbreviated: *Y.M.C.A., FBI, m.p.h.* (*miles per hour*). One important exception is *No.* for *number.* (See also Section **11.**)

Note: Proper names and their derivatives sometimes lose significance as names of particulars and thus become common names of a general class and are no longer capitalized. For example, *quixotic* is derived from *Don Quixote; malapropism, Mrs. Malaprop; quisling, Major Vidkun Quisling.*

Caution: Some words may be used correctly as either common nouns or as proper names: "the *God* of Moses," "a *god* of the pagans"; "a *democratic* system," "the *Democratic* Party." Words denoting family relationship (*father, mother, brother, aunt, cousin*) are generally capitalized when used as titles or alone in place of the name, but not when preceded by a possessive: *Brother William; Sister Mary*[2]; *Mary, my sister; my brother; my uncle; a trip with Father; a trip with my father; a letter from Mother; a letter from my mother.*

9b
Capitalize titles preceding, but usually not following, a proper name.

EXAMPLES   Mr. Brown, Judge White, King George, Aunt Mary

Titles immediately following the name, or used alone as a substitute for the name, are capitalized only to indicate preeminence or high distinction: *Lyndon B. Johnson, President of the United States; the President of the United States; the President.* On the other hand, ordinary titles are usually not capitalized: *William Smith, president of the First National Bank; the president of the bank.*

9c
In titles of books, plays, student papers, etc., capitalize the first and last word and all other words except articles (*a, an, the*), short conjunctions, and short prepositions.

EXAMPLES   *Crime and Punishment, To the Lighthouse, Midnight on the Desert, The Man Without a Country, What Men Live By* [A conjunction or preposition of five or more letters (*Without*) is usually capitalized.]

[2]This rule also applies to names of members of religious orders.

9d

Capitalize the pronoun *I* and the interjection *O* (but not *oh* except when it begins a sentence).

EXAMPLE   If *I* forget thee, *O* Jerusalem, let my right hand forget
her cunning.   —PSALMS

9e

Capitalize the first word of every sentence (including quoted sentences and direct questions within sentences).

EXAMPLES

We were late.

My friend said, "We are late," and added, "very late."

My friend said that we were "very late." [A fragmentary quotation does not begin with a capital.]

The question is, Will others be late, too?

We both had one worry: What explanation could we give our host? [After the colon, complete sentences usually begin with a capital, but not always unless they are quoted.]

9f

Avoid unnecessary capitals.

Many students err in using too many rather than too few capitals. If you have a tendency to overuse capitals, you should study the five principles treated above (**9a, b, c, d, e**) and use a capital letter only when you can justify it. You should also carefully study the following STYLE SHEET.

STYLE SHEET FOR CAPITALIZATION

CAPITALS	NO CAPITALS
Proper Names and Derivatives	*Names of Classes of Persons, Places, Things*
Demosthenes	the famous orator
Chicago, Cook County	a city in that county
Texas, Alaska	a big state, a new state

Proper Names and Derivatives	Names of Classes of Persons, Places, Things
Boston College, Cisco High School	a college, in high school
the Amazon River, Lake Erie	a large river, a wide lake
Fifth Avenue, Highway 40	a busy street, the new highway
the President of Chile	the president of the bank
flowers for Mother and a book for Cousin Elizabeth	flowers for my mother and a book for my cousin
the First Presbyterian Church	the first church built
the French Revolution	a revolution in design
a Communist	communistic ideas
General Electric Company	an insurance company
the Physics Club	the society
a Baptist	baptism
the Medal of Honor	a medal for bravery
the Lord God	the lord of the manor, the Greek gods
Labor Day	the holiday weekend
a Rolls Royce	a limousine
the Freshman-Sophomore Prom	a freshman and two sophomores
Marxism	socialism

Titles Before	Titles After
Lieutenant William Jones	William Jones, the lieutenant
President C. B. Jones	C. B. Jones, president of the company

Specific Courses	General Courses or Subjects
Chemistry B, Geology 100, History 2	courses in chemistry, geology, and history
to take Mathematics A	to study mathematics

Specific Sections	Directions
the West	to fly west
the South	a wind from the south, a southerly wind
in the East, an Eastern rite, an Easterner	to the east, an eastern college

Months, Days	Seasons
May, July, Friday, Sunday	summer, fall, winter, spring

▶ **EXERCISE 1**   Supply capitals wherever needed in the following sentences. Be prepared to give a reason for the use of each capital.

1. In america, candidates for president frequently make promises to minority groups—such as southern democrats, negroes, farmers, laborers, westerners, and alaskans—because, if united, the minorities can determine the outcome of an election.

2. During the easter vacation, after window shopping on fifth avenue and seeing the sights on broadway, I went to bedloe's island, climbed up into the crown of the statue of liberty, and took pictures of new york harbor.

3. Senator redwine, a republican, spoke on our campus and strongly advocated prohibition in hunt county.

4. We invited judge green to meet uncle henry at the cosmos club to make plans for the annual community chest drive.

5. Before the end of the summer, perhaps during july, the president of the united states will take a vacation in florida.

6. The pacific ocean was discovered in 1513 by a spaniard named balboa.

7. Many americans in the northwest are of polish or scandinavian descent.

8. The battle of new orleans, which made general jackson famous, took place *after* the signing of the peace treaty at ghent.

9. The minister stressed not only the importance of obeying god's laws as set forth in the bible but also the need for trusting in his infinite mercy.

10. The west offers grand sights for tourists: the carlsbad caverns, the grand canyon, yellowstone national park —not to mention the attractions of hollywood, las vegas, and salt lake city.

11. Many new englanders go south for part of the winter, but usually they turn back north before easter.

▶ **EXERCISE 2** Supply capitals wherever needed in the following paragraphs. Be prepared to give the reason for the use of each capital.

¹ Laying aside gilbert highet's *the art of teaching,* helen, my roommate, sighed and mumbled, "this book doesn't solve my problems as a student teacher at elmwood elementary school."

² "Since mother is a teacher," I responded, "and often tells me about her discipline problems, maybe I can help you out. ³ Now that my english assignment is finished, I've got plenty of time to listen to your troubles."

⁴ "I'm so discouraged," moaned helen, "because my pupils are either stupid or hard of hearing. ⁵ For instance, after teaching vowels and consonants for days, I gave a test friday. ⁶ One child put this title on his paper: 'what i know about valves and constants.'"

⁷ "oh," I laughed, "my mother has a big collection of similar boners made by her students at madison high school."

⁸ Too absorbed in serious thought to be cheered by a pollyanna roommate, helen continued, "I wish I could read a book called *how to win students and influence parents.* ⁹ Maybe its advice would help me on days like last monday, when beverly atkins whimpered for hours. ¹⁰ Desperate, I asked dr. jones, principal of elmwood, what to do; he suggested the threat of spanking, which served only to make beverly cry even louder.

¹¹ "On the telephone early tuesday morning, beverly's mother gave me what she called 'the perfect solution to the problem.' ¹² She advised, 'just spank a child sitting near my beverly, who'll then get scared and stop crying.'"

▶ **EXERCISE 3** Write brief sentences correctly using each of the following: (1) *freshman,* (2) *Freshman,* (3) *college,* (4) *College,* (5) *south,* (6) *South,* (7) *avenue,* (8) *Avenue,* (9) *algebra,* (10) *Algebra,* (11) *theater,* (12) *Theater.*

Italics

10

Italicize (underline) titles of publications, foreign words, names of ships, titles of works of art, and words spoken of as words. Use italics sparingly for emphasis.

In longhand or typewritten papers, italics are indicated by underlining. The printer sets all underlined words in italic type.

TYPEWRITTEN

In <u>David Copperfield</u> Dickens writes of his own boyhood.

PRINTED

In *David Copperfield* Dickens writes of his own boyhood.

10a

Titles of separate publications—such as books, bulletins, magazines, newspapers, musical works—are italicized (underlined) when mentioned in writing.

EXAMPLES   Many people still enjoy Mark Twain's *Roughing It.*
[Note that the author's name is not italicized.]

We read *The Comedy of Errors,* which is based on the *Menaechmi* of Plautus. [An initial *a, an,* or *the* is capitalized and italicized only when it belongs to the title.]

Mozart's *Don Giovanni;* Beethoven's *Fifth Symphony*

He pored over *Time,* the *Atlantic Monthly,* the *Saturday Evening Post,* and the *New York Times* (OR: New York *Times*). [Italics are not commonly used for articles standing first in the titles of periodicals, and sometimes not used for the name of the city in the titles of newspapers.]

Occasionally quotation marks are used instead of italics for titles of separate publications. The usual practice, however, reserves quotation marks for short stories, short poems, one-act plays, articles from periodicals, and subdivisions of books. See **16b.**

David Copperfield opens with a chapter entitled "I Am Born."

Exception: Neither italics nor quotation marks are used in references to the Bible and its parts.

The first part of the Bible, the Old Testament, begins with Genesis.

▶ EXERCISE 1   Underline all words below that should be italicized.

1. While waiting in the dentist's office, I thumbed through an old issue of Sports Illustrated and scanned an article entitled "Girls on the Go-Go-Go."
2. My father reads the editorials in the San Francisco Chronicle and the comic strips in the Chicago Tribune.
3. A performance of Verdi's opera La Traviata was reviewed in the Fort Worth Star Telegram.
4. Huxley's Brave New World differs greatly from Plato's Republic and More's Utopia.
5. Ivanhoe is a character in the novel Ivanhoe.

10b

Foreign words and phrases not yet Anglicized are usually italicized (underlined).

Such words are indicated in *Webster's New World Dictionary* by a double dagger (‡) immediately before the word; in *Standard College Dictionary* and *The American*

College Dictionary, by the italicized name of the foreign language immediately after the word.

> If I ever heard a *faux pas,* Ann's remark was one.
> Mexico is sometimes called the land of *mañana.*
> We heartily wish him *bon voyage.*

▶ EXERCISE 2 With the aid of your dictionary, list and underline five foreign words or phrases that are generally written in italics. List five other foreign words or phrases (such as "apropos," "bona fide," "ex officio") that no longer require italics.

10c

Names of ships, trains, and aircraft and titles of motion pictures and works of art are italicized (underlined).

EXAMPLES The *Queen Mary* and the *Queen Elizabeth* sailed from New York.

From Chicago we took the *Denver Zephyr* across the plains to Colorado.

Rodin's *The Thinker* stands in one of the Parisian gardens.

On Halloween I enjoy seeing motion pictures like *The Walking Dead.*

10d

Words, letters, or figures spoken of as such or used as illustrations are usually italicized (underlined).

EXAMPLES The article *the* has lost much of its demonstrative force.

In England *elevators* are called *lifts.* [Sometimes quotation marks ("the," "elevators," "lifts") are used instead of italics. See **16c.**]

The final *e* in *stone* is silent.

The first *3* and the final *0* of the serial number are barely legible.

10e

As a rule do not use italics (underlining) to give special emphasis to a word or a group of words. Do not underline the title of your own paper.

Frequent use of italics for emphasis defeats its own purpose and becomes merely an annoyance to the reader. This use of italics has been largely abandoned by good contemporary writers. Emphasis on a given word or phrase is usually best secured by careful arrangement of the sentence. See Section **29**.

A title is not italicized when it stands at the head of a book or an article. Accordingly, a student should not italicize (underline) the title standing at the head of his own paper (unless the title happens to be also the title of a book). See also **8b(4)**.

▶ EXERCISE 3   Underline all words below that should be italicized.

1. My handwriting is difficult to read because each o looks like an a and each 9 resembles a 7.
2. In the early 1920's, Rudolph Valentino starred as "the great lover" in The Sheik.
3. To Let was completed in September, 1920, before Galsworthy sailed from Liverpool on the Empress of France to spend the winter in America.
4. Galsworthy's novels have been reviewed in such periodicals as Harper's Magazine and the Saturday Review and such newspapers as the New York Herald Tribune.
5. According to Greenough and Kittredge, in their book entitled Words and Their Ways in English Speech, "it is more natural for us to say divide (from L. divido) than cleave (from A.S. cleofan)."
6. A Manual of Style, published by the University of Chicago Press, recommends that such Latin words or

abbreviations as *vide, idem, ibid.,* and *op. cit.* be italicized when used in literary references.

7. In the *Spirit of St. Louis,* Charles A. Lindbergh made the first solo nonstop transatlantic flight from New York to Paris.

8. The original of Benjamin West's *Penn's Treaty with the Indians* is in the Pennsylvania Academy of Fine Arts in Philadelphia.

9. The embassy aide was declared *persona non grata* and asked to leave the country at once.

10. There are two acceptable ways to spell such words as *judgment, catalogue,* and *gruesome.*

11. Stevenson is said to have revised the first chapter of *Treasure Island* no fewer than thirty-seven times.

12. Michelangelo's *Battle of the Centaurs* and his *Madonna of the Steps* are among the world's finest sculptures.

▶ **EXERCISE 4** Copy the following passage, underlining all words that should be italicized.

¹ I was returning home on the America when I happened to see a copy of Euripides' Medea. ² The play was of course in translation, by Murray, I believe; it was reprinted in Riley's Great Plays of Greece and Rome. ³ I admire Medea the play and Medea the woman. ⁴ Both of them have a quality of atrocitas which our contemporary primitivism misses. ⁵ Characters in modern plays are neurotic; Medea was sublimely and savagely mad.

Abbreviations and Numbers

11

In ordinary writing avoid abbreviations (with a few well-known exceptions), and write out numbers that can be expressed in one or two words.

Abbreviations

11a

In ordinary writing spell out all titles except *Mr., Messrs., Mrs., Mmes., Dr.,* and *St.* (*saint,* not *street*). Spell out even these titles when not followed by proper names.

INAPPROPRIATE   The Dr. made his report to the Maj.
APPROPRIATE   The doctor (OR Dr. Smith) made his report to the major (OR to Major Brown).

Note: *Hon.* and *Rev.* may be used before the surname when it is preceded by the first name or initials, never before the surname alone.

INAPPROPRIATE   Hon. Smith, Rev. Jones
APPROPRIATE   Hon. George Smith, Hon. G. E. Smith, Rev. Thomas Jones, Rev. T. E. Jones
MORE FORMAL   The Honorable George Edward Smith, the Reverend Thomas Everett Jones, the Reverend Mr. Jones

For forms of address in writing or speaking to officials and other dignitaries of church and state, see "Forms of Address" in *Webster's New World Dictionary,* pp. 1717–19, and *Webster's Seventh New Collegiate Dictionary,* pp. 1173–76.

11b

In ordinary writing spell out names of states, countries, months, days of the week, and units of measurement.

INAPPROPRIATE   He left Ia. on the last Sun. in Jul.
APPROPRIATE   He left Iowa on the last Sunday in July.

INAPPROPRIATE   On Oct. 15 James arrived in Mex.
APPROPRIATE   On October 15 James arrived in Mexico.

INAPPROPRIATE   Only five ft. tall, Susan weighs about a hundred lbs.
APPROPRIATE   Only five feet tall, Susan weighs about a hundred pounds.

11c

In ordinary writing spell out *Street, Road, Park, Company,* and similar words used as part of a proper name.

EXAMPLE   The procession moved down Lee Street between Central Park and the neon signs of the Ford Motor Company.

Note: Avoid the use of *&* (for *and*) and such abbreviations as *Bros.* or *Inc.* except in copying official titles: *A & P; Goldsmith Bros.; Best & Co., Inc.; Doubleday & Company, Inc.*

11d

In ordinary writing spell out the words *volume, chapter,* and *page* and the names of subjects.

INAPPROPRIATE   The notes on chem. are taken from ch. 9, p. 46.
APPROPRIATE   The notes on chemistry are taken from chapter 9, page 46.

11e

In ordinary writing spell out first names.

INAPPROPRIATE   Jas. Smith, Geo. White
APPROPRIATE   James Smith, George White

Permissible abbreviations: In addition to the abbreviations mentioned in **11a,** the following are permissible and usually desirable.

1. *After proper names:* Jr., Sr., Esq., and degrees such as D.D., Ph.D., M.A., M.D.

    Mr. Sam Jones, Sr.; Sam Jones, Jr.; Thomas Jones, M.D.

2. *With dates or numerals:* A.D., B.C., A.M., P.M. (OR a.m., p.m.), No., $

APPROPRIATE	In 450 B.C.; at 9:30 A.M.; in room No. 6; for $365
INAPPROPRIATE	Early this A.M. he asked the No. of your room. [The abbreviations are appropriate only with the numerals.]
APPROPRIATE	Early this morning he asked the number of your room.

3. *For names of organizations and government agencies usually referred to by their initials:* DAR, GOP, FBI, AMA, NASA, UN, FHA

4. *For certain common Latin expressions, although the English term is often spelled out in formal writing, as indicated in parentheses:* i.e. (*that is*), e.g. (*for example*), viz. (*namely*), cf. (*compare*), etc. (*and so forth*), vs. (*versus*)

Note: Use *etc.* sparingly. Never write *and etc.* The abbreviation comes from *et cetera,* of which *et* means *and.*

Special exceptions: Many abbreviations are desirable in footnotes, in tabulations, and in certain types of technical writing. In such special writing the student should follow the practice of the better publications in the field. If he has any doubt regarding the spelling or capitalization of any abbreviation, he should consult a good dictionary such as the *Standard College Dictionary* or *Webster's New World Dictionary* (in the main vocabulary).

▶ EXERCISE 1   Decide which form in each of the following items is appropriate in ordinary writing, and check the letter (*a* or *b*) of the correct form. If both forms are permissible, check both *a* and *b*. Use each appropriate form in a sentence.

1. a. in the U. S.
   b. in the United States
2. a. Rev. H. E. McGill
   b. The Reverend H. E. McGill
3. a. on Hickory St.
   b. on Hickory Street
4. a. etc.
   b. and etc.
5. a. FBI
   b. Federal Bureau of Investigation
6. a. on August 15
   b. on Aug. 15

7. a. for Jr.
   b. for John Evans, Jr.
8. a. e.g.
   b. for example
9. a. at 6:15 A.M.
   b. early in the A.M.
10. a. in Bangor, Me.
    b. in Bangor, Maine

Numbers

11f

Although usage varies, writers tend to spell out numbers that require only one or two words; they regularly use figures for other numbers.

EXAMPLES   after twenty years; only thirty-four dollars; more than four million votes; two thirds of the voters
after 124 years; only $34.15; exactly 4,568,305 votes [Note the commas used to separate millions, thousands, hundreds.]

Special usage regarding numbers:

1. *Use figures for dates.*

   May 1, 1967; 1 May 1967; July 12, 1763

Such endings as *-st, -nd, -rd, -th* should not be added to the day of the month when the year follows; they need not be added even when the year is omitted.

August 2, 1967; August 2

Ordinal numbers to designate the day of the month may be written out or expressed in figures. The year is never written out except in very formal social announcements or invitations.

the fifth (*or* 5th) of May, June first

2. *Use figures for street numbers, for pages and divisions of a book, for decimals and percentages, and for the hour of the day when used with* A.M. *or* P.M.

26 Main Avenue, 460 Fourth Street
The quotation is from page 80.
The bar is .63 of an inch thick.
She gets 10½ percent of the profits.
He arrived at 4:30 P.M.

3. *Be consistent in spelling out or using figures. Normally use figures for a series of numbers.*

The garden plot was 125 feet long and 50 feet wide and contained an asparagus bed 12 feet square.

4. *Normally spell out any numeral at the beginning of a sentence. If necessary, recast the sentence.*

INAPPROPRIATE   25 boys made the trip.
APPROPRIATE   Twenty-five boys made the trip.

INAPPROPRIATE   993 freshmen entered the college last year.
APPROPRIATE   Last year 993 freshmen entered the college.

5. *The practice of repeating in parentheses a number that is spelled out (now generally reserved for legal and commercial writing) should be used correctly if at all.*

I enclose twenty (20) dollars.   I enclose twenty dollars ($20).

▶ EXERCISE 2   Correct all errors in the use of numbers in the following sentences. Write *C* after each sentence that needs no correction.

1. The Thanksgiving holidays begin at one p.m.
2. On June 27th, 1959, Hawaiians voted 18 to 1 for statehood.
3. 500 freshmen are expected at the bonfire tonight.
4. On September 15 I wrote a check for $35.40.
5. On the fifteenth of September I wrote a check for thirty-five dollars.
6. Lex enjoyed the nineteen sixty Olympics.
7. At the age of 14 I spent 12 days hunting and fishing with a group of Boy Scouts in the Ozarks.
8. The reception, to be held at 27 Jackson Street, will begin about 8 o'clock.
9. 18,000 fans watched the Eagles win their 7th victory of the season.
10. The Tigers gained only 251 yards on the ground and 35 in the air.

▶ EXERCISE 3   Correct all errors in the use of abbreviations and numbers in the following sentences.

1. My father moved to Cal. about 10 years ago.
2. He is now living at sixty-five Sandusky St. in Frisco.
3. Geo. Washington, our first Pres., was born in seventeen hundred and thirty-two.
4. When he was 20 years old, he inherited Mt. Vernon from his half bro.
5. He assumed command of the Continental armies in Cambridge, Mass., on Jul. 3, 1775.
6. 125 men were stationed in the mts. to serve as guides.
7. These one hundred and twenty-five men have been in service for nearly 5 years.
8. Our class in math. did not meet last Wed.
9. Do you know the No. of the prof.'s office?
10. Rev. Williams will preach next Sun.

PUNCTUATION

The Comma

12

Use the comma (which ordinarily indicates a pause and a variation in voice pitch) where it is required by the structure of the sentence.

Punctuation helps to clarify the meaning of the written sentence. The writer must supply, as well as he can with marks of punctuation, what the speaker does naturally with his stops and pauses and with his voice variations or pitch. Read the following sentences aloud, noticing how commas indicate differences in the way sentences are spoken:

When I tried to help Ben, I failed at first.
When I tried to help, Ben, I failed at first.

The starter does not function properly, however the mechanic repairs it.
The starter does not function properly; however, the mechanic repairs it.

It is evident that the sound of the spoken sentence can serve as a guide in the punctuation of the written sentence.

But the principles governing punctuation can be stated most exactly in terms of the structure of the sentence. Anyone who understands this structure can master with comparative ease the very few principles governing the different uses of the comma. (If you cannot readily distinguish main clauses, subordinate clauses, and the various kinds of phrases, review Section 1, Sentence Sense.) These principles, which cover the normal practice of the best contemporary writers, are adequate for the needs of the average college student. He may note that skilled writers sometimes employ the comma in unusual ways to express delicate shades of meaning. Such variations can safely be made by the writer who has first learned to apply the following major principles:

Use commas

a. To separate main clauses joined by *and, but, or, nor,* or *for.*
b. To set off certain introductory elements.
c. To separate items in a series (including coordinate adjectives).
d. To set off nonrestrictive and other parenthetical elements.

Main Clauses

12a

Main clauses joined by one of the coordinating conjunctions (*and, but, or, nor, for*)[1] are separated by a comma.

PATTERN   **MAIN CLAUSE,** $\begin{Bmatrix} \text{and} \\ \text{but} \\ \text{or} \\ \text{nor} \\ \text{for} \end{Bmatrix}$ **MAIN CLAUSE.**

We were sitting before the fire in the big room at Twin Farms, and Lewis had rudely retired behind a newspaper.
—DOROTHY THOMPSON

It was not actually raining, but the air had the heavy smell of ozone produced by the lightning of the previous night.
—JEREMY BERNSTEIN

Justice stands upon Power, or there is no justice.
—WILLIAM S. WHITE

The peoples of the Sahara have never been united, nor have they even considered uniting in any common cause.
—JAMES R. NEWMAN

[1] *Yet* is occasionally used as a coordinating conjunction equivalent to *but.* Informal writing frequently uses *so* as a coordinating conjunction, but careful writers usually avoid the *so*-sentence by subordinating one of the clauses.

Note: A comma precedes a coordinating conjunction joining the main clauses of a compound-complex sentence (which has at least two main clauses and one subordinate clause).

> I was glad to agree, for I feel that showing live animals arouses people's interest in their local fauna and its preservation.
> —GERALD DURRELL

Caution: Do not confuse the compound sentence (two main clauses) with the simple sentence (one main clause) containing a compound predicate.

COMPOUND SENTENCE   On the steppe one is electrified, and one can feel one's life burn faster.   —V. S. PRITCHETT

COMPOUND PREDICATE   On the steppe one is electrified and can feel one's life burn faster. [No comma before *and*]

At times professional writers use the comma to set off what seems to be merely the second part of a compound element, especially in long sentences. Closer examination usually discloses, however, that the material following the comma is actually a regular main clause with some words "understood"; the use of the comma emphasizes the distinction between the principal ideas in the sentence. Note the following sentences, in which the implied matter is inserted in brackets:

> There is no other way for the world's living standards to be raised to anything like our level, and [there is] no other way to link or merge the economies of the free nations.   —FORTUNE

> The number of high school graduates has been increasing since 1890 about thirteen times as fast as the population, and the number of college graduates [has been increasing] six times as fast.   —THE ATLANTIC MONTHLY

Exceptions to 12a

1. *Omission of the comma:*

When the main clauses are short, the comma is frequently omitted before *and* or *or*. Before the conjunctions *but* and *for*, the comma is usually needed to prevent confusion with the prepositions *but* and *for*. Sometimes, especially in narrative writing, the comma is omitted even when the clauses are long.

> The next night the wind shifted and the thaw began.
> —RACHEL L. CARSON

> This was met with a great din of spontaneous applause and it was at just that instant that Sally Poker looked down at her feet and discovered that in the excitement of getting ready she had forgotten to change her shoes: two brown Girl Scout oxfords protruded from the bottom of her dress.
> —FLANNERY O'CONNOR

2. *Use of the semicolon instead of the comma:*

Sometimes the coordinating conjunction is preceded by a semicolon instead of the usual comma, especially when the main clauses have internal punctuation or reveal a striking contrast. See also **14a**.

> It was childish, of course; for any disturbance, any sudden intruding noise, would make the creatures stop.
> —ALDOUS HUXLEY

> Doormen grow rich blowing their whistles for cabs; and some doormen belong to no door at all—merely wander about through the streets, opening cabs for people as they happen to find them.
> —E. B. WHITE

▶ EXERCISE 1 Use a comma (or a semicolon) where required in the following sentences. Write *C* after any sentence which needs no further punctuation.

¹ In college a smug freshman receives a kind of shock treatment for professors often use surprising facts to pry open complacent or closed minds. ² For example, a history professor may consider William Wirt a greater hero than Patrick Henry or an English teacher may say that a double negative like "don't have no money" does not really make the meaning of a sentence positive. ³ A freshman should not become rebellious nor should he be unduly alarmed when new information threatens old,

cherished opinions.   ⁴ An intelligent student may question surprising facts but he never doubts the value of opening his mind to new ideas.   ⁵ Moreover, he expects to be confused, at least part of the time, in the college classroom for he, like John Ciardi, the poet, knows that a person who is not confused probably has not yet asked the right questions.

⁶ The governor announced that the water supply was dangerously low and he proclaimed that a state of civil emergency existed.   ⁷ The days passed and the drought grew steadily worse.   ⁸ The state fire marshal ordered all parks closed but forest fires broke out in spite of all precautions.   ⁹ City-dwellers watched their gardens shrivel and die and industrial workers were laid off as electric-power output failed.   ¹⁰ But perhaps the worst afflicted were the farmers for there was no hope of saving their crops and even their livestock had to be sold on a glutted market or else left to die in the fields.

▶ EXERCISE 2   Write eight sentences to illustrate **12a** and two sentences to illustrate the exceptions to it. Be sure to use all five coordinating conjunctions. If necessary, refer to the pattern and examples on page 111.

Introductory Elements

12b

Introductory elements such as adverb clauses, long phrases, transitional expressions, and interjections are usually set off by commas.

To set off an introductory element is to put a comma after it. See also **12d.**

(1)   Introductory adverb clauses

PATTERN   **ADVERB CLAUSE, MAIN CLAUSE.**

> Whenever I tried to put chains on a tire, the car would maliciously wrap them around a rear axle. —JAMES THURBER

> If any college man will work intelligently, I guarantee his success. —HARDIN CRAIG

Many writers omit the comma after short introductory clauses, and sometimes after longer ones, when the omission does not make for difficult reading. In the following sentences the commas may be used or omitted at the option of the writer:

> If we leave(,) he will be offended.
> When *he* comes to the end of the lane(,) *he* should turn to the left. [When the subject of the introductory clause is repeated in the main clause, the comma is usually unnecessary.]

Note: When the adverb clause *follows* the main clause, there is usually no pause and no need for a comma.

PATTERN **MAIN CLAUSE ADVERB CLAUSE.**

> I waited there until he returned.
> Ben arrived before the train did.

Such adverb clauses, however, are set off by a comma if they are parenthetical or loosely connected with the rest of the sentence, especially if the subordinating conjunction seems equivalent to a coordinating conjunction (or if a distinct pause is required in the reading).

> Henry is now in good health, although he has been an invalid most of his life. [*Although* is equivalent to *but.*]
> With children and young people his magic never fails, whether he is doing bottle tricks for three-year-olds or counseling teen-agers about courses or careers. —ALICE KIMBALL SMITH

(2) Long introductory phrases

> *In two years of acting in cowboy films,* W. S. Hart earned $900,000. —H. A. OVERSTREET

> *At the critical moments in this sad history,* there have been men worth listening to who warned the people against their mistakes. —WALTER LIPPMANN

Introductory phrases containing a gerund, a participle, or an infinitive, even though short, must often be followed by a comma to prevent misreading.

Before leaving, the soldiers demolished the fort.
Because of his effort to escape, his punishment was increased.

Short introductory prepositional phrases, except when they are distinctly parenthetical expressions (as *in fact* or *for example*), are seldom followed by commas.

At ninety she was still active.
During the night he heard many noises.

(3) Transitional expressions and interjections

Interjections as well as transitional expressions (such as *for example, in fact, on the other hand, in the second place*) are generally considered parenthetical. See **12d(3)**. When used as introductory elements, they are usually followed by commas.

In fact, I hope to leave tomorrow.
For example, most boys enjoy fishing.
Well, just to stand up and face life's problems takes courage.

▶ EXERCISE 3   In each of the following sentences find the main clause and identify the preceding element as a subordinate clause or a phrase. Then determine whether to use or omit a comma after the introductory element. Justify your decision.

¹ In order to pay his way through college George worked at night in an iron foundry.   ² During this time he became acquainted with all the company's operations.   ³ At the end of four years' observation of George's work the foundry owner offered George a position as manager. ⁴ Although George had planned to attend medical school and enter his father's profession he found now that the kind of work he had been doing had a far greater appeal for him. ⁵ In fact he accepted the offer without hesitation.

Items in Series

12c

Words, phrases, or clauses in a series (including coordinate adjectives) are separated by commas.

(1) Words, phrases, or clauses in a series

The room is *bright, clean, quiet.* [Form *a, b, c*]
The room is *bright, clean,* and *quiet.* [Form *a, b,* and *c*]
The room is *bright* and *clean* and *quiet.* [Form *a* and *b* and *c*. Commas are omitted when *and* is used throughout the series.]
He walked *up the steps, across the porch,* and *through the doorway.* [Phrases in a series]
We protested *that the engine used too much oil, that the brakes were worn out,* and *that the tires were dangerous.* [Subordinate clauses in a series]
We rang the bell, we knocked on the door, and *we shouted until we were hoarse.* [Main clauses in a series]

The final comma is often omitted, especially by newspapers, when the series takes the form *a, b,* and *c.* But students are usually advised to follow the practice of the more conservative books and periodicals in using the comma throughout the series, if only because the comma is sometimes needed to prevent confusion.

CONFUSING   The natives ate beans, onions, rice and honey. [Was the rice and honey a mixture?]
CLEAR   The natives ate beans, onions, rice, and honey. OR The natives ate beans, onions, and rice and honey.

(2) Coordinate adjectives

Adjectives are coordinate when they modify the same word or word group. Notice in the following examples that the pauses between coordinate adjectives are indicated by commas.

a clean, quiet room [A *clean* and *quiet* room—both adjectives modify the word *room.*]

> a clean, quiet public dining room [*Clean* and *quiet* modify the word group *public dining room*, which is pronounced as a unit.]

Coordinate adjectives ordinarily have a reversible word order; adjectives which are not coordinate do not.

COORDINATE   colorful, expensive scarves [*Logical:* expensive, colorful scarves]

NOT COORDINATE   many colorful scarves [*Illogical:* colorful many scarves]

▶ **EXERCISE 4**   In the following sentences distinguish each series and each group of coordinate adjectives, inserting commas where needed. Justify each comma used.

¹ Do you remember Pete Moore and that old battered lunch pail he used to carry?   ² He would go past our house every morning wait on the corner for his ride hand his lunch pail up to one of the men on the truck climb up himself and go rolling away.   ³ Year after year—spring summer fall and winter—Pete and his lunch pail would wait on that corner.   ⁴ And every year they both got a little older a little more battered a little nearer used up. ⁵ My brothers my sisters and I used to make bets about which would wear out first.   ⁶ Then one awful day we heard the blast at the plant saw the sky black with smoke and watched the streets fill with frightened hurrying people.   ⁷ That day was the end of old Pete of his battered lunch pail and of the jokes we made about him.

▶ **EXERCISE 5**   Using necessary commas, supply coordinate adjectives to modify each of the following.

EXAMPLE   old fogy—an arrogant, aggressive old fogy

1. office boy
2. oil painting
3. stock market
4. best man
5. salad dressing
6. motion picture
7. crab grass
8. mountain lion

Parenthetical Elements

12d

Nonrestrictive clauses (or phrases) and other parenthetical elements ("interrupters") are set off by commas. Restrictive clauses (or phrases) are not set off.

Use a comma after a parenthetical element at the beginning of a sentence, before a parenthetical element at the end, and both before and after one within a sentence.

> *My friends,* we have no alternative.
> We have no alternative, *my friends.*
> We have, *my friends,* no alternative.
>
> *He said,* "The story has been told."
> "The story has been told," *he said.*
> "The story," *he said,* "has been told."

Caution: When two commas are needed to set off a parenthetical element within the sentence, do not forget the second comma. To use one comma but not the second makes reading more difficult than the omission of both commas.

CONFUSING   Ours is, of course a democratic country.
CLEAR   Ours is, of course, a democratic country. OR Ours is of course a democratic country.

CONFUSING   Ours is, we are told a democratic country.
CLEAR   Ours is, we are told, a democratic country. [The marked pauses in speaking show that commas are needed.]

(1) **Nonrestrictive clauses and phrases are set off by commas. Restrictive clauses and phrases are not set off.**

Adjective clauses and phrases are nonrestrictive (set off by commas) when they merely add information about a word already identified. Such modifiers are parenthetical; they are not essential to the meaning of the main clause and may be omitted.

Henry Smith, *who is lazy,* will lose his job. ["Henry will lose his job" is true without the nonessential *who is lazy.*]
Venice, *which he visited next,* was then torn by rival factions.
Venice, *visited next,* was then torn by rival factions.

Adjective clauses and phrases are restrictive (not set off by commas) when they are needed for identification of the word they modify. Such clauses limit or restrict the meaning of the sentence.

A boy *who is lazy* deserves to lose his job. ["A boy deserves to lose his job" is true only with the essential *who is lazy.*]
The city *that he visited next* was Venice.
The city *visited next* was Venice.

Adjective clauses beginning with *that* are restrictive. Adjective clauses beginning with *who (whom, whose)* and *which* may be restrictive or nonrestrictive.

Your voice can help you distinguish between restrictive and nonrestrictive modifiers. As you read the following sentences aloud, note that you neither pause nor lower the pitch of your voice for the italicized (restrictive) passages.

RESTRICTIVE   A mother *who does not love her children* is unnatural.
RESTRICTIVE   The girl *sitting near the window* laughed at me.

When reading aloud the sentences below, you naturally "set off" the italicized nonrestrictive modifiers (1) by using definite pauses and (2) by lowering the pitch of your voice. (Note also that a nonrestrictive modifier can be omitted without changing the meaning of the main clause.)

NONRESTRICTIVE   My mother, *who loves her children,* is an ideal parent.
NONRESTRICTIVE   Martha Thompson, *sitting near the window,* smiled knowingly.

Study the meaning of the sentences on the next page. Also read each one aloud, and let your voice help you distinguish between restrictive and nonrestrictive clauses and phrases.

NONRESTRICTIVE CLAUSE   Our newest boat, *which is painted red and white,* has sprung a leak. [The *which* clause, adding information about a boat already identified, is parenthetical. It is not essential to the main clause, *Our newest boat has sprung a leak.*]

NONRESTRICTIVE PHRASE   Our newest boat, *painted red and white,* has sprung a leak.

RESTRICTIVE CLAUSE (NO COMMAS)   A boat *that leaks* is of little use. [The clause *that leaks* is essential to the meaning of the main clause.]

RESTRICTIVE PHRASE (NO COMMAS)   A boat *with a leak* is of little use.

NONRESTRICTIVE CLAUSE   My new car, *which is parked across the street,* is ready. [Clause adding information about a car already identified; pauses and change in voice pitch marked by commas.]

NONRESTRICTIVE PHRASE   My new car, *parked across the street,* is ready.

RESTRICTIVE CLAUSE (NO COMMAS)   The car *which is parked across the street* is ready. [Clause essential to the identification]

RESTRICTIVE PHRASE (NO COMMAS)   The car *parked across the street* is ready.

Sometimes a clause (or phrase) may be either restrictive or nonrestrictive; the writer signifies his meaning by the proper use of the comma.

NONRESTRICTIVE   He spent hours caring for the Indian guides, *who were sick with malaria.* [He cared for all the Indian guides. All of them were sick with malaria.]

RESTRICTIVE (NO COMMA)   He spent hours caring for the Indian guides *who were sick with malaria.* [Some of the Indian guides were sick with malaria. He cared for the sick ones.]

▶ EXERCISE 6 In the following sentences determine whether each clause (or phrase) is restrictive or nonrestrictive. Set off only the nonrestrictive clauses (or phrases).

1. The James Lee who owns the bank is a grandson of the one who founded it.
2. James Lee who owns this bank and five others is one of the wealthiest men in the state.

3. The coach called out to Higgins who got up from the bench and trotted over to him.
4. The coach who chewed on cigars but never lighted them threw one away and reached for another.
5. Anyone who saw him could tell that something was troubling him.
6. All banks which fail to report will be closed.
7. All banks failing to report will be closed.
8. Henry betrayed the man who had helped him build his fortune.
9. James White who had helped Henry build his fortune died yesterday.
10. My father hoping that I would remain at home offered me a share in his business.

▶ EXERCISE 7 Compose and punctuate five sentences containing nonrestrictive clauses or phrases. Compose five sentences containing restrictive clauses or phrases and underline the restrictive elements.

(2) Nonrestrictive appositives, contrasted elements, geographical names, and items in dates and addresses are set off by commas.

Note that most appositives may be readily expanded into nonrestrictive clauses. In other words, the principle underlying the use of commas to set off nonrestrictive clauses also applies here; see pages 119–21.

APPOSITIVES AND CONTRASTED ELEMENTS

Jesse, *the caretaker,* is a good fellow. [The appositive *caretaker* is equivalent to the nonrestrictive clause *who is the caretaker.* Note the distinct pauses and change in voice pitch.]

Sandburg, *the biographer of Lincoln,* was awarded the Pulitzer Prize. [The appositive is equivalent to the nonrestrictive clause *who is the biographer of Lincoln.*]

My companions were James White, *Esq.,* William Smith, *M.D.,* and Rufus L. Black, *Ph.D.* [Abbreviated titles after a name are treated as appositives.]

The cook, *not the caretaker,* will assist you. [The contrasted
element is a sort of negative appositive.]
Our failures, *not our successes,* will be remembered.
Trade comes with peace, *not with war.*

Appositives are usually nonrestrictive (parenthetical),
merely adding information about a person or thing already
identified. Such appositives are set off by commas, which
mark distinct pauses and change in voice pitch. But when
an appositive is restrictive, commas are usually omitted.

The poet Sandburg has written a biography. [*Sandburg* restricts
the meaning, telling what poet has written a biography.]
His son James is sick. [*James,* not his son *William*]
William the Conqueror invaded England in 1066. [An appositive
that is part of a title is restrictive.]
The word *malapropism* is derived from Sheridan's *The Rivals.*
Do you refer to Samuel Butler the poet or to Samuel Butler the
novelist?

▶ **EXERCISE 8**   Use commas to set off contrasted elements
and nonrestrictive appositives in the following paragraph.
Underline restrictive appositives.

[1] Years ago I read *The Marks of an Educated Man* an
interesting book by Albert Wiggam.   [2] According to
Wiggam, one outstanding characteristic of the educated
man is that he "links himself with a great cause" one that
requires selfless service.   [3] Certainly many famous men
whether scientists or artists or philosophers have dedicated
their lives to the cause of serving others.   [4] For example,
Louis Pasteur the famous French chemist devoted his life
to the study of medicine to benefit mankind.   [5] And the
artist Michelangelo served humanity by creating numerous
works of lasting beauty.   [6] Francis of Assisi a saint of
the twelfth century was also devoted to a great cause.
[7] His life was the mirror of his creed a reflection of his
ardent love for others.   [8] Among twentieth-century philosophers was Albert Schweitzer a well-known missionary
and physician.   [9] Schweitzer a person who worked for

both peace and brotherhood was like Pasteur, Michelangelo, and St. Francis because he linked himself with a great cause not with transitory, selfish aims.   [10] I think that the author Wiggam should use the adjective *great* not *educated* to describe the man who devotes himself to a noble cause.

▶ **EXERCISE 9**   Compose ten sentences to illustrate the punctuation of appositives and contrasted elements.

GEOGRAPHICAL NAMES, ITEMS IN DATES AND ADDRESSES

Pasadena, California, is the site of the Rose Bowl. [*California* may be thought of as equivalent to the nonrestrictive clause *which is in California.*]

Address the letter to Mr. J. L. Karnes, Clayton, Delaware 19938. [The zip code is not separated by a comma from the name of the state.]

Tuesday, May 8, 1967, in Chicago; 8 May 1967; May, 1967, in Boston OR May 1967 in Boston. [Commas are often omitted when the day of the month is not given, or when the day of the month precedes rather than follows the month. Students are usually advised not to follow the less conservative practice of dropping the comma after the year, as in "May 8, 1967 in Chicago."]

▶ **EXERCISE 10**   Copy the following sentences, inserting commas where they are needed.

1. The letter was sent to a special agent at 6222 North Central Expressway Dallas Texas 75206.
2. Their son was born on Friday June 18 1954 at Baptist Hospital Knoxville Tennessee.
3. He was inducted into the army at Fort Oglethorpe Georgia on 30 September 1942.
4. William Congreve was born in Bardsey England on January 24 1670.

5. The accident occurred in De Soto Parish Louisiana on Saturday January 1 1966.
6. Please send all communications to 757 Third Avenue New York New York 10017.
7. Pearl Harbor Hawaii was bombed on December 7 1941.

(3) Parenthetical words, phrases, or clauses (inserted expressions), words in direct address, and absolute elements are set off by commas.

PARENTHETICAL EXPRESSIONS

As a matter of fact, the term "parenthetical" is correctly applied to everything discussed under **12d**; but the term is more commonly applied to such expressions as *on the other hand, in the first place, in fact, to tell the truth, however, that is, for example, I hope, I report, he says.* The term would apply equally well to expressions inserted in dialogue: *he said, he observed, he protested,* etc. Expressions that come at the beginning of a sentence are treated both by **12b** and by **12d**.

> You will, *then,* accept our offer?
> *To tell the truth,* we anticipated bad luck.
> The work is, *on the whole,* very satisfactory.
> "We believe," *he replied,* "that you are correct."
> We believe, *however,* that you should go. [When *however* means "nevertheless," it is usually set off by commas. But when *however* means "no matter how," it is not a parenthetical word but a subordinator: "The trip will be hard, *however* you go."]

Some parenthetical expressions causing little if any pause in reading are frequently not set off by commas: *also, too, indeed, perhaps, at least, likewise,* etc. The writer must use his judgment.

> I am *also* of that opinion.
> He is *perhaps* the best swimmer on the team.
> Your efforts will *of course* be appreciated. OR, Your efforts will, *of course,* be appreciated.

DIRECT ADDRESS

Come here, *Mary,* and help us.
I refuse, *sir,* to believe the report.
This, *my friends,* is the whole truth.

ABSOLUTE ELEMENTS

Win or lose, play by rule. [Absolute phrase]
I fear the encounter, *his temper being what it is.* [Nominative absolute]
Well, let him try if he insists. [Mild interjection]
Leslie doesn't play the tuba, *does she?* [Echo question]

12e

Note: **Occasionally a comma, though not called for by any of the major principles already discussed, may be needed to prevent misreading.**

Use **12e** sparingly to justify your commas. In a general sense, nearly all commas are used to prevent misreading or to make reading easier. Your mastery of the comma will come through the application of the more specific major principles (**a, b, c, d**) to the structure of your sentences.

CONFUSING   Inside the room was gaily decorated. [*Inside* may be at first mistaken for the preposition.]

CLEAR   Inside, the room was gaily decorated. [*Inside* is clearly an adverb.]

CONFUSING   After all the conquest of malaria is a fascinating story.

CLEAR   After all, the conquest of malaria is a fascinating story.

▶ EXERCISE 11   All commas in the following passage are correctly used. Justify each comma by referring to **12a** (main clauses joined by a coordinating conjunction), **12b** (introductory elements), **12c** (a series or coordinate adjectives), or **12d** (parenthetical elements).

[1] In the cold months there are few visitors, for northern Minnesota is not a winter playground. [2] And yet the intrepid traveler would be well rewarded by the natural beauty surrounding him. [3] The skies and the undulating fields merge as one; unreality assails the mind and the eye. [4] The sun swings in a low arc, and at sunrise and sunset it is not hard to imagine what the world may be like in many distant aeons when ice and snow envelop the earth, while the sun, cooled to the ruddy glow of bittersweet, lingeringly touches the clouds with warm colors of apricot, tangerine, lavender, and rose.

[5] Night skies may be indescribably clear. [6] The stars are sharp and brilliant, pricking perception; the northern constellations diagramed with utmost clarity upon the blackest of skies. [7] There is no illusion here that they are hung like lanterns just beyond reach. [8] The vast distances of space are as clear to see as the barbed points of light.

[9] When the aurora borealis sweeps in to dominate the night, it elicits a quite different and emotional reaction, not unlike the surging, impressive sight itself. [10] If the luminous, pulsing scarves of light were tangible streamers, certainly it would be possible to become entangled in and absorbed into the celestial kaleidoscope.

—FRANCES GILLIS[2]

▶ EXERCISE 12 Insert commas where needed in the following sentences (selected and adapted from the *New Yorker*). Be prepared to justify each comma used.

1. He was in truth slightly bowlegged but he concealed the flaw by standing with one knee bent.
2. What living American has had a mountain a bird a fish a spider a lizard and a louse named after him?
3. A teacup balanced on a chair tumbled to the floor and immediately our attention turned to poltergeists.

[2] From "Winter North of the Mississippi" by Frances Gillis, reprinted from the *Atlantic Monthly*, March, 1961. By permission of the author.

4. A black cloud crossed the city flashed two or three fierce bolts rumbled halfheartedly and passed on.

5. When Miss Meltzer reminded Feder that there existed neither sufficiently powerful lamps nor properly designed fixtures for the project he said "Of course they don't exist Meltzer. We're going to create them."

6. He dies of pneumonia shortly afterward but returns as a robust ghost to steal the overcoats off the backs of half the citizens in the city triumphantly righting one wrong with a dozen wrongs.

7. Although histoplasmosis is now established as a disease of nearly universal distribution it appears to be most prevalent in the United States.

8. Still something had to be done and Mother and Aunt Berta not being inventive decided to do what all the world was doing.

9. For a week suspended in air we had given thought to becoming engaged—I more than she perhaps for she was engaged already.

10. Clara collapsed into laughter gasping her two hands thrust to her face in a spasm.

11. Two girls one of them with pert buckteeth and eyes as black as vest buttons the other with white skin and flesh-colored hair like an underdeveloped photograph of a redhead came and sat on my right.

12. After officials have measured the jump the result is flashed on the bulletin board but that isn't as satisfactory as seeing the high-jump bar tremble and then stay up or fall.

Superfluous Commas

13

Do not use superfluous commas.

Necessary commas indicate appropriate pauses and voice pitch and thus help to clarify the meaning of a sentence. Unnecessary or misplaced commas, however, are false or awkward signals that often confuse the reader. Compare the punctuation of the following sentences.

> The boys, go to the gymnasium, at two o'clock. [Unnecessary commas]
> The boys go to the gymnasium at two o'clock. [No commas needed]
> Boys, go to the gymnasium at two o'clock. [Comma needed to indicate direct address—see **12d**]
> Helen enjoys tennis but, she cannot play well. [Misplaced comma]
> Helen enjoys tennis, but she cannot play well. [Comma *before* coordinating conjunction—see **12a**]

If you tend to use superfluous commas, consider the need for every comma you are tempted to use and omit it unless you can justify it by Section **12**.

13a

Do not use a comma to separate the subject from its verb, the verb from its object, or an adjective from the noun it precedes.

In the following sentences the encircled commas should be omitted:

> Rain at frequent intervals⊙ is productive of mosquitoes. [Needless separation of subject and verb]

He learned at an early age⊙ the necessity of economizing. [Needless separation of verb and object]

The book says⊙ that members of the crew deserted. [Indirect discourse: needless separation of verb and object]

He was a bad, deceitful, unruly⊙ boy. [Incorrect separation of adjective and its noun]

Note: A comma before the verb sometimes makes for clarity when the subject is heavily modified.

Rain coming at frequent intervals and in sufficient amounts to fill the ponds, the cisterns, and the many small containers near the house**,** is productive of mosquitoes.

13b

Do not use a comma to separate two words or two phrases joined by a coordinating conjunction.

In the following sentences the encircled commas should be omitted:

The poem has nobility of sentiment⊙ and dignity of style.

The players work together⊙ and gain a victory. [Compound predicate: *and* joins two verbs.]

He had decided to work⊙ and to save his money. [*And* joins two infinitive phrases.]

13c

Do not use commas to set off words or short phrases (especially introductory ones) that are not parenthetical or that are very slightly so.

In the following sentences the encircled commas should be omitted:

Last Monday⊙ I went to a baseball game⊙ too.

Maybe⊙ he had a better reason for leaving.

Yet⊙ it is easy to talk⊙ by wire⊙ to any continent.

13d

Do not use commas to set off restrictive (necessary) clauses, restrictive phrases, or restrictive appositives.

In the following sentences the encircled commas should be omitted:

A man⊙ *who hopes to succeed*⊙ must work hard. [Restrictive clause]

Any man⊙ *willing to work*⊙ can make a living there. [Restrictive phrase]

Only in ancient Spanish was *k* used, and the letter⊙ *w*⊙ has never had a place in the Spanish alphabet. [Restrictive appositive]

13e

Do not put a comma before the first item of a series, after the last item of a series, or after a coordinating conjunction.

In the following sentences the encircled commas should be omitted:

I enjoy the study of⊙history, geography, and geology. [Needless comma before the first item of a series. A colon here would also be needless since there is no formal introduction. See **17d**.]

History, geography, and geology⊙are interesting subjects.

I enjoy these subjects, but⊙for others I have less appreciation.

Field work is required in a few sciences, such as⊙botany and geology.

▶ EXERCISE 1   Some of the following sentences contain commas that would usually be omitted in good contemporary writing. Draw a circle around each unnecessary comma. Be prepared to justify each comma that you allow to stand.

1. I gave the note to Helen, and George asked her to read it aloud.

2. I gave the note to Helen, and asked her to read it aloud.
3. Any teacher, who is enthusiastic, deserves a lively class.
4. Professor Brown, who is enthusiastic, has a lively class.
5. One of the debaters, had apparently read Castell's *College Logic.*
6. My brother, one of the debaters, had never heard of the poet, Sandburg.
7. I like to celebrate Christmas quietly, but, my family prefers parties, and fireworks.
8. An old proverb states, that love and a cough are difficult to hide.
9. Remembering a line, from Pascal, I replied, "Noble deeds that are concealed are most esteemed."
10. During the half, we drank coffee, and talked about the close, exciting, football game, especially crucial plays, such as, the pass interference, the untimely fumbles, and the surprising, field goal.

▶ EXERCISE 2   In the following sentences (adapted from Thoreau) draw a circle around each superfluous comma and be prepared to justify each needed comma.

¹ We admire Chaucer, for his sturdy, English wit. ² The easy height, he speaks from, in his "Prologue," to the *Canterbury Tales,* as if he were equal to any of the company there assembled, is as good as any particular excellence in it.   ³ But, though it is full of good sense, and humanity, it is not transcendent poetry. ⁴ For picturesque descriptions, of persons, it is, perhaps, without a parallel in English poetry.   ⁵ Yet, it is, essentially, humorous, as the loftiest genius never is.   ⁶ Humor, however broad and genial, takes a narrower view than enthusiasm.   ⁷ To his own finer vein, he added all the common wit, and wisdom, of his time, and everywhere in his works, his remarkable knowledge of the world, and nice perception of character, his rare, common sense, and proverbial wisdom, are apparent . . . .

[8] The lover learns at last, that there is no person quite transparent and trustworthy, but every one has a devil in him, that is capable of any crime, in the long run.   [9] Yet, as an oriental philosopher has said, "Although friendship between good men, is interrupted, their principles remain unaltered.   [10] The stalk of the lotus, may be broken, and the fibers remain connected."

The Semicolon

14

Use the semicolon (a) between two main clauses not joined by *and, but, or, nor,* or *for* and (b) between coordinate elements containing commas. (Use the semicolon only between parts of equal rank.)

The pause in speaking required for the semicolon is almost as full as that for the period; in fact, the semicolon may be called a weak period. (Read the preceding sentence aloud, noting the very distinct pause marked by the semicolon and the lesser pause marked by the comma.)

The pause test can help you place the semicolon as well as the comma, but you should rely chiefly on your knowledge of the structure of the sentence. If you can distinguish between phrases and clauses, between main and subordinate clauses (see Section **1d** and **1e**), you should have little trouble using the semicolon.

14a

Use the semicolon between two main clauses not joined by one of the coordinating conjunctions (*and, but, or, nor, for*).

PATTERN MAIN CLAUSE; MAIN CLAUSE.[Compound sentence]

We didn't abolish truth; even we couldn't do that.
—WILLIAM FAULKNER

Essentially the form of art is an imitation of reality; it holds the mirror up to nature.   —WILL DURANT

I had great anxiety and no means of relieving it; I had vehement convictions and small power to give effect to them.
—WINSTON CHURCHILL

Note: The semicolon also separates main clauses not joined by a coordinating conjunction in compound-complex sentences.

No society can survive if everything changes but its institutions; no society can stay sane if no one is to innovate except the technologists. —BARBARA WARD

[Main clause subordinate clause; main clause subordinate clause.]

Conjunctive adverbs (e.g., *accordingly, also, anyhow, besides, consequently, furthermore, hence, however, indeed, instead, likewise, moreover, nevertheless, still, then, therefore, thus*) and such transitional phrases as *for example, in fact, in other words, on the contrary, on the other hand,* and *that is* are not grammatically equivalent to coordinating conjunctions. See **3b.** Therefore, use a semicolon before these conjunctive adverbs and transitional phrases when they connect main clauses.

PATTERN

CONJUNCTIVE ADVERB
MAIN CLAUSE;   *or*   MAIN CLAUSE.
TRANSITIONAL PHRASE,

Kon-Tiki, on his original voyage across the sea, had no asphalt or hermetically sealed tins; nevertheless he had no serious food problems. —THOR HEYERDAHL

The organism gets a chance to function according to its own laws; in other words, it gets a chance to realize such good as it is capable of. —ALDOUS HUXLEY

Note that a comma follows the transitional phrase *in other words* but not the conjunctive adverb *nevertheless.* After transitional phrases the pause in reading is usually sufficient to require a comma but often not so after conjunctive adverbs. The pause test is the best guide. See also **12b.**

Caution: Do not overwork the semicolon. Often compound sentences are better revised according to the principles of subordination. See Section **24** and also **14c**.

Exception to 14a: Coordinating conjunctions between main clauses are often preceded by a semicolon (instead of the usual comma) if the clauses have internal punctuation or reveal a striking contrast. See also **12a**.

> American education may be sometimes slapdash and fantastic, with its short-story and saxophone courses, its strange fraternities and sororities, its musical-comedy co-ed atmosphere, its heavily solemn games departments; but at least it has never departed from the fine medieval tradition of the poor scholar. —J. B. PRIESTLEY

14b

The semicolon is used to separate a series of equal elements which themselves contain commas.

This use of the semicolon makes for clarity, showing the reader at a glance the main divisions, which would be more difficult to distinguish if only commas were used throughout the sentence.

> I came to this conclusion after talking in Moscow last spring with three kinds of people concerned: foreign diplomats, students, and correspondents; the new Rector of Friendship University; and the harried Afro-Asian students themselves.
> —PRISCILLA JOHNSON

> The challenge of facing a large audience, expectant but unaroused; the laughter that greets a sally at the outset, then the stillness as the power of imagery and ideas takes hold; the response that flows, audibly or inaudibly, from the audience to the speaker; the fresh extemporizing without which a lecture is dead; the tension and timing as the talk nears the hour; and the unexpected conclusion—this is what every professional speaker comes to know.   —EDWARD WEEKS

14c

Caution: Use the semicolon between parts of equal rank only, not between a clause and a phrase or a main clause and a subordinate clause.

PARTS OF EQUAL RANK

> A bitter wind swept the dead leaves along the street; it cast them high in the air and against the buildings. [Two main clauses]
>
> I hope to spend my vacation in Canada; I enjoy the fishing there.

PARTS OF UNEQUAL RANK

> A bitter wind swept the dead leaves along the street, casting them high in the air and against the buildings. [Main clause and phrase, separated by a comma]
>
> I hope to spend my vacation in Canada, where I enjoy the fishing. [Main clause and subordinate clause, separated by a comma]

Note: At times a semicolon is apparently used between parts of unequal rank. However, closer examination usually reveals that the semicolon is in reality a mark of coordination: following the semicolon is a group of words which, with "understood" words carried over from the preceding clause, constitutes a main clause.

> Popularization is one thing; dedicated music-making [is] another.
> —HARPER'S MAGAZINE
>
> The theory applied equally well to Mrs. Kerr's case; perhaps [the theory applied] even better since it also confirmed the deep-rooted public conviction that no woman really knows what a car is for. —IBID.

▶ EXERCISE 1 In the following sentences (selected from the *Atlantic Monthly*), all semicolons are used correctly. Be prepared to give the reason for the use of each semicolon.

1. The narrow windows and the steeply sloping roof oppressed me; I wished to turn away and go back.

2. Even stillness is a positive factor; it is to motion what silence is to sound.

3. We are not as careful or cherishing of our artists as Europeans; nevertheless, what with television, movies, and shows, it is possible for outstanding dancers to make a living, while choreographers, directors, and dancing actors can make fortunes.

4. The rhymes are filled with fun and good humor; the music, arranged by Cecil Sharp, is a fine accompaniment; but the superb part of the book is the hilarious array of pictures in rainbow colors.

5. Beyond this are the three objectives of the American space program: "to understand the nature of the control exerted by the sun over events on the earth; to learn the nature and origin of the universe, including the solar system; and to search for the origin of life and its presence outside the earth."

6. Everybody was confused; no one knew what to do.

7. "As a historian," wrote De Voto, "I have interested myself in the growth among the American people of the feeling that they were properly a single nation between two oceans; in the development of what I have called the continental mind."

8. Treitschke confirmed him in his belief in blood and iron; Nietzsche in his veneration for the Aryan "blond beast," the superman who would conquer and decimate the subject races.

9. It is beyond possibility to mention all the outstanding books; however, some of the highlights are suggested in the chronological list that follows.

10. It was an inland country, with the forlorn look of all unloved things; winter in this part of the South is a moribund coma, not the Northern death sleep with the sure promise of resurrection.

▶ EXERCISE 2   In the following sentences insert semicolons where they are needed. Remove semicolons standing between parts of unequal rank. Write *C* after each sentence that needs no revision.

1. Although I did my best to explain why I had failed; my parents scolded me for failing the history test.
2. Mac goes around in par now, he has trimmed several strokes off his game since we played together last.
3. I hear it said by the people hereabouts that the old mansion is haunted, in fact, there are some who swear that it is.
4. Hank had dismantled his motor; intending to give it a complete overhaul for the following week's races.
5. He is fairly even-tempered most of the time, and you should have no difficulty getting along with him but whatever you do, don't ever let him get you into a political argument.
6. He lamented that he had no suggestions to offer, however, he spent the next forty minutes offering them.
7. It's all right for you to be here, I crashed this party myself.
8. I went to the address you gave me; if your brother lives there, he lives upstairs over a vacant lot.
9. In our unit at that time there were Lieutenant Holmes, a criminologist by profession and a university lecturer on penology, Captain Sturm, in peacetime a U.S. Steel executive, two old majors, previously retired and now still writing their memoirs, and Lieutenant Colonel Beale, a Mississippi cotton planter.
10. If you expect me to be here in time, or even to get back at all; you had better send somebody to help me.

▶ EXERCISE 3   From your reading, copy any five sentences in which the semicolon is properly used. Explain the reason for each semicolon.

▶ EXERCISE 4   Compose five sentences to illustrate the proper use of the semicolon.

[*See also the general exercises immediately following and the general exercises following Section 17.*]

GENERAL EXERCISES ON THE COMMA
AND THE SEMICOLON

▶ EXERCISE 5   Commas are used correctly in the following sentences. Explain each comma by writing above it the appropriate letter from Section **12: a, b, c,** or **d.**

1. After crossing the river we built no more fires, for we were now in hostile Indian country.
2. Having nothing very important to do, I simply did nothing at all.
3. If he says he'll be there, he'll be there.
4. The smith straightened up, the horse's hoof still between his knees, and then he bent back to his work.
5. Although there are a few adjustments yet to be made, the main part of the work is finished, and the next few days should see it completed altogether.
6. The panting, tormented bull lowered his head for another charge.
7. The kit contains cement, balsa, paper, and instructions for assembly.
8. You will, I suppose, be back tomorrow.
9. The old opera house, which has stood unused for years, will finally be torn down.
10. It was a long, hot, tiresome trip, and I was sorry that I had promised to go.

▶ EXERCISE 6   Insert all necessary commas and semicolons in the following sentences. Above each mark of punctuation write the appropriate rule number.

1. If I were in your position however I would be extremely cautious about believing what I heard.
2. Taking everything into consideration I believe that Robinson should have a better season this year than ever before however you understand that this is only an opinion and that I reserve the right to amend it after I have seen him work out a few times.
3. After we wash the dishes we must wash the towels.

4. Two or three scrawny mangy-looking hounds lay sprawled in the shade of the cabin.

5. While Frank was unpacking the cooking gear and Gene was chopping firewood I began to put up our shelter.

6. Phil meanwhile had gone down to the lake to try to get a few bass for our supper.

7. After perhaps an hour or so of waiting they may go away but don't expect them to go far and don't think they aren't still watching.

8. Bales of cotton hogsheads of sugar and salted meats barrels of flour and cases and crates of goods of every kind imaginable crowded the busy landing as far up and down the river as the eye could reach.

9. In complete disregard of the machine-gun bullets that were nipping through the grass tops all around us Jerry wriggled on his belly all the way out to where I was put a tourniquet on my leg and then began dragging me back to the shelter of the ditch.

10. If I am expected to arrive by eleven o'clock someone should volunteer to wake me up otherwise I shall probably sleep until noon.

The Apostrophe

15

Use the apostrophe to indicate the possessive case (except for personal pronouns), to mark omissions, and to form certain plurals.

15a

Do not carelessly omit the apostrophe in the possessive case of nouns and indefinite pronouns.

The apostrophe indicates a relationship that may be otherwise expressed by the substitution of an *of* phrase or a similar modifier.

> The girls' mother (the mother of the girls); Ted's dog (the dog owned by Ted); tomorrow's assignment (the assignment for tomorrow); no one's fault (the fault of no one); everybody's friend (the friend of everybody)

For inanimate objects the *of* phrase is more commonly used than the *'s: the back of the chair, the top of the desk.*

(1) If the ending (either singular or plural) is not in an *s* or *z* sound, add the apostrophe and *s*.

> The man's hat; the boy's shoes; a dollar's worth; today's problems [Singular]
> The men's hats; the women's dresses; the children's playground [Plural]
> One's hat; another's coat; someone's shirt; anybody's room [Indefinite pronouns—singular]

(2) If the plural ends in an *s* or *z* sound, add only the apostrophe.

Ladies' hats (hats for ladies); boys' shoes (shoes for boys); the Joneses' boys (the boys of the Joneses); three dollars' worth; Farmers' (OR Farmers) Cooperative Society [The names of organizations frequently omit the apostrophe, as in *Ball State Teachers College.*]

(3) If the singular ends in an *s* or *z* sound, add the apostrophe and *s* for words of one syllable. Add only the apostrophe for words of more than one syllable unless you expect the pronunciation of the second *s* or *z* sound.

James's book; Moses' law; Xerxes' army; Hortense's coat

(4) Compounds or nouns in joint possession show the possessive in the last word only. But if there is individual (or separate) possession, each noun takes the possessive form.

My brother-in-law's house; my brothers-in-law's houses; someone else's hat
Helen and Mary's piano [Joint ownership]
Helen's and Mary's clothes [Individual ownership]

▶ EXERCISE 1   Copy the following, inserting apostrophes to indicate the possessive case:

1. the girls (*sing.*) coat
2. the girls (*pl.*) coats
3. a months pay
4. two months pay
5. everybodys business
6. everyone elses clothes
7. the childs mother
8. the childrens mother
9. babys toys
10. babies toys

▶ EXERCISE 2   Rewrite the following as possessives with the apostrophe:

1. the home of my neighbor
2. homes of my neighbors
3. a book for a boy
4. books for boys
5. the car of my sister
6. the cars of my sisters
7. the ideas of a woman
8. the ideas of women
9. the boat of Robert and Jim

10. the boats of Robert and Jim (individual possession)

11. the hat of the lady

12. the hats of the ladies

15b

Do not use the apostrophe with the pronouns *his, hers, its, ours, yours, theirs, whose* or with plural nouns not in the possessive case.

EXAMPLES   He is a friend of *yours* and *theirs.*
He makes *hats* for *ladies.* (BUT He makes *ladies'* hats.)

Do not confuse the possessive pronoun *its* with the contraction *it's,* which means *it is,* or the possessive pronoun *whose* with the contraction *who's,* which means *who is.*

POSSESSIVE   The bird returned to *its* nest.
CONTRACTION   *It's* a small, well-hidden nest.

POSSESSIVE   There is the man *whose* son has been elected to Congress.
CONTRACTION   There is the man *who's* going to be our new congressman.

15c

Use an apostrophe to mark omissions in contracted words or numerals.

EXAMPLES   Can't; didn't; he's (he is); it's (it is); you're (you are); o'clock (of the clock); the class of '70 (1970)

Caution: Place the apostrophe exactly where the omission occurs: *isn't, haven't* [NOT *is'nt, have'nt*].

15d

Use the apostrophe and *s* to form the plural of letters, figures, symbols, and words referred to as words.

EXAMPLES   Congreve seldom crossed his *t*'s, his *7*'s looked like *9*'s, and his *and*'s were usually *&*'s.

Note: This apostrophe is sometimes omitted when there is no danger of ambiguity: the 1930's, or the 1930s; two *B*'s and three *C*'s, or two *B*s and three *C*s.

▶ **EXERCISE 3**   Write brief sentences correctly using (a) the possessive singular, (b) the plural, and (c) the possessive plural of each of the following words.

EXAMPLE
   1. *student*
      a. A student's attitude is important.
      b. Several students dropped the course.
      c. The students' parents were invited.

1. woman
2. father
3. other
4. family
5. lawyer
6. jockey
7. sailor
8. goose
9. brother-in-law
10. genius
11. army
12. Brooks

▶ **EXERCISE 4**   Copy the following sentences, inserting necessary apostrophes and omitting needless or faulty ones. Underline each possessive once and each contraction twice.

1. Who's going to do the dishes? Who's turn is it?
2. The choice is our's to make, not your's.
3. Shes writing copy for a new program on one of the local station's.
4. On Thursday's the childrens' department does'nt open.
5. That boys one of the worlds' worst. Whats he doing now?
6. Its a dogs' life—jeweled collars, T-bone steaks, and fur wraps!
7. *Ifs, buts,* and *maybes* wont satisfy a young swains ardent proposal.
8. They have'nt said the property is theirs'.
9. I did'nt go to sleep until after two oclock.
10. Its a mans right to see that he gets his dollars worth.
11. Theyre not coming to see Freds' new house.
12. The books format is it's best feature.

Quotation Marks
(and Quotations)

16

Use quotation marks to set off all direct quotations, some titles, and words used in a special sense. Place other marks of punctuation in proper relation to quotation marks.

Quotations usually consist of (1) passages borrowed from the written work of others or (2) the direct speech of individuals, especially in conversation (dialogue).

QUOTED WRITING   John Ciardi has written: "Dante is a supreme master because he entered the activity of his life-imagination at a heat of passion beyond most men, yet saw through diamond eyes: he could burn and still see." [The words and punctuation within quotation marks are exactly as they appear in "The Relevance of Dante," in *Saturday Review*, May 22, 1965, p. 53.]

QUOTED SPEECH   "My husband won't let me watch TV programs about doctors and hospitals," Donna explained. "As soon as I hear of a disease or even a symptom, I get sick!" [Within quotation marks are the exactly recorded words of the speaker; the punctuation is supplied by the writer.]

Notice above that quotation marks are used in pairs: the first set marks the beginning of the quotation, and the second set marks the end. Be careful not to omit or misplace the second set. Also remember that the verb of saying and the speaker (such as *Donna explained*) should never be within the quotation marks.

16a

Use double quotation marks to enclose direct (but not indirect) quotations; use single marks to enclose a quotation within a quotation.

EXAMPLES

He said, "I have no intention of staying." [Direct quotation—the exact words spoken]

He said that he had "no intention of staying." [Direct quotation of a fragment of the speech]

He said that he had not intended to stay. [Indirect quotation—no quotation marks]

Notice in the example below that the quotation within a quotation is enclosed by single quotation marks; one within that, by double marks.

"It took courage," the speaker said, "for a man to affirm in those days: 'I endorse every word of Patrick Henry's sentiment, "Give me liberty or give me death!" ' "

—WILLIAM LEWIN

(1) **Long quotations (not dialogue).** In printed matter, small type usually sets off quoted material of ten or more lines.[1] No quotation marks are used, unless the original carries quotation marks. In typewritten papers, such quoted passages are single-spaced and indented from both sides five spaces.[2] The first line is indented ten spaces when it marks a paragraph beginning.

---

[1] Recommended by "The MLA Style Sheet," Revised Edition, 1959, p. 8, reprinted from *Publications of the Modern Language Association of America.*

[2] When quotation marks—instead of the usual smaller type or indention—are used for a passage of two or more paragraphs, the quotation marks come before each paragraph and at the end of the last; they do not come at the end of intermediate paragraphs.

In an interesting essay entitled "The Growing Power of Admen," Vance Packard has this to say about American buyers:

> Happily for the marketers, Americans by nature seem to relish learning to want new things. We are a restless people who like continually to hear of new things to do and buy. (Note the recent popularity of bejeweled fly swatters and mousetraps.) Emerson commented on this trait in Americans when he said that they, unlike Europeans, exhibit "an uncalculated, headlong expenditure." This makes them the world's prize consumers.
>
> Recently the president of the Institute for Motivational Research (which conducts psychological studies for marketers) noted with satisfaction "our increasing willingness to give vent to our whims and desires" and offered the opinion that America is "experiencing a revolution in self-indulgence."[3]

(2) **Poetry.** A single line of poetry or less is usually handled like other short quotations, run in with the text and enclosed in quotation marks. Longer passages should be set off from the text, indented, and quoted line by line exactly as they appear in the original.

The last part of "The Leaden Echo," by Gerard Manley Hopkins, offers no hope to those who would like to stay young and beautiful:

> Be beginning; since, no, nothing can be done
> To keep at bay
> Age and age's evils—hoar hair,
> Ruck and wrinkle, drooping, dying, death's worst, winding sheets,
>   tombs and worms, and tumbling to decay;
> So be beginning, be beginning to despair.
> Oh, there's none—no, no, no, there's none:
>   Be beginning to despair, to despair,
>   Despair, despair, despair, despair.

In the companion poem, "The Golden Echo," however, Hopkins presents a cure for despair, one that is **"**Only not within seeing of the sun.**"**

(3) **Dialogue (conversation).** Written dialogue represents

---

[3] Copyright © by The Atlantic Monthly Company, Boston, Massachusetts. Reprinted with permission.

the directly quoted speech of two or more persons talking together. Standard practice is to write each person's speech, no matter how short, as a separate paragraph. Verbs of saying, as well as closely related bits of narrative, are included in the paragraph along with the speech.

"You remember Kate Stoddard, Mother?" Georgia asked. "This is Kate to pay us a little visit."

Mrs. Stanton rocked and closed her eyes. "What's everybody shouting for?" she asked.

"Sit down, Kate," Georgia said.

Mrs. Stoddard pulled a chair close to Mrs. Stanton. "Well, I will, but I can't stay. I came for a reason."

"We paid our yearly dues," Georgia said.

"I don't know what makes you say that," Mrs. Stoddard said. "I don't think you've ever known me to solicit *personally.* I came about quite another matter. I wanted you to look at this." She fished in her bag and brought out the diary, which she held out rather grudgingly to Georgia. "Be careful of it! It's quite old!" —SALLY BENSON[4]

In the last paragraph, note that although a narrative passage interrupts the dialogue, the speaker is Mrs. Stoddard throughout.

(4) **Punctuation of dialogue.** Note that such expressions as "he said," when introducing a *short* speech, are usually followed by a comma; that they are set off by commas when interpolated (see **12d**[3]); that they are preceded by a comma when added at the end of a speech (unless the speech is a question or an exclamation, when the question mark or the exclamation point replaces the comma). Such expressions as "he said" before *longer* speeches are usually followed by a colon (see **17d**[1]).

---

[4] From "Spirit of '76" by Sally Benson. Originally published in the *New Yorker,* December 25, 1954.

► EXERCISE 1   Compose five sentences to illustrate the proper use of double and single quotation marks.

16b

Use quotation marks for minor titles (short stories, essays, one-act plays, short poems, songs, articles from magazines) and for subdivisions of books.

EXAMPLES

The January 3, 1966, issue of *Sports Illustrated* contains a lively article entitled **"A Snook Hunt on the Spanish Main."**

In this book are numerous short poems and stories, such as **"The Raven"** and **"The Fall of the House of Usher."**

Last summer I read **"L'Allegro,"** a short lyric, and parts of *Paradise Lost.*

Stevenson's *Treasure Island* is divided into six parts, the last of which, called **"Captain Silver,"** opens with a chapter entitled **"In the Enemy's Camp."**

Note: Quotation marks are sometimes used to enclose titles of books, magazines, and newspapers, but italics are usually preferred. See **10a.**

► EXERCISE 2   Compose five sentences showing use of quotation marks with minor titles and subdivisions of books.

16c

Words used in a special sense are sometimes enclosed in quotation marks.

EXAMPLES

The printer must see that quotation marks are **"cleared"**— that is, kept within the margins.

"Sympathy" means **"to suffer with."** [OR: *Sympathy* means *to suffer with. Sympathy* means "to suffer with." See also **10d.**]

16d

Do not overuse quotation marks.

Do not use quotation marks to enclose titles of themes or to mark bits of humor. In general do not enclose in quotation marks common nicknames, technical terms, and trite or well-known expressions. Instead of placing slang and colloquialisms inside quotation marks, use formal English. Above all, do not use quotation marks for emphasis.

NEEDLESS PUNCTUATION   "Old Hickory" was wrought up over the loss of his friend.

BETTER   Old Hickory was wrought up over the loss of his friend.

INAPPROPRIATE IN FORMAL WRITING   He must have been "nuts." The tiny pink telephone is "as cute as a bug's ear."

APPROPRIATE   He must have been insane. The tiny pink telephone is an attractive novelty.

16e

In using marks of punctuation with quoted words, phrases, or sentences, follow the arbitrary printers' rules by placing:

(1) The period and the comma always within the quotation marks.

(2) The colon and the semicolon always outside the quotation marks.

(3) The dash, the question mark, and the exclamation point within the quotation marks when they apply to the quoted matter only; outside when they refer to the whole sentence.

"I will go," he insisted. "I am needed." [Comma and period always inside quotation marks]

He spoke of his "old log house"; he might have called it a mansion. [Semicolon (and colon) always outside quotation marks]

He asked, **"When did you arrive?"** [Here the question mark applies only to the part of the sentence within quotation marks.]

Why did he ask, **"When did you arrive?"** [A second question mark does not follow the quotation.]

What is the meaning of **"the open door"?** [Here the question mark applies to the whole sentence.]

The captain shouted, **"Halt!"** [Here the exclamation point applies only to the quotation.]

Save us from his **"mercy"!** [Here the exclamation point applies to the whole sentence.]

▶ EXERCISE 3 Add correctly placed quotation marks where needed in the following sentences.

1. Surely, I replied facetiously, you know the difference between prose and poetry.
2. Dan asked, Did you accept Beverly's invitation?
3. Have you read the short poem To an Athlete Dying Young?
4. One angry spectator yelled, That blockhead!
5. Who is the author of the line A spark disturbs our clod?
6. Thomas Gray did write 'Tis folly to be wise; however, he qualified the statement with Where ignorance is bliss.
7. How he enjoyed reading the short story The Luck of Roaring Camp!
8. Only one main character appears in Poe's short story The Tell-Tale Heart: the mad murderer.
9. Was it Knox or a Hebrew writer who asked Why is man, mere earth and ashes, proud?
10. The lip of truth shall be established forever, states an ancient proverb, but a lying tongue is but for a moment.

▶ EXERCISE 4 After you have studied **16a(3)**, giving special attention to the punctuation of the dialogue on page 149, and have reviewed **16e**, write a short, original dialogue of approximately two hundred words. Place all quotation marks properly.

▶ EXERCISE 5 Insert quotation marks where they are needed in the following sentences.

1. Campus fads come and go, I commented to Carl as we sat down to lunch in the cafeteria. But, as far as your friend Helen is concerned, this current fad of acting like Mrs. Malaprop will probably never die.

2. Be patient with Helen! Carl snapped as he unrolled his napkin and sorted his silverware. I actually like Helen's bad jokes. Her word play—

3. Please pass the salt, I interrupted.

4. Ignoring my frown, Carl continued, I'll grant you that Helen's puns are usually as old and as clever as the joke ending with Squawbury Shortcake; but here she comes. Let's change the subject pronto.

5. Clearing my throat pretentiously, I took his advice and said, Perhaps your parents should buy a perambulator.

6. A perambulator! Helen happily took up my cue as she plopped down in the chair near Carl. My parents bought me an eight-cup perambulator for my birthday. Just plug it in, and coffee is ready in four minutes!

7. Aren't you thinking of a percolator? I asked her in mock seriousness. An electric percolator heats quickly.

8. Yeah, Helen replied, winking at Carl. It's the same thing as an incubator.

9. You don't mean *incubator!* I barked sharply and then added a bit of my own nonsense: You mean *incinerator.* After a moment of silence, I yawned and said, Incinerator bombs are really fiery weapons. They cause much perturbation.

10. This time Helen had no ready answer. Admitting defeat at her own ridiculous word game, she grinned and announced, Repartee like this is for immature freshmen who like the Malaprop fad—not for me.

The Period
and Other Marks

17

Use the period, the question mark, the exclamation point, the colon, the dash, parentheses, and brackets in accordance with standard usage.

End marks indicate those pitches and stops of the voice which help to reveal the meanings of sentences.

No man is an island. [Statement]
No man is an island? [Question]
No man is an island! [Exclamation]

Dashes, colons, parentheses, and brackets are signals for pauses or voice variations which usually indicate degrees of emphasis within a sentence.

Man is a piece of the continent — not an island.
Consider this idea: no man is an island.
John Donne (1573–1631) said that man is not an island.
The metaphor closes with "because I [John Donne] am involved in mankind."

The Period (.)

17a

Use the period after declarative and mildly imperative sentences, after indirect questions, and after most abbreviations. Use the ellipsis mark (three spaced periods) to indicate omissions from quoted passages.

(1) Use the period to mark the end of a declarative sentence, a mildly imperative sentence, or an indirect question.

DECLARATIVE   They changed the rules.

MILDLY IMPERATIVE   Change the rules. Let's change the troublesome rules.

INDIRECT QUESTION   He asked whether the rules had been changed.

(2) Use periods to follow most abbreviations.

Mr., Mrs., Dr., Jr., Ph.D., etc., B.C., A.D. R.S.V.P. or r.s.v.p., C.O.D. or c.o.d., A.M. or a.m., P.M. or p.m.

Frequently current usage omits periods after many abbreviations, especially of organizations and national or international agencies.

TV, CBS, CIO, ROTC, VA, FBI, USN, FHA, UN

If you have any doubt about the punctuation of a given abbreviation, consult a good college dictionary.

Caution: Do not use periods to indicate that such words as *I've, can't, 2nd, 15th,* and *gym* are contractions or abbreviations.

(3) Use the ellipsis mark (three spaced periods) to indicate an omission of one or more words within a quoted passage.

If the omission ends with a period, use four spaced periods (one to mark the end of the sentence and three to show the omission).

QUOTATION

No man is an island, entire of itself; every man is a piece of the continent, a part of the main. If a clod be washed away by the sea, Europe is the less, as well as if a promontory were, as well as if a manor of thy friend's or of thine own were.

Any man's death diminishes me because I am involved in mankind, and therefore never send to know for whom the bell tolls; it tolls for thee. —JOHN DONNE

QUOTATION WITH ELLIPSES

No man is an island **. . .** every man is a piece of the continent, a part of the main**. . . .** Any man's death diminishes me because I am involved in mankind **. . . .** —JOHN DONNE

The Question Mark (**?**)

17b

Use the question mark to follow direct (but not indirect) questions.

EXAMPLES

Who started the riot**?**

Did he ask who started the riot**?** [The sentence as a whole is a direct question despite the indirect question at the end.]

"Who started the riot**?**" he asked.

He asked, "Who started the riot**?**"

You started the riot**?** [Question in the form of a declarative sentence]

You told me—did I hear you correctly**?**—that you started the riot. [Interpolated question]

Did you hear him say, "What right have you to ask about the riot**?**" [Double direct question followed by a single question mark]

Did he plan the riot, employ assistants, and give the signal to begin**?**

Did he plan the riot**?** employ assistants**?** give the signal to begin**?** [Question marks used between the parts of the series cause full stops and throw emphasis on each part.]

Caution: Do not use the question mark to indicate the end of an indirect question. See also **17a(1)**.

He asked who started the riot. To ask why the riot started is unnecessary. I want to know what the cause of the riot was. How foolish it is to ask what caused the riot!

OTHER USES OF THE QUESTION MARK

A question mark (within parentheses) is used to express the writer's uncertainty as to the correctness of the preceding word, figure, or date: "Chaucer was born in 1340(?) and died in 1400." But the question mark is not a desirable means of expressing the author's wit or sarcasm.

QUESTIONABLE   This kind (?) proposal caused Gulliver to take refuge in nearby Blefuscu. [Omit the question mark. If the context does not make the irony clear, either revise your sentence or give up your attempt to strike an ironic note.]

Courtesy questions common to business letters may be followed by question marks but are usually followed by periods: "Will you (= Please) write me again if I can be of further service."

Caution: Do not use a comma or a period after a question mark.

"Are you ready?" he asked.
He asked, "Are you ready?"

The Exclamation Point (!)

17c

Use the exclamation point after an emphatic interjection and after a phrase, clause, or sentence to express a high degree of surprise, incredulity, or other strong emotion.

EXAMPLES
What! I cannot believe it! How beautiful! [*What* and *how* often begin exclamations.]
Oh! You have finally come! (OR: Oh, you have finally come!)
March! Halt! Get out of this house! [Sharp commands—vigorous imperatives]

Forbid it, Almighty God! I know not what course others may take, but as for me, give me liberty, or give me death!
—PATRICK HENRY

Caution 1: Avoid overuse of the exclamation point. Use a comma after mild interjections, and end mildly exclamatory sentences with a period.

> Well, you are to be congratulated.
> Oh, I cannot do that.

Caution 2: Do not use a comma or a period after the exclamation point.

> "Halt!" shouted the corporal.
> The corporal shouted, "Halt!"

▶ **EXERCISE 1**   Illustrate the chief uses of the period, the question mark, and the exclamation point by composing and correctly punctuating brief sentences as directed below.

EXAMPLE
> *a declarative sentence containing a quoted direct question*
> "Is Fred a ventriloquist?" she asked.

1. a declarative sentence containing a quoted exclamation
2. a direct question
3. an indirect question
4. a double direct question
5. a declarative sentence containing an interpolated question
6. a vigorous imperative
7. a mild imperative
8. a direct question having the form of a declaration
9. an ellipsis at the beginning of a quoted sentence
10. an ellipsis at the end of a quoted sentence

▶ **EXERCISE 2**   Correctly punctuate the following sentences by supplying needed periods, question marks, and exclamation points. Be prepared to give a reason for each mark you add. (*In this exercise* place all end marks that appear together with quotation marks *inside* the quotation marks; see **16c.**)

1. Frank asked me why I did not take Ellen to the dance
2. Frank asked, "Why didn't you take Ellen to the dance"

3. Did Frank ask you why I did not take Ellen to the dance

4. "What will you sell that wreck for" Mr Lacy asked

5. Stumbling toward the telephone, I wondered who could be calling me after 11:30 PM

6. The joker on the other end of the line chirped softly, "Honey, how many hours each week do you watch TV"

7. After a short silence the voice asked me what channel I was watching then

8. What a surprise that was

9. On April 15th I arrived in Washington, DC

10. Members of the YMCA smiled when the speaker was introduced; his name was Dr A J Byrd

The Colon (**:**)

17d

Use the colon after a formal introductory statement to direct attention to what is to follow. Avoid needless colons.

The colon and the semicolon, notwithstanding the similarity of the names, differ greatly in use. The semicolon (see Section 14) is a strong *separator* almost equal to a period, and is used only between equal parts. The colon after a statement or a main clause is a formal *introducer,* calling attention to something that is to follow. The colon usually means *as follows.*

(1) **The colon may direct attention to an appositive (or a series of appositives) at the end of a sentence, to a formal list or explanation, or to a long quotation.**

All her thoughts were centered on one objective **:** marriage. [A dash or a comma, which might be used instead of the colon, would be less formal.]

We may divide poems into three classes **:** narrative, lyric, and dramatic. [A dash might be used instead of the colon; because of the series a comma would be confusing.]

> Competition in the steel industry is described by one of the Corporation's competitors as follows: "Your ability to win when competition for business gets tough comes in the entire setup of your operation, the quality of your management . . . and so on. You have to play a judgment game. This is no 2-cent poker."
> —FORTUNE

(2) **The colon may separate two main clauses when the second clause explains or amplifies the first.**

> The scientific value of even the most recent contributions to this literature, however, is seriously qualified: The sole witness to the dream is the dreamer himself.
> —SCIENTIFIC AMERICAN

> There is something like a Puritan's restraint in the scientist who seeks truth: he keeps away from anything voluntaristic or emotional.
> —ALBERT EINSTEIN

Note: After the colon a quoted sentence regularly begins with a capital, but other sentences (as the examples above show) may begin with either a capital or a small letter.

(3) **Use the colon after the salutation of a business letter, between a title and a subtitle, between figures indicating the chapter and verse of a Biblical reference or the hour and minute of a time reference.**

> Dear Sir:
> *Creative Pattern Practice: A New Approach to Writing*
> according to Matthew 6:10   exactly at 10:35 P.M.

(4) **Avoid needless colons.**

When there is no formal introduction or summarizing word, the colon is usually a needless interruption of the sentence.

NEEDLESS   All her thoughts were centered on: marriage.
BETTER   All her thoughts were centered on marriage.

NEEDLESS	Three kinds of poems are: narratives, lyrics, and dramas. [Awkward separation of verb and its complement]
BETTER	Three kinds of poems are narratives, lyrics, and dramas.

▶ **EXERCISE 3** Punctuate the following sentences by adding appropriate colons or semicolons. When deciding whether a colon or a semicolon should separate two main clauses, use the colon only when the second main clause explains or amplifies the first. Write *C* after any sentence that needs no change.

1. Within two hours we had a strange variety of weather rain, hail, sleet, snow.
2. Promptly at 815 P.M. the minister began his sermon by quoting John 2021.
3. Two questions well worth asking yourself every day are these What must I do? Have I done it?
4. The conference had only one purpose agreement upon a suitable topic for a research paper.
5. Professor Boaz smiled a quick greeting I sat down and tried to look like an intelligent sophomore.
6. My roommate has a simple formula for looking like a sophomore Act depressed.
7. At first I merely looked gloomy later, however, I had good reason to feel depressed.
8. Professor Boaz started suggesting fantastic subjects "Causes of the Korean War," "An Analysis of the 1961 Recession," "Early Poetry of W. B. Yeats."
9. I then dared to mention that the only interests I have are cars, sports, and girls.
10. At the end of the conference I acted like the freshman that I am ironically enough, it was the professor who looked as depressed as an intelligent sophomore.

The Dash (—)

17e

Use the dash to mark a sudden break in thought, to set off a summary, or to set off a parenthetical element that is very abrupt or that has commas within it.

On the typewriter the dash is made by two hyphens without spacing before, between, or after. In handwriting the dash is an unbroken line about the length of two or three hyphens.

PUNCTUATION OF PARENTHETICAL MATTER

Dashes, parentheses, commas—all are used to set off parenthetical matter. Dashes set off parenthetical elements sharply and therefore tend to emphasize them:

> Rifle cartridges and shotgun shells — measured by today's prices — were cheap in 1905.   —DAVID L. COHN

Parentheses tend to minimize the importance of the parts thus set off:

> Rifle cartridges and shotgun shells (measured by today's prices) were cheap in 1905.

Commas are the mildest, most commonly used separators and tend to leave the parts more closely connected with the sentence. Dashes and parentheses should be used sparingly, only when commas will not serve equally well. (For the use of the comma to set off parenthetical matter, see **12d**; for the use of parentheses, see **17f.**)

(1) Use the dash to mark a sudden break in thought.

> "It is hard to explain—" he said, and paused as they composed themselves.   —LIONEL TRILLING

> Can I — I mean, where do you get a saw like that?
>   —GERALD WARNER BRACE

> In fact, she was always right — in a way.   —J. F. POWERS

(2) **Use the dash to set off a brief summary or appositive.**

> The German borrowings are also homely and everyday — wieners, pretzels, hunk, and dunk. —BERGEN EVANS

> The long neck, the small head, the knickers whose cuffs were worn down near his ankles — all these points, often observed by caricaturists, were visible in the flesh. —JOHN UPDIKE

(3) **Use dashes to set off a parenthetical element that is very abrupt or that has commas within it.**

> A telltale suggestion of relief — or was it gratitude? — brightened their eyes. —JOHN MASON BROWN

> He stood up — small, frail, and tense — staring toward things in his homeland. —NORA WALN

> I was mediocre at drill, certainly — that is, until my senior year. —JAMES THURBER

Caution: The dash should be used carefully in formal writing. It is more in keeping with an informal style, but even there it becomes ineffective when overused.

Parentheses ( )

17f

Use parentheses (1) to enclose figures, as in this rule, and (2) to set off parenthetical, supplementary, or illustrative matter.

EXAMPLES

> Dashes are used (1) to mark breaks, (2) to set off summaries, and (3) to set off parenthetical elements. [Parentheses enclose figures used to enumerate items.]

> Mr. Brown's horses (the best, no doubt, in the whole state) were exhibited at the fair. [Dashes would be used if the writer wished to emphasize the parenthetical matter.]

> It is strange (as one reviews all the memories of that good friend and master) to think that there is now a new generation beginning at Haverford that will never know his spell. —CHRISTOPHER MORLEY

When the sentence demands other marks of punctuation with the parenthetical matter, these marks are placed after the second parenthesis. The comma is never used before the first parenthesis. If a whole sentence beginning with a capital is in parentheses, the period or other terminal mark is placed inside the second parenthesis. A parenthetical statement not beginning with a capital is not followed by a period within the parentheses.

Brackets **[ ]**

17g

Use brackets to set off editorial corrections or interpolations in quoted matter.

EXAMPLES

At the office he found a note from the janitor: "Last night i [*sic*] found the door unlocked." [A bracketed *sic* (meaning *thus*) tells the reader that the error appears in the original— is not merely a misprint.]

Every man who loved our vanished friend [Professor Gummere] must know with what realization of shamed incapacity one lays down the tributary pen.   —CHRISTOPHER MORLEY

▶ EXERCISE 4   Correctly punctuate each of the following sentences by supplying commas, dashes, parentheses, or brackets. Be prepared to justify all marks you add, especially those you choose to set off parenthetical matter.

1. Gordon Gibbs or is it his twin brother? plays left tackle.
2. Joseph who is Gordon's brother is a guard on the second string.
3. "Dearest" his voice broke; he could say no more.
4. This organization needs more of everything more money, brains, initiative.
5. Some of my courses for example, French and biology demand a great deal of work outside the classroom.

6. A penalty clipping cost the Steers fifteen yards.
7. This ridiculous sentence appeared in the school paper: "Because of a personal fool *sic* the Cougars failed to cross the goal line during the last seconds of the game."
8. The word *Zipper* a trade-mark like Kodak is now used frequently without the initial capital as a common noun.
9. Rugged hills, rich valleys, beautiful lakes these things impress the tourist in Connecticut.
10. Our course embraced these projects: 1 the close reading of *Hamlet,* 2 the writing of critiques on various aspects of this tragedy, and 3 the formation of a tentative theory of tragedy.

▶ EXERCISE 5   Punctuate the following sentences (selected and adapted from the *Atlantic Monthly*) by supplying appropriate end marks, commas, colons, dashes, and parentheses. Do not use unnecessary punctuation. Be prepared to justify each mark you add, especially when you have a choice of correct marks (e.g., commas, dashes, or parentheses).

1. Emily formerly Mrs Goyette caught McAndless' sleeve where no one could see and tugged it briefly but urgently
2. "Do they still have good food at the Automat" he asked
3. "Oh I know" Granny exclaimed "Let me think about it"
4. "I know" I said "But that's not the real bed what happened to it"
5. For forty-eight years 1888–1936 he taught at Harvard
6. I tell you again What is alive and young and throbbing with historic current in America is musical theatre
7. Louise had then she has it still something near to genius for making improbable persons, places, and situations sound attractive
8. *Good and* can mean *very* "I am good and mad" and

"a hot cup of coffee" means that the coffee not the cup is to be hot

9. At last she had become what she had always wished to be a professional dancer

10. Prestige call it status if you like is in great demand these days

11. At last Marvin stood up, uneasily. "You you think we'd better take him to the vet"

12. There are three essential qualities for vulture country a rich supply of unburied corpses, high mountains, a strong sun

13. They failed forgivably! to see the less happy results of their enthusiasm

14. A significant little adage which circulates in Michigan athletic circles says in effect that there are three aspects of college life at Michigan intellectual, social, and athletic but that the student has time for only two

15. Women sit in their corner discussing items out of their exclusively feminine world children, servants, gardens, gossip

16. An older law was operating at the box office if you try to please everybody, you don't please anybody

17. As one man put it "Rose Bowl, Sugar Bowl, Orange Bowl all are gravy bowls"

18. Industrialization of Red China with German machines and German technology what a prize

19. We are told and we believe women more than men that to win love but more imperatively to retain love we must be beautiful

20. There is a democratic process the box office that determines the success and eminence of an artist

SPELLING AND DICTION

Spelling

18

Spell every word according to established usage as shown by a good dictionary.[1]

If you are the typical college student, you will misspell about fifty words as you write your freshman English papers. And of these fifty, only two or three will be found in another student's list of fifty misspellings. Thus it is evident that spelling is a highly individual problem, to be solved by attention to one's own particular difficulties. By writing down in your INDIVIDUAL SPELLING LIST (see the model at the end of this section) all the words you misspell during your first college year, and by analyzing and mastering these words as they are called to your attention, you can make steady improvement in your spelling.

In college you cannot count upon much class time devoted to spelling. But by following independently the program outlined in this section, you can improve your spelling tremendously. *Ignorance of the correct spelling of ordinary words is now, and will probably continue to be, the one universally accepted sign of the uneducated man.*

As aids in fixing the correct spelling of the word in your memory, use chiefly the EAR and the EYE.

THE EAR—FOR WORDS SPELLED AS PRONOUNCED   Pronounce the word aloud several times, clearly and distinctly, in accordance with the pronunciation shown by the dictionary. Be careful not to omit, add, change, or transpose any letter or syllable. Then write the word down in your INDIVIDUAL SPELLING LIST.

[1] Careful study of Section **18** will help to eliminate one of the two most common errors in the average student paper.

THE EYE—FOR WORDS NOT SPELLED AS PRONOUNCED   Look carefully at the word (1) as it appears in the dictionary and (2) as
you write it *correctly* in your INDIVIDUAL SPELLING LIST. Note
the differences between pronunciation and spelling. Photograph the word with your eye so that you can visualize it later.

SPELLING RULES   Use a few spelling rules if you find them helpful.
See **18d** and **18e.** (For more detailed rules see the section en-
titled "Orthography" in *Webster's New International Diction-
ary*, Second Edition, or "Spelling" in *Webster's Third New
International Dictionary* or *Webster's Seventh New Collegiate
Dictionary*.)

18a

**Do not allow mispronunciation to cause misspelling. (The
ear is especially helpful in overcoming such misspelling.)**

At least two problems arise when one uses pronunciation
as a guide to correct spelling. First, the spellings of many
words reflect the pronunciations used two or three hundred
years ago because changes in pronunciation take place
more rapidly than changes in spelling. Second, one spelling may symbolize a half dozen sounds (like *ough* in
though, rough, through, etc.), and one sound may have
numerous spellings (like *sh* in *ration, tissue, ocean*.)[2]
In spite of these problems, however, mispronunciation can
and does cause the misspelling of words such as those in
the following lists.

▶ EXERCISE 1   Find in the four lists on page 170 the
words you tend to mispronounce—and to misspell.

(1) Careless omission

Pronounce this first list distinctly, making it a point *not
to omit* the sound represented by the italicized letters.

[2] See Mario Pei, "The Problem of Spelling Reform," *The Story of English*,
J. B. Lippincott Co., Philadelphia, 1952.

candidate	library	quantity
environment	literature	recognize
everybody	occasionally	surprise
generally	probably	usually

(2) Careless addition

Pronounce this second list distinctly, making it a point *not to add* any syllable or letter.

athlete	entrance	lightning
disastrous	grievous	mischievous
drowned	height	remembrance
elm	hindrance	umbrella

(3) Careless change

Pronounce this third list distinctly, making it a point *not to change* letters, particularly letters in italics.

| accumulate | introduce | particular |
| accurate | optimistic | prejudice |

(4) Careless transpositions of letters

Pronounce this fourth list distinctly, making it a point *not to transpose* italicized letters.

cavalry	irrelevant	prefer
children	perhaps	prescription
hundred	perspiration	preserve

Add to your INDIVIDUAL SPELLING LIST any of the words in the four lists that you have a tendency to misspell. Follow the model spelling list at the end of this section.

18b

Distinguish between words of similar sound and spelling, and use the spelling demanded by the meaning. (The eye is the chief aid in avoiding such misspelling.)

▶ EXERCISES 2–7 Study the following list, ten word groups at a time, to improve your ability to select the word needed to express your meaning. With the aid of your dictionary compose a sentence to illustrate the correct use of each word. Add to your INDIVIDUAL SPELLING LIST any word that you misspell.

[2]

accent, ascent, assent
accept, except
advice, advise
affect, effect
all ready, already
all together, altogether
allusive, elusive, illusive
altar, alter
berth, birth
born, borne

[3]

capital, capitol
choose, chose
cite, sight, site
coarse, course
complement, compliment
conscience, conscious
council, counsel, consul
decent, descent, dissent
desert, dessert
device, devise

[4]

dual, duel
dyeing, dying
fair, fare
formally, formerly
forth, fourth
freshman, freshmen
hear, here
holy, wholly
instance, instants
irrelevant, irreverent

[5]

its, it's
know, no
later, latter
lead, led
lessen, lesson
lose, loose
moral, morale
of, off
passed, past
peace, piece

[6]

personal, personnel
plain, plane
precede, proceed
presence, presents
principal, principle
prophecy, prophesy
quiet, quite, quit
respectfully, respectively
right, rite, wright, write
sense, since

[7]

shone, shown
stationary, stationery
than, then
there, their, they're
threw, through
to, too, two
weak, week
weather, whether
whose, who's
your, you're

18c

Distinguish between the prefix and the root.

The root is the base to which prefix or suffix is added. Take care not to double the last letter of the prefix (as in *disappear*) when it is different from the first letter of the root or to drop the last letter of the prefix when the root begins with the same letter (as in *immortal* and *unnecessary*.)

dis- (prefix)	+	appear (root)	=	disappear
grand-	+	daughter	=	granddaughter
im-	+	mortal	=	immortal
un-	+	necessary	=	unnecessary

18d

Apply the rules for spelling in adding suffixes.

(1) Drop final e before a suffix beginning with a vowel but not before a suffix beginning with a consonant

Drop final *e* before a suffix beginning with a vowel.

bride	+	-al	=	bridal
combine	+	-ation	=	combination
come	+	-ing	=	coming
fame	+	-ous	=	famous
plume	+	-age	=	plumage
precede	+	-ence	=	precedence
prime	+	-ary	=	primary

Retain final *e* before a suffix beginning with a consonant.

care	+	-ful	=	careful
care	+	-less	=	careless
entire	+	-ly	=	entirely
place	+	-ment	=	placement
rude	+	-ness	=	rudeness
stale	+	-mate	=	stalemate
state	+	-craft	=	statecraft
sure	+	-ty	=	surety

Some Exceptions: *due, duly; true, truly; awe, awful; hoe, hoeing, singe, singeing.* After *c* or *g* the final *e* is retained before suffixes beginning with *a* or *o: notice, noticeable; courage, courageous.* Note that pronunciation will help you with this rule; "soft" *c* and *g* are followed by *e* before *a* and *o*, while "hard" *c* and *g* are not. Compare *noticeable* and *despicable, courageous* and *analogous.*

▶ EXERCISE 8   For each word below cite the rule governing dropping or retaining final *e*.

1. confine	+	-ing	6. love	+	-ly
2. confine	+	-ment	7. peruse	+	-al
3. arrange	+	-ing	8. like	+	-ness
4. arrange	+	-ment	9. like	+	-ing
5. love	+	-ing	10. like	+	-ly

(2) Double a final single consonant before a suffix beginning with a vowel (a) if the consonant ends a word of one syllable or an accented syllable and (b) if the consonant is preceded by a single vowel. Otherwise, do not double the consonant.

drop, drop*p*ing [In a word of one syllable preceded by a single vowel. But preceded by a double vowel: *droop, drooping.*]

admit, admit*t*ed [In accented syllable preceded by a single vowel. But in unaccented syllable: *benefit, benefited.*]

▶ EXERCISE 9   Note the importance of the last rule in forming the present participle and the past tense of verbs. Example: *regret, regretting, regretted.* Supply the present participle for each of the following verbs, justifying the spelling by the rule: *appear, compel, differ, happen, occur, plan, profit, refer, remit, scoop.*

(3) Except before *ing*, final *y* is usually changed to *i*.

defy	+	-ance	=	defiance
happy	+	-ness	=	happiness

mercy	+	-ful	=	merciful
modify	+	-er	=	modifier
modify	+	-ing	=	modifying [Not changed before *ing*]

Note: Verbs ending in *y* preceded by a vowel do not change the *y* to form the third person singular of the present tense or the past participle: *array, arrays, arrayed.* Exceptions: *lay, laid; pay, paid; say, said.*

▶ EXERCISE 10   Cite the rule to justify retaining or dropping final *y* before the suffixes of the following words: *alloys, craftiness, employed, employs, fanciful, fancying, studied, studying, volleys, volleying.*

(4) Form the plural by adding *s* to the singular, but by adding *es* if the plural makes an extra syllable.

boy, boys; cap, caps; radio, radios
bush, bushes; match, matches [The plural makes an extra syllable.]

Exceptions:

a. If the noun ends in *y* preceded by a consonant, change the *y* to *i* and add *es: sky, skies; comedy, comedies.* But after final *y* preceded by a vowel, *y* is retained and only *s* is added: *joy, joys.*

b. If the noun ends in *fe*, change the *fe* to *ve* and add *s: knife, knives.*

c. A few nouns ending in *o* take the *-es* plural, although the plural does not make an extra syllable: *potato, potatoes; Negro, Negroes.*

d. For plurals of compound words such as *father-in-law* usually add the *-s* to the chief word, not the modifier: *fathers-in-law, maids of honor.*

For other plurals formed irregularly, consult your dictionary.

Note: Add *'s* to form the plurals of letters, signs, and figures. See also **15d**.

▶ EXERCISE 11   Supply plural forms for words listed below. If words are not covered by the rules given under **18d**, consult your dictionary.

cup	army	foot	passer-by
wife	cameo	son-in-law	room
box	marsh	valley	leaf
child	ox	alumnus	goose
key	sheep	radius	mouse

18e ·
Apply the rules for spelling to avoid confusion of *ei* and *ie*.

When the sound is *ee*, write *ie* (except after *c*, in which case write *ei*).

				(after *c*)	
chief	grief	pierce	wield	ceiling	deceive
field	niece	relief	yield	conceit	perceive

When the sound is other than *ee*, usually write *ei*.

eight	height	heir	reign	sleigh	vein
foreign	deign	neighbor	feign	weigh	stein

Exceptions: Fiery, financier, leisure, seize, species, weird.

▶ EXERCISE 12   Write out the following words, filling out the blanks with *ei* or *ie*. Justify your choice for each word.

bes—ge	dec—t	fr—ght	r—gned	s—ve
conc—ve	f—nd	pr—st	s—ne	th—f

Hyphenated Words

18f
Hyphenate words chiefly to express a unit idea or to avoid ambiguity. (For division of words at the end of a line, see **8b.**)

A hyphenated word may be either two words still in the process of becoming one word or a new coinage made by the writer to fit the occasion. In the former case a recent dictionary will assist in determining current usage. Many words now written as one were originally separate words and later hyphenated in the transitional stage. For example, *post man* first became *post-man* and then *postman.* More recently *basket ball* has passed through the transitional *basket-ball* to *basketball.* The use of the hyphen in compounding is in such a state of flux that authorities often disagree. Some of the more generally accepted uses are listed below. ＼

(1) **The hyphen may be used to join two or more words serving as a single adjective before a noun.**

[The dictionary ordinarily cannot help with this use of the hyphen. The writer joins recognized words to coin a new unit idea to fit the occasion.]

     A know-it-all expression, a bluish-green dress

But the hyphen is omitted when the first word of the compound is an adverb ending in *-ly* or when the words follow the noun.

     A slightly elevated walk, a gently sloping terrace
     His expression suggested that he knew it all.
     The dress was a bluish green.

(2) **The hyphen is used with compound numbers from twenty-one to ninety-nine.**

     twenty-two, forty-five, ninety-eight

Note: Hyphenate a fraction when it functions as an adjective and is placed before the word modified.

     A *two-thirds* vote is needed. [*Two-thirds* is an adjective modifying *vote.*]
     Two thirds of the voters endorsed the amendment. [*Two thirds* is the subject, not an adjective.]

(3) **The hyphen is used to avoid ambiguity or an awkward union of letters or syllables between prefix or suffix and root.**

His re-creation of the setting was perfect. [BUT Fishing is good recreation.]

He re-covered the leaky roof. [BUT He recovered his health.]

Micro-organism, re-enter, semi-independent, shell-like, thrill-less, sub-subcommittee.

(4) **The hyphen is used with the prefixes ex- (meaning "former"), self-, all-, and the suffix -elect.**

ex-governor, self-made, all-American, mayor-elect

EXERCISES ON SPELLING

The general list of words most frequently misspelled is made up of 654 (651 + *it's, too, two*) common words that everyone needs in his business and social life. The list is drawn, by kind permission of Dean Thomas Clark Pollock, from his study of 31,375 misspellings in the written work of college students.[3] In the list as given below the words *its, it's* and *to, too, two* are treated as word groups; all other words are listed individually, usually omitting any word that is spelled the same as a part of a longer word. For example, the list includes *definitely* but not *definite, existence* but not *exist, performance* but not *perform.* Each of the first hundred words in the general list below was misspelled more than forty-three times (or more than an *average* of forty-three times in the case of words grouped in Dean Pollock's report).

▶ **EXERCISES 13–25** With the aid of your dictionary study the words in the general list in units of fifty words at a

[3] See Thomas Clark Pollock, "Spelling Report," *College English,* XVI (November, 1954), 102–09; and Thomas Clark Pollock and William D. Baker, *The University Spelling Book,* Prentice-Hall, Inc., Englewood Cliffs, N. J., 1955, pp. 6–12.

time until you feel sure (1) of the meaning and (2) of the spelling of each word. Then without the aid of your dictionary test yourself by writing sentences in which each word is correctly used and spelled. Add to your INDIVIDUAL SPELLING LIST each word that you misspell.

GENERAL SPELLING LIST

I. *The Hundred Words Most Frequently Misspelled*[4]

[13]

1. accommodate
2. achievement
3. acquire
4. all right
5. among
6. apparent
7. argument
8. arguing
9. belief°
10. believe°
11. beneficial
12. benefited
13. category
14. coming
15. comparative
16. conscious
17. controversy
18. controversial
19. definitely
20. definition
21. define
22. describe
23. description
24. disastrous
25. effect
26. embarrass
27. environment
28. exaggerate

29. existence°
30. existent°
31. experience
32. explanation
33. fascinate
34. height
35. interest
36. its (it's)
37. led
38. lose
39. losing
40. marriage
41. mere
42. necessary
43. occasion°
44. occurred
45. occurring
46. occurrence
47. opinion
48. opportunity
49. paid
50. particular

[14]

51. performance
52. personal
53. personnel
54. possession
55. possible

56. practical
57. precede°
58. prejudice
59. prepare
60. prevalent
61. principal
62. principle
63. privilege°
64. probably
65. proceed
66. procedure
67. professor
68. profession
69. prominent
70. pursue
71. quiet
72. receive°
73. receiving°
74. recommend
75. referring°
76. repetition
77. rhythm
78. sense
79. separate°
80. separation°
81. shining
82. similar°
83. studying
84. succeed

[4] An asterisk indicates the most frequently misspelled words among the first hundred. The most troublesome letters for all 651 words are indicated by italics.

85. succession
86. surprise
87. technique
88. than
89. then
90. their°
91. there°
92. they're°
93. thorough
94. to° (too,° two°)
95. transferred
96. unnecessary
97. villain
98. woman
99. write
100. writing

II. The Next 551 Words Most Frequently Misspelled

[15]
101. absence
102. abundance
103. abundant
104. academic
105. academically
106. academy
107. acceptable
108. acceptance
109. accepting
110. accessible
111. accidental
112. accidentally
113. acclaim
114. accompanied
115. accompanies
116. accompaniment
117. accompanying
118. accomplish
119. accuracy
120. accurate
121. accurately
122. accuser
123. accuses
124. accusing
125. accustom
126. acquaintance
127. across
128. actuality
129. actually
130. adequately
131. admission
132. admittance

133. adolescence
134. adolescent
135. advantageous
136. advertisement
137. advertiser
138. advertising
139. advice
140. advise
141. affect
142. afraid
143. against
144. aggravate
145. aggressive
146. alleviate
147. allotted
148. allotment
149. allowed
150. allows

[16]
151. already
152. altar
153. all together
154. altogether
155. amateur
156. amount
157. analysis
158. analyze
159. and
160. another
161. annually
162. anticipated
163. apologetically

164. apologized
165. apology
166. apparatus
167. appearance
168. applies
169. applying
170. appreciate
171. appreciation
172. approaches
173. appropriate
174. approximate
175. area
176. arise
177. arising
178. arouse
179. arousing
180. arrangement
181. article
182. atheist
183. athlete
184. athletic
185. attack
186. attempts
187. attendance
188. attendant
189. attended
190. attitude
191. audience
192. authoritative
193. authority
194. available
195. bargain
196. basically

197. basis
198. beauteous
199. beautified
200. beautiful

[17]

201. beauty
202. become
203. becoming
204. before
205. began
206. beginner
207. beginning
208. behavior
209. bigger
210. biggest
211. boundary
212. breath
213. breathe
214. brilliance
215. brilliant
216. Britain
217. Britannica
218. burial
219. buried
220. bury
221. business
222. busy
223. calendar
224. capitalism
225. career
226. careful
227. careless
228. carried
229. carrier
230. carries
231. carrying
232. cemetery
233. certainly
234. challenge
235. changeable

236. changing
237. characteristic
238. characterized
239. chief
240. children
241. Christian
242. Christianity
243. choice
244. choose
245. chose
246. cigarette
247. cite
248. clothes
249. commercial
250. commission

[18]

251. committee
252. communist
253. companies
254. compatible
255. competition
256. competitive
257. competitor
258. completely
259. concede
260. conceivable
261. conceive
262. concentrate
263. concern
264. condemn
265. confuse
266. confusion
267. connotation
268. connote
269. conscience
270. conscientious
271. consequently
272. considerably
273. consistency
274. consistent

275. contemporary
276. continuous(ly)
277. controlled
278. controlling
279. convenience
280. convenient
281. correlate
282. council
283. counselor
284. countries
285. create
286. criticism
287. criticize
288. cruelly
289. cruelty
290. curiosity
291. curious
292. curriculum
293. dealt
294. deceive
295. decided
296. decision
297. dependent
298. desirability
299. desire
300. despair

[19]

301. destruction
302. detriment
303. devastating
304. device
305. difference
306. different
307. difficult
308. dilemma
309. diligence
310. dining
311. disappoint
312. disciple
313. discipline

314. discrimination
315. discussion
316. disease
317. disgusted
318. disillusioned
319. dissatisfied
320. divide
321. divine
322. doesn't
323. dominant
324. dropped
325. due
326. during
327. eager
328. easily
329. efficiency
330. efficient
331. eighth
332. eliminate
333. emperor
334. emphasize
335. encourage
336. endeavor
337. enjoy
338. enough
339. enterprise
340. entertain
341. entertainment
342. entirely
343. entrance
344. equipment
345. equipped
346. escapade
347. escape
348. especially
349. etc.
350. everything

[20]

351. evidently
352. excellence
353. excellent
354. except
355. excitable
356. exercise
357. expense
358. experiment
359. extremely
360. fallacy
361. familiar
362. families
363. fantasies
364. fantasy
365. fashions
366. favorite
367. fictitious
368. field
369. finally
370. financially
371. financier
372. foreigners
373. forty
374. forward
375. fourth
376. friendliness
377. fulfill
378. fundamentally
379. further
380. gaiety
381. generally
382. genius
383. government
384. governor
385. grammar
386. grammatically
387. group
388. guaranteed
389. guidance
390. guiding
391. handled
392. happened
393. happiness
394. hear
395. here
396. heroes
397. heroic
398. heroine
399. hindrance
400. hopeless

[21]

401. hoping
402. hospitalization
403. huge
404. humorist
405. humorous
406. hundred
407. hunger
408. hungrily
409. hungry
410. hypocrisy
411. hypocrite
412. ideally
413. ignorance
414. ignorant
415. imaginary
416. imagination
417. imagine
418. immediately
419. immense
420. importance
421. incidentally
422. increase
423. indefinite
424. independence
425. independent
426. indispensable
427. individually
428. industries
429. inevitable
430. influence
431. influential
432. ingenious

433. ingredient
434. initiative
435. intellect
436. intelligence
437. intelligent
438. interference
439. interpretation
440. interrupt
441. involve
442. irrelevant
443. irresistible
444. irritable
445. jealousy
446. knowledge
447. laboratory
448. laborer
449. laboriously
450. laid

[22]

451. later
452. leisurely
453. lengthening
454. license
455. likelihood
456. likely
457. likeness
458. listener
459. literary
460. literature
461. liveliest
462. livelihood
463. liveliness
464. lives
465. loneliness
466. lonely
467. loose
468. loss
469. luxury
470. magazine
471. magnificence
472. magnificent

473. maintenance
474. management
475. maneuver
476. manner
477. manufacturers
478. material
479. mathematics
480. matter
481. maybe
482. meant
483. mechanics
484. medical
485. medicine
486. medieval
487. melancholy
488. methods
489. miniature
490. minutes
491. mischief
492. moral
493. morale
494. morally
495. mysterious
496. narrative
497. naturally
498. Negroes
499. ninety
500. noble

[23]

501. noticeable
502. noticing
503. numerous
504. obstacle
505. off
506. omit
507. operate
508. oppose
509. opponent
510. opposite
511. optimism
512. organization

513. original
514. pamphlets
515. parallel
516. parliament
517. paralyzed
518. passed
519. past
520. peace
521. peculiar
522. perceive
523. permanent
524. permit
525. persistent
526. persuade
527. pertain
528. phase
529. phenomenon
530. philosophy
531. physical
532. piece
533. planned
534. plausible
535. playwright
536. pleasant
537. politician
538. political
539. practice
540. predominant
541. preferred
542. presence
543. prestige
544. primitive
545. prisoners
546. propaganda
547. propagate
548. prophecy
549. psychoanalysis
550. psychology

[24]

551. psychopathic
552. psychosomatic

553. quantity
554. really
555. realize
556. rebel
557. recognize
558. regard
559. relative
560. relieve
561. religion
562. remember
563. reminisce
564. represent
565. resources
566. response
567. revealed
568. ridicule
569. ridiculous
570. roommate
571. sacrifice
572. safety
573. satire
574. satisfied
575. satisfy
576. scene
577. schedule
578. seize
579. sentence
580. sergeant
581. several
582. shepherd
583. significance
584. simile
585. simple
586. simply

587. since
588. sincerely
589. sociology
590. sophomore
591. source
592. speaking
593. speech
594. sponsor
595. stabilization
596. stepped
597. stories
598. story
599. straight
600. strength

[25]

601. stretch
602. strict
603. stubborn
604. substantial
605. subtle
606. sufficient
607. summary
608. summed
609. suppose
610. suppress
611. surrounding
612. susceptible
613. suspense
614. swimming
615. symbol
616. synonymous
617. temperament
618. tendency

619. themselves
620. theories
621. theory
622. therefore
623. those
624. thought
625. together
626. tomorrow
627. tragedy
628. tremendous
629. tried
630. tries
631. tyranny
632. undoubtedly
633. unusually
634. useful
635. useless
636. using
637. vacuum
638. valuable
639. varies
640. various
641. view
642. vengeance
643. warrant
644. weather
645. weird
646. where
647. whether
648. whole
649. whose
650. yield
651. you're

INDIVIDUAL SPELLING LIST

▶ **EXERCISE 26** No doubt you have been keeping your INDIVIDUAL SPELLING LIST from the beginning of the course and have been mastering each misspelled word as it has come to your attention. If by any chance you have not, begin now by listing, in the form shown below, all words that you have misspelled thus far in your written work. These should be in the spelling column of your "Record of Errors." (See page 90 at the end of Section 8.) Add to these all words misspelled as you have worked through Exercises 1–25 of this section. Continue throughout the course to add to your LIST every misspelled word that is called to your attention.

In the first column, write the word (correctly spelled); in the second, write the word by syllables, with accent marked; and in the third, show what you consider the best method for mastering the spelling of the word. Study the words in your LIST from time to time to make sure that you do not misspell any of them again.

MODEL FORM FOR SPELLING LIST

Word (correctly spelled)	*Word (spelled by syllables)*	*Best Method for Mastery of Spelling*
candidate	can'di date	Ear—letter omitted in pronunciation
prejudice	prej'u dice	Ear—letter changed in pronunciation
its	its	Eye—confused with *it's*
athlete	ath'lete	Ear—letter added in pronunciation
bridal	brid'al	Rule—drop final *e* before vowel
perspiration	per spi ra'tion	Ear—letters transposed in pronunciation
principal	prin'ci pal	Eye—confused with *principle*
accidentally	ac ci den'tal ly	Ear—letters omitted in pronunciation
merciful	mer'ci ful	Rule—change final *y* to *i* except before *ing*

Good Use—Glossary

19

Use a good dictionary to help you select the words best suited to express your ideas.

A dictionary is a storehouse of words. It is a good storehouse to the extent that it brings together words used in the English language and gives the reliable information you need about those words.

19a
Use only a good dictionary, and be sure to use it intelligently.

A good English dictionary is based upon the scientific examination of the writing and speaking habits of the English-speaking world; it records the origin, development, and changing use of words. Any dictionary is reliable only to the extent that it is soundly based on usage. But even the best dictionary cannot be perfect, as Dr. Johnson observed long ago.

The "unabridged" dictionaries, those that try to include the half million words in the language, must run to several thousand pages in a single volume or to a number of volumes. Among these large dictionaries, the following are especially useful.

New Standard Dictionary. New York: Funk & Wagnalls Company, Inc., 1959. 2815 pages.

Webster's New International Dictionary. Second Edition. Springfield, Massachusetts: G. & C. Merriam Company, 1934. 3194 pages.

Webster's Third New International Dictionary. Springfield,
Massachusetts: G. & C. Merriam Company, 1961. 2662 pages.
A Dictionary of American English on Historical Principles.
4 volumes. Chicago: University of Chicago Press, 1936–44.
The Oxford English Dictionary. 12 volumes and Supplement.
Oxford: Clarendon Press, 1933. (A corrected reissue of *A
New English Dictionary on Historical Principles,* 10 volumes
and Supplement, 1888–1928)—Abbreviated *OED* or *NED*.

Most students must consult these large dictionaries in
the library. But even if a student owns a large dictionary, he will need one of the smaller dictionaries on the
college or adult level, such as the following:

American College Dictionary (1947).—*ACD*
Standard College Dictionary (1963).—*SCD*
Webster's New World Dictionary (1953).—*NWD*
Webster's Seventh New Collegiate Dictionary (1963).—*NCD*

Note: Dictionaries are usually kept up to date by frequent
slight revisions, sometimes with supplementary pages for
new words. The last thorough revision of each dictionary
listed above is shown by the date in parentheses.

Intelligent use of a dictionary requires some knowledge
of its plan and special abbreviations as given in the introductory matter. This knowledge will help you understand
a typical entry, such as that for *expel.*

(1) Spelling, Pronunciation   (2) Parts of Speech, Inflected Forms

ex·pel (ik·spel′)   *v.t.* **·pelled, ·pel·ling**   **1.** To drive out by
force; force out; eject: to *expel* something from the mouth.
2. To force by decision of the proper authorities to end
(3) Meanings — attendance at a school, etc., or to terminate membership
(4) Origin — in an organization, etc.; oust.   [< L *expellere* < *ex-* out
Synonyms — + *pellere* to drive, thrust]   **— ex·pel′la·ble** *adj.*
— Syn. *Expel, eject, dislodge, evict, oust,* and *dismiss* mean to
send away forcibly. A school *expels* an unruly pupil; water in the
lungs must be promptly *expelled.* A rifle *ejects* a shell automati-
cally; a squid *ejects* an inky fluid. To *dislodge* is to move something heavy or resisting from its place; an avalanche may *dislodge* a large boulder. A man is *evicted* from his house; an official is
ousted from office; an employee is *dismissed* from his job.

(1) Spelling and pronunciation. The spelling of *expel* (by syllables separated by a dot) is given first, with pronunciation indicated (within parentheses) immediately following. The sound of each letter is shown by the short key to pronunciation at the bottom of the page (and by the detailed key in the front introductory matter). The accent in *expel*, as shown by the mark (′), falls on the last syllable.

(2) Parts of speech and inflected forms come next: *v. t.* classifies *expel* as a "verb, transitive"; the words in boldface give the inflected forms for the past participle and the present participle; another part of speech formed from the base word (the adjective *expellable*) is given in the last line of the entry.

(3) Meanings (including synonyms). Two separate meanings of *expel* are shown after the numbers *1* and *2*. In the *NCD* and in the *NWD* such definitions are arranged in the historical order of development, thus enabling the reader to see at a glance something of the history of the word. *But he should note that the meaning which developed first, and is consequently placed first, may no longer be the most common.* For example, the *NCD* and the *NWD*, in defining *prevent*, begin with the original but obsolete meaning "to anticipate" and come later to the present meaning "to keep from happening." The *SCD* and *ACD*, which put the most common meaning first, begin with "to keep from happening" and come later to the obsolete meaning. With *expel*, as with many words, the meaning that first developed is still the most common.

The meaning is made clearer by comparing the word to other words of similar meaning (synonyms, abbreviated **Syn.**). Note the special paragraph in which *expel* and five synonyms are differentiated.

For more detailed information about *expel* the student may consult one of the unabridged dictionaries in the library. In *Webster's New International Dictionary*, Second Edition, the entry for this word is more than twice as long as that in the shorter dictionaries and includes a quotation from Spenser. In *Webster's Third New International Dictionary* the entry is nearly four times as long and gives nine quotations to illustrate the various uses of the word. *The Oxford English Dictionary*, the most detailed of all dictionaries of the English language, quotes some fifty English writers of the past five or six hundred years to show the exact meaning of *expel* at each stage of its history.

(4) Origin: development of the language. The origin of the word—also called its *derivation* or *etymology*—is shown in square brackets: [< L *expellere* < *ex-* out + *pellere* to drive, thrust]. This bracketed information means that *expel* is derived from (<) the Latin (L) word *expellere*, which is made up of *ex-*, meaning "out," and the combining form *pellere*, meaning "to drive or thrust." Breaking up a word, when possible, into prefix and combining form, as in the case of *expel*, (and also suffix, if any) will often help to get at the basic meaning of a word.

	Prefix		Combining Form		Suffix
circumvention	*circum-*, around	+	*venire*, to come	+	*-ion*, act of
dependent	*de-*, down	+	*pendere*, to hang	+	*-ent*, one who
intercede	*inter-*, between	+	*cedere*, to pass		
preference	*pre-*, before	+	*ferre*, to carry	+	*-ence*, state of
transmit	*trans-*, across	+	*mittere*, to send		

The bracketed information given by a good dictionary is especially rich in meaning when associated with the historical development of our language. English is one of the Indo-European (IE.)[1] languages, a group of languages apparently derived from a common source. Within this

[1]The parenthetical abbreviations for languages here and on the next few pages are those commonly used in the bracketed derivations in dictionaries.

group of languages, many of the more familiar words are remarkably alike. Our word *mother*, for example, is *mater* in Latin (L), *meter* in Greek (Gk.), and *matar* in the ancient Persian and in the Sanskrit (Skt.) of India. Our pronoun *me* is exactly the same in Latin, in Greek, in Persian, and in Sanskrit. Words in different languages which apparently go back to a common parent language are called *cognates*. The large number of cognates and the many correspondences in sounds and structures indicate that most of the languages of Europe and some of the languages of Asia are derived from a common language, called by linguists Indo-European, which was spoken in the east-central region of Europe about five thousand years ago. By the opening of the Christian era the speakers of this language had spread themselves over most of Europe and as far east as India. Of the eight or nine language groups into which they had developed (see the inside back cover of the *NWD*, the entry "Indo-European" and "A Brief History of the English Language" in *SCD*, or "Indo-European languages" in *NCD*), English is chiefly concerned with the Greek (Hellenic) on the eastern Mediterranean, with the Latin (Italic) on the central and western Mediterranean, and with the Germanic in northwestern Europe. English is descended from the Germanic.

Two thousand years ago the Greek, the Latin, and the Germanic each comprised a more or less unified language group. After the fall of the Roman Empire in the fifth century, the several Latin-speaking divisions developed independently into the modern Romance languages, chief of which are Italian, French, and Spanish. Long before the fall of Rome the Germanic group was breaking up into three groups: (1) East Germanic, represented by the Goths, who were to play a large part in the last century of the Roman Empire before losing themselves in its ruins; (2) North Germanic, or Old Norse (ON.), from which we have modern Danish (Dan.) and Swedish (Swed.), Norwegian (Norw.) and Icelandic (Icel.); and

(3) West Germanic, the direct ancestor of English, Dutch (D.), and German (G.).

The English language may be said to have begun about the middle of the fifth century, when the West Germanic Angles and Saxons began the conquest of what is now England and either absorbed or drove out the Celtic-speaking inhabitants. The next six or seven hundred years are known as the Old English (OE.) or Anglo-Saxon (AS.) period of the English language. The fifty or sixty thousand words then in the language were chiefly Anglo-Saxon, with a small mixture of Old Norse words as a result of the Danish (Viking) conquests of England beginning in the eighth century. But the Old Norse words were so much like the Anglo-Saxon that they cannot always be distinguished.

The transitional period—about 1100 to 1500—from Old English to Modern English is known as Middle English (ME.). Changes already under way were accelerated by the Norman Conquest beginning in 1066. The Normans or "Northmen" had settled in northern France during the Viking invasions and had adopted the Old French (OF.) in place of their native Old Norse. The Normans, coming over to England by thousands, made French the language of the King's court in London and of the ruling classes (both French and English) throughout the land, while the masses continued to speak English. Only toward the end of the fifteenth century did English become once more the common language of all classes. But the language that emerged had lost most of its Anglo-Saxon inflections[2] and had taken on thousands of French words (derived originally from Latin). It was, however, still basically English, not French, in its structure.

A striking feature of Modern English (that is, English since 1500) is its immense vocabulary. As already noted, Old English used some fifty or sixty thousand words, very largely native Anglo-Saxon; Middle English used perhaps a hundred thousand, many taken through the French

[2] See pp. 2–3.

from Latin and others directly from Latin; and now our unabridged dictionaries list over four times as many. To make up this tremendous word hoard, we have borrowed most heavily from the Latin, but we have drawn some words from almost every known language. English writers of the sixteenth century were especially eager to interlard their works with words from Latin authors; and as Englishmen pushed out to colonize and to trade in many parts of the globe, they brought home new words as well as goods. Modern science and technology have drawn heavily from the Greek. The result of all this borrowing is that English has become the richest, most cosmopolitan of all languages.

In the process of enlarging our vocabulary we have lost most of our original Anglo-Saxon words. But those that are left make up the most familiar, most useful part of our vocabulary. Practically all of our simple verbs, our articles, conjunctions, prepositions, and pronouns are native Anglo-Saxon; and so are many of our familiar nouns, adjectives, and adverbs. Every speaker and writer uses these native words over and over, much more frequently than the borrowed words. If every word is counted every time it is used, the percentage of native words runs very high, usually between 70 and 90 percent. Milton's percentage was 81, Tennyson's 88, Shakespeare's about 90, and that of the King James Bible about 94. English has been enriched by its extensive borrowings without losing its individuality; it is still fundamentally the *English* language.

▶ EXERCISE 1   Note the origins of the words on a typical page (or on several typical pages) of your dictionary. Copy examples of words derived from (1) Anglo-Saxon; (2) Old French or Latin through Old French; (3) Latin directly; (4) Greek through Latin; (5) Greek directly; (6) other languages.

(5) Dictionary labels—levels of usage. (See also pages 195–99, 203–04.) Most dictionaries use such labels as *Informal* (OR *Colloquial*), *Slang, Dialect, Obsolete* (OR *Archaic*), and *Illiterate* (OR *Substandard*). Labeled words, or labeled meanings of words, should be used with appropriate care, as treated further under **19b–h.**

The labeling or classification of words is often difficult, for the language is constantly changing and many words are on the borderline between the formal (or general) and the informal (or colloquial), between colloquial and slang, between slang and dialect, and between dialectal words and illiterate (or substandard) ones. There are no clearly marked boundaries between the various classes, and naturally even the best dictionaries will not always agree. Although classes of words are often referred to as "levels of usage," we are not to think of one class as always higher or better than another. Any one may be appropriate for a given occasion. Technical language that might not be generally understood is often the clearest and most economical for speech and writing addressed to those in one's profession. The occasion and the purpose of the writer or speaker will determine the best words to select. The unlabeled words, or word meanings (for many words are labeled for one meaning but not for another), which make up the bulk of the English vocabulary, are usually best for general (formal) writing and, along with colloquialisms, for conversation and the more informal types of writing. But it should be noted that *Webster's Third International Dictionary*, followed by the *NCD*, has discontinued the label *Colloquial*, thus leaving to the writer's judgment the problem of avoiding many unlabeled words that would be inappropriate in the usual expository prose. Words commonly unlabeled by dictionaries range from the very learned words appropriate in the most formal situations to the very simple words that are used in both the most dignified and the most informal styles.

▶ **EXERCISE 2** The ten words in the *Standard College Dictionary* beginning with *grind* may be classified as indicated below. *Italics* indicate that a word belongs in the class in respect to one or more of its meanings but not all. Note that all ten of the words are unlabeled for at least one meaning.

FORMAL or GENERAL (not labeled) *grind,* grindelia, *grinder, grindery,* grindstone, gringo, *grip*[1], grip[2], *gripe,* grippe
INFORMAL or COLLOQUIAL *grind, grinder, gripe*
SLANG *grind*
BRITISH *grindery* (also FORMAL because in general use throughout one country)
UNITED STATES *grip*[1] (also FORMAL because in general use throughout one country)
ARCHAIC *gripe*

Classify according to the labels in your dictionary the ten words (exclusive of proper names) beginning with *grating.* Note that most of the ten words are unlabeled for at least one meaning.

▶ **EXERCISE 3** Classify according to the labels in your dictionary the ten words beginning with *knock.* Note that nearly all these words are unlabeled for at least one meaning.

FURTHER EXERCISES ON THE USE OF THE DICTIONARY

▶ **EXERCISE 4** What are the etymologies of the following words?

adjective	conjunction	dialogue	monarchy
aristocracy	democracy	emperor	oligarchy

▶ **EXERCISE 5** If a copy of the *Oxford English Dictionary* is available, determine the first English meanings of the following words. What meanings developed later?

doom	inspiration	prevent	sanguine
gallery	knave	proper	silly

▶ EXERCISE 6   List synonyms for each of the following words. (For synonyms and antonyms you may find that your dictionary should be supplemented by a book of synonyms such as *Roget's International Thesaurus,* New York, 1965, which is available also in a pocketbook size.)

act	change	fight	see
anger	eat	go	think

▶ EXERCISE 7   List antonyms for each of the following words.

awkward	clever	gallantry	quiet
clear	fast	greed	study

▶ EXERCISE 8   Study the following pairs of words in your dictionary (in the special paragraphs, if any, that compare and contrast the pairs) and write sentences to illustrate the shades of difference in meaning.

cause—reason	help—aid	push—shove
freedom—liberty	position—situation	valid—sound

▶ EXERCISE 9   Determine the most common American spelling of the following words: *connexion, gypsy, labour.* Which of the following words should be written separately, which should be written solid, and which should be hyphenated?

cropeared	girlscout	heartfelt	postoffice
cubbyhole	heartbroken	heartfree	vestpocket

▶ EXERCISE 10   Determine the pronunciation for each of the following words. Which of the words change the accent to indicate a change in grammatical function?

absent	exquisite	Montaigne	vehement
contest	impious	object	Vietnam

▶ EXERCISE 11   Classify each of the following words as a verb (transitive or intransitive), a noun, an adjective, an adverb, a preposition, or a conjunction. Give the principal parts of each verb, the plural (or plurals) of each noun, and the comparative and superlative of each adjective or adverb. (Note that some words are used as two or more parts of speech.)

bad	drag	often	since	stratum
bite	into	sheep	sing	tomato

▶ EXERCISE 12   Which of the following words are usually capitalized? Which are capitalized only for certain meanings?

easter	italic	platonic	spanish
italian	liberian	roman	stoical

▶ EXERCISE 13   Divide the following words into syllables.

analytic	industrious	liberty	vindictive
indistinguishable	laboriously	supplement	vocabulary

▶ EXERCISE 14   Get from your dictionary specific information about each of the following. Note the source of information as (a) general vocabulary, (b) list of abbreviations, (c) gazetteer, (d) biographical list, or (e) appendix.

Annam	Esau	Melpomene	*vive le roi*
Attila	Escorial	Louis Pasteur	WAC

19b

Avoid informal (colloquial) words in the more formal types of writing.

Words or expressions labeled *Informal* or *Colloquial* in most dictionaries are appropriate to conversation and to informal writing. For these purposes colloquialisms often give a desirable tone of informality. But colloquial expressions tend to bring a discordant note into expository or other formal types of writing.

INFORMAL	The repeated *phone* calls only *aggravated* me but made my sister *plenty mad*.
FORMAL	The repeated *telephone* calls only *annoyed* me but made my sister *very angry*.
INFORMAL	I *got away with it* then, but it's *plumb no go* now.
FORMAL	I *was not discovered* then, but I *could not do* it now.

Contracted forms (*won't, I'd, he'll, hasn't*) are proper for informal writing and equally proper for all but the most extremely formal speech. In formal expository writing, such contractions are normally written out—*will not, I would* or *I should, he will, has not*.

| INFORMAL | *It's* really too bad that *he's* been held up and *can't* be here for the opening. |
| FORMAL | *It is* unfortunate that he *has been* detained and *cannot* be here for the opening. |

▶ **EXERCISE 15** Consult your dictionary for informal meanings of the following words: *brass, dig, fizzle, kick, way*. For each word compose a sentence in which the word is used with an informal meaning. Then in each sentence substitute a formal word with the same meaning.

19c

Use slang only when appropriate; in general, avoid jargon.

(See **19g** for technical words.)

Slang is defined by the *Standard College Dictionary* as "language, words, or phrases of a vigorous, colorful, facetious, or taboo nature, invented for specific occasions or uses, or derived from the unconventional use of the standard vocabulary." Some slang words have a pungent quality: *goon* and *moocher* may soon join *van, sham, mob,* and *banter* as standard words of the English language. Such slang may be effective on certain informal occasions.

But much slang is trite and tasteless, and is used in an ineffective attempt to mask an inadequate vocabulary. For some people everything disapproved of is "lousy," when they could be more exact with "contemptible," "unfair," "mean," or "worthless." Most of the objection to slang, then, is based not upon arbitrary *don'ts* but upon slang's habitual alliance with lazy thinking. Slang is the sluggard's way of avoiding the search for the exact, meaningful word.

Perhaps more objectionable than slang are certain types of jargon—language which is meaningless, or at least very confusing except to a special group. Almost every trade or occupation has its own jargon. A man with recent military experience might write the following jargon about his first day in college:

The mustering-in was snafu.

This sentence would be easily understood by his army friends; other readers might require a formal statement:

The registration was confused.

A particularly confusing type of jargon is found in much government writing. (See also **21a, Wordiness.**)

BUREAUCRATIC JARGON   All personnel functioning in the capacity of clerks will indicate that they have had opportunity to take due cognizance of this notice by transmitting signed acknowledgment of receipt of same.

IMPROVED   All clerks will acknowledge in writing the receipt of this notice.

COMMERCIAL JARGON   Allow us to express our appreciation of your esteemed favor.

IMPROVED   Thank you for your letter.

Note: Jargon in the sense of technical terms used by the learned professions can be very useful. See **19g.**

19d

Dialectal words should be used appropriately.

Dialectal words (also called *localisms* or *provincialisms*) should normally be avoided in speaking and writing outside the limited region where they are current. Speakers and writers may, however, safely use dialectal words known to the audience they are addressing.

DIALECT   I *reckon* he filled the *poke* with apples.
STANDARD   I *suppose* he filled the *bag* with apples.

19e

Illiteracies and improprieties should be avoided.

Illiteracies (also called *vulgarisms*) are the *nonstandard* expressions of uneducated people and are usually not listed in the dictionary.

NONSTANDARD   The boys *ain't* going. *They's* no use asking them.
STANDARD   The boys *are not* going. *There's* no use asking them.

An *impropriety* is a good word used with the wrong sense or function.

WRONG SENSE   I *except* your invitation. [Wrong meaning]
RIGHT WORD   I *accept* your invitation.
QUESTIONABLE   She sang *good*. [Wrong function—adjective used as adverb]
STANDARD   She sang *well*.

19f

Obsolete, archaic, or obsolescent words should be avoided.

All dictionaries list words (and meanings for words) that have long since passed out of general use. Such words as *ort* (fragment of food) and *yestreen* (last evening) are still found in dictionaries because these words, once the standard vocabulary of great authors, occur in our older literature and must be defined for the modern reader.

Some archaic words—like *wight, methinks,* and *quoth*—have been used for purposes of humor. Modern practice tends to label such usage as juvenile.

19g

Technical words should be used only when appropriate to the audience.

When you are writing for the general reader, avoid all unnecessary technical language. Since the ideal of the good writer is to make his thought clear to as many people as possible, he will not describe an apple tree as a *Malus pumila* or a high fever as *hyperpyrexia*. (Of course technical language, with its greater precision, is highly desirable when one is addressing an audience that can understand it, as when a physician addresses a group of physicians.)

Whenever technical terms come to be generally understood, as they often do (*phosphate* and *atomic energy*, for example), they may be used, of course, as freely as the unlabeled words in the dictionary.

19h

Avoid (1) "fine writing," (2) "poetic" expressions, and (3) unpleasing combinations of sound or overuse of alliteration.

(1) Avoid "fine writing." "Fine writing" is the unnecessary use of ornate words and expressions. It is generally fuzzy and repetitious; it tends to emphasize words rather than ideas. A simple, direct statement like "From childhood I have looked forward to a journey" can become by fine writing something like this: "From the halcyon days of early youth I have always anticipated with eagerness and pleasure the exciting vistas of distant climes and mysterious horizons."

(2) Avoid "poetic" expressions. Genuine poetry has its very proper place, and the vivid language of simile and metaphor enriches even colloquial prose. But the sham poetry of faded imagery (*eye of night* for *moon*) and inappropriate expressions like *oft, eftsoons, 'twas,* and *'neath* are misplaced in the usual prose style.

(3) Avoid unpleasing combinations of sound or overuse of alliteration. Good prose has rhythm, but it does not rhyme. If you write, "In foreign relations, the western nations are subject to dictation," you distract the reader's attention from your meaning. Equally offensive to the average reader is the overuse of alliteration (repetition of the same consonant sound), as in "Some people *s*hun the *s*ea*s*hore."

OTHER EXERCISES ON USAGE

▶ EXERCISE 16   In the following list put *C* after any sentence that requires no revision, even for formal writing. Write *Inf.* for each sentence approved for informal use only. Label each violation of good usage. Then rewrite all sentences (except those marked *C*) to make them conform to formal English. You may find the **Glossary of Usage** (**19i**) helpful in determining some inappropriate usages.

1. If I had of known you was coming, I would of waited longer.
2. Everyone suspicioned the old man of stealing our apples.
3. The ad in the paper was sort of hazy.
4. The sifting snow screened our view of the highway.
5. George was not dumb, though he looked like he was.
6. The profs dished out more than we could take.
7. Has your neighbor done sold his house?
8. The boy had a keen desire to win the game.
9. You do things different from anybody I know.
10. We filled the bucket with H_2O.
11. The poor man was in a sad fix.
12. I suppose that your findings are correct.
13. "You are batty," I yelled. "Now scram!"
14. I am terribly aggravated with your doings.
15. Ten miles is all the farther that I can live away from my store.
16. Where do you live at now?
17. The general was completely sold on the private who had some spunk.

18. 'Twas a clear, cool eve, and the moon shed an effulgent glow.
19. A first-rate farmer raises heaps of farm produce.
20. I am kind of late today, for I do not feel so good.
21. He took and snatched the parcel from her hands although he knew that he hadn't ought.
22. Since Richard hopes to become a musician, he is taking piano lessons.
23. Because of the depression he lost considerable in his business.
24. Her folks live in the country ten miles outside the city limits.
25. He calculated he could win out in the election.

▶ EXERCISE 17   Rewrite the following passages of bureaucratic, legal, or academic jargon in simple formal English.[3]

1. It is obvious from the difference in elevation with relation to the short depth of the property that the contour is such as to preclude any reasonable developmental potential for active recreation.
2. Verbal contact with Mr. Blank regarding the attached notification of promotion has elicited the attached representation intimating that he prefers to decline the assignment.
3. Voucherable expenditures necessary to provide adequate dental treatment required as adjunct to medical treatment being rendered a pay patient in in-patient status may be incurred as required at the expense of the Public Health Service.
4. I hereby give and convey to you, all and singular, my estate and interests, right, title, claim and advantages of and in said orange, together with all rind, juice, pulp and pits, and all rights and advantages therein.
5. I prefer an abbreviated phraseology, distinguished for its lucidity.

[3]Quoted, by permission, from Stuart Chase's *Power of Words*, Harcourt, Brace & World, New York, 1953, pp. 250–53.

6. Realization has grown that the curriculum or the experiences of learners change and improve only as those who are most directly involved examine their goals, improve their understandings and increase their skill in performing the tasks necessary to reach newly defined goals.

Glossary of Usage

19i

Consult the following glossary to determine the standing of a word or phrase and its appropriateness to your purpose.

The glossary below can include only a few of the words likely to cause difficulty. If the word you are looking for is not included, or if you need more information about any word in the list, consult a good recent college dictionary, remembering that dictionaries do not always agree. The following list does not represent the usage of any one dictionary, but justification for each usage label can usually be found in at least two of the leading dictionaries.

This glossary follows the *Standard College Dictionary* (page xxiii) in classifying all English words as STANDARD or NONSTANDARD.

STANDARD words are those in general use throughout the English-speaking world, or in one country (with such dictionary labels as *U.S.* or *Brit.*), or at least in a large section of a country (with such labels as *Western U.S.*). A relatively few standard words, or word meanings, are labeled *Informal* or *Colloquial* by most dictionaries to distinguish words better suited for conversation and familiar writing than for more formal expository writing, such as that usually expected in college. (See also **19b**.) These standard but "colloquial" words are called INFORMAL in this glossary to distinguish them from all other standard words, a much larger group called FORMAL. This term, as here used, has almost the meaning "general" since FORMAL includes both our most learned words and also such simple words as *boy, cat, dog, go, see, come, good, bad* and our pronouns, prepositions, conjunctions, and articles (*a, an, the*).

NONSTANDARD is the term applied to all other words in the dictionary—that is, to all words not classified as STANDARD. These "nonstandard" words, for one reason or another, have only a limited use. They make up but a minor part of words listed and generally have such dictionary labels as the following (some of which are used in this glossary):

SLANG.   Vivid, recently coined, highly colloquial words. See also **19c.**

DIALECT.   Words common to a very limited region. See also **19d.**

OBSOLETE or ARCHAIC.   Words not in current use. See also **19f.**

LAW, MEDICINE, etc.   Technical terms not generally understood. See also **19g.**

ILLITERATE, SUBSTANDARD, or VULGAR.   Substandard words used in dialogue to illustrate the speech of the uneducated. See also **19e.**

Note that some meanings of a word may be STANDARD while other meanings of the same word have a NONSTANDARD label.

a, an   Use *a* before a consonant sound, *an* before a vowel sound.

a heavy load   *a* nap   *a* uniform   *a* one-man show
an honest boy   *an* ape   *an* umpire   *an* only child

accept, except   The verb *accept* means "to give an affirmative answer to" or "to receive." The verb *except,* seldom used, means "to exclude"; as a preposition, *except* means "with the exclusion of."

Mary *accepted* the invitation to dinner.
They *excepted* Mary from the invitation.
All the boys *accept* John as their leader.
All the boys *except* John are leaders.

accidentally, incidentally   When using these adverbs, remember that *-ly* is added to the adjective forms *accidental* and *incidental*, not to the noun forms *accident* and *incident*.

NONSTANDARD   Mr. Kent accidently overheard the report.
STANDARD   Mr. Kent *accidentally* overheard the report.

ad, exam, gym, math   Informal shortening of *advertisement, examination, gymnasium,* and *mathematics.* Formal writing requires the full word.

advice, advise   Pronounced and spelled differently, *advice* is a noun, *advise* a verb.

Patients should follow their doctors' *advice.*
Patients should do what their doctors *advise.*

affect, effect   *Affect,* meaning "to influence," is a verb only. *Effect* may function as a verb or a noun. The verb *effect* means "to bring about" or "to achieve"; the noun *effect* means "the result."

The reforms *affected* many citizens.
The citizens *effected* a few reforms.
He said that wars *affect* the economy.
He stressed the *effect* of wars on the economy.

aggravate   Formally *aggravate* means "to make worse or intensify." Informally it means "to provoke or annoy."

INFORMAL   The children's noise aggravated Mrs. Faber.
FORMAL   Lack of water aggravated the suffering.

ain't   A nonstandard contraction avoided by the educated, unless used for humorous effect.

alibi   Informal for *excuse.* In formal English, used only with the legal meaning.

all the farther, all the faster   Nonstandard substitutes for *as far as, as fast as.*

NONSTANDARD   A mile is all the farther we can walk.
STANDARD   A mile is *as far as* we can walk.

allusion, illusion   Do not confuse *allusion,* "an indirect reference," with *illusion,* "an unreal image or false impression."

Timothy made an *allusion* to the Trojans.
The Trojan horse was no optical *illusion*.

almost, most   *Most* is informal when used as a substitute for *almost*.

INFORMAL   Most all referees strive to be fair.
FORMAL   Almost all referees strive to be fair.

a lot, lots   Informal for "very much," "a great deal," or "many." *Alot* is a misspelling of *a lot*.

already, all ready   *Already* means "before or by the time specified." *All ready* means "completely prepared."

The theater was *already* full by seven o'clock.
The cast was *all ready* for the curtain call.

all right   *Alright* is still an unacceptable spelling of *all right*.

altogether, all together   *Altogether* means "wholly, thoroughly." *All together* means "in a group."

That type of rule is *altogether* unnecessary.
They were *all together* in the lobby.

alumnus, alumna   *Alumnus*, a male graduate; *alumni*, two or more male graduates. *Alumna*, a female graduate; *alumnae*, two or more female graduates. *Alumni*, male and female graduates grouped together.

A.M., P.M. (also **a.m., p.m.**).   Use only with figures. "He came at 10:00 A.M. (*not* in the A.M.) and left at 4:00 P.M." "He came in the morning and left in the afternoon (*not* in the P.M.)."

among, between   *Among* always implies more than two, a group; *between* literally implies only two. *Between*, however, is now often used for three or more when each is regarded individually.

What honor was there *among* the forty thieves?
What is the difference *between* a thief and a robber?
"This secret," said Uncle Rex, "is *between* you and me and the gate post."

amount, number   Use *amount* to refer to things in bulk or mass; *number* refers to the countable.

A large *amount* of rice is consumed annually.
A large *number* of disgruntled men barred the entrance.

an, a See **a, an.**

and etc. Never place *and* before *etc.* The *and* is redundant since *etc.* is an abbreviation of *et* (and) + *cetera* (other things).

anyone, any one *Anyone* means "any person at all." *Any one* singles out one person or thing in a group. Similarly with *every-one, every one, someone, some one.*

Anyone can wax a floor.
Any one of those maids can wax a floor.

anyways, anywheres Dialectal for *anyway, anywhere.*

DIALECTAL   Janice cannot drive anywheres.
STANDARD   Janice cannot drive *anywhere.*

as Avoid using *as* instead of *because, for, since, that, which, who,* or *whether.*

DIALECTAL   I do not know as I should go.
STANDARD   I do not know *whether* I should go.
AMBIGUOUS   As it was snowing, we played basketball.
PRECISE   *While* it was snowing, we played basketball.
PRECISE   *Because* it was snowing, we played basketball.

In negative statements some writers prefer *so . . . as* to *as . . . as:* The poet is not *so* popular *as* he once was. See also **like, as, as if.**

as to A vague substitute for *about.*

She spoke to me about (*not* as to) her plans.

at Although *from* after *where* is standard, *at* after *where* is not standard.

NONSTANDARD   Where did the Brownings live at?
STANDARD   Where did they live? Where were they from?

at about *About* is preferable.

WORDY   He arrived at about noon.
BETTER   He arrived about noon.

awful, awfully *Awful* in the sense of "very great, bad, ugly," as well as *awfully* in the sense of "extremely," is not only informal but trite.

INFORMAL   That costume jewelry looks awful.
FORMAL   That costume jewelry looks ostentatious.

INFORMAL   The price of the car is awfully high.
FORMAL   The price of the car is extremely high.

awhile, a while   Distinguish between the adverb *awhile* and the article and noun *a while*.

> Rest *awhile* before you leave.
> Rest for *a while* before you leave.

bad, badly   Although either *bad* or *badly* is now standard in the sense of "ill, sorry," writers usually prefer *bad* after such verbs as *feel* or *look*.

STANDARD   Charles feels *bad*.   Charles feels *badly*.

bank on   Informal expression for *rely on*.

because   See **reason is because**.

being as, being that   Nonstandard for *since, because*.

beside, besides   When meaning "except," *beside* and *besides* are interchangeable prepositions. Distinguish, however, between *beside* meaning "by the side of" and *besides* meaning "in addition to."

STANDARD   I sat *beside* the window.
STANDARD   Herbert has income *besides* his salary.

Notice the difference in the meaning below:

> He owns the car *beside* the house.
> He owns the car *besides* the house.

better   See **had better, had rather, would rather**.

between, among   See **among, between**.

bursted, bust, busted   The obsolete *bursted* is not standard usage; *bust* and *busted* are slang. The principal parts of *burst* are *burst, burst, burst*.

but, hardly, scarcely   "Can't help but" is now standard, both formally and informally, but such negatives as "can't hardly" and "don't scarcely" are still nonstandard.

STANDARD   I *couldn't help but* laugh. OR I *couldn't help* laughing.
NONSTANDARD   I couldn't hardly read his handwriting.
STANDARD   I *could hardly* read his handwriting.

but what   Informal for *that* in negative expressions.

> INFORMAL   Brad has no doubt but what the Lions will win.
> FORMAL   Brad has no doubt *that* the Lions will win.

calculate   Dialectal for *think* or *expect*.

can, may   Informal usage substitutes *can* for *may* in questions and negations. Formal usage still requires that *can* be used to denote ability to perform and *may* to denote permission to do.

> INFORMAL   *Can* I use your class notes?
> FORMAL   *May* I use your class notes?

can't hardly   A double negative in implication. Use *can hardly*. See **but, hardly, scarcely.**

case, line   Often used in wordy expressions.

> WORDY   In the case of Jones there were good intentions.
> CONCISE   Jones had good intentions.
> WORDY   Buy something in the line of fruit.
> CONCISE   Buy some fruit.

complected   Dialectal for *complexioned*.

> DIALECT   They are light-complected children.
> STANDARD   They are light-*complexioned* children (OR children of light complexion).

considerable   Used formally as an adjective, informally as a noun. Nonstandard as an adverb.

> NONSTANDARD   Prices have dropped considerable.
> INFORMAL   Considerable has been donated to the civic fund.
> FORMAL   A *considerable* amount has been donated.

contact   Frequently overused for more exact words or phrases such as *ask, consult, inform, query, talk with, telephone, write to.*

continual, continuous   *Continual* implies "occurring in steady, rapid but not unbroken succession"; *continuous* means "complete absence of interruption."

> *Continual* interruptions delayed the rehearsal.
> The *continuous* roar of the waterfall was disturbing.

could of   Nonstandard for *could have.*

data, criteria, phenomena   Plurals of *datum* (rarely used), *criterion*, *phenomenon*. *Criterion* and *phenomenon* have alternate plurals: *criterions, phenomenons.* The plural *data* is often construed as a collective noun: "This *data has* been verified."

deal   Informal for "business transaction." Frequently overworked for more exact words such as *sale, agreement, plan, secret agreement.*

definitely   Often overused as a vague intensifier.

differ from, differ with   *Differ from* means "to stand apart because of unlikeness." *Differ with* means "to disagree."

> Poe's stories *differ from* those of Hemingway.
> On that point I *differ with* you.

different from   In America, the preferred preposition after *different* is *from*. But *different than* is accepted by many writers if the expression is followed by a clause.

> The Stoic philosophy is *different from* the Epicurean.
> The outcome was *different from* what I expected (OR, more informally, *different than I had expected*).

done   Standard as an adjective and as the past participle of the verb *do*. Nonstandard as an adverb and as a substitute for *did*.

NONSTANDARD	The bread is done sold.
STANDARD	The bread is *already* sold. The bread is *done*.
NONSTANDARD	Do the police know who done it?
STANDARD	Do the police know who *did* it? Who *has done* it?

don't   A contraction for *do not* rather than for *does not*.

NONSTANDARD	He don't smoke. (He do not smoke.)
STANDARD	He *doesn't* smoke. (*He does* not smoke.)

each other, one another   Used interchangeably. Some writers prefer *each other* when referring to only two, and *one another* when referring to more than two.

effect, affect   See **affect, effect.**

either, neither   Used to refer to one or the other of two. (As subjects, the words are singular.)

> Either a bicycle or a car will please him.
> Neither of the paintings is finished.

emigrate, immigrate   *Emigrate* means "to leave a place of abode for residence in another country." *Immigrate* means "to come for permanent residence into a country of which one is not a native."

> Conrad *emigrated* from Poland.
> He *immigrated* to England.

enthuse, enthused   Informal as a verb for "to show enthusiasm" and as a synonym for *enthusiastic.*

> INFORMAL   We were all enthused about the new club.
> FORMAL   We were all *enthusiastic* about the new club.

etc.   See **and etc.**

everyone, every one   See **anyone, any one.**

everywheres   Dialectal for *everywhere.*

except, accept   See **accept, except.**

expect   Informal if used for *suppose* or *think.*

> INFORMAL   I expect James voted yesterday.
> FORMAL   I *suppose* James voted yesterday.

farther, further   Although these words are often used interchangeably to express geographic distance, some writers prefer *farther. Further* is used to express additional time, degree, or quantity.

> Denver is *farther* north than Dallas.
> Will there be *further* improvements in city government?

faze   Informal for "disturb, worry, disconcert." Not related to the noun *phase,* standard English for *aspect* or *stage.*

fewer, less   Informally, interchangeable. Formal English makes this distinction: *less* refers to value, degree, or amount; *fewer* refers to number, to the countable.

INFORMAL Less children are born during a depression.
FORMAL   *Fewer* children are born during a depression.

fine Informal when used as an adverb meaning "well, excellently." *Fine* is a vague, overused adjective; choose a more exact expression.

flunk Informal for *fail*.

folks Informal for *parents, relatives*.

former Refers to the first named of two.

> The Folger and the Huntington are two famous libraries; the *former* is in Washington, D.C., and the latter is in California. [If three items are referred to, do not use *former* or *latter* but *first* and *last*.]

funny Informal for *strange, queer, odd*. In general usage *funny* means "amusing."

further, farther See farther, further.

gentleman, lady Generally preferable: *man, woman*. Use *gentleman, lady* when your purpose is to distinguish persons of refinement and culture from the ill-bred. Use the plural forms in addressing an audience: "Ladies and Gentlemen."

get, got The verb *to get* is one of the most useful words in standard English. It is common in such good idioms as *get along with* (someone), *get the better of* (someone), *get at* (information), *get up* (a dance), *get on* (a horse), or *get over* (an illness). Avoid, however, *get* or *got* in expressions considered slang or too informal.

INFORMAL I do not get the professor half the time.
FORMAL   I do not *understand* the professor half the time.

good Nearly always used as an adjective. Generally considered informal when used as an adverb.

INFORMAL Mrs. Nevins cooks good.
FORMAL   Mrs. Nevins cooks *good* meals. She cooks *well*.

gotten Past participle of *get*, the principal parts of which are *get* (present), *got* (past), *got*, or *gotten* (past participle). In England *gotten* is now old-fashioned, but in the United States both *got* and *gotten* are in general use.

grand A vague, trite adjective. Describe what you mean with more specific words.

guy Informal for *man* or *boy*.

had better, had rather, would rather Good idioms used to express advisability (with *better*) or preference (with *rather*). *Better* is an informal shortening of *had better*.

INFORMAL Members better pay their dues.
FORMAL Members *had better* pay their dues.

had of, had ought Nonstandard for *had, ought*.

half a, a half, a half a Use *half a* or *a half*, but avoid the redundant *a half a*.

REDUNDANT He worked a half a day.
STANDARD He worked *half a* day.
STANDARD He worked *a half* day. [Perhaps more formal and more specific]

hanged, hung Informally, the distinction between *hanged* and *hung* is often no longer made, but formal usage still makes a distinction: *hanged* is used in referring to executions; *hung*, to objects.

The outlaw was *hanged*.
The lodge is *hung* with African trophies.

hardly See **but, hardly, scarcely.**

have, of See **of, have.**

healthful, healthy Although both *healthful* and *healthy* are standard words meaning "conducive to health," *healthy* is most frequently used to mean "having health"; *healthful*, "giving health."

That is a *healthful* (OR *healthy*) climate.
Healthy (NOT healthful) pets are sold in that shop.

himself, myself See **myself, himself.**

hisself Nonstandard for *himself*.

Honorable, Reverend See **Reverend, Honorable.**

if, whether   Some writers prefer *whether* to *if* after such verbs as *say, learn, know, understand, doubt,* especially when followed by *or.*

> Forecasters did not know *whether* it would rain or snow.

illusion, allusion   See **allusion, illusion.**

immigrate, emigrate   See **emigrate, immigrate.**

imply, infer   The writer or speaker *implies;* the reader or listener *infers. Imply* means "to suggest without stating"; *infer* means "to reach a conclusion based upon evidence." Often used interchangeably in informal English.

> His statement *implies* that he will resign.
> From his statement I *infer* that he will resign.

in, into   Do not confuse. *In* indicates "location within." "He was *in* the room." *Into* indicates "motion or direction to a point within." "He came *into* the room." Compare the meaning of these sentences:

> We flew *in* another jet.
> We flew *into* another jet.

in back of, in behind, in between   Wordy for *back of, behind, between.*

incidentally, accidentally   See **accidentally, incidentally.**

incredible, incredulous   *Incredible* means "too extraordinary to admit of belief." *Incredulous* means "inclined not to believe on slight evidence."

> The hunters told *incredible* stories.
> The hunters' stories made me *incredulous.*

individual, party, person   *Individual* refers to a single thing, animal, or person. In legal writing, *party* may refer to a group of people or to a single person, but in other formal writing, *party* designates a group only. *Person* is preferred for general reference to a human being.

> INFORMAL   Paul is the only interested party.
> FORMAL   Paul is the only interested *person.*

infer, imply   See **imply, infer.**

inferior than   Nonstandard. Use *inferior to* or *worse than.*

ingenious, ingenuous   *Ingenious* means "clever, resourceful," as "an ingenious device." *Ingenuous* means "open, frank, artless," as "ingenuous actions."

> The electric can opener is an *ingenious* device.
> Don's *ingenuous* smile disarms the critics.

in regards to   Use either of the correct idioms, *in regard to* or *as regards.*

inside of, outside of   The *of* is often unnecessary. *Inside of* is informal for *within. Outside of* is informal for *except, besides.*

> FORMAL   We live *inside* the city limits.
> FORMAL   The job will be finished *within* (NOT inside of) ten days.

into, in   See **in, into.**

invite   Slang when used as a substitute for *invitation.*

irregardless   Nonstandard for *regardless.*

its, it's   *Its* is a possessive pronoun; *it's* is a contraction of *it is* or *it has.*

just   Informal for *truly, very, accurately.* Choose an exact word.

> INFORMAL   The earthquake was just dreadful.
> FORMAL   The earthquake was unbelievably dreadful.

kind, sort   Singular forms, which may be modified by *that* or *this.* Use *those* or *these* to modify only plural forms, such as *these kinds.*

> INFORMAL   Mr. Pratt prefers these kind.
> FORMAL   Mr. Pratt prefers *this kind.*

kind of, sort of   Informal when used as an adverb meaning "somewhat, rather, after a fashion."

> INFORMAL   The kitchen floor seems kind of uneven.
> FORMAL   The kitchen floor seems *somewhat* uneven.

kind of a   Omit the *a* in your formal writing.

lady, gentleman   See **gentleman, lady.**

later, latter Referring to time, *later* is the comparative form of *late*. *Latter* refers to the last named of two. If more than two are named, use *last*, not *latter*.

lay, lie Do not confuse these verbs. See **7a**, pages 69–70.

learn, teach *Learn* means "to acquire knowledge"; *teach* means "to impart knowledge."

STANDARD Miss Evans *taught* Earl only one week, but he *learned* how to study during that time.

leave, let Do not use *leave* for *let*. *Leave* means "to depart from"; *let* means "to permit." But "Leave (*or* Let) me alone" is a standard idiom.

NONSTANDARD I will not leave you go today.
STANDARD I will not *let* you go today.

less, fewer See **fewer, less.**

let's us Redundant for *let's*, which is the contraction of *let us*.

lie, lay Do not confuse. See **7a**, pages 69–70.

like, as, as if Informal English uses *like* either as a preposition or as a conjunction: "Work like a man." "This tastes like it should." Formal written English still prefers *as* or *as if* for the conjunction: "This tastes *as* it should." "He eats *as if* he were starving."

likely, liable Informally, *liable* is substituted for *likely*. Formally, *likely* means "probable, to be expected," but *liable* means "susceptible to something unpleasant" or "legally responsible."

INFORMAL My favorite program is liable to win an award.
FORMAL My favorite program is *likely* to win an award.
FORMAL John is *liable* to cut his foot with the ax.

line, case See **case, line.**

locate Informal for "settle, to make one's residence."

INFORMAL He located in Texas.
FORMAL He *settled* in Texas; he *located* his factory there.

lose, loose Do not confuse. *Lose* means "to cease having." *Loose* (verb) means "to set free." *Loose* (adjective) means "free, not fastened."

lots, lots of, a lot   Informal for *many, much, a great deal.*

lovely   Informal for *delightful, highly pleasing.* Choose the exact word to fit your meaning.

mad   Still considered informal for *angry, furious.*

math   Informal for *mathematics.*

may be, maybe   Distinguish between the verb form *may be* and the adverb *maybe,* meaning "perhaps."

> April *may be* the best time for a vacation.
> *Maybe* the family will take a vacation in April.

may, can   See **can, may.**

mighty   Informally used for *very, exceedingly.*

> INFORMAL   The Wards are mighty good neighbors.
> FORMAL   In Rhodes stood the *mighty* statue of Colossus.

moral, morale   The noun *moral* means "lesson, maxim"; the adjective *moral* means "pertaining to right conduct, ethical." *Morale,* a noun, refers to "a cheerful, confident state of mind."

> What is the *moral* of Thurber's fable?
> Has the *morale* of the team improved?

most   See **almost, most.**

myself, himself, yourself   Properly intensive or reflexive pronouns. "I myself will go; I will see for myself." In general *myself* is not a proper substitute for *I* or *me;* but it is substituted informally (1) for *I* after comparisons with *than* or *as* ("Everyone worked as well as myself") or (2) for *me* when it is the second member of a compound object ("He allowed my brother and myself to go home.").

nice   Overworked as a vague word of approval. Find an exact word.

nohow   Nonstandard for *not at all.*

nowheres   Dialectal for *nowhere.*

number   See **amount, number.**

of, have   The preposition *of* is nonstandard when substituted in writing for the verb form *have.*

| NONSTANDARD | Mary could of (would of, may of, might of, must of, ought to of) done that last week. |
| STANDARD | Mary could *have* (would *have*, may *have*, might *have*, must *have*, ought to *have*) done that last week. |

off of   Informal for *off*.

| INFORMAL | The clock fell off of the desk. |
| FORMAL | The clock fell *off* the desk. |

OK, O.K., okay   All three are accepted as standard forms expressing general approval. A more specific word, however, usually replaces *OK* in formal writing.

one another, each other   See **each other, one another.**

ought   See **had ought.**

outside of   See **inside of, outside of.**

party, person, individual   See **individual, party, person.**

per   Careful writers generally avoid *per*, except in business English or in Latin phrases.

phenomena   Plural of *phenomenon*. See **data, criteria, phenomena.**

phone   Informal for *telephone*. Formally, use the full word.

photo   Informal shortening of *photograph*. Use the full word in your formal writing.

plenty   Informal as an adverb meaning *very*.

| INFORMAL | The chemistry test was plenty hard. |
| FORMAL | The chemistry test was *very* hard. |

P.M., A.M.   See **A.M., P.M.**

practical, practicable   *Practical* means "useful, sensible, not theoretical." *Practicable* means "feasible, capable of being put into practice."

The sponsors are *practical*, and their plans are *practicable*.

principal, principle   Distinguish between *principal*, an adjective or noun meaning "chief" or "chief official," and the noun *principle*, meaning "fundamental truth."

prof Informal for *professor*. Use the full word in your formal writing.

quite An adverb meaning "entirely, positively." Used informally to mean "very, to a great extent, noticeably."

INFORMAL The lake is quite near.
FORMAL His guess was *quite* wrong.

raise, rise See **rise, raise.**

real Informal for *very, extremely.*

INFORMAL The victorious team was real tired.
FORMAL The victorious team was *extremely* tired.

reason is because Formal English usually completes the construction *The reason is (was)* with a *that* clause or recasts the sentence.

INFORMAL The reason why he missed his class was because (*or* on account of) he overslept.
FORMAL The reason why he missed his class was *that* he overslept.
FORMAL He missed his class because he overslept.

reckon Informal or dialectal for *guess, suppose, think.*

respectfully, respectively *Respectfully* means "in a manner showing respect." *Respectively* means "each in the order given."

Tom rose *respectfully* when Mrs. Hughes entered.
The President commended the Army, Navy, and Air Force, *respectively.*

Reverend, Honorable To be followed not only by the surname but also by the initials or some other title (such as *Mr.*) of the person referred to.

The *Honorable Mr. Wilson* presided.
The next speaker was *Rev. J. C. Boyle.*

right along Informal for "without interruption, continuously."

INFORMAL Road construction moved right along.
FORMAL Road construction moved forward without interruption.

rise, raise An intransitive verb, *rise (rose, risen)* means "to move upward." A transitive verb, *raise* (*raised*) means "to cause to move upward, to place erect."

> Franklin *rises* promptly at seven.
> Franklin *raises* his hand often in English class.

same, said, such Except in legal documents, questionable substitutes for *it, this, that, before-mentioned.*

says, said Not interchangeable. *Says* is present tense; *said*, past.

> NONSTANDARD   Allen dashed into the cafeteria and says, "Helen won the essay contest."
> STANDARD   Allen dashed into the cafeteria and *said*, "Helen won the essay contest."

scarcely See **but, hardly, scarcely.**

seldom ever, seldom or ever Use *seldom if ever, hardly ever.*

sit, set See **Section 7,** pages 69–70.

so, so that *So* is an overworked word. Do not overwork *so* to join main clauses. In clauses denoting purpose, *so that* is usually preferred to *so.*

> AMBIGUOUS   Ralph left so I could study.
> CLEAR   Ralph left *so that* I could study.
> CLEAR   Ralph left; *therefore*, I could study.

some Informal for *remarkable, striking, extraordinary.*

> INFORMAL   The St. Bernard is some dog!
> FORMAL   The St. Bernard is a *remarkable* dog!

someone, some one See **anyone, any one.**

somewheres Dialectal for *somewhere.*

sort, sort of, sort of a See **kind, kind of, kind of a.**

speak, speech The verb *speak* means "to talk"; the noun *speech* is "the act of speaking."

> Hamlet told the actors to "*speak* the *speech* trippingly on the tongue."

such Note carefully the formal uses of *such* listed in the dictionary. Avoid the vague, weak use of *such* or *such a.* When *such* is completed by a result clause, it should be followed by *that.*

INFORMAL	Twain has such a remarkable sense of humor.
FORMAL	Twain has a remarkable sense of humor.
FORMAL	There was *such* a rain *that* we could not drive.

See also **same, said, such.**

sure Informal for *surely* or *certainly.*

| INFORMAL | The sunrise sure was beautiful. |
| FORMAL | The sunrise *surely* was beautiful. |

sure and Informal for *sure to.*

suspicion Dialectal when used as a verb in place of *suspect.*

| DIALECTAL | I did not suspicion anything. |
| STANDARD | I did not *suspect* anything. |

take In your formal writing, avoid such informal expressions as *take it out on, to take up with, take in a movie.* Choose instead expressions such as *vent one's anger on, be friendly with, attend a movie.*

teach See **learn, teach.**

terrible, terribly *Terrible* is informal for *unpleasant, very bad. Terribly* is informal in the sense of *extremely, exceedingly.*

than, then *Than* and *then* are not interchangeable. Do not confuse the conjunction *than* with the adverb or adverbial conjunction *then,* which relates to time.

Nylon wears better *than* rayon.
First it snowed; *then* it sleeted.

their, there, they're Do not confuse. *Their* is a possessive pronoun; *there* is an adverb or an expletive; *they're* is the contraction of *they are.*

There is no explanation for *their* refusal.
They're installing a traffic light *there.*

theirself, theirselves Nonstandard for *themselves.*

these kind, these sort See **kind, sort.**

this here, that there, these here, them there Nonstandard expressions. Use *this, that, these, those.*

to, too, two Distinguish the preposition *to* ("*to* the store") from the adverb *too* ("*too* cold") and the numeral *two* ("*two* apples").

try and Informal for *try to.*

type of Do not omit the *of* in expressions such as "that type of film" or "that type of hero."

used to, supposed to Be sure to add the -*d* to *use* and *suppose* when writing, although the -*d* is often dropped in speech.

> Horses *used to* be indispensable.
> James was *supposed to* be in charge.

used to could Nonstandard or facetious for *used to be able.*

wait on Means *to attend, to serve.* Informal for *wait for.*

> FORMAL   I *waited for* the lecturer to begin.

want Nonstandard if a *that* clause is its object.

> NONSTANDARD   I want that he should have a chance.
> STANDARD   I want him to have a chance.

want in, out, down, up, off, through. Informal or dialectal for *want to come in* or *get in, out, down, up, off, through.*

ways Informal for *way* referring to distance.

> INFORMAL   It's a long ways to Chicago.
> FORMAL   It is a long *way* to Chicago.

where Informal for *that.*

> INFORMAL   I saw in the newspaper where the strike had been settled.
> FORMAL   I saw in the newspaper *that* the strike had been settled.

where . . . at Redundant. Omit the *at.*

which, who Use *who* or *that* instead of *which* to refer to persons.

while Do not overuse as a substitute for *and* or *but.* The conjunction *while* usually refers to time.

who, which See **which, who.**

worst way *In the worst way* is slang for *very much.*

NONSTANDARD	Mrs. Simmons wanted a color TV in the worst way.
STANDARD	Mrs. Simmons wanted a color TV *very much.*

would of   Nonstandard for *would have.*

would rather   See **had better, had rather, would rather.**

you   Avoid the awkward use of *you* as an indefinite pronoun.

AWKWARD	When a person eats too much before bedtime, you may have nightmares.
BETTER	A person who eats too much before bedtime may have nightmares.

you all   A standard plural, now used generally in various sections of the United States, particularly in the South. Unacceptable if used to indicate the singular *you.*

you was   Nonstandard for *you were.*

Exactness

20

Select words that are exact, idiomatic, and fresh.

Especially when writing, you should strive to choose words which express your ideas exactly, precise words which convey the emotional suggestions you intend. The choice of a right word will depend on your purpose, your point of view, and your reader.

If you can make effective use of the words you already know, you need not have a remarkably large vocabulary. In fact, as shown by the example below, professional writers often choose short, familiar words.

> I saw her sitting at her desk, taking the rubber band off the roll-call cards, running it back upon the fingers of her right hand, and surveying us all separately with quick little henlike turns of her head. . . . She was forever climbing up the margins of books and crawling between their lines, hunting for the little gold of phrase, making marks with a pencil.
>
> —JAMES THURBER[1]

Of course, as you gain experience in writing and reading, you will become increasingly aware of the need to add new words, both short and long, to your vocabulary. When you discover a valuable new word, make it your own by mastering its spelling, its meaning, and its exact use.

[1] From "Here Lies Miss Groby" by James Thurber, reprinted from the *New Yorker*, March 21, 1942, by permission of the *New Yorker*.

20a

Consult a good dictionary for the exact word needed to express your idea.

(1) Make sure that the dictionary gives the exact meaning you have in mind.

WRONG WORD   I hope my mother will find the mountain air *enervating*. [*Enervating* means "weakening or destroying the vigor of."]

RIGHT WORD   I hope my mother will find the mountain air *invigorating*. [*Invigorating* means "animating or giving vigor to."]

INEXACT   A registration official *brainwashed* the freshmen for forty-five minutes. [*Brainwashing* is "the alteration of personal convictions, beliefs, habits, and attitudes by means of intensive, coercive indoctrination."]

EXACT   A registration official *briefed* the freshmen for forty-five minutes. [To *brief* is "to prepare in advance by instructing or advising."]

Be careful to use the right conjunction to express the exact relation between words, phrases, and clauses.

INEXACT   The halfback is clumsy *and* speedy. [*And* adds or continues.]

EXACT   The halfback is clumsy *but* speedy. [*But* contrasts.]

Caution: Do not confuse words that are similar in spelling or meaning. If necessary, review the list of similar words in Section 18, Exercise 2. See also **19i**.

WRONG WORD   Early Christians stressed the *immorality* of the soul.

RIGHT WORD   Early Christians stressed the *immortality* of the soul.

▶ EXERCISE 1   First, consult your dictionary in order to find the exact meaning of each word below. Then write a sentence using each word correctly.

1. eminent, imminent
2. persuade, dissuade
3. repentance, remorse
4. subconscious, unconscious
5. paradox, enigma
6. astronomy, astrology
7. opaque, translucent
8. imply, insinuate
9. jargon, dialect
10. sophomore, sophomoric

(2) Select the word with the connotation, as well as the denotation, proper to the idea you wish to express.

The denotation of a word is what the word actually points to. According to the dictionary, the word *birthday* denotes "the day of one's birth or its anniversary." The connotation of a word is what the word suggests or implies. For example, the word *birthday* may connote a cake with lighted candles, gifts, parties, a special date to remember —or forget.

Connotation includes the emotions or associations that surround a word. For instance, *taxi, tin lizzie, limousine, convertible, station wagon, dump truck, hot rod*—all denote much the same thing to a traffic officer. But to various readers, and in various contexts, each word may have a special connotation. *Taxi* may suggest a city rush hour; *tin lizzie,* an historical museum; *limousine,* an airport; *convertible,* a homecoming parade; *station wagon,* children and dogs; *dump truck,* highway construction; *hot rod,* noisy fun. Similarly, *jalopy, bus, sedan, bookmobile, moving van, ambulance, squad car*—all denote a means of transportation, but each word carries a variety of connotations.

A word may be right in one situation, wrong in another. *Female parent,* for instance, is a proper expression in a biology laboratory, but it would be very inappropriate to say "John wept because of the death of his female parent." *Female parent* used in this sense is literally correct, but the connotation is wrong. The more appropriate word, *mother,* not only conveys the meaning denoted by *female parent;* it also conveys the reason why John wept. The first expression simply implies a biological relationship; the second is full of imaginative and emotional suggestions.

▶ EXERCISE 2   Give one dictionary definition (denotation) and one connotation for each of the following words.

1. yellow
2. Christmas
3. tolerance
4. grandfather
5. New York City
6. dog
7. China
8. orchids
9. library
10. existentialism

▶ EXERCISE 3   Be prepared to explain why the italicized words in the following sentences, although literally correct, might be inappropriate because of their connotations.

1. At the sound of the organ, the professors in full regalia *scampered* down the aisle and *tramped* to their assigned seats.
2. We are building our new home on the rim of a most delightful little *gulch.*
3. The soloist *tucked* his *fiddle* under his chin.
4. For the *enlightenment* of the other ladies, Mrs. Bromley measured upon her *belly* the area of her recent operation.
5. Homer squeezed a quantity of *chlorophyllaceous extrusion* onto his toothbrush.
6. Small fry at the Saturday movies *consume* scads of popcorn and peanuts.
7. The conclusion of the Gettysburg Address indicates that President Lincoln *hankered* for a new *spurt* of freedom.

▶ EXERCISE 4   Be prepared to discuss those words below which because of their connotative value intensify the author's meaning.

1. In all America, no one was so lucky as the Southerner who was a part of this social revolution, of this determi-

nation to reaffirm the principles of what we have called the American dream.   —RALPH MC GILL

2. A man with courage knows how to die standing up; he's got more guts than you could hang on a fence, gravel in his gizzard, and is as salty as Lot's wife and as gritty as fish eggs rolled in sand.   —GEORGE D. HENDRICKS

(3) **Select the specific word and the concrete word rather than the general and abstract.**

A *general* word is all-inclusive, indefinite, sweeping in scope. A *specific* word is precise, definite, limited in scope.

general	specific	more specific
food	dessert	apple pie
prose	fiction	short stories
people	Americans	Mr. and Mrs. Smith

An *abstract* word deals with concepts, with ideas, with what cannot be touched, heard, or seen. A *concrete* word has to do with particular objects, with the practical, with what can be touched, heard, or seen.

ABSTRACT WORDS   democracy, loyal, evil, hate, charity
CONCRETE WORDS   mosquito, spotted, crunch, wedding, car

All writers must sometimes use abstract words, like *wisdom* or *integrity*, and occasionally resort to generalizations, like "Men through the ages have sought freedom from tyranny." These abstractions and generalizations are vital to communication of ideas and theories. To be effective, however, the use of these words must be based upon clearly understood and well-thought-out ideas.

Professional writers usually have little difficulty handling general and abstract words. Inexperienced writers, however, tend to use too many general and abstract words. The writing becomes drab and lifeless, because of the scarcity of specific, concrete words. Be as specific as you can. For example, instead of writing "a *thin* speaker," consider the possibility of using *gaunt, slender, lanky,* or *frail.*

When you are tempted to write *pretty,* ask yourself whether *graceful, delicate, stunning, shapely, becoming, ravishing,* or *picturesque* would not be more appropriate.

The test for the specific word is contained in one or more of these questions: Exactly who? Exactly what? Precisely when? Exactly where? Precisely how? As you study the examples below, notice what a difference specific, concrete words can make in the expression of an idea.

DULL   The Army team finally advanced the ball. [*How* did they do it?]

SPECIFIC   Adams, the Army quarterback, received the ball from center Jim Hawkins, retreated to his ten-yard line, and threw a pass to left-end Smith, who was tackled on the Army thirty-five-yard line. [Specific details expand the idea.]

DULL   After going up the famous mountain, we went on down and saw the sights of Pompeii.

SPECIFIC   After exploring the crater of Mount Vesuvius, we wandered through the streets of Old Pompeii and saw the lava-covered bodies of four men and a dog that had been buried alive by the eruption of 79 A.D.

DULL   She worked in her flower bed, digging around in it and looking over the plants. She always saw to it that no bugs or other pests got into her flowers.

SPECIFIC   She took off a glove and put her strong fingers down into the forest of new green chrysanthemum sprouts that were growing around the old roots. She spread the leaves and looked down among the close-growing stems. No aphids were there, no sowbugs or snails or cutworms. Her terrier fingers destroyed such pests before they could get started.   —JOHN STEINBECK[2]

▶ **EXERCISE 5**   Using a dictionary of synonyms if you wish, choose five specific words which might be appropriately substituted for each of the following: (1) *see,* (2) *walk,*

---

[2] From *The Long Valley* by John Steinbeck. Copyright 1937, 1965 by John Steinbeck. Reprinted by the permission of The Viking Press, Inc.

(3) *great*, (4) *bad*, (5) *happy*, (6) *man*, (7) *get*, (8) *nice*
(9) *think*, (10) *love.*

EXAMPLE *eat:* munch, nibble, bolt, gulp, feast on

▶ EXERCISE 6 Select from the words inside parentheses the specific word which best fits the context of the sentence.

1. Her moral indignation was always (high, evident, on the boil).   —ALDOUS HUXLEY
2. A janitor collects garbage in a cart that (sounds, rumbles, squeaks) on the broken tile like a tumbril.
    —JOHN BARTLOW MARTIN
3. Her beauty was (outstanding, fabulous, paralyzing)— beyond all words, all experience, all dream.
    —CONRAD AIKEN
4. He had (flaxen, yellow, light) hair, weak blue eyes, and the general demeanor of a saintly but timid (person, animal, codfish).   —P. G. WODEHOUSE
5. The plumber lifted his strong, (weathered, tough, dark) face and looked curiously at her.   —KAY BOYLE
6. He (threw away, got rid of, flipped away) the dead match and blew (a puff of smoke, a stream of gray) into the evening.   —FLANNERY O'CONNOR
7. Presently there came a spectacle of a man (getting, working, churning) himself into the deepest rage over the immobility of a house.   —STEPHEN CRANE
8. From the main street outside came the echoes of holiday (celebration, hysteria, noises).
    —CARSON MC CULLERS
9. Two girls went (skittering, running, hurrying) by in short transparent raincoats, one green, one red, their heads (tucked, bent, held) against the drive of the rain.   —KATHERINE ANNE PORTER
10. The women were disposed about a table of plate glass and their nine handbags lay in (polkadots, a pile, an archipelago) upon its great (lucid, opaque, serene) surface.   —LIONEL TRILLING

▶ **EXERCISE 7** Using specific words, rewrite the following sentences.

1. My father looked at my grade in science and said what I least expected to hear.
2. At the store we priced a number of items.
3. The boy made a bad mistake the morning of his first day at school.
4. My relatives gave me two gifts which pleased me.
5. Only Fred was in the room; he sat slumped in a chair reading a magazine.
6. Marvin's car needs new parts before the family uses it for a trip.
7. Various aspects of the television show were criticized in the newspaper.
8. Many things in our back yard are unattractive.
9. The player moved forward quickly and caught the ball.
10. During that time the traffic officer arrested more than twenty people for the same violation.

(4) Use appropriate figurative language to create imaginative or emotional impressions.

A figure of speech is the use of a word in an imaginative rather than in a literal sense. The two chief figures of speech are the simile and the metaphor. A *simile* is an explicit comparison between two things of a different kind or quality, usually introduced by *like* or *as*. A *metaphor* is an implied comparison of dissimilar things; words of comparison, such as *like* and *as,* are not used.

SIMILES This land is still there. The motorist on Highway 66 sees it swim toward him *like the blur of a microscope's field sharpening toward focus.*
—WALLACE STEGNER

As a parasol with many flounces, as a peacock with many feathers, shuts its flounces, folds its feathers, so she subsided and shut herself as she sank down in the leather armchair. —VIRGINIA WOOLF

METAPHORS   Thought is *the weariest of all the Titans.*

—J. FRANK DOBIE

There was some talk of expulsion, but his record
showed *a neat picket fence of A's broken only
twice by filigree B's.*   —JOHN ANTHONY WEST

Metaphors and similes are especially valuable because
they are concrete and tend to point up essential relationships that cannot otherwise be communicated. (For faulty
metaphors see **23c.**)

Two other frequently used figures of speech are hyperbole and personification. *Hyperbole* is deliberate over-
statement or fanciful exaggeration. *Personification* attributes
to the nonhuman (inanimate objects, animals, ideas) those
characteristics possessed only by the human.

HYPERBOLES

At our house, washing dishes is a *Sisyphean* task.

I, for one, don't expect till I die to be so good a man as I am at
this minute, for just now I'm *fifty thousand feet high—a
tower with all the trumpets shouting.*   —G. K. CHESTERTON

PERSONIFICATIONS

The hurricane perversely changed her course, slashing her way
through Louisiana swamps with malicious determination.

They sleep and the moon and the sun sleep and even the ocean
sleeps sometimes on certain days when there is no current and
a flat calm.   —ERNEST HEMINGWAY

▶ EXERCISE 8   Test the exactness and force of the metaphors, similes, hyperboles, and personifications in the following sentences by attempting to state the same ideas
literally.

1. All these people zipped and caromed about the pristine
   world of the screen as jazzily as a convention of water
   bugs.   —JAMES AGEE
2. Outside, evening had laid its blanket on the city.
   —ANDREW SINCLAIR

3. As the trout's back came up out of the water the minnows jumped wildly. They sprinkled the surface like a handful of shot thrown into the water.
   —ERNEST HEMINGWAY

4. When a headache and he went to bed together, they were a noisy pair.   —CLARENCE DAY

5. Her eyes, lost in the fatty ridges of her face, looked like two small pieces of coal pressed into a lump of dough as they moved from one face to another while the visitors stated their errand.   —WILLIAM FAULKNER

6. The odd thing about truth is that it keeps changing its clothes.   —CURTIS BOK

7. She was ready half an hour before the time of departure and she paid some visits on the floor in her powder-blue gown and her hat that looked like one minute after an April shower.   —F. SCOTT FITZGERALD

8. Every time a Cooper person is in peril, and absolute silence is worth four dollars a minute, he is sure to step on a dry twig.   —MARK TWAIN

9. Ushers standing at fixed intervals wave their torches like regimented fireflies.   —FRANCIS RUSSELL

10. To tell *all* about ourselves in one vast breath is really to press the whole round world in the lemon-squeezer of our minds . . . .   —J. B. PRIESTLEY

▶ EXERCISE 9   Complete each of the following by using a simile, metaphor, hyperbole, or personification. Use effective figures of speech. (For instance, instead of the familiar metaphor *Time is money!* you might use *Time is a physician.*)

1. My first in-class theme, as the professor read it to the class, sounded like . . . .
2. The father of the valedictorian was as proud as . . . .
3. The ragweed in Texas . . . .
4. Death is . . . .

5. Like a bewildered freshman during registration, the Pacific cold front . . . .
6. As it glistened in the sun, the jet was . . . .
7. Fans pushing into the stadium reminded me of . . . .
8. As George left art lab he resembled . . . .
9. Moaning in front of the full-length mirror, Gladys said, "I . . . ."
10. To Farmer Selby, that mangy, flea-ridden hound is . . . .
11. The steamer . . . .
12. Helen's hat looked like . . . .
13. As confident as . . . , I stepped forward.
14. Like . . . , the class sat speechless.
15. Driving on a crowded freeway, Uncle Robert is . . . .

20b

Use the exact idiom demanded by English usage.

At the very heart of the English language are idioms. These are everyday expressions which distinctly characterize a language and make it different from any other language. They are acceptable patterns of usage that do not conform to rules. One type of English idiom (such as *for many a year*) cannot be analyzed or justified grammatically; another type (such as *I completely lost my head!*) cannot be taken literally, cannot be sensibly translated word for word into another language. Dictionaries treat many idiomatic phrases. See, for instance, the idioms built around *go* and listed after *go* in your dictionary.

Ordinarily native speakers use idiomatic English naturally and effectively, but once in a while they may have difficulty choosing idiomatic prepositions. Be careful to use the exact phrasing for each idiom, not some unidiomatic approximation.

UNIDIOMATIC   comply to, superior than, buy off of
IDIOMATIC   comply with, superior to, buy from

When you are in doubt about what preposition to use after

a given word, look up that word in the dictionary. Take, for instance, the word *angry*. The *Standard College Dictionary* lists these idiomatic phrases: "*angry with* (or *at*) his brother; *angry at* (or *about*) an insult."

Dictionaries also classify many idioms as *formal, informal, dialectal,* etc. For example, the *Standard College Dictionary* makes usage distinctions such as the following:

INFORMAL   Try and catch me.
FORMAL   Try to catch me.
DIALECTAL I'll wait on you if it won't take long.
STANDARD   I'll wait for you if it won't take long.

Always choose the idiom that is both exact and appropriate.

▶ EXERCISE 10   Consult a good college dictionary to determine what prepositions are idiomatically used with (1) *agree,* (2) *compare,* (3) *differ,* (4) *consist,* and (5) *deal.* Use each of these verbs correctly in two sentences, each with a different preposition.

▶ EXERCISE 11   In a good college dictionary study the idiomatic phrases treated under *catch, put, set, tie,* and *win.* Select three different idioms formed with each verb, and illustrate each idiom in a sentence.

▶ EXERCISE 12   Choose the idiomatic preposition in each set of parentheses below. If you are not sure whether a given phrase is idiomatic, consult a good college dictionary.

1. Buy your car (from, off of) the man next door.
2. There was no sales tax prior (to, than) 1961.
3. That regiment is equal (for, to) the assignment.
4. Does Mr. Mason agree (with, on) the president's opinion?
5. Jo stays angry (with, at) himself.
6. We expect to be (at, to) home all day.
7. Barbara is utterly oblivious (about, of) noise when she studies chemistry.

8. In return for their labor, Americans expect to have the necessities (of, for) life.
9. Robert has gone in search (of, for) a secondhand car.
10. Drivers are expected to comply (with, to) traffic laws.

20c

Select fresh expressions instead of trite, worn-out ones.

Such trite expressions as *a word to the wise, as clear as mud, the almighty dollar,* and *the long arm of the law* were once striking and effective. What you may not know is that excessive use has made them trite. They are now stock phrases in the language, automatic clichés that have lost their effectiveness. Good writers do not use trite, well-known phrases when fresh, original expressions are more effective. Compare the effectiveness of the following sentences.

TRITE   *It goes without saying* that we often feel *as helpless as a baby* when we try to *hitch our wagon to a star.*

ORIGINAL   When we reach out for the stars, our limitations become grotesquely apparent.   —ARTHUR KOESTLER

To avoid trite phrases you must be aware of current usage. Catch phrases and slogans pass quickly from ephemeral popularity into the Old Words' Home. Glittering political shibboleths like *grass roots, pulse of public opinion,* and *the common man* are notoriously short-lived. Commercial advertising also bestows its *kiss of death* on an honorable phrase. When a mattress company bids you *sleep in peace* or promises a *midsummer night's dream* on their *airy fairy beds,* when blankets are publicized as *soft as down* or *gentle as a baby's breath,* mark the italicized words as trite expressions, for the time being at least.

Every writer uses a few clichés, such as *the weaker sex* or *beating about the bush.* And nearly every writer occasionally quotes familiar proverbs, Biblical verses, and lines from poetry—for example, "Who steals my purse steals trash . . . ." or "Three may keep a secret if two of them are dead." It is not unusual for a professional writer to give a new twist to an old saying—for instance, *easier done than said, to make a short story long,* or *There's madness in his method.* No good writer, however, relies heavily on the phraseology of others; he chooses his own words to communicate his own ideas.

▶ EXERCISE 13   Construct sentences which contain accept-able substitutes for ten of the hackneyed expressions listed below. In your sentences include within brackets the hackneyed expressions you replace. Be careful not to re-place one hackneyed expression with another.

1. after all is said and done
2. agree to disagree
3. all work and no play
4. better late than never
5. cold as ice
6. easier said than done
7. green with envy
8. last but not least
9. white as a sheet
10. on the ball (on the beam)
11. bitter end
12. busy as a bee
13. by leaps and bounds
14. slow but sure
15. straight from the shoulder
16. sweat of his brow
17. this day and age
18. too funny for words
19. wee small hours
20. none the worse for wear
21. good personality
22. needless to say

▶ EXERCISE 14   First make a list of ten hackneyed expres-sions that you often use; then rewrite each by using exact, straightforward words of your own.

▶ EXERCISE 15   As you revise the following sentences, use original, specific diction in place of the italicized trite and general words.

TRITE (AND GENERAL)   I took the collie to chase rabbits in the upper fields, but its actions showed that it *did not have enough sense to come in out of the rain.*

ORIGINAL (AND SPECIFIC)   I took the one-eyed collie to chase rabbits in the upper fields, but it barked at ducks and brought me a tramp's shoe from a hedge, and lay down with its tail wagging in a rabbit hole. —DYLAN THOMAS

1. *In this day and age* too much emphasis is placed on *filthy lucre.*
2. The telephone rang *at just the psychological moment.*
3. At the blast of the siren, the culprits *beat a hasty retreat.*
4. The professor spoke *straight from the shoulder.*
5. Fred was grateful to *the powers that be* for escaping the accident.
6. Father saw to it that my plans were *nipped in the bud.*
7. The *tall, dark, and handsome* actor was *on the ball.*
8. Examination week approached *slowly but surely.*
9. When the *blushing bride* entered the room, she was *the center of attraction.*
10. His *better half* was *busy as a bee* getting the house ready for company.
11. Though the score was forty to ten, the Eagles fought hard *to the bitter end.*
12. The ice cream was soup, and the hamburgers were *as cold as ice.*
13. *After all is said and done,* a student normally gets the grade he makes.
14. *Last but not least,* high taxes ought not discourage the small businessman.
15. *It stands to reason that* gravity is an important factor in space exploration.
16. On one side of the stage stood the American flag *in all its glory.*
17. Henry earns $52 a week by *the sweat of his brow.*
18. That highly ambitious secretary believes in *all work and no play.*
19. Knowing he was *doomed to disappointment,* he sank to *the depths of despair.*

20. After *working all day like a Trojan*, Mr. Gladwater *was tired but happy* as he *wended his way homeward*.

OTHER EXERCISES ON EXACTNESS

▶ EXERCISE 16   Look up the definitions of the following words in your dictionary; then use each word appropriately in an original sentence.

1. fabulous	6. cute	11. exotic	16. expedient
2. scandal	7. latent	12. dialect	17. equivocal
3. aspire	8. exploit	13. liberal	18. alleviate
4. judgment	9. amoral	14. simony	19. temperance
5. psychic	10. cynical	15. ironical	20. universality

▶ EXERCISE 17   The following passage from G. K. Chesterton is an excellent example of precise writing. Study the italicized expressions first with the aid of a dictionary and then in the context of the sentence and the paragraph. Substitute a synonym for each italicized word and compare its effectiveness with that of the original.

If a *prosperous* modern man, with a high hat and a frock-coat, were to solemnly *pledge* himself before all his clerks and friends to count the leaves on every third tree in Holland Walk, to hop up to the City on one leg every Thursday, to repeat the whole of Mill's "Liberty" seventy-six times, to collect three hundred dandelions in fields belonging to any one of the name of Brown, to remain for thirty-one hours holding his left ear in his right hand, to sing the names of all his aunts in order of age on the top of an omnibus, or make any such unusual undertaking, we should immediately *conclude* that the man was mad, or as it is sometimes expressed, was "an artist in life." Yet these *vows* are not more extraordinary than the vows which in the Middle Ages and in similar periods were made, not by *fanatics* merely, but by the greatest figures in civic and national civilization—by kings, judges, poets, and priests. One man swore to chain two mountains together, and the great chain hung there, it was said, for ages as a monument of that *mystical folly.* Another swore that he would find his way to Jerusalem with a patch over his eyes, and died looking for it. It is not easy to see that these two *exploits,* judged from a *strictly rational standpoint,* are any saner than the acts above suggested. A mountain is commonly a stationary and reliable object which it is not necessary to chain up at night like a dog. And it is not easy at first sight to see that a man pays a very high compliment to the Holy City by setting out for it under conditions which render it *to the last degree improbable* that he will ever get there.[3]

▶ EXERCISE 18   Carefully read the following paragraph, which sets forth in humorous fashion one of the home cures used by the English for the common cold. Be prepared for a class discussion of the author's appropriate diction, of his figurative language, of his choice of concrete, specific words.

[1] The Fresh-Air treatment is practiced only by those large red-faced men in check suits who look you in the eye, slap their chests, and declare they've never owned an overcoat or been to a doctor in their lives, as if claiming freedom from original sin. [2] They have a simple attitude to illness: it's all "psychological," from smallpox to fractured femurs. [3] But they are only human, and in time claimed by both death and colds. [4] The first sneeze affects them like a starter's pistol: they tear off their ties and waistcoats, stamp around the house throwing open the windows, jump into a cold bath, and upset their wives by doing breathing exercises all night in bed. [5] The discomfort in which they wallow for a fortnight makes no difference to the course

[3] From "A Defence of Rash Vows" by G. K. Chesterton, reprinted by permission of J. M. Dent & Sons, Ltd.

of the disease, but by rendering their surroundings unfit for human habitation they rarely manage to infect anyone else.[4]

▶ EXERCISE 19   Analyze Paragraph 28 of Section 31, page 345, for choice of words.

▶ EXERCISE 20   Choose the word inside parentheses which best suits the context of each item below.

1. To be an American and unable to play baseball is comparable to being a Polynesian unable to (swim, debate, drive).   —JOHN CHEEVER
2. Moonbeams (splash, twinkle, glow) and spill wildly in the rain.   —VIRGINIA WOOLF
3. Every evening at the rush hour the subway (releases, disgorges, gives out) its millions.   —JACQUES BARZUN
4. The scarecrow gave them an (unusual, eerie, elated) feeling when they saw it from the bedroom window at twilight.   —WILLIAM MAXWELL
5. Mr. Brook was a somewhat (pastel, ordinary, insipid) person.   —CARSON MC CULLERS
6. There was a roaring in my ears like the rushing of (music, rivers, breezes).   —STEPHEN VINCENT BENÉT
7. Superstitions, as Bacon said, like (birds, moths, bats) fly best in twilight, and the twilight of confused liberalism seems particularly favorable to them.   —BERGEN EVANS

[4] From "The Common Cold" by Richard Gordon, reprinted from the *Atlantic Monthly*, January, 1955. By permission of the *Atlantic Monthly* and Curtis Brown, Ltd.

Wordiness

21

Avoid wordiness. Repeat words only when needed for emphasis or clarity.

Today the best professional writers make each word count, avoiding the telegraphic as well as the verbose style. As you write and revise your composition, make sure that every word has a reason for being there, and eliminate all deadwood. When striking out unnecessary, meaningless, inappropriate words, keep in mind Allan Simpson's observation: "Every slaughtered syllable is a good deed."

21a

Omit words or phrases that add nothing to the meaning.[1]

Notice below that the words in brackets contribute nothing to meaning. Avoid such wordiness in your own writing.

1. all [of the] new styles [in this day and age]
2. yellow [in color], small [in size], eleven [in number]
3. circulated [around], cooperated [together], inside [of]
4. [true] facts, [erroneous] fallacies, a widow [woman]
5. [it was] in 1965 [that], at 9 A.M. [in the morning]

▶ EXERCISE 1   Without changing the meaning, strike out unnecessary words in the following sentences. Write *C* after each sentence that needs no revision.

[1] Bureaucratic jargon, called "gobbledygook," is often extremely wordy. See the example on page 197.

1. As a usual rule, all of the new cars of today have factory guarantees.
2. About midnight Halloween evening, Lucille dropped in for a short, unexpected visit.
3. It was in the year of 1964 that the joint partnership began to dissolve.
4. Architect James Hoban, the designer of the White House, was born in Dublin.
5. The venetian blind factory is close to the point of bankruptcy.
6. One reason why we honor Lincoln is because of the fact that he saved the Union.
7. The skillful English director made ruthless murder and flagrant blackmail the absurd hobbies of hilarious comedians.
8. The usual consensus of the majority is that Columbus discovered America.
9. Los Angeles is very different in various ways from the city of San Francisco.
10. In this day and time, it is difficult to find in the field of science a chemist who shows as much promise for the future as Joseph Blake shows.

21b

If necessary, revise the structure of the sentence to avoid wordiness.

Notice in the following examples how changes in sentence structure reduce two sentences of sixteen words to one sentence of eleven, ten, nine, and finally six words.

> There was a mist which hung like a veil. It obscured the top of the mountain.
>
> The mist *hung like a veil* and obscured the mountain top. [Part of a compound predicate]
>
> The mist, *hanging like a veil*, obscured the mountain top. [Participial phrase]

> The mist, *like a veil,* obscured the mountain top. [Prepositional phrase]
>
> The mist *veiled* the mountain top. [Word]

Any one of these sentences may, depending on the context, meet the special needs of the writer. By studying these examples, you can learn methods of revising the structure of your sentences to eliminate undesirable wordiness.

▶ EXERCISE 2　Revise the structure of the following sentences to eliminate wordiness.

1. There were six freshmen who volunteered.
2. When the Indians made tools, they used flint and bone as materials.
3. A new addition has been built at the side of the house, and this addition has been developed into a library.
4. Another thing is good health. It is one of our great blessings. It may be had through proper diet and exercise. Rest is also desirable.
5. My uncle was a tall man. He had a long nose. Over his right eye he had a deep scar.
6. If any workers were disgruntled, they made their complaints to the man who was in charge as manager.
7. Personally I believe it was the Spaniards rather than the Indians who first brought horses and ponies to America.
8. The grass was like a carpet. It covered the whole lawn. The color of the grass was a deep blue.
9. When anyone wants to start a garden, it is best to begin in the early part of the spring of the year.
10. Near the center of the campus of our university a new building has been erected, and it is constructed of red brick.

21c

Avoid careless or needless repetition of words or ideas.

Unless you are repeating intentionally for emphasis or for clarity in transitions, be careful not to write the same word twice or to write the same thing twice in slightly different words.

AWKWARD   Since the committee has already made three *reports,*
            only one *report* remains to be *reported* on.
BETTER   Since the committee has already made three reports,
            it has only one more to present.

REPETITIOUS Julia delights in giving parties; entertaining guests is
            a real pleasure for her.
CONCISE   Julia delights in giving parties.

Use a pronoun instead of needlessly repeating a noun. Several pronouns in succession, even in successive sentences, may refer to the same antecedent noun, so long as the reference remains clear.

NEEDLESS REPETITION   The upper-middlebrow consumer takes his
    culture seriously, as seriously as his job allows, for *the consumer*
    is gainfully employed. In *the consumer's* leisure hours he reads
    Toynbee or Osbert Sitwell's serialized memoirs. *The upper-
    middlebrow consumer* goes to museum openings and to the
    theater, and *the consumer* keeps up on the foreign films.

BETTER   The upper-middlebrow consumer takes his culture seri-
    ously, as seriously as his job allows, for he is gainfully em-
    ployed. In his leisure hours he reads Toynbee or Osbert Sitwell's
    serialized memoirs. He goes to museum openings and to the
    theater and he keeps up on the foreign films.

                                                    —RUSSELL LYNES

▶ EXERCISE 3   Revise the following sentences to eliminate wordiness and useless repetition.

1. In the last act of the play there is the explanation of the title of the play.
2. In the decade from 1950 to 1960, enrollments at universities doubled; in 1960 there were twice as many students as in 1950.
3. That morning we went to Jones Beach so that we could enjoy all the pleasures that that famous playground affords.

4. The National Gallery of Art, which is in Washington, D.C., and which contains the Mellon, Kress, and Widener collections of paintings and sculpture, is one of the largest marble structures in the entire world.

5. The radio announcer repeatedly kept saying, "Buy Peterson's Perfect Prawns," over and over and over again.

6. There were fifty people in the hospital ward who were among those who received great benefit from the new drug.

7. I had an advantage over the other contestants because of the fact that I had just looked up the word myself in a dictionary.

8. I got busy and got my assignment.

9. He found the problem of discovering the legal status of the migrant workers an almost insoluble problem.

10. In order that a man may apply to become a citizen of the United States he must make out an application stating his intention to become a citizen.

▶ **EXERCISE 4**   Rewrite the following passage to eliminate wordiness and useless repetition.

¹ Samuel Clemens (Mark Twain) was born in 1835 at Florida, County of Monroe, State of Missouri; but while he was still quite young, his family moved to Hannibal, a small Mississippi River town, where Samuel as a boy spent the days of his youth, and he grew up to young manhood there. ² In 1853 Samuel Clemens left this small Mississippi River town of Hannibal to see something of the world. ³ In his itinerant wandering during the next four years which followed, Clemens worked at the printing trade in printing shops of various cities in the East and Middle West from the Mississippi to the Atlantic seaboard. ⁴ In Cincinnati, Ohio, in the year of 1857 Clemens took passage on a river steamboat bound down the river for New Orleans, Louisiana. ⁵ On this trip down the river Clemens met the

pilot who steered the boat, named Mr. Horace Bixby, who agreed for the sum of five hundred dollars in money to teach young Clemens (Mark Twain) the art of piloting boats up and down the river. [6] One may read of Mark Twain's experience as a cub pilot apprentice in his book which he wrote about it and called *Life on the Mississippi.*

Omission of Necessary Words

22

Do not omit a word or phrase necessary to the meaning of the sentence.

Two reasons usually account for omissions of necessary words in student writing. The main reason is that the writer's mind is ahead of his pen; he thinks the word but does not write it. A second reason is that habits of informal speech reveal themselves in writing; an omission which may go unnoticed in spoken English may make a written sentence awkward or confusing.

> The analyst talked about the tax dollar goes. [The writer thought "talked about where" but did not write *where*.]
> I been considering changing my major. [Omission of *v* sound in saying *I've been* causes the omission of *have* in writing.]

To avoid omitting necessary words, you should not only carefully proofread your papers but also study the rules in this chapter.

22a

Do not omit an article, a pronoun, a conjunction, or a preposition that is necessary to make your meaning clear.

(1) Omitted article or pronoun

AWKWARD   Fog grounded all planes only week ago.
BETTER   Fog grounded all planes only *a* week ago.
CONFUSING A man has a job there makes good money.
CLEAR   A man *who* has a job there makes good money.

Note: If it is necessary to indicate plural number, repeat a pronoun or an article before the second part of a compound.

> My mother and father were there. [Clearly two persons—repetition of *my* before *father* not necessary]
> A friend and *a* helper stood nearby. [Two persons clearly indicated by repetition of *a*]

(2) Omitted conjunction

CONFUSING   They noticed the young men who made up the crew were eager to start. [*Young men* can be momentarily mistaken for the object of *noticed*.]

BETTER   They noticed *that* the young men who made up the crew were eager to start.

Note: The conjunction *that* is frequently omitted as an introduction to clauses when the omission is not confusing.

> Sid thinks the National League will win.

(3) Omitted preposition

AWKWARD   Winter the Bakers ski at Chestnut Lodge.

BETTER   In winter the Bakers ski at Chestnut Lodge.

Note: Some idiomatic phrases indicating time or place regularly omit the preposition.

> The package was mailed Friday (*on Friday*).
> Mrs. Melton stayed home (*at home*).

22b

Do not omit a necessary verb or a necessary auxiliary.

AWKWARD   The play is good and the characters interesting. [Singular *is* may be used with singular *play* but not with plural *characters*.]

BETTER   The play is good and the characters *are* interesting. [The correct verb is supplied for *characters*.]

AWKWARD He never has and never will be given proper recognition. [*Be* is the correct auxiliary for *will* but not for *has*.]

BETTER He never has *been* given proper recognition, and he never will be. [The correct auxiliary is supplied for *has*.]

22c

Do not omit words necessary to complete comparisons (or other constructions).

INCOMPLETE Ed's income is less than his wife.
COMPLETE Ed's income is less than *that of* his wife.

INCOMPLETE Snow here is as scarce as Miami.
COMPLETE Snow here is as scarce as *it is in* Miami.

CONFUSING Bruce likes me more than Ann.
CLEAR Bruce likes me more than *he likes* Ann (OR more than Ann *does*).

INCOMPLETE Harry is as old, if not older, than Paul.
COMPLETE Harry is as old *as*, if not older than, Paul.
BETTER Harry is as old *as* Paul, if not older.

INFORMAL Mr. Perkins is as shrewd as any man in the office.
FORMAL Mr. Perkins is as shrewd as any *other* man in the office.

Note: Incomplete comparisons often occur in advertising copy.

Inferior detergents are far more expensive. [More expensive than what?]

Note: Once a frame of reference has been established, an intelligible comparison may be made without explicit mention of the second term of the comparison.

From here, it is forty miles to the nearest ranch. The nearest town is even farther.

Formal writing avoids such intensives as *so, such,* and *too* without a completing phrase or clause.

INFORMAL	Peter was too ill.
FORMAL	Peter was too ill *to stay on the job.*
INFORMAL	Sue is so tone deaf.
FORMAL	Sue is so tone deaf *that she cannot tell "Three Blind Mice" from "The Star-Spangled Banner."*

▶ EXERCISE 1 Supply words that are omitted in the following sentences. Write *C* after every sentence that needs no revision.

1. The mystery of the stolen jewels reminds me of other mysteries like Sherlock Holmes.
2. The paint on sale is better than any paint on the market.
3. I found the performance too dull.
4. A girl has a face like that ought to win a beauty contest!
5. Our new car uses more gasoline.
6. In our state the winter is as mild as Louisiana.
7. Some people like cars with bucket seats much better.
8. Chifford cars are longer, faster, more economical to operate.
9. I always have and always will live in Kansas City.
10. The plains are mostly given over to cattle raising, not farming.
11. If Jack is in a profession he is not trained, he will not succeed.
12. The lawyer had to prove whatever the witness said was false.
13. You are as good, if not better, than anyone else.
14. Jim's wife and mother are standing beside him.
15. The merchandise is finest quality but the prices high.
16. Mr. Carter paid me more than Jim.
17. The pine trees here are as tall as Vermont.
18. Our city park is as attractive, if not more attractive, than yours.
19. The novels of Graham Greene are so controversial.
20. The work of the farmer requires longer hours than a plumber.

▶ EXERCISE 2   Supply words needed in the following paragraph.

¹ According to manual for drivers, every operator should know the state laws and traffic rules.   ² For example, he should know legal speeds both in town and out of town, state highways and city streets.   ³ He should also be aware of meaning of hand signals and blinking lights.   ⁴ Every good driver knows that safety is so important.   ⁵ He keeps at a safe distance from the ahead on the highway, he slows down before entering an intersection, and he is always in the proper lane for turning.   ⁶ A safe driver understands policemen who give traffic orders take precedence over signs or lights that give conflicting directions.   ⁷ Moreover, a driver who is safe is far more courteous, for he knows that at times discourtesy can actually break a law or even take a life.   ⁸ Knowledge and courtesy have and always will be among the characteristics of an excellent driver.

EFFECTIVE SENTENCES

Unity and Logical Thinking

Unity, coherence, emphasis, variety—these are fundamental qualities of effective prose. Unity and coherence in sentences help to make ideas logical and clear. Emphasis makes them forceful. Variety lends interest. All these are usually found in good writing.

23

Write unified, logical sentences.

A sentence is unified when all its parts contribute to one clear idea or impression. The ideal sentence is, of course, one with parts that form a perfect whole so that a clause, a phrase, or even a word cannot be changed without disturbing the clarity of thought or the focus of the impression. A study of this section should help you to write logical, unified sentences, sentences which are not cluttered with obscurities, irrelevancies, or excessive details.

23a

Bring into the sentence only related thoughts; use two or more sentences for thoughts not closely related.

As you write a sentence, make sure that the ideas in it are related and that the relationship is immediately clear to the reader. Use two or more sentences to develop ideas which do not belong in one sentence because of the lack of close relationship.

UNRELATED   The ancient name for Paris, a city which today has about 2,800,000 inhabitants, was Lutetia.

IMPROVED   Paris today has about 2,800,000 inhabitants. The ancient name of the city was Lutetia. [The two unrelated ideas are put into separate sentences, possibly in different parts of the paper.]

UNRELATED   Yesterday Ted sprained his ankle, and he could not find his chemistry notes anywhere.

RELATED   Accident-prone all day yesterday, Ted not only sprained his ankle but also lost his chemistry notes. [The relationship of the two ideas is made clear by the addition of the opening phrase.]

▶ EXERCISE 1 All ten sentences below contain ideas which are apparently unrelated. Adding words when necessary, rewrite each of the sentences to indicate clearly a relationship between ideas. If you can establish no close relationship, put the ideas in separate sentences.

1. I hate strong windstorms, and pecans pelted my bedroom roof all night.
2. The fence and barn need repairs, and why are property taxes so high?
3. There are many types of bores at social gatherings, but personally I prefer a quiet evening at home.
4. A telephone lineman who works during heavy storms can prove a hero, and cowards can be found in any walk of life.
5. Although barbers are not often found in the unemployed ranks, haircuts contribute to the economy of the nation.
6. Jones was told to hire a tutor in French immediately, but the long hours of work at a service station kept his grades low.
7. Macbeth was not the only man to succumb to ambition, and Professor Stetson, for example, likes to draw parallels between modern men and literary characters.
8. Brad sent his sweetheart a dozen red roses, and she sang on a fifteen-minute program over KTUV.

9. The food in the cafeteria has been the subject of many jokes, and most college students do not look underfed.
10. Birds migrate to the warmer countries in the fall and in summer get food by eating worms and insects which are a pest to the farmer.

23b

Excessive detail and clumsy, excessive subordination should not be allowed to obscure the central thought of the sentence.

Bring into a sentence only pertinent details. Omit tedious minutiae and numerous side remarks. Avoid also clumsy, overlapping subordination, the house-that-Jack-built construction.

EXCESSIVE SUBORDINATION   Never before have I known a student who was so ready to help a friend who had gotten into trouble which involved money.

BETTER   Never before have I known a student so ready to help a friend in financial trouble.

EXCESSIVE DETAIL   In 1788, when Andrew Jackson, then a young man of twenty-one years who had been living in the Carolinas, still a virgin country, came into Tennessee, a turbulent place of unknown opportunities, to enforce the law as the new prosecuting attorney, he had the qualities in him which would make him equal to the task.

BETTER   In 1788, when Andrew Jackson came into Tennessee as the new prosecuting attorney, he had the necessary qualifications for the task.

As you strive to eliminate irrelevant details, remember that length alone does not make a sentence ineffective. Good writers can compose very long sentences, sometimes of paragraph length, without loss of unity. The use of parallel structure, balance, rhythm, careful punctuation, well-placed connectives can bind a sentence into perfect unity. Observe the effective repetition (indicated by italics) in Winston Churchill's famous sentence:

We shall go on to the end, *we shall fight* in France, *we shall fight* on the seas and oceans, *we shall fight* with growing confidence and growing strength in the air, *we shall defend* our Island, whatever the cost may be, *we shall fight* on the beaches, *we shall fight* on the landing grounds, *we shall fight* in the fields and in the streets, *we shall fight* in the hills; *we shall never surrender,* and even if, which I do not for a moment believe, this Island or a large part of it were subjugated and starving, then our Empire beyond the seas, armed and guarded by the British Fleet, *would carry on the struggle,* until, in God's good time, the New World, with all its power and might, steps forth to the rescue and the liberation of the old.   —WINSTON CHURCHILL[1]

In the following sentence Henry James maintains unity by balancing the "grand hotel" with the "small Swiss pension." (Italics have been added.)

The shore of the lake presents an unbroken array of establishments of this order, of every category, *from the "grand hotel" of the newest fashion,* with a chalk-white front, a hundred balconies, and a dozen flags flying from its roof, *to the small Swiss pension of an elder day,* with its name inscribed in German-looking lettering upon a pink or yellow wall and an awkward summer-house in the angle of the garden.

—HENRY JAMES[2]

▶ **EXERCISE 2**   Recast the following sentences to eliminate excessive subordination or detail.

1. During the first period last Monday in Room 206 of the English building, we freshmen enjoyed discussing various dating codes.
2. The fan which Joan bought for her son who frets about any temperature that exceeds seventy arrived today.
3. When I was only four, living in a Colonial house, little of which remains today, I often walked alone the two miles from my house to the lake.

[1] From *Their Finest Hour* by Winston Churchill. By permission of Houghton Mifflin Company.
[2] From *Daisy Miller.*

4. Four cars of various designs and makes jammed together on the freeway, which was completed in 1961
at a cost of over a half million dollars.

5. In a dark, pin-striped suit the senator advocated drastic
reforms, occasionally taking time out for applause or a
sip of water.

6. The dilapidated boat, though seaworthy ten years ago
but badly in need of repairs now, moved out into the
bay.

7. Flames from the gas heater given us by Aunt Tina before she died three years ago licked at the chintz
curtains.

8. After finishing breakfast, which consisted of oatmeal,
toast, and coffee, Martha called the tree surgeon, a
man approximately fifty years old.

9. At last I returned the book that I had used for my report which I made Tuesday to the library.

10. A course in business methods helps the young man to
get a job in order that he may prove whether he is
fitted for business and thus avoid postponing the test,
as so many do, until it is too late.

23c

Mixed, obscure, or illogical constructions should be avoided.

(1) **Do not mix figures of speech by changing too rapidly from one to another.**

MIXED   Playing with fire can get a man into hot water.
BETTER   Playing with fire can result in burned fingers.

MIXED   Her plan to make it rain on Walter's parade was nipped
in the bud.
BETTER   Walter thwarted her plan to make it rain on his parade.

(2) **Do not mix constructions. Complete each construction logically.**

MIXED When Mr. Green plays the hypochondriac taxes his wife's patience. [Adverb clause, part of a complex sentence, is here combined with the predicate of a simple sentence.]

CLEAR Mr. Green's playing the hypochondriac taxes his wife's patience. [Simple sentence]

CLEAR When Mr. Green plays the hypochondriac, he taxes his wife's patience. [Complex sentence]

Note: In defining, professional writers tell *what* the thing defined is, not when it is or where it is.

AWKWARD A sonnet is when a poem has fourteen lines.
BETTER A sonnet is a poem of fourteen lines.

AWKWARD Banishing a person is where he is driven out of his country.
BETTER Banishing a person is driving him out of his country.

(3) **Make each part of the sentence agree logically with the other parts.**

Often a sentence is absurd because of failure in logical agreement resulting from a confusion of singular and plural words.

ILLOGICAL Many of those attending the convention brought their wife with them.
BETTER Many of those attending the convention brought their *wives* with them.

(4) **Do not use the double negative.**

NONSTANDARD I don't want none.
STANDARD I don't want any.

See **19i** under **but, hardly, scarcely.**

▶ **EXERCISE 3** Revise the following sentences to eliminate mixed, obscure, or illogical constructions.

1. For Don, money does grow on trees, and he lets it go down the drain easily.
2. Because raindrops are not the same size explains the difference in the speed of their falling.

3. Friction is when one surface scrapes another.
4. These women we freshmen would not want for a mother.
5. I wouldn't take nothing for that experience!
6. Like a bat guided by radar, Hilda toes the mark.
7. To be discreet is where a person carefully avoids saying or doing something wrong.
8. Does anyone here know why Mr. James resigned or where did he find a better job?
9. Tourists are not permitted to bring their camera inside the area.
10. When a man needs glasses causes him to make mistakes.

23d

Do not make illogical statements.

One of the most important tests of good writing is the soundness of its reasoning. You should make sure that all your sentences are well thought out and contain no slips or weaknesses in your chain of reasoning. Be especially careful to avoid the common fallacies by observing the following principles of sound thinking.

(1) Be sure your generalizations are sufficiently supported.

FAULTY None of the children in my family drink coffee; children do not like coffee. [The writer has jumped to a conclusion without finding a sufficient number of examples or instances to support his belief.]

FAULTY When an automobile accident occurs in this city, the police are never on hand. [Unless the writer has himself seen or read an authoritative account of every automobile accident in the city, he cannot sensibly make this assertion. By avoiding such words as *never* and *always*, using instead such qualifiers as *sometimes* or *often*, the writer can generalize more safely.]

(2) **Be sure your evidence is objective and relevant to your assertion.**

FAULTY   Henry is an honest boy; he will make a success of anything he tries. [Obviously, Henry's honesty cannot guarantee his success at a task for which he may be intellectually unsuited. The writer's inference does not follow from the evidence.]

FAULTY   Donald is an atheist and a profligate; his arguments against a sales tax are worthless. [The writer here tries to discredit Donald's ideas by attacking him as a man. Donald might be a dissolute man, however, and still have excellent views on economic problems such as the sales tax.]

FAULTY   Joseph Jones, our distinguished candidate for mayor, has been endorsed by Miss Leila Lovely, Hollywood's brightest star. [This fallacy is the opposite of the previous one. The writer is using Miss Lovely's prestige as an actress to enhance the political reputation of Joseph Jones. But what are Miss Lovely's qualifications to be considered an expert on politics?]

▶ EXERCISE 4   Be prepared to contribute to a class discussion of the faulty reasoning in the sentences below.

1. Everybody goes to Florida in the winter.
2. Breaking a mirror will bring on seven years of bad luck.
3. Do not vote for my opponent as mayor; his parents were not born in America.
4. Young people nowadays do not obey their parents.
5. Joseph will be a good class president because all his classmates like him.
6. Of course the other car was at fault: the driver was a woman.
7. I am certain that all Germans like opera; I have never met one who did not like it.
8. I ate shrimp last night, and therefore I am sick today.
9. I always buy these razor blades because all the baseball players use them.

10. After the first atomic bomb was exploded, it rained for a week in my home town, and yet the scientists maintain that atomic explosions do not affect the weather!

▶ EXERCISE 5 Write approximately a hundred words either supporting or refuting one of the following statements. Make sure that you bring into each sentence only related ideas and pertinent details. Carefully avoid mixed or obscure constructions as you clearly present logical, convincing evidence in support of your point of view.

1. The learned think themselves superior to the common herd. —W. T. STACE
2. Today Christmas is a major factor in our capitalist economy. —ALDOUS HUXLEY
3. Few people see the long-range implications of juvenile delinquency. —JUDGE ELIJAH ADLOW
4. Not one of us who has thought about it expects man as we know him to be on this planet a million years from now. —HARLOW SHAPLEY
5. The notion that advertising can somehow "manipulate" people into buying products which they should not buy is both arrogant and naïve. —MARTIN MAYER

Subordination

(An Aid to Unity)

24

Use subordination to relate ideas concisely and effectively; use coordination only to give ideas equal emphasis.

In grammar, subordination relates ideas by combining dependent elements with independent ones. (See Section 1, pages 14–23.) The principle of subordination is of great importance in composition since it is one of the best means of achieving sentence unity.

One of the marks of a mature style is effective use of subordination, particularly modifying phrases and clauses which give grammatical focus to main clauses. Inexperienced writers tend to use too many short simple sentences or stringy compound sentences. Compare the style of the groups of sentences below.

COORDINATION   Frank was listening to the radio. He heard the news then. His mother was killed in an automobile accident. The accident had occurred at ten o'clock.

SUBORDINATION   *Listening to the radio,* Frank heard *that his mother had been killed in an automobile accident at ten o'clock.* [A participial phrase, a noun clause, and a prepositional phrase replace three simple sentences.]

COORDINATION   Some students cheat, and they receive high grades, but they should be caught and penalized.

SUBORDINATION Students *who cheat* should be caught and penalized *instead of receiving high grades.* [An
adjective clause and a preposition with a
gerund-phrase object replace two main clauses.]

As the subordinate clauses in the examples above indicate, grammatically subordinate structures may contain
very important ideas.

24a

**Use subordination to combine a related series of short,
ineffective sentences into longer units.**

When combining a series of related choppy sentences,
first choose one complete idea for your sentence base;
then use subordinate structures (such as modifying phrases
or clauses, parenthetical elements, and appositives) to relate the ideas in the other simple sentences to the base.

CHOPPY We must learn two things. We have to control ourselves.
We must live in peace with our neighbors. If not, we
shall not even be in a position to regret it.

BETTER Unless we learn to control ourselves and to live in peace
with our neighbors, we shall not even be in a position
to regret it. —DANA L. FARNSWORTH

CHOPPY He stood there in his buckskin clothes. One felt in him
standards and loyalties. One also felt a code. This code
is not easily put into words. But this code is instantly
felt when two men who live by it come together by
chance.

BETTER As he stood there in his buckskin clothes, one felt in him
standards, loyalties, a code which is not easily put into
words, but which is instantly felt when two men who
live by it come together by chance. —WILLA CATHER

Caution: Avoid excessive or clumsy, overlapping subordination. See **23b.**

► EXERCISE 1 Combine the following short sentences into longer sentences in which ideas are properly subordinated.

¹ The miller was a large man. ² He weighed well over two hundred pounds. ³ He wore a red beard. ⁴ It was thick and broad and was shaped like a spade. ⁵ On his nose grew a wart. ⁶ Red bristles sprouted out of the wart. ⁷ This miller was a quarrelsome man. ⁸ He was proud of his bull-like strength. ⁹ He missed no chance to display it. ¹⁰ He especially liked to show off by tearing down doors. ¹¹ He would jerk them off their hinges. ¹² He could also butt them to pieces with his head. ¹³ Sometimes there was no door convenient. ¹⁴ Then he would get attention in other ways. ¹⁵ He was a loud-mouth. ¹⁶ He always had a story ready to tell. ¹⁷ His stories were ones he had picked up in barrooms. ¹⁸ Usually they were filthy. ¹⁹ It didn't matter that decent people were nearby. ²⁰ He would tell his story anyhow. ²¹ He had to make a noisy display of himself in one way or another. ²² He never ran out of ways of doing it. ²³ He might not be able to find a door to wreck. ²⁴ People sometimes wouldn't listen to his stories. ²⁵ He played a bagpipe. ²⁶ His behavior had its reward. ²⁷ It kept him from being a very well-liked man.

24b

Do not write a series of main clauses strung together with *and*, *so*, or *but* when ideas should be subordinated. Use coordination only to give ideas equal emphasis.

WEAK   There was a perfect full moon with theatrically silver light, and this should be a must for all future power failures, and so people peered into the faces of passersby, but they acted like children at a Halloween party, and they appeared to be trying to guess which friends were hiding behind which masks.

BETTER   In the theatrically silver light of a perfect full moon (a must for all future power failures) people peered into the faces of passersby like children at a Halloween party trying to guess which friends hide behind which masks.

—LOUDON WAINWRIGHT

ACCEPTABLE   The offer was tempting, but I did not accept it. [Coordination used to stress equally the offer and the refusal]

USUALLY BETTER   Although the offer was tempting, I did not accept it. [Stress on one of the two—the refusal]

The conjunctive adverbs *however, therefore,* and *consequently* are often used in transitions when subordination would be preferable. Main clauses linked by these conjunctive adverbs can usually be combined and the proper relationship indicated by a subordinating conjunction. Subordinating conjunctions express such relationships as cause (*because, since*), concession (*although*), time (*after, before, since, whenever, while, until*), place (*where*), or condition (*if, unless*).

COORDINATION   I became increasingly uneasy; however, I kept my seat.

SUBORDINATION   Although I became increasingly uneasy, I kept my seat. [Subordination is usually better.]

COORDINATION   Fred knows almost nothing about farming; therefore I do not expect him to enjoy much success.

SUBORDINATION   Since Fred knows almost nothing about farming, I do not expect him to enjoy much success.

▶ EXERCISE 2   Revise the following sentences to achieve unity by way of effective subordination.

1. Jean Henri Dunant was a citizen of Switzerland, and he felt sorry for wounded Austrian soldiers in the Napoleonic Wars; therefore, he started an organization, and it was later named the Red Cross.
2. Yesterday I was daydreaming, so I did not hear the physics assignment, but anyway I passed the test today.
3. First he selected a lancet and sterilized it, and then he

gave his patient a local anesthetic and lanced the infected part.

4. Father Latour was at a friend's house, and he saw two fine horses, and he induced the owner to part with them.

5. I graduated from high school, and then I worked in a bank, and so I earned enough to go to college.

6. The president of the bank walked into his office promptly at nine, and just then he saw the morning paper, and the headlines startled him.

7. We had just reached the bend in the road, for we were on our way home, and we saw a truckload of laborers crowded off the highway by an oncoming bus.

8. The Spanish started the custom in America of branding cattle, and the Mexicans kept it going, and Americans still brand cattle to show ownership.

9. Daniel Fahrenheit made a thermometer, and he used mercury in it; however, René Réaumur devised one too, but he used alcohol instead of mercury.

10. A wife wears a ring on the third finger of the left hand, for a vein runs from it to the heart, according to an old tale; therefore, the ring symbolizes the giving of the heart with the hand.

24c

Avoid illogical as well as awkward subordination.

When writing sentences such as the following, you are free to choose whatever you please for the subordinate structure. Your decision to subordinate one idea to another will depend upon what you wish to emphasize.

Although I know that the weather reports often err, I listen to them avidly.

Although I listen to the weather reports avidly, I know that they often err.

Placement of ideas in subordinate positions, however, is sometimes fixed. In the following sentence, for example, logic requires that one idea be subordinated rather than the other.

COORDINATION   I struck the match, and at that moment the oven exploded.

ABSURD SUBORDINATION   When the oven exploded, I struck the match.

LOGICAL SUBORDINATION   When I struck the match, the oven exploded. (OR The oven exploded when I struck the match.)

Many writers tend to avoid putting their most significant ideas in subordinate structures.

A cow that kicked a lantern over caused the great Chicago fire. (NOT A cow kicked a lantern over, causing the great Chicago fire.)

Note: Do not thwart subordination by inserting an inappropriate *and* or *but* before *which, who,* or *whom.*

AWKWARD   Law enforcement is a problem and which troubles the mayor.

IMPROVED   Law enforcement is a problem which troubles the mayor.

▶ **EXERCISE 3**   Revise the following sentences as necessary to eliminate awkward or illogical subordination.

1. Louise has had great success but which has not gone to her head.
2. Although David slept soundly, the deafening noise continued.
3. Mr. Dunbar is a good lawyer and who nearly always wins his cases.
4. As soon as we ate turkey, Thanksgiving arrived.
5. My father is an electrician and whom his customers depend on.
6. Even though I will not cut down the ragweed, I have hay fever.
7. Bruce found a lost hound and which needs a home.

▶ EXERCISE 4   Revise the following passage to achieve proper subordination.

¹ I was walking down the street when I found a purse containing fifty dollars.   ² It was just noon.   ³ Thousands of people were on the streets.   ⁴ I could not find the owner.   ⁵ I went into the neighboring stores, and I inquired of the shopkeepers whether anyone had lost the money, and I approached the policeman with the same question.   ⁶ No one could say who had lost the money, and so I thought I was the rightful owner, having found the purse myself.   ⁷ But my father did not approve my keeping the purse.   ⁸ He asked me to advertise it.   ⁹ He said I might use the daily paper.   ¹⁰ Next day I ran an advertisement in the paper, and now a week has passed and I have had no answers, and so I think the money is really mine.

▶ EXERCISE 5   Be prepared to contribute to a class discussion of the subordination of ideas in paragraphs 9 and 41, pages 330 and 354–55, of Section **31**.

Coherence:
Misplaced Parts;
Dangling Modifiers

25

Avoid needless separation of related parts of the sentence. Avoid dangling modifiers.

The meaning of an English sentence depends largely on the position of its parts. Usually these parts—especially the words, phrases, and subordinate clauses serving as modifiers—can be placed in various positions; and they should be placed to give just the emphasis or meaning desired. Note how the meaning in the following sentences changes according to the position of the modifier *only:*

> She said that she loved *only* him.
>   [She loved no one else.]
> She said that *only* she loved him.
>   [No one else loved him.]
> She said *only* that she loved him.
>   [She said nothing else.]
> She *only* said that she loved him.
>   [She didn't mean it.]
> *Only* she said that she loved him.
>   [No one else said it.]
> She said that she *only* loved him.
>   [Even love has its limitations.]

Normally the modifier should be placed as near the word modified as idiomatic English will permit.

Note: If you cannot distinguish readily the various modifiers and the parts of the sentence discussed in this chapter, review Section 1, especially **1d,** and Section 4.

Misplaced Parts

25a

Avoid needless separation of related parts of the sentence.

(1) In standard written English, adverbs such as *almost, only, just, even, hardly, nearly,* or *merely* are regularly placed immediately before the words they modify.

In spoken English, which tends to place these adverbs before the verb, ambiguity can be prevented by stressing the word to be modified.

AMBIGUOUS IN WRITING He is *just* asking for a trifle.
CLEAR He is asking for *just* a trifle.

INFORMAL The house *only* costs $12,500.
FORMAL The house costs *only* $12,500.

▶ EXERCISE 1 Place the adverbs in the following sentences immediately before the words they modify.

1. Some contemporary poets hardly show any interest in making their poems intelligible.
2. I only bet on the horse to take third place.
3. He took the penny home and polished it almost until it looked like new.
4. The man was only willing to sell a part of the farm.
5. He even works during his vacation.

(2) The position of a modifying prepositional phrase should clearly indicate what the phrase modifies.

A prepositional phrase used as an adjective nearly always immediately follows the word modified.

MISPLACED Mother gave date muffins to my *friends with pecans in them.*
CLEAR Mother gave my friends date *muffins with pecans in them.*

The position of a prepositional phrase used as an adverb is ordinarily not so fixed as that of an adjective phrase. Adverb phrases are usually placed near the word modified or at the beginning or end of a sentence. Sometimes, however, the usual placement can be awkward because the intended modification is not clear.

MISPLACED   One student said that such singing was not music but *a throat ailment in class.*

CLEAR   *In class* one student said that such singing was not music but a throat ailment. [OR One student *said in class* that such singing was not music but a throat ailment.]

▶ EXERCISE 2   Recast the following sentences to correct undesirable separation of related parts. Explain exactly what ambiguity each separation causes in each sentence.

1. Newspapers carried the story of the quarterback's fumbling all over the country.
2. At the age of two, my mother put me in a nursery school.
3. Students could not understand why Plato and Socrates were so wise in high school.
4. Gertrude served sundaes at the picnic to hungry guests in paper cups.
5. The professor made it clear why plagiarism is wrong on Monday.

(3) Adjective clauses should be placed near the words they modify.

AWKWARD   We bought gasoline in Arkansas at a small country store *which cost $3.12.* [*Which* does not refer to *store.*]

CLEAR   At a small country store in Arkansas, we bought gasoline *which cost $3.12.* [*Which* refers to *gasoline.*]

AWKWARD   I saw the horse stop at the edge of the precipice *that had raced ahead.*

CLEAR   I saw the horse *that had raced ahead* stop at the edge of the precipice.

(4) Avoid "squinting" constructions—modifiers that may refer either to a preceding or to a following word.

SQUINTING	I agreed *on the next day* to help him.
CLEAR	I agreed to help him *on the next day.*
CLEAR	*On the next day,* I agreed to help him.
SQUINTING	The tug which was whistling *noisily* chugged up the river.
CLEAR	The whistling tug chugged *noisily* up the river.
CLEAR	The tug whistled *noisily* as it chugged up the river.

(5) Avoid awkward separation of parts of verb phrases and awkward splitting of infinitives.

AWKWARD	There stood the old car which we *had* early last autumn *left* by our lake cottage.
IMPROVED	There stood the old car which we *had left* by our lake cottage early last autumn.
AWKWARD	You should now begin *to,* if you wish to succeed, *hunt* for a job.
IMPROVED	If you wish to succeed, you should now begin *to hunt* for a job. [In general avoid the "split" infinitive unless it is needed for smoothness or clarity.]

Note: Although all split infinitives were once considered questionable, those which are not awkward are now acceptable.

Americans seem to always be searching for something new.

—NEWSWEEK

Dangling Modifiers

25b

Avoid dangling modifiers.

Although any misplaced word, phrase, or clause dangles whenever it hangs loosely within a sentence, the term *dangling* is applied especially to incoherent verbal phrases and elliptical clauses. A dangling modifier is one that does not refer clearly and logically to some word in the sentence.

When verbal phrases or elliptical clauses come at the beginning of a sentence, the normal English word order requires that they immediately precede and clearly refer to the subject of the sentence.

PARTICIPLE   *Taking our seats,* we watched the game. [We took our seats.]

GERUND   After *watching the late show,* Nancy was tired. [Nancy watched the late show.]

INFINITIVE   *To avoid the rush-hour traffic,* Mr. Clark left the office early. [Mr. Clark avoided the rush-hour traffic.]

ELLIPTICAL CLAUSE   *When only a small boy,* I went with my father to Denver. [*I was* is implied in the elliptical clause.]

To correct a dangling modifier, (1) rearrange the words in the sentence to make the modifier sensibly refer to the right word, or (2) add words to make the meaning clear and logical.

(1) Avoid dangling participial phrases.

DANGLING   *Taking* our seats, the game started. [*Taking* does not refer to the subject *game,* nor to any other word in the sentence.]

IMPROVED   *Taking* (OR *Having taken*) our seats, *we* watched the opening of the game. [*Taking* refers to *we,* the subject of the sentence.]

IMPROVED   *After we had taken our seats,* the game started. [Participial phrase expanded into a clause]

DANGLING   The evening passed very pleasantly, *eating* candy and *playing* the radio. [*Eating* and *playing* refer to nothing in the sentence.]

IMPROVED   *We* passed the evening very pleasantly, *eating* candy and *playing* the radio. [*Eating* and *playing* refer to *we,* the subject of the main clause.]

Note: Participles do not dangle when they are used in an absolute phrase or used to introduce or refer to a general truth.

> *Weather permitting,* we will have a cookout.
> *Generally speaking,* a pessimist is an unhappy man.

(2) Avoid dangling phrases containing gerunds.

DANGLING *By mowing the grass high and infrequently,* your lawn can be beautiful. [Who is to do the mowing?]

IMPROVED By *mowing* the grass high and infrequently, *you* can have a beautiful lawn.

(3) Avoid dangling infinitive phrases.

DANGLING *To write* well, good books must be read. [The understood subject of *to write* should be the same as the subject of the sentence.]

IMPROVED *To write* well, a *student* must read good books. [*To write* refers to *student,* the subject of the sentence.]

DANGLING *To run* efficiently, proper oiling is needed.

IMPROVED *To run* efficiently, the *machine* must be properly oiled.

Note: Infinitives do not dangle when they introduce a general truth rather than designate the action of a specific person or thing.

> To be brief, rats carry disease.
> To judge from reports, all must be going well.

(4) Avoid dangling elliptical clauses (or phrases).

An elliptical clause—that is, a clause with an implied subject and verb—"dangles" unless the implied subject is the same as that of the main clause.

DANGLING When only a small boy (OR At the age of nine), my father took me with him to Denver. [*I was* is implied in the elliptical clause.]

IMPROVED When I was only a small boy (OR When I was nine years old), my father took me with him to Denver. [Elliptical clause expanded]

IMPROVED When only a small boy (OR At the age of nine), *I* went with my father to Denver. [Subject of the main clause made the same as the implied subject of the subordinate clause]

DANGLING Prepare to make an incision in the abdomen as soon as completely anesthetized.

IMPROVED Prepare to make an incision in the abdomen as soon as the patient is completely anesthetized.

▶ **EXERCISE 3**   Revise the following sentences to eliminate dangling modifiers. Write *C* after each sentence that needs no revision.

1. While wondering about this phenomenon, the sun sank from view.
2. By standing and repeating the pledge, the meeting came to an end.
3. Once made, you must execute the decision promptly.
4. To speak effectively, eye contact is needed.
5. After sitting there awhile, it began to snow, and we went indoors.
6. Darkness having come, we stopped for the night.
7. Having taken his seat, we began to question the witness.
8. To grow good tomatoes, be sure to provide stakes for the vines.
9. Entering Chicago from the west, a whole network of stockyards is the first thing seen.
10. Before eating breakfast, the table had to be cleared.

▶ **EXERCISE 4**   Revise the following sentences to improve coherence. Write *C* after each sentence that needs no revision.

1. The car was advertised in last night's paper which is only two years old and is clean.
2. We have seed in a large can in our garage for sparrows.
3. Marvin wanted to, even during the 6:15 P.M. sports news, finish our game of checkers.

4. An official warned the hunter not to carry a rifle in a car that was loaded.
5. Selby said in the evening he would go.
6. To sum up, the candidate easily won the election.
7. Rusty ought to always be kept on a leash or in the yard.
8. Being in a hurry to leave Denver, the dented fender was not repaired then.
9. Mr. Waters promised again to visit the newcomers.
10. Having a broken arm and nose, I thought the statue was very ugly.
11. The slaves were unwilling to submit to his plans, thinking they could free themselves.
12. After taking only a few steps, I discovered that I had forgotten my keys.
13. You are, considering the whole affair, very fortunate.
14. The first thing a student must learn is to think for himself upon entering college.
15. Located on a mountain top, this made it an ideal place for a summer resort.
16. Henry promised when he was on his way home to stop at the library.
17. To irrigate successfully, water must flow through carefully planned ditches.
18. The Browns returned this morning from their vacation in the mountains on the bus.
19. Before taking a first trip by air, the thought of flying frightens one.
20. Keep stirring the water into the mixture until pale green.

Parallelism

26

Use parallel structure as an aid to coherence.

Words, phrases, clauses, or sentences are parallel when they have balanced grammatical structure. According to Simeon Potter, balanced sentences satisfy "a profound human desire for equipoise and symmetry." Use parallel form, especially with coordinating conjunctions, in order to express your ideas naturally and logically.

26a

For parallel structure, balance a word with a word, a phrase with a phrase, a clause with a clause, a sentence with a sentence.

As you study the following examples of parallelism, notice that a noun is balanced with nouns, an active verb with active verbs, an infinitive phrase with an infinitive phrase, a noun clause with a noun clause, a complex sentence with a complex sentence. Notice also that repetition of words can emphasize the parallel structure. One item in a series may be expanded without marring the total effect of the parallelism.

(1) Words

AWKWARD   The way we write reveals our bent, our inclinations, and what our inner drives are. [Nouns and subordinate clause not parallel]

PARALLEL   The way we write reveals ‖ our *bent*,
‖ our *inclinations*,
‖ our inner *drives*.
—CHARLES W. FERGUSON

AWKWARD   As the forest lives, decays, and is devoured by itself, it spawns exotic creatures. [Active verbs not parallel to passive verb]

PARALLEL   As the forest ‖ *lives,*
           ‖ *decays,* and
           ‖ *devours* itself,

it spawns exotic creatures. —NATIONAL GEOGRAPHIC

(2) Phrases

AWKWARD   It is easier to love humanity as a whole than loving one's neighbor. [Infinitive phrase and gerund phrase not parallel]

PARALLEL   It is easier ‖ *to love humanity* as a whole than
          ‖ *to love* one's *neighbor.* —ERIC HOFFER

(3) Clauses

AWKWARD   What we say and the things that we do somehow seem out of joint. [Noun clause not parallel to noun modified by adjective clause]

PARALLEL   ‖ *What we say* and
        ‖ *what we do*   somehow seem out of joint.
                                  —NORMAN COUSINS

(4) Sentences

PARALLEL   ‖ *The danger of the past was that men became slaves.*
        ‖ *The danger of the future is that men may become*
        ‖ *robots.*   —ERICH FROMM

Caution: Do not use parallel structure for sentence elements not parallel in thought. Never use an awkward or unidiomatic expression for the sake of a parallel. Lack of parallel structure is preferable.

MISLEADING   Our meetings were held on Friday afternoon, on Saturday morning, and on Saturday afternoon we started home.

CLEAR   Our meetings were held on Friday afternoon and on Saturday morning. On Saturday afternoon we started home.

AWKWARD A teacher attempts to teach something, fails to inspire the pupil, kills the desire to learn, and hammers on cold iron. [Parallel structure used for ideas that could be related more clearly and effectively by way of subordination.]

BETTER A teacher who is attempting to teach without inspiring the pupil with a desire to learn is hammering on cold iron. —HORACE MANN

▶ **EXERCISE 1** Underline the parallel structures in the following sentences, and be prepared to participate in a class discussion of the grammatical constructions. (If necessary, review Section 1, especially 1c and 1d.)

1. Not alone our physical acts but our ethics and our very emotions are to be channeled, standardized, massformulated. —J. FRANK DOBIE

2. The birth of language is the dawn of humanity. The line between man and beast—between the highest ape and the lowest savage—is the language line.
   —SUSANNE K. LANGER

3. Without criticism abuses will go unrebuked; without dissent our dynamic system will become static.
   —HENRY STEELE COMMAGER

4. Not for a single moment did he ever compromise with what he believed, with what he dreamed.
   —DEEMS TAYLOR

5. Broadly speaking, human beings may be divided into three classes: those who are toiled to death, those who are worried to death, and those who are bored to death.
   —WINSTON CHURCHILL

▶ **EXERCISE 2** Achieve parallelism in each of the following sentences (adapted from the *National Geographic Magazine*) by using the structure of the italicized words. When revising for parallel structure, do not copy the entire sentence; copy only the parallel items (properly punctuated), as in the example.

EXAMPLE   The trees are magnificent—*twisted by winds, hammered by storms,* and snows press them under.

REVISION   . . . twisted by winds, hammered by storms, pressed under snows.

1. The cameramen spent months *in primitive areas, in African heat, in Alaskan blizzards,* and where there are jungles in South America.
2. I missed the wild loneliness of the Cinqueterre, *its hard-won vineyards, its silent olive trees,* its villages that were isolated.
3. On the machinist's bench stood a variety of plastic birds, *opening and closing their beaks, turning their heads,* and their tails flipped.
4. During Divali festivals, the Indians like *to paint their houses, to buy new clothes,* exchanging visits, and offering prayers for prosperity.
5. They say in Arizona that men *tear down nature's mountains, run them through mills and smelters,* and of the waste new mountains are built.
6. We took advantage of exactly the right combination of *weather, temperature, equipment,* the surface of the mountain, and the moonlight which we were so grateful for.
7. We aimed to show the mothers the importance of a balanced diet—*that unpolished wheat has virtues, that vitamin B prevents beriberi,* and the value of protein foods.
8. Mainly *from the Central Highlands, from the Indian river section,* and the groves located near Tampa come a quarter of the world's oranges and tangerines.
9. Genoa is the *geographical, historical,* and logically the capital of the Ligurian coast.
10. *The lake was only a small sapphire glinting behind a tiny wall;* there were the canals which looked as if they were only silver threads as they wound across a plain.

26b

Whenever necessary to make the parallel clear, repeat a preposition, an article, an auxiliary verb, the sign of the infinitive, or the introductory word of a long phrase or clause. (See also **22c**.)

AWKWARD   I admire Tennyson *for the ideals* in his poems but not *his style.*

IMPROVED   I admire Tennyson ‖ *for the ideals* in his peoms
                                but not
                                for his style.

AWKWARD   In the wreck the circus lost *a camel* and *elephant.*

IMPROVED   In the wreck the circus lost ‖ *a camel* and
                                        an elephant.

OBSCURE   He explained *that* the advertising campaign had been successful, business had increased more than fifty per cent, and additional capital was sorely needed.

CLEARER   He explained ‖ *that* the advertising campaign had been successful,
                          that business had increased more than fifty per cent, and
                          that additional capital was sorely needed.

▶ EXERCISE 3   Insert words that will bring out the parallel structure in the following sentences.

1. Take as much time as you need—a day, hour, year.
2. I intend to do two things: to try and succeed.
3. I told Katherine that I could not go and I had good reasons.
4. The professor assigned this poem and short story by Poe.
5. The sentences are difficult to understand, not because they are long but they are obscure.
6. The child learns in nursery school to take his turn, to respect the rights of others, and take care of his materials.

7. They would lie on the battlefield for hours and sometimes days.
8. Not only has he visited the patients, but also sung ballads for them.
9. One can learn much more by studying than worrying.
10. The hunter was outwitted by a tiny raccoon and buffalo herd.

26c

Correlatives (*either . . . or, neither . . . nor, both . . . and, not only . . . but also, whether . . . or*) should be followed by elements that are parallel in form.

FAULTY   He was not only *kind* but also *knew* when to help people.
          [Adjective paralleled with verb]
BETTER   He was ‖ *not only kind*
                 but also helpful.

FAULTY   I debated whether *I should give* the beggar money or *to offer* him food.
          [Subordinate clause paralleled with infinitive]
BETTER   I debated ‖ *whether to give* the beggar money
                 or to offer him food.

26d

Be sure that a *who* (or *which*) clause precedes *and who* (or *and which*).

FAULTY   Inez Carter is a woman of great charm and who is popular. [A *who* clause does not precede the *and who;* the *of* phrase is not parallel to the *who* clause.]
BETTER   Inez Carter is a woman ‖ *who has great charm* and
                             who is popular.

▶ EXERCISE 4   Revise the following sentences by using parallel structure to express parallel ideas. Write *C* after each sentence that needs no revision.

1. I like a detective story with exciting action and which keeps me guessing.
2. You will enjoy painting a favorite corner of the room, showing an armchair, drop-leaf table, and lamp.
3. Someone has said that Americans cannot enjoy life without a TV set, an automobile, and a summer cottage.
4. My friend told me that the trip would be delayed but to be ready to start on Friday.
5. William is a boy with a good mind and who has the highest principles.
6. A sea lion watches carefully the action of his fellows and how they obey their trainer.
7. He was quiet and in a serious mood after the talk.
8. I did not know whether I should go to some technical school or to enter a liberal arts college.
9. The secretary must attend all meetings, call the roll, and keep the minutes.
10. People fall naturally into two classes: the workers and those who like to lean on others.

▶ EXERCISE 5   First carefully read the paragraphs below, observing all parallel constructions. Then write a similar composition of your own on a subject such as the importance of music, the value of travel, the beauty of friendship, or the impact of automation.

¹ Man's greatest source of enlightenment lies in the printed word.   ² No amount of persuasion can forever take away its imprint on the minds of a searching public. ³ Passing years cannot dilute its great truths nor still its gifts of laughter.   ⁴ It alone passes from generation to generation the sum of mankind's knowledge and experience.

⁵ Through the medium of printing you can live a thousand lives in one.   ⁶ You can discover America with Columbus, pray with Washington at Valley Forge, stand with Lincoln at Gettysburg, work in the laboratory with Franklin,

Edison, Pasteur or Salk and walk the fields with St. Francis.
[7] Through printing you can encompass in your imagination
the full sweep of world history.   [8] You can watch the rise
and fall of civilizations, the ebb and flow of mighty battles
and the changing pattern of life through the ages.
[9] Through printing you can live a mental life of adventure.
[10] You can roam with Marco Polo, sail the seas with
Magellan, be a swashbuckling Musketeer, a member of
Robin Hood's band of merry men, a Knight of King
Arthur's Round Table or a conqueror of space.

[11] Printing lets you enrich your spirit with the Psalms,
the Sermon on the Mount, the Beatitudes and all the other
noble writings that are touched with divine fire.   [12] You
can know the majesty of great poetry, the wisdom of great
philosophers, the findings of the scientists.

[13] You can start today where the great thinkers of yesterday left off because printing has immortalized man's
knowledge.   [14] Thinkers dead a thousand years are as alive
in their works today as when they walked the earth.
[15] Through printing you can orient your life to the world
you live in, for printing links the past, the present and the
future.   [16] It is ever-changing and immutably constant, as
old as civilization and as new as this morning's newspaper.

[17] It is man's enduring achievement.[1]

▶ **EXERCISE 6**   Indicate parallelism in Lincoln's Gettysburg
Address. See Section 1, Exercise 14.

[1] By permission of the Padgett Printing Corporation, Dallas.

Point of View

27

Maintain a consistent point of view as an aid to coherence.

Sudden and illogical shifts in point of view tend to obscure the meaning and thus to cause needless difficulty in reading.

27a

Avoid needless shifts in tense. (See also **7d.**)

SHIFT   The boy *closed* his book and *hurries* away to the playground. [A shift from past tense to present tense]

BETTER   The boy *closed* his book and *hurried* away to the playground. [Both verbs in the past tense]

Note: When the historical present is used, as in summarizing plots of narratives, care will be needed to avoid slipping from the present tense into the past tense.

Romeo *goes* in disguise to a Capulet feast, *falls* in love with Juliet, and *marries* (not *married*) her secretly.

27b

Avoid needless shifts in mood. (See also **7d.**)

SHIFT   First *rise* to your feet and then you *should address* the chairman. [A shift from imperative to indicative mood]

BETTER   First *rise* to your feet and then *address* the chairman. [Both verbs in the imperative mood]

27c

Avoid needless shifts in subject or voice.

A shift in subject often involves a shift in voice. A shift in voice nearly always involves a shift in subject.

SHIFT James liked fishing, but hunting was also enjoyed by him. [The subject shifts from *James* to *hunting*. The voice shifts from active to passive.]

BETTER James liked fishing, but he also enjoyed hunting. [The subject does not shift. Both verbs active]

SHIFT Mary took summer courses and her leisure hours were devoted to tennis. [The subject shifts from *Mary* to *hours*. The voice shifts from active to passive.]

BETTER Mary took summer courses and devoted her leisure hours to tennis. [One subject only. Both verbs active]

SHIFT Paul hurried up the mountain path, and soon the laurel came into his sight. [The subject shifts from *Paul* to *laurel*.]

BETTER Paul hurried up the mountain path and soon caught sight of the laurel. [One subject only]

27d

Avoid needless shifts in person.

SHIFT *We* have reached a point where *one* ought to face the possibility of a great and sudden change. [A shift from first to third person]

BETTER *We* have reached a point where *we* ought to face the possibility of a great and sudden change.

SHIFT *Students* will find the University Book Shop a great convenience. *You* need not leave the campus to purchase any school supplies *you* may need. [A shift from third to second person]

BETTER *The student* will find the University Book Shop a great convenience. *He* need not leave the campus to purchase any school supplies *he* may need.

27e

Avoid needless shifts in number. (See also agreement of pronoun and antecedent, **6b.**)

SHIFT   A *person* should be thoughtful of *their* neighbors. [A shift from singular *person* to plural *their*]

BETTER   A *person* should be thoughtful of *his* neighbors.

SHIFT   The United Nations *deserves* encouragement. Indeed *they deserve* much more than that. [If *United Nations* takes a singular verb (*deserves*), it should not be referred to by a plural pronoun (*they*).]

BETTER   The United Nations *deserves* encouragement. Indeed, *it deserves* much more than that.

27f

Avoid needless shifts from indirect to direct discourse.

SHIFT   My friend asked whether I knew the coach and will he be with the team. [Mixed indirect and direct discourse]

BETTER   My friend asked whether I knew the coach and whether he would be with the team. [Indirect discourse]

BETTER   My friend asked, "Do you know the coach? Will he be with the team?" [Direct discourse]

27g

Maintain the same tone or style throughout the sentence.

INAPPROPRIATE   Analysis of the principal obstacles to harmony in the United Nations reveals that Russia and her satellites refuse to *play ball* with the rest of the world. [A shift from formal to colloquial style. Substitute *cooperate*, or a similar word, for the italicized expression.]

INAPPROPRIATE   After distributing the grass seed evenly over the lawn, rake the ground at least twice and then *gently bedew it* with fine spray. [The italicized expression is too "poetic" in a sentence with a prosaic purpose. Substitute *water it lightly*.]

INAPPROPRIATE   It seemed to Juliet, as she gazed down from the balcony, that Romeo's face was as white as *the underside of a fish*. [The italicized expression clashes with the romantic beginning of the sentence.]

27h

Maintain a consistent perspective throughout the sentence (and also throughout the larger elements of discourse).

FAULTY PERSPECTIVE   From the top of the Washington Monument, the government offices seemed to be so many beehives, and the workers droned at their tasks behind long rows of desks. [The perspective shifts from the monument to the interior of government buildings.]

CONSISTENT PERSPECTIVE   From the top of the Washington Monument, the government buildings seemed to be so many beehives, and it was easy to imagine the workers droning at their tasks behind long rows of desks.

▶ **EXERCISE 1**   Correct in the following sentences all needless shifts in tense, mood, subject, voice, person, number, tone, or perspective. Explain each revision by writing the number of the appropriate rule in this chapter: **a, b, c, d, e, f, g,** or **h.** Write *C* after each sentence that needs no revision.

1. According to Helen Leath, Mr. Blake knows how to deal with annoying door-to-door salesmen; they are quickly frightened away by him.
2. Pretending to be a seller of knives, Mr. Blake waves a long butcher knife near the throat of the salesman. You can well imagine what they think.
3. When the policeman gave me a ticket for rolling past a stop sign, I ask him what the fine would be.
4. A woman stepped forward, grabs the culprit by the collar, and demands that he apologize to the child.
5. He said he had a convertible model in stock and would I like to try it out.
6. Jane likes to cook, but house cleaning is not a pleasant occupation.
7. Each person has some distinctive mannerism of their own.
8. When she saw him in the room, she thinks that she is dreaming.

9. If there is little enthusiasm among the students, we might ask, "Why they should be enthusiastic?"

10. No matter what her mother may say, Jane always took the opposite view.

11. It is a book everyone should read, for you can derive much good from it.

12. Gentlemen, we have finished our discussion about balancing the budget; bear with me awhile until I have said a few words about budgeting the balance.

13. The foreign ministers held their conference in Paris, and contrary to rumors, the peace pipe is passed around.

14. Pick the roses in the morning, and then they should be placed in water.

15. A vacation is enjoyed by all because it refreshes the mind and the body.

16. He told his aunt that there is someone in the room.

17. Every citizen should do his duty as they see it.

18. Aunt Jane spent her summers in Wisconsin, but Arizona is her favorite winter climate.

19. Jim wondered whether Jack had left and did he say when he would return?

20. Standing before the house, he thought of the many happy years he had spent there and how quickly they are passing.

▶ EXERCISE 2   Revise the following paragraph to avoid all needless shifts. If necessary, expand the paragraph.

¹ From behind the desk the shopkeeper emerged and comes toward me. ² He is a heavy-set man, and his brown tweed coat was badly worn. ³ An assistant gave me a chair and leaves the room, but not before he had welcomed us and even told me where one might find lodging. ⁴ "First, look around in this vicinity and then you should find a comfortable place in a nearby hotel," he says. ⁵ I hurried out of the shop and soon the hotel comes into view. ⁶ Be thankful for suggestions when offered you. ⁷ It usually helps one.

▶ **EXERCISE 3**   Follow the directions for Exercise 2.

¹ He was an artful old codger, it always had seemed to me.   ² He has a deceptively open face and his manner is that of a simple farmer.   ³ He tried to appear humble and said that "I am opposed to all pretense."   ⁴ Nevertheless he will let it be known that he has great influence with important people.   ⁵ Take these impressions for what they are worth; it may help one in your dealings with this reptile.

Reference of Pronouns

28

Make a pronoun refer unmistakably and definitely to its antecedent.[1]

A pronoun whose antecedent is not immediately obvious is at best an annoyance to the reader, who must pause to clarify the meaning, and at worst a cause of serious misunderstanding. You may find the faulty use of pronouns one of the easiest errors to let slip by in your writing. Because you know just who or what you mean by *he, she, it; who, which, what; this, that; the same, such,* etc., you may not realize that you have not made your meaning obvious to the reader. Always check, therefore, to see that you have placed all pronouns as close as possible to their antecedents. If, having done this, you find that the reference of a pronoun is still not clear, repeat the antecedent or use a synonym for it. If repetition proves awkward, recast your sentence.

28a

Avoid ambiguous reference. Construct the sentence in such a way that the reader can easily distinguish between two possible antecedents.

AMBIGUOUS	John told William that he had made a mistake. [Who made the mistake?]
CLEAR	John said to William, "You have made a mistake."
CLEAR	John admitted to William that he had made a mistake.

[1] For agreement of pronoun and antecedent see **6b**.

AWKWARD   The books were standing on the shelf which needed
           sorting. (See also **25a[3]**.)
BETTER   The books which needed sorting were standing on
           the shelf. [Pronoun placed near its antecedent]

28b

**Avoid remote reference—reference to an antecedent
(1) too far removed from the pronoun or (2) so placed in
a subordinate construction that it is not central in the
mind of the reader.**

Make your meaning immediately clear to the reader.
Save him the annoyance of searching about for the
antecedent.

REMOTE   The *lake* covers many acres. Near the shore water lilies
           grow in profusion, spreading out their green leaves
           and sending up white blossoms on slender stems. *It*
           is well stocked with fish. [The pronoun *it* is too far
           removed from the antecedent *lake*.]
IMPROVED   The *lake* covers many acres. Near the shore water lilies
           grow in profusion, spreading out their green leaves
           and sending up white blossoms on slender stems.
           The *lake* is well stocked with fish. [Repetition of the
           antecedent *lake*]
VAGUE   He sat by the little window all day and worked steadily
           at his translating. *It* was too small to give much
           light. [Temporarily confusing: antecedent of *it* not
           clear until reader finishes the sentence]
CLEAR   He sat by the little window all day and worked steadily
           at his translating. The *window* was too small to give
           much light. [Repetition of the noun]
OBSCURE   When *Johnson's* club was organized, *he* asked Gold-
           smith to become a member. [Reference to anteced-
           ent in the possessive case]
IMPROVED   When *Johnson* organized his club, *he* asked Goldsmith
           to become a member. (See also **27c**.)

Caution: As a rule avoid pronoun reference to the title of a theme, or to a word in the title.

> *Title:* Is Work a Curse or a Blessing?

AWKWARD To a man who is harassed by a nagging wife and undisciplined children, *it* can be a great blessing, a welcome escape.

BETTER To a man who is harassed by a nagging wife and undisciplined children, *work* can be a great blessing, a welcome escape.

28c

Use broad reference only with discretion.

Informal English allows much latitude in the use of antecedents that must be inferred from the context. Even formal English accepts the general idea of a clause as an antecedent when the reference is unmistakable. But students who overuse *this, that, it,* or *which* to refer to the general idea of the preceding clause or sentence may be advised, as a means of insuring greater clarity, to make each of their pronouns refer to a specific noun (or noun substitute).

(1) Avoid reference to the general idea of a preceding clause or sentence unless the meaning is clear and unmistakable.

VAGUE William was absent from the first performance, which caused much comment. [*Which* has no antecedent.]

CLEAR William's absence from the first performance caused much comment. [Pronoun eliminated]

VAGUE The story referred to James, but Henry misapplied it to himself. This is true in real life. [*This* has no antecedent.]

CLEAR The story referred to James, but Henry misapplied it to himself. Similar mistakes occur in real life.

(2) As a rule do not refer to a noun not expressed but merely inferred from some word.

VAGUE	My mother is a music teacher. It is a profession I know nothing about.
CLEAR	My mother is a music teacher, but the teaching of music is a profession I know nothing about.
VAGUE	He wanted his teachers to think he was above average, as he could have been if he had used it to advantage.
CLEAR	He wanted his teachers to think he was above average, as he could have been if he had used his ability to advantage.

(3) **Avoid the use of the indefinite** *it, you,* **or** *they* **in your formal writing.**

INFORMAL (OR FORMAL)	If you break the law, you may be arrested. [Informal when *you* means "anyone," formal when *you* is addressed to a specific person or persons]
FORMAL	If a person breaks the law, he may be arrested. OR Anyone breaking the law may be arrested.
INFORMAL	When *you* cannot swim, a leaking boat tossing in deep, stormy waters frightens *you.* I admit that I am afraid.
FORMAL	Since I cannot swim, I admit that a leaking boat tossing in deep, stormy waters frightens me.
INFORMAL	In France *they* could not understand William.
FORMAL	In France William could not be understood.
AWKWARD	In the book *it* says that many mushrooms are edible.
IMPROVED	The book says that many mushrooms are edible.

Note: The pronoun *it* is correctly used in such idiomatic expressions as *it seems, it is cold, it is raining, it is useless to go,* and *it is five miles to town.*

28d

Avoid the confusion arising from the repetition in the same sentence of a pronoun referring to different antecedents.

CONFUSING	Although *it* is very hot by the lake, *it* looks inviting. [The first *it* is an idiomatic pronoun; the second *it* refers to *lake.*]
CLEAR	Although it is very hot by the lake, the water looks inviting.

| CONFUSING | We should have prepared for our examinations earlier. *It* is too late to do *it* now. |
| CLEAR | We should have prepared for our examinations earlier. It is too late now. |

▶ **EXERCISE** Reconstruct the following sentences as necessary to correct faults in reference. Write *C* after each sentence that needs no revision.

1. Howard was more intelligent than the average student, but he did not use it properly.
2. I did not even buy a season ticket, which was very disloyal to my school.
3. Her ladylike qualities were reflected in the graciousness of her manner. This was apparent in her every act.
4. Package wrapping has always been my job, because they say that I can do it better than anyone else.
5. When building roads the Romans tried to detour around valleys as much as possible for fear that flood waters might cover them and make them useless.
6. If you are taken to the courthouse, they will fine you.
7. In the article it states that the inland sea is salt.
8. Our language is rich in connectives which express fine distinctions of meaning.
9. One summer while visiting my grandparents I was attracted by three pigeons that decided to settle in their barn loft.
10. If all impurities are not removed from the iron, it will deprive steel of its ductility and prevent it from being rolled into bars or drawn into wire.
11. The speaker was eloquent, but he was annoyed by the intense heat in the auditorium.
12. My worst fault is the inability to express myself clearly in the presence of other people. But this is not true when I am with close friends.
13. I left home and hitchhiked to Chicago. This means of travel is not satisfactory, for it requires much waiting at the side of the road.

14. When the termite eggs are hatched, they grow wings and fly about the country in swarms.
15. Mary told Ann that she would be accepted as a member of the club.
16. The story awakens your interest in radium, which continues to the end of the book.
17. Visitors should heed the notice that is on the outside of the door.
18. Mary showed Jane that she had not made a mistake.
19. It may freeze tonight and damage the pipe, and it should be protected.
20. If a driver is guilty of violating a traffic law, the cost of your car insurance goes up.

Emphasis

29

Select words and arrange the parts of the sentence to give emphasis to important ideas.

Since your ideas vary in importance, your expression of them should vary in stress. Short factual statements and routine description or narration cannot always be varied for emphasis without doing violence to the natural order of the English language. For example, it would be absurd for a sportswriter to describe a football play in this fashion: "Short was the pass that Randy caught, and across the goal line raced he." But in most types of writing, some sentences may be rearranged to achieve emphasis without sacrificing naturalness of expression.

You may gain emphasis through the use of concrete words, especially verbs and nouns (Section 20), through economy of language (Section 21), and through subordination (Section 24). You may also emphasize ideas:

   a. By placing important words in the important positions at the beginning and end of the sentence.
   b. By changing loose sentences into periodic sentences.
   c. By arranging ideas in the order of climax.
   d. By using the active instead of the passive voice.
   e. By repeating important words.
   f. By putting words out of their usual order.
   g. By using balanced construction.
   h. By abruptly changing the sentence length.

29a

Gain emphasis by placing important words at the beginning or end of the sentence—especially at the end.

UNEMPHATIC   Science from the dawn of history has been intimately associated with war, and probably longer. [Parenthetical qualifier placed in an important position weakens the sentence.]

EMPHATIC   Science from the dawn of history, and probably longer, has been intimately associated with war.
                                                —BERTRAND RUSSELL

UNEMPHATIC   In my opinion, the spirit of science is the spirit of progress, above all. By that I mean that science does not seek a utopia or heaven that is static. Generally speaking, there are ever newer horizons and higher peaks for men to climb, mentally, spiritually, materially. [The most important words are not placed at the beginning or end of the sentences. Word padding, such as *In my opinion* and *By that I mean that,* is unemphatic. In the last sentence, *materially* is the least important item in the series.]

EMPHATIC   Above all, the spirit of science is the spirit of progress. Science seeks no static utopia or heaven. It can afford men ever newer horizons and higher peaks to climb, materially, mentally, and spiritually.
                                                —HERMANN J. MULLER

Note: Since semicolons are equivalent to weak periods, words placed before semicolons also have an important position.

▶ EXERCISE 1   Be prepared for a class discussion of emphasis in the following paragraph, giving special attention to the choice of words which begin and end sentences.

¹ By a strange perversity in the cosmic plan, the biologically good die young. ² Species are not destroyed for their shortcomings but for their achievements. ³ The

tribes that slumber in the graveyards of the past were not the most simple and undistinguished of their day, but the most complicated and conspicuous. ⁴ The magnificent sharks of the Devonian period passed with the period, but certain contemporaneous genera of primitive shellfish are still on earth. ⁵ Similarly, the lizards of the Mesozoic era have long outlived the dinosaurs who were immeasurably their biologic betters. ⁶ Illustrations such as these could be endlessly increased. ⁷ The price of distinction is death.
—JOHN HODGDON BRADLEY[1]

▶ EXERCISE 2 Revise each of the following sentences to gain emphasis for important ideas. (The sentences are adapted from the works of modern professional writers.)

1. In my opinion, rudeness luxuriates in the absence of self-respect more or less.
2. Frequently, dipping a paddle was like offering the torrent a toothpick, however.
3. Higher education has become a juvenile branch of the entertainment industry, if we may believe Mr. Daniels.
4. In any event, nothing in the fishing world makes as little sense as a short-sleeved fishing shirt, in the first place.
5. Shimmering buildings arrowed upward and glinted through the treetops, just ahead of us. ·
6. In the final analysis all he could see were the three double chins that her husband wore at the back of his neck conspicuously.
7. The search for truth is a subversive activity, and always has been.
8. In all probability not to engage in this pursuit of ideas is to live like ants instead of like men, however you look at it.
9. What they need is an awareness of their opportunities and potentialities, in fact; what they need is a philosophy, really.

[1] From "Is Man an Absurdity?" by John H. Bradley, *Harper's Magazine*, October, 1936.

10. One of the most exciting sports is whale watching, now in the prime of its season of course.

29b

Gain emphasis by changing loose sentences into periodic sentences. (Section 29b is an extension of 29a.)

A loose sentence is easily scanned, since the main idea comes toward the beginning and the reader can omit details, often parenthetical, placed later in the sentence. To get the meaning of a periodic sentence, however, the reader cannot stop until he reaches the period.

LOOSE Thousands of feet above the earth, the air is crowded with living creatures, drifting, flying, gliding, ballooning, or involuntarily swirling along on the high winds. [Notice how many effective details follow the main clause *the air is crowded with living creatures*.]
—RACHEL L. CARSON

PERIODIC Once Columbus had shown the way to the West Indies and the Americas, once Balboa had seen the Pacific and Magellan had sailed around the globe, there arose, and long persisted, two new ideas. [The main idea comes at the end of the sentence.]
—RACHEL L. CARSON

Both types of sentences are effective. The loose sentence is, and should be, the more commonly used. But the periodic sentence, by holding the reader in suspense and reserving the main idea until the end, is more emphatic. Note the difference in tone in the following sentences.

LOOSE There cannot be peace on earth as long as you see your fellow man as a being essentially to be feared, mistrusted, hated, and destroyed. [Main idea first—a good sentence]

PERIODIC   As long as you see your fellow man as a being essentially to be feared, mistrusted, hated, and destroyed, there cannot be peace on earth. [Main idea last—a more emphatic sentence]   —THOMAS MERTON

LOOSE   History has proved amply that mere numbers may be defeated by smaller forces who are superior in arms, organization, and morale.

PERIODIC   That mere numbers may be defeated by smaller forces who are superior in arms, organization, and morale history has amply proved.

Caution: Do not overuse the periodic sentence to the point of making your style unnatural. Variety is desirable. See Section **30**.

▶ EXERCISE 3   Study the structure of the following sentences, and then label each as either *loose* or *periodic*.

1. On the moon, inside the air-filled domes that the future colonists will erect, a man could fly like a bird.
   —ARTHUR C. CLARKE

2. So passionately do I love the usual, the commonplace, the everyday, that I turn off the television instantly if an adventure program comes on.   —PEARL BUCK

3. Polyphemus continued to melt round the room, staring malignly at nothing.   —ELIZABETH BOWEN

4. Out of this pain of loss, this bitter ecstasy of brief having, this fatal glory of the single moment, the tragic writer will therefore make a song for joy.
   —THOMAS WOLFE

5. If great comedy must involve something beyond laughter, Lloyd was not a great comedian.
   —JAMES AGEE

6. There are blustering signatures that swish across the page like cornstalks bowed before a tempest.
   —F. L. LUCAS

7. Obscurity is the very opposite of culture as it is the opposite of good breeding.   —JACQUES BARZUN

8. Earline was a big, bouncy, uncomplicated girl who poked you in the ribs to make sure you got the point of her jokes. —FRANCES GRAY PATTON

9. A small tree, rising between him and the light, stood there saturated with the evening, each gilt-edged leaf perfectly drunk with excellence and delicacy.
—E. B. WHITE

10. No one who has felt the fury of the fish charging like electric current through line and rod, who has heard the cacophonous screech of backing being ripped through guides, who has reeled with a madman's frenzy in the final seconds before boat and angler plunge into the Rogue's crashing, foaming white water, who has held on, bruised and shaken, until that sudden, inexplicable moment when the line goes slack and the contest is over as abruptly as it began—no one who has experienced such an encounter is ever the same again. —VIRGINIA KRAFT[2]

▶ **EXERCISE 4** Convert the loose sentences in Exercise 3 to periodic sentences, and then convert the periodic to loose; notice how your revisions make for varying emphasis.

29c

Gain emphasis by arranging ideas in the order of climax.

Notice in the examples below that words, phrases, clauses, and sentences are arranged in the order of importance, in stair-step fashion, with the strongest idea last.

Mr. Raleigh fears poverty, illness, and death. [Words placed in order of importance]
We could hear the roar of cannon, the crash of falling timbers, and the shrieks of the wounded. [Climax reached in *shrieks of the wounded*]

---

[2] From "Steelheads on a Rough River" by Virginia Kraft (*Sports Illustrated*, November 1, 1965) © 1965 Time Inc.

Sometimes their anguish was my anguish; sometimes their cussedness was my fury; occasionally their pleasure was my despair. [Clauses in order of importance]   —RUSSELL LYNES

In the language of screen comedians four of the main grades of laugh are the titter, the yowl, the belly laugh and the boffo. The titter is just a titter. The yowl is a runaway titter. Anyone who has ever had the pleasure knows all about a belly laugh. The boffo is the laugh that kills. [First words and then sentences are placed in climactic order.]   —JAMES AGEE

Note: A striking arrangement of ideas in reverse order of climax, called anticlimax, is sometimes used for comic effect.

To a distant cousin the rich old man willed his ranch, three oil wells, five apartment houses, and innumerable alley cats.

▶ **EXERCISE 5**   Arrange the ideas below in what you consider to be the order of climax.

1. Franklin used the ant as a symbol of industry, wisdom, and efficiency.

2. Everything on wheels—trains, bicycles, hot rods, roller skates—Archibald loved.

3. Images in the poem involve sun-drenched orchards, diamond-eyed children, and golden-flecked birds.   .

4. Like Patrick Henry, the young soldier wanted death or liberty.

5. He left the city because of his rapidly failing health, lack of success in business, and the loss of his club membership.

6. His confident manner, his knowledge of men, and his friendliness made him the logical man for the office.

7. Something must be done at once. The commission is faced with a deficit.

8. I gathered together the souvenirs of college days: my diploma, a textbook on mathematics, my fraternity pin, and a battered book bag.

9. His actions, his language, his clothes—these help reveal a man's character.
10. The would-be governor shook hands with the man on the street, autographed books for teenagers, promised prosperity to all, and wrote letters to senior citizens.

▶ **EXERCISE 6** Be prepared for a class discussion of the arrangement of ideas in the following paragraphs.

I began to think about personal liability insurance the morning Mrs. Ehrlich, our cleaning woman, suddenly screamed down to me from her perch on the windowsill: "Mr. J., come help! I got another one of those dizzy spells!"

I had asked Mrs. Ehrlich time and again to stop climbing around on the windowsills. I had also asked her not to run so fast while carrying the big plate-glass top of the coffee table across the waxed floors, and to try not to pour quite so much water into the electrical outlets. These restrictions may seem harsh, but I don't think I am what you could call a tyrannical employer. I've left her plenty of room for fringe-benefit fun. I've said nothing about blowing out the pilot light, sticking her fingers into the vacuum cleaner's turbo-jet engine, or tossing all the naphthalene, paint cans, and oil-soaked rags she pleases into the incinerator. —HAYES B. JACOBS[3]

29d

Gain emphasis by using the strong active voice instead of the weak passive voice.

UNEMPHATIC   Our picture window was punctured by hail, our frame garage was flattened by winds, and our basement was turned into a muddy swamp by the flash flood.

EMPHATIC   Hail punctured our picture window, winds flattened our frame garage, and the flash flood turned our basement into a muddy swamp.

[3] From Martin Levin's "The Phoenix Nest," *Saturday Review*, May 15, 1965, p. 6.

Exception: If the receiver of the action is more important than the doer, the passive voice is more effective.

EMPHATIC   His only son was killed in Vietnam.
EMPHATIC   Any driver who exceeds the speed limit will be fined.

▶ **EXERCISE 7**   Substitute the active for the passive voice.

1. The speech on the state of domestic affairs was delivered by the President of the United States.
2. It is taken for granted by students in Dr. Boyer's class that a weekly quiz will be given to them.
3. Victorian literature is being reevaluated by modern scholars.
4. As the station is reached, the train is seen coming around a curve.
5. A mink wrap was worn by the actress.
6. Paul was hesitant to enter the room, for he saw that a poster was being made by Jane.
7. Two maxims are often preached by Uncle Theodore: no moss will be gathered by a rolling stone; and, worms are always caught by early birds.
8. It was decided by the members that the meetings were to be held at their homes.
9. When the play was brought to an end, the actors were greeted with a loud burst of applause by the audience.
10. It is greatly feared by the citizens that adequate punishment will not be meted out by the judge.

29e

Gain emphasis by repeating important words.

Note the great difference between the careless repetition in **21c** and the effective repetition in the following passages. See also **31b(3)**.

EMPHATIC   The poet enters his world as an *as if*: he writes *as if* he were plowing a field, *as if* he were conducting a

chemical experiment, *as if* he were analyzing a real
man seated before him.　　　—JOHN CIARDI

EMPHATIC　　In this whole matter of War and Peace especially, we
have been at various times and in various ways *false*
to ourselves, *false* to each other, *false* to the facts of
history and *false* to the future.　　—HENRY R. LUCE

See also the quotation from Winston Churchill in **23b**.

▶ EXERCISE 8　From your reading, copy three passages in
which emphasis is gained by the repetition of an important
word or phrase.

29f

**Gain emphasis by putting a word or phrase out of its
natural order.**

EMPHATIC　*Trust her* I dare not.
EMPHATIC　*Never* will I vote for such a change!

Caution: This method of securing emphasis, if overused,
will make the style distinctly artificial. And of course the
order of the parts of the sentence should never be such as
to make for ambiguity. (See **25a**.)

▶ EXERCISE 9　Copy from your reading and bring to class
five passages in which emphasis is secured by putting
a word or phrase out of natural order.

29g

Use balance to gain emphasis.

A sentence is balanced when identical or similar grammatical structure is used to express contrasted ideas. A
balanced sentence uses parallel structure (see Section 26)
and emphasizes the contrast between parts of similar length
and movement.

UNBALANCED   Love is positive, but consider the negative aspects of tolerance. Passion is involved in love, and yet how humdrum and dull tolerance is.

BALANCED   Love is positive; tolerance negative. Love involves passion; tolerance is humdrum and dull.

—E. M. FORSTER

BALANCED   The slightest sense perception—a falling leaf, a twinkling star, a smiling child—awakens our minds as well as arouses our feelings, and forces us to ask: Why? What? Whence? Whither?

—MORTIMER ADLER

Caution: Do not overuse balance, which can make for artificiality rather than emphasis.

▶ **EXERCISE 10**   Copy from your reading and bring to class five examples of the balanced sentence.

▶ **EXERCISE 11**   Copy all examples of balanced structure from Lincoln's Gettysburg Address (at the end of Section 1, Exercise **20.**)

▶ **EXERCISE 12**   Use balanced sentences to show the contrast between the following: Men and women, youth and age, success and failure.

29h

Abruptly change the sentence length to gain emphasis.

EXAMPLE   Across an expanse of new-turned earth stretches a new public housing project, with a playyard for the children, and at 32nd Street begins the new campus of the Illinois Institute of Technology, sleek brick-and-glass buildings surrounded by new trees and new grass. And just beyond the Institute rises a great gray hulk of brick, four stories high, topped by an ungainly smokestack, ancient and enormous, filling half the block north of 34th Street between State and Dearborn. It is the Mecca Building.   —JOHN BARTLOW MARTIN

[The last short sentence, which abruptly follows a group of longer sentences, is emphatic; the author stresses *Mecca Building* because the purpose of his essay is to describe this strange place.]

▶ EXERCISE 13   Revise the following sentences as necessary to give greater emphasis. Write *C* after each sentence that needs no revision.

1. The chairman will give his report after the meeting has been called to order.
2. The soldiers were outnumbered two to one, as you may have heard.
3. It was no fault of hers that the program was a failure.
4. Forceful prose was created by Hemingway because of his sensitivity to the real speech of Americans, however.
5. The zero hour had come. Already the armies were marching.
6. On the other hand, he had done the best he could, according to his story.
7. At any time I shall be ready, no matter how late the hour is.
8. He saw much to interest him: the Statue of Liberty, the art galleries, the tall buildings, and the crowds on the street.
9. A fast pass was thrown to Milburn, and a twenty-five yard gain was made by him before the whistle was blown by the referee.
10. Scouting develops a boy morally, mentally, and physically.
11. Convince her against her will I cannot.
12. The storm broke in all its fury at the close of a hot day.
13. Mr. Brown knew that he had made wrong decisions, that he should apologize, that he had made a mistake.
14. I asked her to marry me, many years ago, in a shop on Tremont Street, late in the fall.
15. Around her shoulders was draped a gorgeous Spanish shawl.

16. The art of the Indians was crude, but a great deal of originality was shown by some of them.

17. Her charm, her friendliness, her generosity, and her neat appearance made her a favorite with the girls.

18. As we approached the house, lights were turned on and faces appeared at the windows.

19. Make the most of it if this be treason.

20. The car overturned when we struck a rut in the road.

▶ EXERCISE 14 By pointing to specific sections of this chapter, indicate the methods of gaining emphasis used in the following sentences.

1. A rhythm, a musical motif, a brush stroke, a color can be malicious. But the melody in a work, sonata, picture or poem cannot be malicious.   —JACQUES MARITAIN

2. What money he could lay his hands on he spent like an Indian rajah.   —DEEMS TAYLOR

3. Beds he slept in are relics, stones he stepped on are sacred, battles he lost are victories.

    —MARSHALL FISHWICK

4. The radio, except as it serves mariners, is a decivilizing achievement. It has destroyed the illusion of distance, invaded the privacy of walled enclosures, and coated the tongue of music.   —E. B. WHITE

5. When the loudspeaker announces "The Two-Fisted Killer from Ecuador," he rises on short, crooked legs, lowers his shaggy black head, aims himself and charges onto the court.   —MARSHALL SMITH

6. Why lands sink under the sea and rise again nobody knows.   —WOLFGANG LANGEWIESCHE

7. If a man can write a better book, preach a better sermon, or make a better mouse-trap than his neighbor, though he builds his house in the woods, the world will make a beaten path to his door.

    —EMERSON

8. Gone are the people who owned these farms, their

most lasting works faded like old ink, their names nothing but an echo in the land records.

—KENNETH ANDLER

9. Jet planes flashed a glance at us, after apparently ripping the old blue canvas of the sky. The monstrous voices roared out the half-time and three-quarter-time scores of other games. The cannon was fired at every touchdown. The tumblers somersaulted. The cheerleaders continued their idiot ballet.   —J. B. PRIESTLEY

10. The impression seems to be that the age we live in is the age of the masses. Half the times you open a book or start a discussion you find yourself dealing with mass production, mass consumption, mass media and mass culture. We blame the masses for all our ills: the vulgarization of culture and politics, the meaninglessness of our way of life, the ferocity of our wars and, of course, the population explosion.   —ERIC HOFFER[4]

[4] From "Making a Mass Elite," *Holiday Magazine*, March, 1966.

Variety

30

Vary the structure and the length of your sentences to make your whole composition pleasing and effective.

The two following paragraphs have the same content, but the first is made up of eight short sentences, all simple or compound; the second has four sentences varied in length and structure: one simple, one complex, and two compound-complex. Note how variety in the second paragraph makes it more effective than the first.

UNVARIED   Even a climatic change can affect the rate of rotation. The earth's weather becomes warmer, for example, and some of the ice concentrated at the North and South poles melts. This releases water into the world's oceans. The mass of ice near the earth's axis of rotation is reduced, and the amount of water in the oceans is increased. The oceans are farther from the axis. As a result, the earth's movement of inertia becomes greater, and its speed of rotation decreases. This is like a twirling ice skater. He moves his arms out from his body; his speed of rotation decreases.

VARIED   Even a climatic change can affect the rate of rotation. When the earth's weather becomes warmer, for example, some of the ice concentrated at the North and South poles melts, releasing water into the world's oceans. The mass of ice near the earth's axis of rotation is reduced, and the amount of water in the oceans (which are farther from the axis) is increased. As a result, the earth's movement of inertia becomes greater and—like a twirling ice skater who moves his arms out from his body—its speed of rotation decreases.   —TIME[1]

[1] From "Toward a Longer Day," *Time*, February 25, 1966. Courtesy *Time*; © Time Inc. 1966.

Except for the loose, stringy sentences in **30c**, this section deals only with *good* sentences. Throughout Section 30 you are cautioned against monotonous repetition of any one type of sentence, not because these sentences are not good ones, but because they do not combine to form a pleasing and effective pattern. Even the best sentence can be boring if it follows a long series of sentences similar in design.

Note: Can you distinguish readily between main clauses and subordinate clauses, clauses and phrases, compound sentences and compound predicates? If necessary, review the fundamentals of the sentence treated in Section 1, **Sentence Sense,** especially **1d;** then study **Variety.**

30a

Usually avoid a series of short, simple sentences. Vary the length. (See also **29h.**)

UNVARIED   Consider what might happen on Venus. We could step off our rocket and meet a spider. Suppose he is ten feet tall. The spider might well be a creature of good will. He might be capable of right action. He might have an I.Q. incomparably higher than our own. But his terrible spider aspect would surprise us. We might not wait to test the creature's friendship. We might stomp on him with the largest boot available. [A series of choppy sentences]

VARIED   Consider what might happen should we step off our rocket on Venus to meet a 10-foot-tall spider. The spider might well be a creature of good will, capable of right action, and with an I.Q. incomparably higher than our own. But, surprised by his terrible spider aspect, we might not wait to test the creature's friendship. We might stomp on him with the largest boot available.   —RAY BRADBURY[2]

▶ **EXERCISE 1** Revise the following paragraph to achieve variety in sentence length.

[2] From "Cry the Cosmos," *Life*, September 14, 1962.

¹ A salesman's speech, recently recorded, has an interesting thesis. ² A man should solve problems. ³ And a man should create problems to solve. ⁴ For instance, a woman's car will not start. ⁵ She has a problem. ⁶ An auto-parts man solves it by selling her a battery. ⁷ I think that by nature man is a solver of problems. ⁸ A teacher baffles his class with problems. Then he helps the students solve them. ⁹ A doctor solves the problems of his patients by recommending drugs or surgery. ¹⁰ In fact, even a garbage collector helps housewives clear their kitchens. ¹¹ And a ditch digger eliminates the drainage problems of a city. ¹² How to spend leisure hours in an age of computers is a problem for many Americans. ¹³ Singers, dancers, actors, and writers help solve this problem. ¹⁴ Man can see problems everywhere. ¹⁵ And he does something about them.

30b

Avoid a long series of sentences beginning with the subject. Vary the beginning.

The best writers begin about half their sentences with the subject—far more than in any other one way. But some students use this kind of beginning almost exclusively. To avoid overuse, they should vary the subject-first beginning.

Basic Sentence Patterns	*Variations*
SUBJECT—VERB.	VERB—SUBJECT.
The professor walked in.	In walked the professor.
A man lay beside the road.	Beside the road lay a man.
SUBJECT—VERB—OBJECT.	OBJECT—SUBJECT—VERB.
Henry scorned honest men.	Honest men Henry scorned.
I will not do that again.	That I will not do again.

SUBJECT—LINKING VERB —COMPLEMENT.	COMPLEMENT—SUBJECT —LINKING VERB.
Bruce was a bungler then.	A bungler Bruce was then.
We shall never be completely secure.	Completely secure we shall never be!

In addition to shifting the word order of basic patterns, you can vary the beginnings of sentences in the following ways:

(1) Begin with an adverb or an adverb clause.

ADVERB   *Suddenly* the professor walked in.
ADVERB CLAUSE   *Although Bruce has good manners now,* he was a bungler then.

(2) Begin with a prepositional phrase or a participial phrase.

PREPOSITIONAL PHRASE   *At that moment* the professor walked in.
PARTICIPIAL PHRASE   *Waiting patiently for help,* a man lay beside the road.

(3) Begin with a coordinating conjunction such as *but, and, or, nor,* or *yet.*

Effective sentences can often begin with a coordinating conjunction, but only when the conjunction shows the proper relation of the sentence to the preceding sentence. See **31b(4)**.

COORDINATING CONJUNCTION   The young woman wept and wrung her hands. *But* the injured man, lying beside the road, waited patiently for help. [*But* makes a contrast.]

▶ **EXERCISE 2**   Compose a good sentence that begins with the subject. Then revise the sentence to vary the beginning in as many ways as you can.

▶ **EXERCISE 3**   Classify the beginnings of the sentences in paragraph 32, page 347, into the types designated above.

30c

Avoid the loose, stringy compound sentence. (See also 24b.)

The ineffective compound sentence may be revised:

(1) **By converting it to a complex sentence.**

AIMLESSLY COMPOUND   The Mississippi River is one of the longest rivers in the world, and in the springtime it often overflows its banks, and many people are endangered.

COMPLEX   The Mississippi River, which is one of the longest rivers in the world, often endangers many people during the springtime by overflowing its banks.

(2) **By using a compound predicate in a simple sentence.**

COMPOUND   He put on his coat, and next he picked up his hat and cane, and then he hurried from the house.

SIMPLE   He put on his coat, picked up his hat and cane, and hurried from the house.

(3) **By using an appositive or a modifier in a simple sentence.**

COMPOUND   The town is north of the Red River, and a tornado struck it, and it was practically demolished.

SIMPLE   The town, located north of the Red River, was struck by a tornado and practically demolished.

COMPOUND   He was the mayor of the town, and he was a genial fellow, and he invited the four boys into his study.

SIMPLE   The mayor of the town, a genial fellow, invited the four boys into his study.

(4) **By using phrases in a simple sentence.**

COMPOUND   The streets were icy and we could not drive the car.

SIMPLE   Because of the icy streets we could not drive the car.

COMPOUND   You will reach your destination tomorrow, and then you can take a long rest.

SIMPLE   After reaching your destination tomorrow, you can take a long rest.

30d

Vary the conventional subject-verb sequence by occasionally separating subject and verb by words or phrases.

SUBJECT—VERB   The *auditorium is* across from the park and it is a gift of the alumni. [A compound sentence]

VARIED   The *auditorium,* across from the park, *is* a gift of the alumni. [A simple sentence]

SUBJECT—VERB   The *crowd sympathized* with the visitors and *applauded* every good play.

VARIED   The *crowd,* sympathizing with the visitors, *applauded* every good play.

Caution: Avoid awkward or needless separation of subject and verb.

30e

Vary a series of declarative statements by using an occasional exclamation, exhortation, command, or question.

STATEMENT   We will fight to the end.

EXCLAMATION   Imagine our nation not fighting to the very end!

EXHORTATION   Let us fight, then, to the very end.

COMMAND   Fight on. Fight to the end.

QUESTION   Who of us will not fight to the end? [A rhetorical question usually should not be answered.]

▶ EXERCISE 4   Be prepared for a class discussion of sentence variety in the following paragraphs.

1. ¹ I will not dwell on the trials I endured from this horse. ² She was mean and never mean the same way twice. ³ She would tolerate two automobiles and bolt from the third, the same with mailboxes or even a stone beside the road. ⁴ At times she would stop and eye a telephone pole with such trembling, ears-cocked, ears-back panic that even I began to think the pole was doing something to scare her; if not at that moment, perhaps it had on some previous occasion. ⁵ At that instant, after seem-

ing to compose herself, she would bolt again. ⁶ She very nearly threw me when the sleeve of my slicker, neatly tied on behind me, came adrift and touched her flank, to which her reaction was one of bucking and sun-fishing. ⁷ If I left her at a hitching rack, she would lean back and pull until she broke the reins. ⁸ It was suicidal to light a cigarette while riding her in the dark. ⁹ My worst moment with her came when we put up suddenly from the road just in front of us an eagle or a hawk which had been enjoying a dust bath. ¹⁰ She went through her entire repertoire. —CHARLES W. MORTON[3]

2. ¹ It was never a pilot that started the idea that night falls. ² A pilot knows that it does not. ³ It oozes up out of the ground, fills the hollows and low places with purple pools of shadow that spread and rise to the tops of the trees and the houses. ⁴ Long before the sky has darkened, the world below is swimming in night. ⁵ And then finally darkness begins washing up over the sky from the east, climbing over the zenith, closing down at last over the final gleams of the sunset. ⁶ Here and there stars begin to prick through, larger and more liquid than ever seen from the ground, and the moon, big and white, outlines the earth. ⁷ Below the plane, lights map the town, race along the roads, accenting but not relieving the blackness, for darkness clings to the ground. ⁸ Whatever light there is clings to the sky to the last. —ALMA HEFLIN[4]

3. ¹ Any Mediterranean knows what he wants, what it should be like, where it comes from. ² In a restaurant he asks searching questions about each item of the food, how it is cooked, and he will complain on principle if there is the smallest doubt or disappointment, so that often the chef nervously comes up from the kitchen halfway through a meal to see how his customers are taking it. ³ It is a

[3] From *It Has Its Charms* ... by Charles W. Morton. Published by J. B. Lippincott Company. Copyright © 1966 by Charles W. Morton.

[4] From *Adventure Was the Compass* by Alma Heflin McCormick. By permission of the author.

point of honor to complain.   [4] In a shop he makes the same demands; patiently the assistant brings out all the cloth, all the shoes, and is not in the least upset if the customer refuses all.   [5] On the contrary, the assistant admires the discrimination.   [6] For life is not buying or selling; it is getting what you exactly wish for, what you can afford. [7] The wish is everything, and for that, patience is indispensable and life is timeless.   —V. S. PRITCHETT[5]

4. [1] All around the lakeshore the tormented water raced— not 80 feet high but, in places, clawing up to *800 feet* above lake level.   [2] It thundered at the dam—and the dam held. [3] But the water went over the dam not five feet high but up to 300 feet high, and smashed to the bottom of the gorge 800 feet below.   [4] There it was constricted as in a deadly funnel, and its speed fearfully increased.   [5] It shot out of the short gorge as from a gun barrel and spurted across the wide Piave riverbed, scooping up millions of deadly stones.   [6] Ahead of it raced a strange icy wind and a storm of fragmented water, like rain, but flying *upward.*   [7] By now it was more than a wave, more than a flood.   [8] It was a tornado of water and mud and rocks, tumbling hundreds of feet high in the pale moonlight, leaping straight at Longarone.   —GORDON GASKILL[6]

5. [1] Can you imagine any better example of divine creative accomplishment than the consummate flying machine that is a bird?   [2] The skeleton, very flexible and strong, is also largely pneumatic—especially in the bigger birds. [3] The beak, skull, feet, and all other bones of a 25-pound pelican have been found to weigh but 23 ounces.   [4] Yet the flesh too is pneumatic, and in some species there are air sacs around viscera, muscles, and, where balance and streamlining permit, immediately under the skin.   [5] The

[5] From "Europe's Mediterranean Coast" by V. S. Pritchett, *Holiday,* January, 1966.

[6] From "The Night the Mountain Fell" by Gordon Gaskill. Reprinted from *The Reader's Digest,* May, 1965, by permission.

lungs are not just single cavities as with mammals but whole series of chambers around the main breathing tubes, connected also with all the air sacs of the body, including the hollow bones.   [6] Thus the air of the sky literally permeates the bird, flesh and bone alike, and aerates it entirely.   [7] And the circulation of sky through the whole bird acts as a radiator or cooling system of the flying machine, expelling excess humidity and heat as well as exchanging carbon dioxide for oxygen at a feverish rate.

—GUY MURCHIE[7]

[7] From Guy Murchie, *Song of the Sky,* 1954, reprinted by permission of and arrangement with Houghton Mifflin Company, the authorized publishers.

LARGER ELEMENTS

The Paragraph

31

Make paragraphs unified and coherent; develop them adequately.

A paragraph is a distinct unit of thought—usually a group of related sentences, though occasionally no more than one sentence—in a written or printed composition. The form of a paragraph is easy to recognize: the first line is indented. The content of a unified paragraph deals with one central idea; every sentence contributes to this idea. Moreover, each sentence fits into a logical pattern of organization and is therefore carefully related to other sentences in the paragraph.

Below is an example of a unified, coherent, adequately developed paragraph. As you read it, observe (1) the clear statement of the controlling idea in the first sentence, (2) the development of that idea in the sentences which follow, (3) the orderly arrangement of the supporting facts, and (4) the close relationship of the sentences to the central idea and to one another. (For easy reference, each of the fifty-nine specimen paragraphs in this chapter is numbered.)

1 As a matter of fact, the educated man uses at least three languages. With his family and his close friends, on the ordinary, unimportant occasions of daily life, he speaks, much of the time, a monosyllabic sort of shorthand. On more important occasions and when dealing with strangers in his official or business relations, he has a more formal speech, more complete, less allusive, politely qualified, wisely reserved. In addition he has some acquaintance with the literary speech of his language. He understands this when he reads it, and often enjoys it, but he hesitates to use it. In times of emotional stress hot fragments of it may come out of him like lava, and in times of feigned emotion, as when giving a commencement address, cold, greasy gobbets of it will ooze forth.

—BERGEN EVANS[1]

The central idea of the above paragraph is "the educated man uses at least three languages." The sentences developing the central idea classify the languages and describe their uses; these points are well organized, progressing from informal speech in ordinary situations to formal speech on rare occasions. Repeated references to times and situations, the comparison of the languages, and transitional devices (such as the phrase "in addition") link the sentences within the paragraph and thus contribute to its coherence.

Since each paragraph in a composition is a distinct unit of thought, the beginning of a new paragraph is an important signal to the reader. It serves as a signpost of an approaching curve in the avenue of thought; or it warns him that he must take a new avenue of thought. It announces a new time, place, person, or thing in the course of a narrative, a different point of view in description, a new step in an exposition, or an advance in argument.

Length. Expository or argumentative paragraphs in current books and magazines are usually from 50 to 250 words in length, with the average perhaps 100 words. Paragraphs tend to run longer in books and shorter in the narrow columns of newspapers. Shorter paragraphs are more frequent in narrative writing, especially dialogue, in which each speech is paragraphed separately.

Indention. The first lines of paragraphs are indented uniformly, about one inch in longhand and five spaces in typewritten copy.

---

[1] From "Grammar for Today" by Bergen Evans, reprinted from the *Atlantic Monthly*, March, 1960. By permission of the author.

31a

Give unity to the paragraph by making each sentence contribute to the central thought.

A paragraph is said to have unity when each sentence contributes to the central thought. Any sentence that fails to contribute violates the unity of the paragraph and should be omitted. The central thought is usually expressed in a *topic sentence.* Although a topic sentence may come anywhere within a paragraph, the central idea of an expository paragraph is often stated in the first sentence.

In the illustrations of unified paragraphs below, the central idea, when expressed, is indicated by italics.

2 *We strolled across the campus after the last class one afternoon late in May, when the magnolia blossoms and the gentlemen were both out in force enjoying the balmy air.* A pair of men in running shorts and spiked shoes trotted by, not speeding, merely limbering up. Down by the rough stone wall that enclosed the campus another pair tossed a baseball languidly. Sheltered by low-swinging magnolia boughs, a group engaged in what looked suspiciously like a poker game. In the shade of a giant oak lay one man who actually had a book; but unfortunately the book, spread open, rested on his chest, and he slept blissfully.

—GERALD W. JOHNSON[2]

To achieve unity, you may find it helpful to make a plan for a paragraph, carefully listing points that clearly support your central topic. Paragraph 2, for example, reveals the following plan:

CENTRAL TOPIC   Observations during a campus stroll in May

DEVELOPMENT
1. two runners
2. ball tossers
3. card players
4. sleeping scholar

[2] From *Hod-Carrier: Notes of a Laborer on an Unfinished Cathedral* by Gerald W. Johnson. Reprinted by permission of William Morrow & Co., Inc. Copyright © 1963, 1964 by Gerald W. Johnson.

When the topic sentence comes at or near the beginning, the conclusion of the paragraph may not only restate the central idea—and thus repeat key words or the main point of the topic sentence—but also emphasize its significance:

3 *Father got holes in his socks even oftener than we boys did in our stockings.* He had long athletic toes, and when he lay stretched out on his sofa reading and smoking, or absorbed in talking to anyone, these toes would begin stretching and wiggling in a curious way by themselves, as though they were seizing on this chance to live a life of their own. I often stared in fascination at their leisurely twistings and turnings, when I should have been listening to Father's instructions about far different matters. Soon one and then the other slipper would fall off, always to Father's surprise, but without interrupting his talk, and a little later *his busy great toe would peer out at me through a new hole in his sock.*

—CLARENCE DAY[3]

Occasionally the central idea of a paragraph may be stated in the last sentence only, especially when the writer progresses from particulars to a generalization:

4 When we watch a person walk away from us, his image shrinks in size. But since we know for a fact that he is not shrinking, we make an unconscious correcting and "see" him as retaining his full stature. Past experience tells us what his true stature is with respect to our own. Any sane and dependable expectation of the future requires that he have the same true stature when we next encounter him. *Our perception is thus a prediction; it embraces the past and the future as well as the present.*

—WARREN J. WITTREICH[4]

When not expressed in a topic sentence, the central idea of a unified paragraph is distinctly implied:

[3] From *Life with Father* by Clarence Day. Reprinted by permission of the publishers, Alfred A. Knopf, Inc.

[4] From "Visual Perception and Personality" by Warren J. Wittreich, reprinted from *Scientific American*, April, 1959. By permission of the publishers.

5 A man in cuffless shirt-sleeves with pink armgarters, wearing a linen collar but no tie, yawned his way from Dyer's Drug Store across to the hotel. He leaned against the wall, scratched a while, sighed, and in a bored way gossiped with a man tilted back in a chair. A lumber-wagon, its long green box filled with large spools of barbed-wire fencing, creaked down the block. A Ford, in reverse, sounded as though it were shaking to pieces, then recovered and rattled away. In the Greek candy-store was the whine of a peanut-roaster, and the oily smell of nuts.

—SINCLAIR LEWIS[5]

[Topic implied: *Such were the activities in Main Street.*]

▶ EXERCISE 1 Point out, or supply, the topic sentence for paragraph 16, pages 335–36, and for any other paragraphs assigned by your instructor.

Caution: Do not make rambling statements that are vaguely related to your topic sentence. As you write a paragraph, hold to the main idea. For instance, if the controlling idea of a paragraph is "My roommate Bill Jones cannot keep a secret," irrelevant sentences about Bill Jones or about secrecy will disrupt the unity. Every statement should pertain to Bill Jones's inability to keep a secret.

CHECK LIST FOR REVISING A PARAGRAPH
WHICH LACKS UNITY

1. Does the paragraph have a central idea clearly stated or implied? (If not, supply a topic sentence.)
2. Does the topic shift one or more times? (If so, either develop each topic in a separate paragraph, or supply a topic sentence to which each of the ideas can be made to contribute.)
3. Does every sentence contribute to the central idea? (If not, cross out each irrelevant sentence. If any sentence is related to the central idea, but not clearly so, revise it to make the relationship clear.)

[5] From *Main Street* by Sinclair Lewis, copyright, 1920, by Harcourt, Brace & World, Inc.; renewed, 1948, by Sinclair Lewis. Reprinted by permission of the publishers.

REVISION OF A FAULTY PARAGRAPH

My friend Cliff is often late on important occasions because of his excessive courtesy. — *Topic sentence needed*

On Christmas Eve, for example, Cliff was late to dinner. His unusually courteous habits had delayed him on a shopping trip. At the entrance of a large bargain basement, he had stood for a quarter of an hour holding doors open for last-minute shoppers. Once inside, he lost more time standing aside so that clerks could serve others first. ~~Cliff bought a billfold for his brother.~~ — *Omit — irrelevant*

When Cliff at last left the store, he took time out to carry heavy packages for a woman whose car was parked two blocks away. *When he finally arrived* ~~At~~ home, his family was eating — *Make reference to central idea clear*

dessert. The very next week, Cliff was late for an important business conference. He had stood outside a busy elevator letting everyone else on first; then he lost even more time insisting that he be the last person off. Who else besides Cliff would so courteously put others first? ~~Cliff is the type of person who cannot sleep if a thank-you note remains unwritten.~~ — *Omit — topic shifts*

▶ **EXERCISE 2** To achieve unity, revise the following faulty paragraph. Be prepared to give reasons for your revisions.

At my place last night, a tornadic wind played several mischievous pranks. Whistling loudly through the weather stripping, it sprayed dirty water all over the freshly mopped kitchen floor. Next, as though chiding me for my earlier complaints about stuffy air, it created enormous drafts by breaking a half dozen window panes. The moment an announcer on television started reading a special bulletin from the weather bureau, the wind knocked down my television antenna and, just as I reached for the radio, blacked out the whole house. Later I learned that a pilot flying above the turbulent weather had reported that he had never seen such a violent thunderstorm. Traveling at ninety miles an hour, the wind leveled a two-car garage belonging to Mr. Fulton, my neighbor. The wind also turned on an outdoor water faucet, flooding my pansy bed, overturned the dog house, imprisoning my fox terrier, and dumped a stolen boat into the back yard, after ripping the motor off and breaking the oars. After that savage storm, my family and I are most grateful to be alive and uninjured.

31b

Give coherence to the paragraph by so interlinking the sentences that the thought may flow smoothly from one sentence to the next.

A paragraph is said to have coherence when the relationship between sentences is clear, when the transition from one sentence to the next is easy and natural. The reader should be able to follow the thought without difficulty. In order to secure this coherence, this easy flow of the thought from sentence to sentence, the writer should rely first of all on (1) arrangement of the sentences in a clear order, and then on the use of (2) pronouns referring to the preceding sentence, (3) repeated words or ideas, (4) transitional expressions, and (5) parallel structure.

(1) **Arrange the sentences of the paragraph in a clear, logical order.**

There are several common, logical ways to order the sentences in a paragraph; the choice of an appropriate order depends upon the writer's purpose and the nature of his material. Perhaps the simplest and most common order is "time" order.

POOR ARRANGEMENT OF SENTENCES

After the death of Saul, David ruled Israel for forty years. Once he incurred the king's anger and was driven ignominiously from court. As a shepherd lad he had lived in the hills of Judea. He had vanquished the mighty Philistine with his slingshot. The sad-faced Saul was charmed with his songs. He was the sweetest singer in all Israel.

[Confused time order]

ORDERLY SEQUENCE OF SENTENCES

6 David, the shepherd lad who lived in the hills of Judea, was the sweetest singer in all Israel. It was he who charmed the sad-faced Saul with his songs. It was he, too, who vanquished the mightly Philistine with his slingshot. Later he incurred the anger of Saul and was driven from court. But upon Saul's death David came back and ruled Israel for forty years.

[David's (1) *youth in Judea,* (2) *experiences with Saul,* and (3) *reign over Israel*]

This paragraph about David is made clearer by re-arrangement in time order. Narrative paragraphs lend themselves naturally to such arrangement, and other types of paragraphs often have a time element that makes possible and natural a chronological arrangement. For example, in explaining a process—how something is done or made—the writer can follow the process through, step by step, as in the following paragraph.

7 In *engraving,* the artist grooves out clean strips of metal from the plate with a steel instrument called a burin. The artist is actually drawing with the burin. After the picture is engraved, printing ink is rubbed over the entire plate. The surface is then wiped clean, leaving ink in the incised portions of the copper. A dampened sheet of paper is placed over the plate and together they are run through a roller press. The paper is dampened to retain the ink better and to avoid cracking or tearing, since a great deal of pressure must be exerted to force the paper into the incised areas. —MARVIN ELKOFF[6]

Sentences that have no evident time order can sometimes be arranged in "space" order, in which the paragraph moves from east to west, from west to east, from the near to the distant, from the distant to the near, from the left to the right, etc. This order is used especially for descriptive paragraphs. Note the movement from the warm, low coastal gardens to the cold, high areas in the following paragraph.

8 Late winter color heralds the approach of spring in all areas of the Southwest. In mild coastal gardens, this happens gradually as spring sneaks up without much fanfare. Farther inland, bulbs and flowering trees attract more attention. And in colder areas of the mountains and high desert, the appearance of the first buds on a deciduous shrub or tree is downright exciting after winter's snow.[7]

Another good arrangement of sentences is in order of "climax," according to which the least important idea is stated first and the others in order of increasing importance, as in the following paragraph. See also **29c**.

9 An ant cannot purposefully try anything new, and any ant that accidentally did so would be murdered by his colleagues. It is the ant colony as a whole that slowly learns over the ages. In contrast, even an earthworm has enough flexibility of brain to enable it to be taught to turn toward the left or right for food. Though rats are not able to reason to any considerable degree, they can solve such problems as separating round objects from triangular ones when these have to do with health or appetite. Cats, with better brains, can be taught somewhat more, and young dogs a great deal. The higher apes can learn by insight as well as by trial and error. —GEORGE R. HARRISON[8]

[6] From "Collecting Original Art Prints" by Marvin Elkoff, *Holiday*, February, 1966.

[7] From "The Earliest Color," reprinted from *Sunset*, January, 1959. By permission of the publishers.

[8] From "How the Brain Works" by G. R. Harrison, reprinted from the *Atlantic Monthly*, September, 1956. By permission of the author.

Sometimes the movement within the paragraph may be from the general to the particular, from the particular to the general, or from the familiar to the unfamiliar. A paragraph may begin with a general statement which is then supported by particular details, or, reversing the process, it may begin with a striking detail or series of details and conclude with a summarizing statement. Note the movement from the general to the particular in paragraph 10 and from particular to general in paragraph 11:

10 In the ten years we have been married, I have yet to see Maurine act deviously. Although caginess is presumed to be a prerequisite for politics, she has marched to the top of the ballot by blurting out exactly what is in her mind. When she was asked to back a bill allocating a portion of dog-racing revenues for 4-H clubs, Maurine scolded her constituents for tying a worthy cause to pari-mutuel gambling. The special interests which she has offended would terrify most politicians—utility companies, dairy farmers, the Bar-Tenders' Union, the fairs in all thirty-six Oregon counties, slot-machine operators, the Farm Bureau Federation, even the American Legion.   —RICHARD L. NEUBERGER[9]

[The first sentence states the topic: *Maurine never acts deviously*. The second sentence begins the development with a general statement about her positive action. The third sentence shows specifically how she faced up to the 4-H clubs, and the fourth lists other special interests defied in the same way.]

11 Many years ago a graduate student inconvenienced himself greatly to come a long distance to see me to ask if I could help him secure some information about the term "poll tax." He was preparing a doctor's thesis, he told me, and needed to know how long this term had been in the language, what its basic meaning was, and what other meanings it may have had in the course of its use in English. He was most surprised when I opened the *OED* to the appropriate place and showed him that all he needed to know about this term had been available within a few feet of his desk in the school where he was studying. It is not at all likely that any but the exceptional student will ever need all the information about words that the larger dictionaries afford, but it is well worth the

[9] From "My Wife Put Me in the Senate," *Harper's Magazine*, June, 1955.

while of every student to become acquainted with the fact that such information is available for those who at any time need to make use of it. —MITFORD M. MATHEWS[10]

[This paragraph explains how one particular graduate student learned his lesson and then suggests the value of the lesson to all students.]

Paragraphs 6, 7, 8, 9, 10, and 11 above illustrate four of many possible types of clear sentence arrangement within the paragraph. Any order of sentences, or any combination of orders, is satisfactory so long as it makes the sequence of thought clear. Proper arrangement of the sentences is the first, the basic, step to insure good transitions from sentence to sentence. All other steps presuppose that the sentences have first been arranged in the clearest possible order.

▶ EXERCISE 3 Analyze paragraph 4 above and paragraphs 32 and 39 below to determine the order used.

(2) Link sentences by means of pronouns referring to antecedents in preceding sentences. (See also Section 28.)

In the following paragraphs italics are used to indicate the pronouns serving as links between sentences. Such pronouns should usually come near the beginning of the sentence if they are to be of much use in paragraph coherence.

12 I was becoming conditioned by what I saw each day on Pahlavi Avenue as I walked to the university. I would pass a squatting merchant on a blanket, his wares before him, chanting to attract business. *He* had for sale thirty empty Carter's ink bottles; it was puzzling to imagine where *he* had gotten them. Farther along a man specializing in art objects was selling a page from an old copy of the *Saturday Evening Post. It* was a four-color advertisement for Hotpoint showing a father, mother, and two crisply dressed daughters smugly regarding the legend in needlework on the wall behind them: "Bless Our Happy Hotpoint Home." Now *it*

---

[10] From "The Freshman and His Dictionary" by Mitford M. Mathews, reprinted from *College Composition and Communication*, December, 1955. By permission of the National Council of Teachers of English.

was handsomely encased behind glass with a gold baroque frame.
—CURTIS HARNACK[11]

13 Amoebae are gray bits of jelly speckled with multitudes of grains and crystals. *They* have no particular form, although when *they*'re sleeping off a jag or just floating around passing the time of day, *they* assume a sort of star shape, like a splash of ink. Mostly *they* pour *themselves* along like a lava flow. Every once in a while *they* sit down on something and when *they* get up that something is inside *them*. —ALFRED BESTER[12]

▶ **EXERCISE 4** Underline the pronouns used to link sentences in paragraphs 24, 27, and 42, or in any others assigned by your instructor. Check the antecedent (in a preceding sentence) to which each pronoun refers. Underline the pronouns used to link sentences in your last paper or in your last two papers.

(3) **Link sentences by repeating words or ideas used in the preceding sentences.**

Notice in the next paragraph the repetition of the key words—*liberal, radical, leftist, left; conservative, rightist, right*—and of an idea—*labels, distinction, classifications,* "*ideological* positions," "This system of classifying political *philosophies*." Notice also that the repetition of *world* and the use of *French* and *France's* link sentences within the paragraph.

14 The *liberal-conservative labels* parallel the *left-right distinction* that grew out of the *French* Revolution. In *France's* National Assembly of 1789, the *conservatives* sat to the *right* of the speaker, and became known as *rightists*, and the *radicals* sat at the *left* and became known as *leftists*. From then on, it was commonly assumed that you could place *ideological positions* somewhere on a list ranging from the *left* to the *right*. *This system of classifying political philosophies* is attractive because it seems so tidy. But it

[11] From "The Wasteful Savers" by Curtis Harnack, first published in *The Reporter*, September 29, 1960. Reprinted by permission of the author.

[12] From "The Compleat Hobbyist" by Alfred Bester, *Holiday*, December, 1965.

is woefully inadequate, since it is one-dimensional, whereas the *world* is three-dimensional. The *world* today is much too complex to hold still for the *left* versus *right* and the *liberal* versus *conservative* classifications. —BOB SENSER[13]

▶ EXERCISE 5 In paragraphs 25 and 34, or in any others assigned by your instructor, underline each word or idea that is repeated in order to link the sentences within the paragraph. In your last paper underline words or ideas that are repeated as a means of linking sentences.

(4) Link sentences by using such transitional expressions as the following:

ADDITION   moreover, further, furthermore, besides, and, and then, likewise, also, nor, too, again, in addition, equally important, next, first, secondly, thirdly, finally, last, lastly

CONTRAST   but, yet, and yet, however, still, nevertheless, on the other hand, on the contrary, after all, notwithstanding, for all that, in contrast to this, at the same time, although this may be true, otherwise

COMPARISON   similarly, likewise, in like manner

PURPOSE   to this end, for this purpose, with this object

RESULT   hence, therefore, accordingly, consequently, thus, thereupon, as a result, then

TIME   meanwhile, at length, immediately, soon, after a few days, in the meantime, afterward, later

PLACE   here, beyond, nearby, opposite to, adjacent to, on the opposite side

SUMMARY, REPETITION, EXEMPLIFICATION, INTENSIFICATION   to sum up, in brief, on the whole, in sum, in short, as I have said, in other words, to be sure, as has been noted, for example, for instance, in fact, indeed, in any event

Note the transitional expressions in the following paragraph. See also paragraph 17.

15   Since the major cost of advanced education, if the student is away from home, is board and lodging, one can argue that as far as possible the expansion of public education beyond

[13] From "Don't Get Obsessed with Labels" by Bob Senser, reprinted from *Our Sunday Visitor*, May 7, 1961. By permission of the publishers.

high school should be arranged locally. *Otherwise* in order to offer equal opportunities we should have to envisage using public funds to provide years of free board and room for a considerable fraction of our high school graduates. *But* there are various types of professional and vocational education which can be given at only a few centers in even a very populous state. It is literally impossible, *for example*, to give adequate instruction in clinical medicine except in cities of sufficient size to support large hospitals. *Similarly*, advanced work in the arts, sciences, and letters can be done only where adequate libraries and laboratories are at hand. It is clearly in the national interest to find all the latent talent available for the lengthy training that research careers demand. *Yet* to establish research centers at every point in the United States where general education beyond the high school is desired would be not merely uneconomical, but impossible.   —JAMES BRYANT CONANT[14]

▶ EXERCISE 6   In paragraph 37, or in any others assigned by your instructor, underline all transitional expressions used to link sentences within the paragraph. In your last paper underline all transitional expressions used to link sentences.

(5) Link sentences by means of parallel structure—that is, by repetition of the sentence pattern.

Note how the following paragraph is made coherent by the parallel structure of the last four sentences.

   16   In the minds and in the ideals of Americans we have untouched natural resources that need developing just as much as the material treasures still tucked away in unused patents, in undeveloped river valleys, and in the atomic nuclei. For the next war, if one is still required to iron out national vanities, we shall need not so much manpower as brain power and alertness. For the continuing fight against disease, we shall need trained technical skills and unlimited resources in laboratory equipment and service. For the advancement of knowledge generally, we need a deliberate plan to free contemplative men for quiet and respected contemplation. For the realization of "fuller and more fruitful employment and

---

[14] From "The University," reprinted from *Education in a Divided World* by James Bryant Conant. By permission of Harvard University Press.

a fuller and more fruitful life," we need a National Science Foundation and a country-wide awareness that governmental support for knowledge-research is henceforth basic in the national policy.

—HARLOW SHAPLEY[15]

▶ EXERCISE 7 In paragraph 27, or in any others assigned by your instructor, point out instances of parallel structure used to link sentences within the paragraph. Can you find instances in your own writing?

We have observed that easy transition from sentence to sentence within the paragraph depends on clear arrangement of the sentences and then on linking these sentences by means of pronouns, repeated words or ideas, transitional expressions, and parallel structure. Usually several of these aids to coherence are found in a single paragraph. In the following paragraph the linking devices are underlined and are explained in the margins.

17 It would seem that the great

virtue of <u>writing</u> is its power to

Repetition of word arrest the swift process of thought

for steady contemplation and analy-

sis. Writing is the translation of

Parallel structure <u>the audible into the visual.</u> In *Pronoun (referring to writing)*

large measure <u>it</u> is the spatiali-

zation of thought. Yet <u>writing</u> on *Repetition of word*

Transitional word papyrus and parchment fostered a

very different set of <u>mental habits</u> *Repetition of idea (process of thought)*

from those we associate with print

[15] From "Status Quo or Pioneer," *Harper's Magazine*, October, 1945.

336 Larger Elements

and books. <u>In the first place</u>, si- *Transitional expression*

lent reading was unknown until the

macadamized, streamlined surfaces

of the printed page arrived to per- *Parallel structure*

mit the <u>swift traverse of the eye</u>

Repetition of idea (silent reading) <u>alone</u>. <u>In the second place</u>, diffi-

culty of access of manuscripts *Transitional expression*

impelled students to memorize so

far as possible everything they

Pronoun referring to necessary memorization read. <u>This</u> led to encyclopedism,

but also to having on tap in oral

discourse one's entire erudition.[16]

▶ EXERCISE 8 In paragraph 36 below, or in any other paragraphs assigned by your instructor, point out all devices used to insure easy transition from sentence to sentence.

(6) Transitions between paragraphs.

Transitions from one paragraph to the next are even more necessary than those between sentences within the paragraph. The reader takes it for granted that all sentences in one paragraph are on the same topic. But the paragraph break signals a new topic or a new phase of the preceding one, and the reader wants to know at once what

[16] From "Sight, Sound, and Fury" by Marshall McLuhan, reprinted from *Commonweal*, April 9, 1954, the weekly journal of opinion edited by Catholic laymen. By permission of *Commonweal*.

the new one is to be. In the three connected paragraphs (18, 19, and 20) below, note how each opening sentence ties in with the preceding paragraph and also indicates the direction in which the new paragraph is to go.

18 In Philadelphia, the advantage of a small car was recently illustrated in a court of law. A baffled cop had dragged before a magistrate the owners of two MGs which had both been parked in the motor space designed for a single vehicle. It was the view of the cop that this arrangement resulted in an illicit mulcting of the city at the rate of a dime an hour. The magistrate disagreed; he commended the drivers for their ingenuity.

19 Another and no less precious asset arises not so much from size as from lighter and differently distributed weight. A small car is supremely handy in icy weather. It is almost never trapped by snow or mud, and it will almost never lose traction on a slippery grade. Its skids are rare and gentle. And its driver can enjoy the soul-satisfying experience of wending his way up a steep and snowy hill at an even speed among big cars which have skidded into the gutter or which lie helplessly athwart the highway.

20 For many of the more than a million Americans who own two or more cars, these and other advantages have dictated the choice of a small car as a supplement to the basic big car. The combination of, say, a station wagon and an MG provides a nice balance between capacity and chic and provides an escape from the status of a two-car family with all the financial and social implications it involves. A small car doesn't seem to be *exactly* a car; its sheepish owner can treat it as a gadget and explain that it costs next to nothing to operate.

—LAURENCE LAFORE, R. W. LAFORE, AND R. W. LAFORE, JR.[17]

The topics of the three paragraphs may be stated thus: (18) *Ease of parking small cars was recently illustrated in Philadelphia.* (19) *The light weight of small cars is especially advantageous in icy weather.* (20) *The small car needs hardly to be considered a "second" car.* The opening sentence of paragraph 18 refers, by *advantage,* to the

[17] From "The Small Cars: Fun on Wheels," *Harper's Magazine*, March, 1955.

previously discussed ease of parking small cars and also leads up to the illustration to be used in the paragraph. The next paragraph begins with *another . . . asset,* showing at once that an additional advantage of small cars is to be pointed out (at the same time that *another* calls attention to the one just discussed). And *these and other advantages* in the opening sentence of paragraph 20 ties in with what has preceded while leading to what is to follow.

Sometimes a paragraph is used to make a transition. Paragraph 22 below is an example of a transitional paragraph.

21 I am overwhelmed by our material and material-istic culture—and its accomplishments. We have developed manufacturing and marketing techniques unsurpassed by any other country. The editors of *Fortune* magazine have observed, "The foreign visitor is drenched with sights and sounds and smells emanating from a man-made environment to which almost all Americans appear to give all their energies."

22 What are some of the factors that make us differ-ent from the rest of the world?

23 Our *standard of living* is considerably higher than that of any other nation. In fact, the American way of living is one in which an ever-increasing standard of living is considered our birthright. And with a high standard of living, we have not only great physical and material well-being but also an opportunity to expand our economy still further, especially in the last part of the twentieth century. —STEUART HENDERSON BRITT[18]

[Note how paragraph 22 links paragraph 21 (which stresses our difference from the rest of the world) with paragraph 23 (which discusses one factor that makes us different). The paragraphs after 23 take up and develop separately the other factors.]

▶ EXERCISE 9 Analyze all of the transitions, not only those between sentences within a paragraph but also those between the paragraphs.

---

[18] By permission from *The Spenders,* by Steuart Henderson Britt. Copy-right 1960. McGraw-Hill Book Company, Inc.

24 Language must convey all the complex organization of observations, ideas, and plain prejudices on which society and culture rest. It must reveal our individual moods, social status, origin, and appraisal of the situation in which we find ourselves. It must enable us to interact both with close friends and total strangers promptly and effectively. All this is complicated enough.

25 But language must do more than this. It must continually adjust itself to new needs. No language can be a fixed system of words and patterns. It must be open to receive new words and new structures, and to change the old. Change is inevitable, since language functions in a society in ceaseless flux. The continual change in language produces inevitable maladjustments in the system. The language must repeatedly repair itself, restoring and maintaining equilibrium by additional changes to counterbalance those forced upon it by changed environment. A language that could not adjust would deteriorate.   —H. A. GLEASON, JR.[19]

31c

Develop the paragraph adequately. Supply enough information to satisfy the reader but avoid excessively long paragraphs.

(1) Supply enough information to satisfy the reader.

Avoid inadequately developed paragraphs. A topic sentence is not in itself a paragraph. In ordinary writing a very short paragraph is sometimes used for emphasis or for transition between longer paragraphs. But a *series* of paragraphs each less than fifty words in length (except in dialogue and other special types of writing) suggests inadequate development of the thought. If such choppy paragraphs deal with the same topic, they should be combined into one or more longer paragraphs. If not, each paragraph should be expanded to the point where the thought is adequately developed.

[19] From *Linguistics and English Grammar*, New York, 1965, p. 107.

PARAGRAPHS THAT SHOULD BE COMBINED

The line of demarcation between capitalism and socialism is sharp and clear.

Capitalism is that form of organization in which the means of production—and by that is meant the machine and the funds required to utilize the machine—are controlled by private individuals or by privately owned organizations.

Under a socialistic regime the control of the means of production, the control of capital—for even socialists concede the need for capital—is by the group. Under capitalism the profits accrue to the private individual; under socialism, to the group.

[These three short paragraphs, read together, actually make one unified paragraph of ninety words and should be so written. Taken separately, the paragraphs are short and choppy; together they form a paragraph of average length developing a clearly stated topic sentence: *The line of demarcation between capitalism and socialism is sharp and clear.*]

PARAGRAPHS THAT SHOULD BE EXPANDED

During his first term of office President Roosevelt introduced many laws to promote national recovery. These laws covered all phases of the national life.

[The reader wants to know specifically what some of these laws were.]

Forestry work is healthful, educational, and financially rewarding. A forester, for example, soon learns how to prevent and to fight forest fires.

[The reader expects to find out about three aspects of forestry work, and the writer comments briefly on only one. How is the work healthful? What else does a forester learn? What are the financial rewards?]

The football game was much more like a movie than like real life. The most improbable things happened.

[Some of the improbable happenings should be mentioned, and the implied contrast between the movies and real life elaborated.]

Each of these short paragraphs begins with a promising topic sentence and then stops before supplying enough information to satisfy the reader. In other words, the paragraphs are not adequately developed. If the paragraphs in your compositions tend to be inadequately developed, study the seven methods of paragraph development described and illustrated in **31d**, pages 344–57.

(2) Avoid excessively long paragraphs.

In current writing, paragraphs seldom run to more than two or three hundred words, and the average is much shorter, perhaps not more than one hundred words. Whenever a writer finds that he needs more than 250 words to develop his central thought, he should, if possible, divide his material into two or more paragraphs. Let us notice, for example, how we may divide the following long paragraph, which Richard Steele wrote more than two hundred years ago when readers were less hurried than those of our generation.

¹ When a good artist would express any remarkable character in sculpture, he endeavors to work up his figure into all the perfections his imagination can form, and to imitate not so much what is, as what may or ought to be. ² I shall follow their example, in the idea I am going to trace out of a fine gentleman, by assembling together such qualifications as seem requisite to make the character complete. ³ In order to do this I shall premise in general, that by a fine gentleman I mean a man completely qualified as well for the service and good as for the ornament and delight of society. ⁴ When I consider the frame of mind peculiar to a gentleman, I suppose it graced with all the dignity and elevation of spirit that human nature is capable of. ⁵ To this I would have joined a clear understanding, a reason free from prejudice, a steady judgment, and an extensive knowledge. ⁶ When I think of the heart of a gentleman, I imagine it firm and intrepid, void of all inordinate passions, and full of tenderness, compassion, and benevolence. ⁷ When I view the fine gentleman with regard to his manners, methinks I see him modest without bashfulness, frank and affable without impertinence, obliging and complaisant without servility, cheerful and in good humor without noise. ⁸ These amiable qualities are not easily obtained; neither are there many men that have a genius to excel this way. ⁹ A finished gentleman is perhaps the most un-

common of all the great characters in life. ^{10} Besides the natural endowments with which this distinguished man is to be born, he must run through a long series of education. ^{11} Before he makes his appearance and shines in the world, he must be principled in religion, instructed in all the moral virtues, and led through the whole course of the polite arts and sciences. ^{12} He should be no stranger to courts and to camps; he must travel to open his mind, to enlarge his views, to learn the policies and interests of foreign states, as well as to fashion and polish himself, and to get clear of national prejudices, of which every country has its share. ^{13} To all these more essential improvements he must not forget to add the fashionable ornaments of life, such as are the languages and the bodily exercises most in vogue; neither would I have him think even dress itself beneath his notice.

A careful reading shows that this whole paragraph of 404 words develops Steele's concept of the ideal gentleman. The paragraph has unity; except for the excessive length, there would be no reason for dividing it. Fortunately it can (like most overlong paragraphs) be divided into shorter paragraphs, each developing a specific part of the general topic. Steele's long paragraph can be divided, without any rewriting, into three good paragraphs as follows:

FIRST PARAGRAPH (sentences 1–3) The method to be used in depicting the ideal gentleman and a general definition of him.
SECOND PARAGRAPH (sentences 4–7) The ideal gentleman's specific qualities of mind, heart, and manners.
THIRD PARAGRAPH (sentences 8–13) The education needed to develop these qualities.

If the long paragraph were thus divided into three, it would be much easier for the reader to comprehend. And each paragraph would be well unified, with good transitions from one to the other. Note especially the excellent transition to the third paragraph: "These amiable qualities are not easily obtained; neither are there many men that have a genius to excel this way."

31d

Master several different methods of paragraph development.

Analysis shows that good paragraphs may be developed by many methods and by innumerable combinations of methods. No one method, or combination of methods, is better than another except as it happens to fit the needs of a given paragraph. The experienced writer may be unaware of the method he is using. The inexperienced writer, however, can learn to develop his own paragraphs by studying the methods of professional writers.

(1) List specific details suggested by the topic sentence.

26 After the refrain she would give the night herding yodel of the cowboy, born of the vast melancholy of the plains; *a yodel to quiet a herd of restless cattle in the deep darkness of a rainy night,* when far-off flashes of lightning and the rumble of distant thunder meant danger. While the cattle milled around and refused to lie down, close to the fringe of the circle of moving animals rode the cowboys giving this wordless cry to the cattle, like the plea of a lonesome wolf calling for his mate, like the croon of a mother trying to quiet a restless babe in the long watches of the night, like the soft moo of a cow wooing her young offspring from its hiding place to come for its milk. "Quiet, cattle, quiet. Darkness is everywhere, but we, your friends, are near. Lie down, little dogies, lie down." The yodel was persuasive, far-reaching. Even in its high notes it was soothing and tender. —JOHN A. LOMAX[20]

[Notice that the carefully selected details bring into focus the nature and effect of the yodel at night. Effective writers choose details with care, and omit irrelevant details no matter how fascinating they may be in themselves.]

27 *My second great fortune was Lily Bess Campbell, professor of English literature at the University of California in Los Angeles.* She taught me to think exactly, to say the precise truth as nearly as I could perceive it. She taught me that there is vitality

[20] From "Songs of the Cowboy," *Atlantic Monthly,* March, 1947.

in logic, that there is logic in humor and in beauty, that in humor the greater the truth the funnier, that in lyricism the more consistent and clear the more moving. She made me brief a Shelley ode as though it were a legal argument. She taught me that a sentence was organic with bones and sinews and for this reason had life, that the power of logic was a passionate power and that Euclid and Grammar were one. And for the first time I recognized Pattern, which is Law as well as Magic. —AGNES DE MILLE[21]

[The paragraph lists nine particulars in which Professor Campbell proved to be a "great fortune."]

28 When it was over and I escaped through the ropes, shaking, bleeding a little from the mouth, with rosin dust on my pants and a vicious throbbing in my head, *I knew all there was to know about being hit in the prize-ring.* It seems that I had gone to an expert for tuition. I knew the sensation of being stalked and pursued by a relentless, truculent professional destroyer whose trade and business it was to injure men. I saw the quick flash of the brown forearm that precedes the stunning shock as a bony, leather-bound fist lands on cheek or mouth. I learned more (partly from photographs of the lesson, viewed afterwards, one of which shows me ducked under a vicious left hook, an act of which I never had the slightest recollection) about instinctive ducking and blocking than I could have in ten years of looking at prizefights, and I learned, too, that as the soldier never hears the bullet that kills him, so does the fighter rarely, if ever, see the punch that tumbles blackness over him like a mantle, with a tearing rip as though the roof of his skull were exploding, and robs him of his senses. —PAUL GALLICO[22]

[Details of this paragraph describe how the author learned what it is like to be a prizefighter. Note that in this paragraph and in paragraphs 26 and 27, the order of development is from the general to the particular.]

▶ EXERCISE 10 Develop one of the following topic sentences by using carefully selected specific details.

[21] From "The Valor of Teaching" by Agnes de Mille, *Atlantic Monthly*, June, 1955.
[22] From *Farewell to Sport* by Paul Gallico. Reprinted by permission of Alfred A. Knopf, Inc.

1. Americans know what two aspirins can do.
2. Television shows are influential babysitters.
3. Music shapes our moods.
4. My uncle was in almost perpetual emotion.
5. The comedian looked as distressed as a freshman on registration day.
6. One teacher influenced my thinking.
7. It was a perfect day for a trip to the lake.
8. At that moment, I knew how it felt to have stage fright.
9. I was the first one to arrive after the accident.
10. It is exciting to travel by jet.

(2) Illustrate the topic sentence by an example or examples.

29 *The belief in punishment at a distance was strikingly illustrated by a report from South Africa last April.* It seems that the caning of offenders was being carried out in a magistrates' court located near the center of Cape Town. Sentences of up to ten cuts were inflicted on malefactors, beginning with eight-year-old boys, in that particular jurisdiction. The matter became newsworthy when the public began to object to the practice. The objection, however, was not to the punishment itself but to the uncomfortable circumstance that it was administered in the business district of the city. One citizen complained, "We can clearly hear the swish and smack of the cane and the pleadings and screams of the people being beaten." It appears that this noise was upsetting women office workers. Not only the women were disturbed. One man said "that his conversations with important clients had been interrupted by the 'howling of somebody being thrashed.'" The problem was solved by police assurances that the beatings would thereafter be administered in the basement, where they would not disturb the public.   —JUDGE DAVID L. BAZELON[23]

[The topic sentence is developed by one striking example. Note that the example of the citizens' reactions to *nearby* punishment makes immediately clear what the author means by the rather abstract idea, "the belief in punishment at a distance." A good

[23] From "The Imperative to Punish" by David L. Bazelon, reprinted from the *Atlantic Monthly*, June, 1960. By permission of the author.

example is clearly related to the generalization it illustrates, and it makes that generalization easily understandable to the reader.]

30   *Tails serve animals as* fly-swatters, as signals, as instruments of communication, as extra hands and *tools of many uses.* A woolly monkey curls the tip of his tail into a circle, plants this loop on the ground, stiffens the rest of the tail into a supporting column, and has a portable chair. A honey bear, raiding a nest of bees, hangs head downward and then, when it wants to make its getaway, climbs its own tail. Pangolins, which are scaly anteaters living in West Africa, block their burrow entrances with their armored tails.   —ALAN DEVOE[24]

[Three sentences, each presenting a separate example, develop the topic sentence.]

31   The average cow hand is so conscious of brands that in season and out of season, appropriately and inappropriately, consciously and unconsciously, *he brands whatever he comes across.* He whittles brands on sticks; he burns them into the planks of branding chutes, on pasture gates, on the anchor posts of windmill towers. He smears them with axle grease across the doors of barns and garages. He paints them with charcoal on the rock walls of canyons in which he has made a campfire. He carves them into his spur traps, leggings, saddle—above all, into his boot tops. More pistols were etched with cattle brands than were ever notched for dead victims. Many a cook has stenciled the ranch coat of arms into the top crust of that gala-day treat—a wild-plum cobbler. Ranchboys are incorrigible when it comes to carving brands on their desks at school. They play ranch, and with bailing wire for running irons brand oak balls, the sawed-off tips of horns, spools, and other objects used to represent cattle and horses.   —J. FRANK DOBIE[25]

[The topic sentence is developed by numerous examples.]

32   *Perhaps the most extraordinary quality the Mohammedan religion developed in Jolo is its fanaticism.* For years, no Moro would attend school for fear of "invisible conversion" to

---

[24] From *This Fascinating Animal World* by Alan Devoe. Copyright 1951 McGraw-Hill Book Company. Used by permission.

[25] From "The Heraldry of the Range," *Adventures in American Literature,* New York, 1958, p. 173.

Christianity. As recently as 1940 the students of one of the schools killed all their non-Moro teachers for no reason that the authorities were ever able to discern. And even today, some people of Jolo will not ride in a car, simply because Christians introduced automobiles to the island. It is also a problem for Moros to go to the hospital, because, according to their reasoning, if they died, a Christian would touch them, and this is not to be borne.

—FAUBION BOWERS[26]

[The topic sentence is developed by four instances or examples, each in a separate sentence.]

▶ EXERCISE 11   Analyze the development of paragraph 12, or any other paragraph selected by your instructor.

▶ EXERCISE 12   Develop one of the following topics by using a long example or several short ones.

1. The collie is a particularly loyal dog.
2. It is easy to coach at a distance.
3. A man uses his thumb in various ways.
4. There is a flower for every occasion.
5. My little brother is always fixing things.
6. Our science teacher encourages us really to see the things we look at.
7. In my collection are many greeting cards.
8. I have considered majoring in several subjects.
9. He makes everyone he meets feel important.
10. Almost anything can be bought on the installment plan.

(3) Develop the topic by definition.

   33   *First, it is desirable to define the intellectuals.* They are all those who create, distribute and apply culture—the symbolic world of man, including art, science and religion. Within this group, three different levels can be set out. There is the hard core who are the creators of culture—authors, artists, philosophers, scholars, editors, some journalists. Second, there are those who

[26] From "The Land-Locked Pirate of the Pacific," *Harper's Magazine*, June, 1955.

distribute what others create—performers of various arts, most teachers, most reporters. Third, and the most peripheral group, are those who apply culture as part of their jobs—professionals such as physicians and lawyers.   —SEYMOUR MARTIN LIPSET[27]

[The topic sentence calls for a definition of *intellectuals;* the other sentences define and explain the word. A formal, or logical, definition such as Lipset uses has two parts: first, the thing being defined is put into a *class* of similar things; then it is differentiated from all other things in that class. Thus, *intellectuals* are defined as "those" men (*class*—i.e., mankind) "who create, distribute and apply culture" (*difference* from other kinds of men).]

34 *A guaranteed annual wage is money paid by an employer to people for all or some part of a year in which they are not making products.* The payments are part of the manufacturer's cost and hence part of the consumer's cost. If the manufacturer has ten employees but work for only eight, he must nevertheless recover in the price he gets for his product the payments he makes to his employees for hours they did not work, or he must go out of business. This is true of any employer, whether he has ten or ten thousand employees.   —LELAND HAZARD[28]

[The topic sentence defines "guaranteed annual wage," and the remaining sentences serve to refine and clarify this definition.]

▶ EXERCISE 13   Select a suitable topic sentence and develop a paragraph by definition.

(4) Develop the topic by using classification.

35 There are three kinds of book owners. The first has all the standard sets and best-sellers—unread, untouched. (This deluded individual owns woodpulp and ink, not books.) The second has a great many books—a few of them read through, most of them dipped into, but all of them as clean and shiny as the day they were bought. (This person would probably like to make books his own,

[27] From "The Egghead Looks at Himself" by Seymour M. Lipset, reprinted from the New York *Times Magazine*, November 17, 1957. By permission of the author.

[28] From "Can We Afford a Guaranteed Wage?" by Leland Hazard, *Atlantic Monthly*, March, 1955.

but is restrained by a false respect for their physical appearance.)
The third has a few books or many—every one of them dog-eared
and dilapidated, shaken and loosened by continual use, marked and
scribbled in from front to back. (This man owns books.)

—MORTIMER J. ADLER[29]

[Classification is like definition in that it develops an idea by
putting things into classes. But it does not differentiate one member of a class from another; instead, it simply gives a complete
or representative listing of the members of the class. Thus,
Adler in the paragraph above classifies book owners into three
main classes and lists each class.]

▶ **EXERCISE 14**   Use classification to develop one of the
following topics:

1. There are various kinds of newspapers (OR columnists,
   editors, comic strips).
2. I have known two (OR three, OR four) distinct types of
   hostesses (OR advisers, artists, lecturers).

(5) Develop the topic by using comparison or contrast.

36   To some of his contemporaries Socrates looked like
a sophist. But *he distrusted and opposed the sophists wherever
possible.* They toured the whole Greek world: Socrates stayed in
Athens, talking to his fellow-citizens. They made carefully prepared
continuous speeches; he only asked questions. They took rich fees
for their teaching; he refused regular payment, living and dying
poor. They were elegantly dressed, turned out like filmstars on a
personal-appearance tour, with secretaries and personal servants
and elaborate advertising. Socrates wore the workingman's clothes,
bare feet and a smock; in fact, he had been a stonemason and
carver by trade, and came from a working-class family. They spoke
in specially prepared lecture-halls; he talked to people at street-
corners and in the gymnasium (like public baths and bathing beaches
nowadays), where every afternoon the young men exercised, and
the old men talked, while they all sun bathed. He fitted in so well
there that he sometimes compared himself to the athletic coach,
who does not run or wrestle, but teaches others how to run and

[29] From "How to Mark a Book" by Mortimer J. Adler, reprinted from
the *Saturday Review,* July 6, 1940. By permission of the publishers.

wrestle better: Socrates said he trained people to think. Lastly, the sophists said they knew everything and were ready to explain it. Socrates said he knew nothing and was trying to find out.

—GILBERT HIGHET[30]

[The first sentence is transitional, linking this paragraph with the author's foregoing one; the second sentence states the topic, which is developed by contrasting the sophists with Socrates. In making a comparison or contrast, a writer will often choose the things he wants to compare or contrast from the same class. Socrates and the sophists both belong to the class "philosopher-teachers." This common class provides the *basis* of the contrast. Thus the two kinds of philosophers can be contrasted not only in their methods and their personal habits but, most important, in the ideas or theories of knowledge they taught.]

37 *In all the countries of Europe I have visited there is a patent difference between metropolises and smaller towns.* In the provinces of France, or Austria, or Germany you notice the difference in every shop window, in every coffee house, in the universities themselves. When, for instance, you go from Paris to Lille or to Orleans or to Bordeaux the dresses, the books, the furniture you see in the windows will lag some months if not years behind those you were used to seeing in Paris. The hotels and restaurants will be more modest, uncomfortable, and rather shabby. Universities will lack the stimulating élan of the Sorbonne. *Nothing of this kind distinguishes Madison from, let us say, New York or Chicago.* Here you see just the same merchandise in the windows as in New York, the same neon lights, the same pictures in the same movie theaters, you read the same columns and comics in the local papers as in those of New York, and the university with its splendid installations, its rich library, its almost luxurious Students' Union certainly does not fall behind any university I saw in New York, though it is smaller.

—PAUL SCHRECKER[31]

[The implied topic sentence, derived from the two italicized sentences, is: In Europe, but not in America, there is a patent difference between metropolises and smaller towns. European conditions (in four sentences following the first italicized sen-

[30] From *The Art of Teaching* by Gilbert Highet. Copyright 1950 by Gilbert Highet. Reprinted by permission of Alfred A. Knopf, Inc.

[31] From "American Diary," *Harper's Magazine,* July, 1944.

The Paragraph **351**

tence) are contrasted with American conditions (in one very long sentence following the second italicized sentence). Note that instances or examples are used to develop the separate parts of the contrast.]

▶ EXERCISE 15 Develop by contrast one of the following topics: (1) the service at a soda fountain and in a hotel dining room; (2) the dialogue of a motion picture and the dialogue of Shakespeare; (3) the architecture of the Washington Monument and of the Lincoln Memorial; (4) the relative effectiveness of radio and television.

38 *The living language is like a cowpath: it is the creation of the cows themselves, who, having created it, follow it or depart from it according to their whims or needs.* From daily use, the path undergoes change. A cow is under no obligation to stay in the narrow path she helped make, following the contour of the land, but she often profits by staying with it and she would be handicapped if she didn't know where it was and where it led to. Children obviously do not depend for communication on a knowledge of grammar; they rely on their ear, mostly, which is sharp and quick. But we have yet to see the child who hasn't profited from coming face to face with a relative pronoun at an early age, and from reading books, which follow the paths of centuries.

—E. B. WHITE[32]

[This paragraph compares the living language to a cowpath and the children who speak the language to the cows that use the path by pointing out similarities regarding creation, usage, change, and profitable knowledge and conformity. Note that, unlike the comparisons in paragraphs 35 and 36, the two things compared here are not members of the same class.]

Note that the last three paragraphs illustrate two different ways of making the contrast. In paragraphs 37 and 38 one side of the contrast is completely developed and then the other; in paragraph 36 both sides are contrasted in almost every sentence. Either way is good, and so is a combination of the two.

[32] From the *New Yorker*, February 23, 1957. Reprinted by permission; Copr. © 1957, The New Yorker Magazine, Inc.

▶ EXERCISE 16   Develop a paragraph by analogy according to the organization used in paragraph 38.

(6) Develop the topic by showing cause or effect.

39   Tragedy was a Greek creation because in Greece thought was free. Men were thinking more and more deeply about human life, and beginning to perceive more and more clearly that it was bound up with evil and that injustice was of the nature of things. And then, one day, this knowledge of something irremediably wrong in the world came to a poet with his poet's power to see beauty in the truth of human life, and the first tragedy was written. As the author of a most distinguished book on the subject says: "The spirit of inquiry meets the spirit of poetry and tragedy is born." Make it concrete: early Greece with her godlike heroes and hero-gods fighting far on the ringing plains of windy Troy; with her lyric world, where every common thing is touched with beauty —her twofold world of poetic creation. Then a new age dawns, not satisfied with beauty of song and story, an age that must try to know and to explain. And for the first time tragedy appears. A poet of surpassing magnitude, not content with the old sacred conventions, and of a soul great enough to bear new and intolerable truth—that is Aeschylus, the first writer of tragedy.

—EDITH HAMILTON[33]

[Miss Hamilton here states that tragedy began when the ancient Greeks discovered, through free inquiry, that evil is an inevitable part of human life. This discovery is, then, the *cause* of the writing of tragedy. But before this cause could have an effect in the creation of tragic plays, a great poet had to come along—that was Aeschylus. A paragraph developed by causal analysis must not only raise the question *why* but answer it to the satisfaction of the reader. The cause or causes must satisfactorily explain the result. Has Miss Hamilton done this?]

40   One might wonder why, after the Norman Conquest, French did not become the national language, replacing English entirely. The reason is that the Conquest was not a national migration, as the earlier Anglo-Saxon invasion had been. Great

---

[33] Reprinted from *The Greek Way* by Edith Hamilton. By permission of W. W. Norton & Company, Inc. Copyright 1930, 1942 by W. W. Norton & Company, Inc.

numbers of Normans came to England, but they came as rulers and landlords. French became the language of the court, the language of the nobility, the language of polite society, the language of literature. But it did not replace English as the language of the people. There must always have been hundreds of towns and villages in which French was never heard except when visitors of high station passed through. —PAUL ROBERTS[34]

[The topic sentence raises the question why the Norman Conquest did not, as might have been expected, make England a French-speaking country. The topic sentence thus states an *effect* or *result* of the Conquest. The sentences that follow develop the topic by showing *causes* to account for the result.]

▶ EXERCISE 17 Notice how paragraphs 39 and 40 are developed by explaining why the opening statement is true. In the same way develop a paragraph from one of the following topics:

1. Higher education has become more important than ever.
2. Our age is a dangerous one in which to live.

(7) Develop the topic by a combination of methods.

Many good paragraphs are developed not by any one specific method but by a combination of methods. Some good paragraphs almost defy analysis. The important consideration is not the specific method used but the adequacy of the development.

41 I wonder why American towns look so much alike that I sometimes mix them up in my memory. The reference to the standard influence of mass production whose agents are the traveling salesman, the mail-order houses, the five-and-ten cent stores, the chain stores, the movies, is not sufficient. If you stay two days in Bologna and in Ferrara, or in Arles and in Avignon, you will never mix them up in all your life. But it may well happen that

[34] From "A Brief History of English," reprinted from *Understanding English* by Paul Roberts. By permission of Harper & Brothers.

after you spend two days in St. Louis and in Kansas City the images of these towns soon merge into one. I think the real reason for this is that these towns have not yet had time enough to individualize and to crystallize visible local traditions of their own. Physiognomically speaking, children are much less differentiated from each other than grown people. —PAUL SCHRECKER[35]

[Note how this effective paragraph combines both cause or effect and comparison or contrast.]

42 I have heard rumors of visitors who were disappointed. The same people will be disappointed at the Day of Judgment. In fact, the Grand Canyon is a sort of landscape Day of Judgment. It is not a show place, a beauty spot, but a revelation. The Colorado River, which is powerful, turbulent, and so thick with silt that it is like a saw, made it with the help of the erosive forces of rain, frost, and wind, and some strange geological accidents; and all these together have been hard at work on it for the last seven or eight million years. It is the largest of the eighteen canyons of the Colorado River, is over two hundred miles long, has an average width of twelve miles, and is a good mile deep. It is the world's supreme example of erosion. But this is not what it really is. It is, I repeat, a revelation. The Colorado River made it, but you feel when you are there that God gave the Colorado River its instructions. It is all Beethoven's nine symphonies in stone and magic light. Even to remember that it is still there lifts up the heart. If I were an American, I should make my remembrance of it the final test of men, art, and policies. I should ask myself: Is this good enough to exist in the same country as the Canyon? How would I feel about this man, this kind of art, these political measures, if I were near that Rim? Every member or officer of the Federal Government ought to remind himself, with triumphant pride, that he is on the staff of the Grand Canyon. —J. B. PRIESTLEY[36]

▶ **EXERCISE 18** Pick out the topic sentence in paragraph 42. Show how Priestley effectively develops his central idea. What specific methods or combination of methods of development are used?

---

[35] From "American Diary," *Harper's Magazine*, July, 1944.
[36] From *Midnight on the Desert* by J. B. Priestley. By permission of the author.

▶ EXERCISE 19   Be prepared for a class discussion of the following paragraphs. Be able to point out topic sentences or central ideas and to designate methods of development.

43   Being a freethinking fisherman who will try anything, I borrowed the colonel's flimsy rod, only to find out that, while bread bait may not be immoral, it was in this case impractical. Mother Slonaker's loaf was so creamy good that it simply melted off the hook, and the trout would gobble it up as it drifted toward the bottom of the pool. At this point a conventional fisherman would have given up, but not an iconoclast with a fish crow to feed. Looking around for a bread substitute, I could hardly fail to see the piles of cigarette butts with which the colonel, while nervously dueling the trout, had littered the bank of the pool. Fortunately, he smoked Brand X, a filtered fag, suitably safe and masculine for a marine. Breaking off a firm, fibrous, buoyant filter, I put it on the hook and threw it in the water. A rainbow immediately rose, trout-lipped the butt, swallowed it, and was pulled out on the grass.   —BIL GILBERT[37]

44   Except for the charred joke of a wall where the fire finally stopped, only our chimney guards the big hole now, and snow blankets most of the wreckage in it. The andirons, their burden of logs consumed along with the room they were supposed to warm, are squatting black in the fireplace. Six feet below, the fire screen is a twisted sculpture where it fell with the floor. Pipes poke at odd angles here and there. Scorched cables snake in and out of the snow piled in the cellar. On a cracked flagstone sits skull-like the metal top of a tape recorder. Near it, a scrap on a little drift, is a circular patch of blue. It is the center of a record, and the printing on it shows that it was Side 2 of Beethoven's *Eroica*. In the shell of the garage a pair of tires and a ping-pong table survive.   —LOUDON WAINWRIGHT[38]

[37] From "The Compleatest Angler" copyright © 1965 by Bil Gilbert. From the book *Bears in the Ladies Room and Other Beastly Pursuits* by Bil Gilbert. Reprinted by permission of the author and Doubleday & Company, Inc.

[38] From "After the Fire, a Sifting of Ashes," *Life* Magazine © 1966, Time Inc.

45 A pecking order has come into existence in science, in which the highest rank is assigned to the "purest" subjects, those whose connection with the directly observable elements of our physical environment is least obvious. Problems relating to the structure of the earth, the origin and history of the solar system, the conditions under which life developed on this planet—all the questions which directly concern the planet earth and man's physical existence on it—are considered impure and of lower intellectual content. Scientific investigations which have a direct bearing on human affairs are ranked at the bottom. The difficult and important problem of the weather is beneath the notice of most physicists.

—ROBERT JASTROW[39]

46 Of the various factors that caused men to come to America, the economic was no doubt the most important. Throughout the period of the migrations, there was no free land in Europe; natural resources were limited; and the population was always in danger of increasing faster than the means of subsistence. Migration always occurred chiefly from areas of Europe where agriculture was still the chief occupation and where (owing to the growth of big estates or to genuine overcrowding) the demand for land was in excess of the supply. This was true of Spain in the sixteenth century, of England in the early seventeenth, and of Ireland, Germany, Scandinavia, Italy, and the Slavic countries of the east in the nineteenth.

—HENRY BAMFORD PARKES[40]

47 Children are poetic. They love to feel of things. I suppose it is necessary to their preservation that they should be, for by random exercise of their organs of feeling they develop them and make them fit for their practical function. But that is not the chief reason why they are poetic; the chief reason is that they are not practical. They have not yet felt the necessity, or got addicted to the trick, of formulating a purpose and then achieving it. There-

[39] From "Intuition in Science: Why Cover It Up?" Science and Humanity Supplement of *Saturday Review,* May 1, 1965.

[40] Reprinted from *The American Experience* by Henry Bamford Parkes, by permission of Alfred A. Knopf, Inc. Copyright 1947, 1955 by Henry Bamford Parkes.

fore, this naive impulse of nature, the impulse toward realization, is free in them. Moreover, it is easy of satisfaction. It is easy for children to taste the qualities of experience, because experience is new, and its qualities are but loosely bound together into what we call "things." Each is concrete, particular, unique, and without an habitual use. —MAX EASTMAN[41]

48 There is Lou Martin, the class comedian, whose forte is facial expressions. No one can look more crestfallen over unprepared homework: hand clasped to brow, knees buckling, shoulders sagging with remorse, he is a penitent to end all penitents. No one can look more thirsty when asking for a pass: tongue hanging out, eyes rolling, a death-rattle in the throat, he can barely make it to the water fountain. No one can look more horrified at a wrong answer issuing from his own traitor lips; or more humble; or more bewildered; or more indignant. I know it's not in the syllabus, but I'm afraid I encourage him by laughing. —BEL KAUFMAN[42]

49 We have always been a small people numerically and we shall remain a small people, unable to compete with our rivals in the size of population, extent of territory, richness of natural resources, and strength and equipment of the armed forces. But our place is in the history of humanity and the place of our country in the world cannot be measured in quantitative terms. Few people have had so profound an influence upon so large a part of the human race. And there are few countries which have played so central a role in world history as the Land of Israel. It must be our aim to achieve a future that can be worthy of our past.

—DAVID BEN GURION[43]

50 This, then, is how one might define jazz: it is a new music of a certain distinct rhythmic and melodic character, one that

[41] From *The Enjoyment of Poetry* by Max Eastman. Reprinted by permission of Charles Scribner's Sons.

[42] From *Up the Down Stair Case* by Bel Kaufman. Copyright 1964 by Bel Kaufman. Published by Prentice-Hall, Inc., Englewood Cliffs, New Jersey.

[43] From *Ben Gurion Looks Back.* Copyright © 1965 by Moshe Pearlman and David Ben Gurion. Reprinted by permission of Simon and Schuster and Weidenfeld & Nicolson, Ltd.

constantly involves improvisation—of a minor sort in adjusting accents and phrases of the tune at hand, of a major sort in creating music extemporaneously, on the spot. In the course of creating jazz, a melody or its underlying chords may be altered. The rhythmic valuations of notes may be lengthened or shortened according to a regular scheme, syncopated or not, or there may be no consistent pattern of rhythmic variations so long as a steady beat remains implicit or explicit. The beat is usually four quarternotes to the bar, serving as a solid rhythmic base for the improvisation of soloists or groups playing eight or twelve measures, or some multiple or dividend thereof. —BARRY ULANOV[44]

51 The essential problem of man in a computerized age remains the same as it has always been. That problem is not solely how to be more productive, more comfortable, more content, but how to be more sensitive, more sensible, more proportionate, more alive. The computer makes possible a phenomenal leap in human proficiency; it demolishes the fences around the practical and even the theoretical intelligence. But the question persists and indeed grows whether the computer will make it easier or harder for human beings to know who they really are, to identify their real problems, to respond more fully to beauty, to place adequate value on life, and make their world safer than it now is.

—NORMAN COUSINS[45]

52 How does an amateur, or a professional, recognize a new comet when he finds one? Most new-found comets are as diffuse and formless as a squashed star, completely devoid of any tail. In this respect they resemble hundreds of faint nebulae that speckle the sky, with this difference: nebulae are fixed, but a comet will inevitably move. Consequently, a second observation made a few hours later will generally reveal a motion if the nebulous wisp is indeed a comet. However, most comet hunters compare the position of their suspected comet with a sky map that charts faint

---

[44] From *A History of Jazz in America* by Barry Ulanov. Copyright 1952 by Barry Ulanov. Reprinted by permission of The Viking Press, Inc.

[45] From "The Computer and the Poet" by Norman Cousins, *Saturday Review,* July, 23, 1966. Reprinted by permission.

nebulae and clusters. Then the discovery is quickly reported to a nearby observatory or directly to the Central Bureau.

—OWEN GINGERICH[46]

53   The herring gull is a creature of sufficient ingenuity that if he picks up a mussel with a shell too hard for his beak to break, he will carry it to a height and drop it on a hard road. He is a creature of sufficient loyalty and perception to guarantee that he will never attack his own mate, and will recognize her among dozens flying into the colony at a distance to defy human binoculars. He is a creature of sufficient social sophistication that, while many arrive in the spring already paired, definite areas in the colony which Tinbergen calls "clubs" will be set aside as meeting places for the unpaired. He is a creature also, as we have seen, of such sensitive social adjustment that the arriving flock will make "decisions" of mood and readiness as if it were one being. So dependent is the herring gull on the community of his citizenship that he would probably be unable to breed were he to return in the spring to the wrong gull town. So powerful and incomprehensible is his attachment for home that, like the albatross, a pair may return year after year to nest in precisely the same spot, although the North Sea's winter storms will have effaced all landmarks to guide his eye.

—ROBERT ARDREY[47]

54   This American devotion to music-making for pleasure is not an overnight development. During the Depression, millions of people attended the free WPA music classes. Thus the movement started. We dreamed of "good times," and when they finally came, amateur music-making on a mass scale followed. Since the end of World War II, the census of adult amateurs has risen considerably: from 16,500,000 in 1947 to 25,000,000 in 1964. In its continuing surveys, the American Music Conference, an organization that promotes amateur music, has found that music-making for the fun of it is now "second only to reading among the nation's leisure-time participative activities."　　　—JAMES T. MAHER[48]

55　Mathematics, the language of science, is not like other tongues. Its symbols are atoms of distilled logic, far more compact than words in some ways but uncolored by any of the associations, sights, and feelings that make words immediately meaningful. As a result, mathematics cannot be translated phrase for phrase or symbol by symbol like French or Sanskrit. Most of its content is no more interesting than a housewife's accounts—pure numbers and quantities. The rest, the part that gradually seeps into the core of a culture, is something that it does not really say at all but only implies. In this it is like poetry. And like a poem, a great formula is not so much translated as it is interpreted—rightly or wrongly according to the judgment and taste of each generation.
　　　—DAVID BERGAMINI[49]

56　At the 1964 meeting of the American Association for the Advancement of Science a University of Colorado researcher named George A. Dulk predicted that a burst of radio signals from the planet Jupiter would be received in Colorado at midnight, December 31, 1964. On New Year's Eve, at 11:40 P.M.—just a few minutes ahead of schedule—a radio signal that sounded like the sizzle of a frying pan was picked up by the eighty-five-foot radio telescope at the National Center for Atmospheric Research. Since the signals did not come from intelligent creatures at the other end—there was never any question of that—the fulfillment of Dulk's prediction caused only a minor stir. For predictions—even startling predictions—of this kind are, of course, the bread and butter of science. They are entirely routine.　　　—ALVIN TOFFLER[50]

---

[48] From "Holiday Handbook: Music-Making at Home" by James T. Maher. Copyright 1966 by Curtis Publishing Company. Reprinted by permission of Harold Matson Company, Inc.

[49] From "The Language of Science" by David Bergamini. Copyright 1960 by Reporter Magazine, Inc. Reprinted by permission of Harold Matson Company, Inc.

[50] From "The Future as a Way of Life" by Alvin Toffler. Reprinted from *Horizon*, Summer, 1965, by permission of the author.

57 Bradley's play has just one somewhat unsound aspect, and it is the result of his mania for throwing the ball to his teammates. He can't seem to resist throwing a certain number of passes that are based on nothing but theory and hope; in fact, they are referred to by the Princeton coaching staff as Bradley's hope passes. They happen, usually, when something has gone just a bit wrong. Bradley is recovering a loose ball, say, with his back turned to the other Princeton players. Before he turned it, he happened to notice a screen, or pickoff, being set by two of his teammates, its purpose being to cause one defensive man to collide with another player and thus free an offensive man to receive a pass and score. Computations whir in Bradley's head. He hasn't time to look, but the screen, as he saw it developing, seemed to be working, so a Princeton man should now be in the clear, running toward the basket with one arm up. He whips the ball over his shoulder to the spot where the man ought to be. Sometimes a hope pass goes flying into the crowd, but most of the time they hit the receiver right in the hand, and a gasp comes from several thousand people. Bradley is sensitive about such dazzling passes, because they look flashy, and an edge comes into his voice as he defends them. "When I was halfway down the court, I saw a man out of the corner of my eye who had on the same color shirt I did," he said recently, explaining how he happened to fire a scoring pass while he was falling out of bounds. "A little later, when I threw the pass, I threw it to the spot where that man should have been if he had kept going and done his job. He was there. Two points." —JOHN MCPHEE[51]

58 In many of the interviews and most of the essays and introductions there are three recurring themes. The first is the nature of poetry. Frost was no untutored swain, though the early interviewers liked to pretend he was, but a conscientious and brilliant student of both the practice and theory of poetry. He resented the suggestion that he was a simple sort of poet, especially when it was made by admirers who polemically contrasted his intelligibility with the obscurity of most of the poets who became influential in the Twenties. He could be impatient enough with what

---

[51] "A Sense of Where You Are" by John McPhee. © 1965, by John McPhee. Reprinted from *The New Yorker*, January 23, 1965, by permission of John McPhee and *The New Yorker*.

seemed to him a faked obscurity, put on to conceal failures of the imagination, but he never suggested that a poem was bad because it was difficult. He knew that his own poems were considerably less simple than most of his admirers believed. In whatever he wrote about the nature of poetry he was careful to avoid dogmatic definitions. He chose to be elusive, even coy, rather than to bind a poet in chains. —GRANVILLE HICKS[52]

59 Mankind in the mass has often been compared, cynically or otherwise, to insects. To the historian proper the image of an ant-heap is almost inevitable. When he looks back into the past, he sees no great men or famous names, but myriads of minute and nameless human insects, hurrying this way and that, making wars and laws, building and destroying cities and civilizations. The swarm ebbs and flows over the earth and through the centuries, the groups converging and coalescing or breaking up and scattering. The story of this ant-heap, of its impersonal groups and communities and of their ebb and flow upon the earth, is history. —LEONARD WOOLF[53]

▶ EXERCISE 20 Indicate an appropriate method or combination of methods of developing each of the following topic sentences:

1. Like history, styles repeat themselves.
2. We are living in the Age of Computers.
3. Students have strange study habits.
4. *Irony* is harder to define than to illustrate.
5. I like Salinger better than Golding.
6. As Tennyson once said, a lie that is half a truth is the blackest lie of all.
7. A circus has many mouths to feed.
8. Before talking about democracy we should at least say what democracy is not.
9. I no longer believe in fortune tellers.

[52] From "Robert Frost Revisited" by Granville Hicks, *Saturday Review*, July 9, 1966. Reprinted by permission.

[53] From *After the Deluge* by Leonard Woolf. Reprinted by permission of The Hogarth Press, Ltd.

10. Some men think our great cities are monuments of progress; others say they are symptoms of social disease.
11. You can solve most problems by taking a walk.
12. Intelligence means the ability to discriminate.
13. At college I have discovered two kinds of friends.
14. A self-reliant person must know his predominant weakness as well as his predominant strength.
15. Automation may revolutionize education.
16. The ability to think and the ability to write are closely allied.
17. There is a great deal of difference between a state college and a state university.
18. When the storm was over we all set to work in earnest.
19. My jalopy reminds me of a frumpy old woman.
20. The itinerary of a typical American tourist will be fascinating in 1980.

Planning and Writing the Whole Composition

32

Arrange and express your ideas effectively.

The four units of composition, in an ascending order, are (1) the word—Sections **19-22**, (2) the sentence—Sections **23-30**, (3) the paragraph—Section **31**, and (4) the whole composition—Section **32**. Words make up the sentence, sentences make up the paragraph, and paragraphs make up the whole composition.

A paragraph is usually a series of sentences developing one topic. A composition is usually a series of paragraphs developing several topics which are closely related. Just as a unified paragraph has a stated or implied topic to which each sentence contributes, a unified composition has a central idea to which each paragraph contributes. Therefore, many of the techniques used to write paragraphs (e.g., developing a central idea, arranging supporting details logically and effectively, making appropriate transitions) are applicable to the composition as a whole. See Section **31**.

In fact, sometimes the major difference between a paragraph and a composition is merely a matter of scale. For example, the topic sentence of paragraph 1 on pages 322–23 could easily be converted to the central idea of a composition. The three points made within paragraph 1 could then be topic sentences for separate paragraphs. Of course, more specific details would be necessary to develop each paragraph adequately; an introductory and a concluding paragraph might also be added.

32a

Choose an appropriate subject and limit it properly.

Be sure to select a topic that will enable you to say something interesting about what you know well. Limit the topic you choose so that you can develop it adequately, specifically.

A subject is appropriate:

1. If it appeals to you, or if you can develop an interest in it as you work on it.
2. If it is acceptable to the intended reader.

A subject is properly limited:

1. If you know enough about it or can learn enough in a reasonable period. (Subjects that require extensive reading should be reserved for the library paper. See Section 33.)
2. If the topic is not too broad to treat in the time or space at your command. ("Amateur Photography" might be a satisfactory title for a paper of several thousand words; but if you must limit yourself to several hundred words, you will do better with "Developing a Film" or "The Growth of My Interest in Photography.")

Let us suppose that you have chosen (or have been assigned) "Sports" as a general subject for a paper of five hundred words. Obviously, you cannot cover everything to be said about sports in five hundred words. You must therefore find a more limited topic. You may be particularly interested in one sport, but "Football" or "Baseball" is still too broad for your short paper. Therefore you should concentrate on a narrow phase of the sport chosen, such as "The Importance of Fumbles in Saturday's Game" or "Characteristics of a Good Shortstop."

PURPOSE

Before making a final decision regarding the specific topic, you should consider your purpose in writing the composition. If your purpose is to inform the reader, either "The Importance of Fumbles in Saturday's Game" or "Characteristics of a Good Shortstop" would be appropriate. If, however, your primary aim is to describe your feelings as you watched a particularly heart-breaking defeat, you might want to title your theme "A Cold Day at Memorial Stadium." On the other hand, you might decide that you want to argue about the merits of watching football as compared with watching baseball. You might then write a theme on the topic "Football or Baseball as a Spectator Sport" or "I Would Rather Watch Football than Baseball." Finally, you might decide to write a narrative account of the most exciting five minutes of a football game. Then your topic might be "With Only Minutes to Go."

Each of the purposes you might select corresponds to one of the four main types of writing as they are conventionally classified in rhetoric—exposition or explanation (to inform), description, argument (or persuasion), and narration. *Exposition* is the most common kind of nonfiction writing and the kind most frequently written by college students. *Argument* is similar to exposition but written with the intention of convincing rather than simply explaining. In *narration,* events are presented in a time sequence, and in *description* a sensory impression of an object or feeling is conveyed. (See paragraph 5, Section **31**.) Very seldom is description written independently. Usually it is only part of a composition in which one of the other types dominates. In fact, few compositions are a single form of discourse. Most are mixtures in which one form predominates. Thus, a paper on "How to Drive a Car" would be primarily exposition but would also contain bits of description (perhaps of the steering mechanism) and narration (perhaps an anecdote about the author's first drive).

Whatever form of discourse a paper may take, it does not fall into order by chance. *Order is the result of careful planning.*

CENTRAL IDEA

After deciding upon your purpose, you will find it helpful to set down, in a single sentence, the central or controlling idea for your paper. If the purpose is to inform, the sentence may read, "A good shortstop thinks and acts quickly." This thesis statement helps to limit the subject and especially helps determine the items to be included in the outline. In fact, if in the beginning you can set down a central idea containing logically arranged main points (see Example 1 below), you will already have the main headings of your outline. If you do not give the main points in your central idea (see Examples 2 through 5 below), you may later wish to reword it in order to show its close relationship to the items in your outline. In dealing with some subjects, you may need to list your ideas and then find and consider more evidence before you can decide upon an appropriate central idea. If not determined in the process of limiting the subject, the central idea should be written out before the outline is completed and then used to test the contents of the outline.

1. *Purpose:* To inform by pointing out ways to appraise a used car [Exposition]
   Title: How to Buy a Good Used Car
   Central Idea: Before selecting a used car, a wise buyer will carefully inspect the car himself, talk to the former owner of it, and engage a good mechanic to examine its motor.

2. *Purpose:* To convince the reader of a need for change [Argument]
   Title: Why Have Final Examinations?
   Central Idea: Final examinations should be abolished.

3. *Purpose:* To describe Rushville and its surroundings [Description]
   Title: Rushville: A Beautiful City in the Mountains
   Central Idea: Rushville is a beautiful city in the mountains.

4. *Purpose:* To tell a story about a childhood experience [Narration]
   Title: I Will Never Play Post Office Again!
   Central Idea: Playing "postmaster," my brother once shocked my friends and me by wiring a group of old post office boxes.

5. *Purpose:* To describe Old Tony and show that he is a colorful individual [Exposition, Description, Narration]
   Title: Old Tony
   Central Idea: Old Tony is the most colorful individual that I know.

Each of the suggestions listed below is a suitable subject for a student paper. Some of the suggestions, as worded, may provide the exact title you need for your paper. In all likelihood, however, you will wish to limit the subject to the scope of your experience and to sharpen the wording to suit your purpose. (For the proper capitalization of titles, see **9c.**)

Suggestions for Written Work

HOME AND THE INDIVIDUAL

1. Automation in the home
2. My home town in 1980
3. Our family's diets
4. Why I like my hobby
5. How children educate parents
6. If I could choose my relatives (OR parents)
7. Types of family friends
8. Our changing neighborhood
9. New styles in clothes
10. Being an only child (OR the youngest OR oldest)
11. My favorite author (book, actor, television show, etc.)

COLLEGE LIFE

1. Campus fads
2. Dating habits of college students
3. College slang
4. Earning one's way
5. My first field trip
6. The course I find most practical (OR difficult, interesting, etc.)
7. The student union
8. Campus politics
9. Why I should (OR should not) join a fraternity (OR sorority)
10. Boners of a freshman
11. The writing laboratory
12. Using a microscope
13. Are examinations fair?
14. The honor system
15. How to be a cheer leader
16. What makes school spirit?
17. Why I am going to college
18. Duties of the quarterback (OR halfback, fullback, etc.)
19. What is sportsmanship?
20. Life in a dormitory (OR fraternity house, sorority house, etc.)

ECONOMICS, HISTORY, SOCIOLOGY

1. Poverty in America
2. A nation of computers
3. Why the Spanish Armada was defeated
4. The Peace Corps
5. A four-hour work day
6. Conservation or Pollution
7. What our taxes buy
8. Our senior citizens
9. Our foreign aid
10. The Iron (or Bamboo) Curtain
11. Help for the retarded
12. Advertising schemes
13. The right to strike
14. The parole system
15. Status symbols
16. Socialized medicine
17. Social service as a career
18. Types of personalities
19. Tourists and the economy
20. Urban renewal
21. The guaranteed annual wage

SCIENCE AND MEDICINE

1. Discoveries in space
2. Underwater explorations
3. Extrasensory perception
4. Discoveries about the memory (OR heart, nerves, blood, etc.)
5. The common cold
6. Synthetic diamonds
7. New wonder drugs
8. Life expectancy
9. Uses of wild plants
10. The oxygen tent
11. Chemical warfare on insects
12. Uses of uranium
13. Plastic surgery
14. Predicting the weather
15. Beneficial bacteria
16. Experiments with animals

MISCELLANEOUS

1. Current English usage
2. Ghosts in literature
3. Poltergeists
4. Unidentified Flying Objects
5. Fads in music
6. Boom in water sports
7. City conveniences in the country
8. Political conventions
9. A choice involving conscience
10. Typical television characters (*such as* doctors, lawyers, etc.)
11. Pop (or Op) Art

▶ EXERCISE 1 After selecting five subjects from the preceding "Suggestions for Written Work," decide how it may be necessary to limit each one and what your purpose would be in writing a composition on each topic. Then write (1) your purpose, (2) an appropriate title, and (3) the central idea for each subject that you choose. (You may find it helpful to refer to the examples on pages 368–69.)

32b

Develop a working plan or an outline before writing a composition. See also 33c.

Although a formal outline may not be required for every paper, learning to make and use a good outline is important to inexperienced writers because it is a working plan that can make the actual writing of a composition easier.

The outline is the blueprint of the composition. Just as the carpenter or the engineer follows his blueprint implicitly in order to avoid costly structural blunders, so the writer—especially the student writer—follows his outline carefully so that he may arrange his ideas effectively.

But blueprints can be changed and improved, and so can outlines. The writer should make the outline his helpful tool; he should not become its slave. He should keep the outline a growing, developing plan which he will not hesitate to change at any stage of his composition whenever he hits upon a way to improve it. He will naturally try to perfect his outline before he starts to write the paper, but the actual writing will almost certainly suggest a few desirable changes in the arrangement of details.

The first step in the preparation of an outline is the jotting down of ideas on the topic. Keeping the purpose of the composition firmly in mind, the student should not hesitate to jot down a long list of ideas; and he should jot them down rapidly, without much concern for the proper order. When he begins to classify his ideas, he will find it easy to reject needless ones; he may find also that he needs to supplement his knowledge by further observation or reading.

Suppose, for example, a student has chosen to write on the subject "Books I Have Read." He first limits the subject to autobiographies. Then he limits it further by deciding upon his purpose: to inform his reader about the types of autobiographies he has read. Next, he selects a tentative title: "Types of Autobiographies." Finally, he writes out a tentative central idea and jots down a list of items closely related to the thesis statement.

LIST OF IDEAS FOR A COMPOSITION
ON AUTOBIOGRAPHIES

Tentative Central Idea: Autobiographies reveal significant facts about the authors' experiences.

Types of Autobiographies	*What They Reveal*
adventure stories	actions
success stories	achievements
journals like Pepys's *Diary*	contemporary life
travel books	explorations, sights
collections of letters	problems, attitudes
religious accounts	temptations
so-called war records	decisions, battles
disguised autobiographies	emotional conflicts
reports of events	personality

The next step in making an outline is the grouping of the listed items under a few main headings. After some thought, the writer will see that if he uses each of the nine types of autobiographies (listed in the first column above) as a main heading, the development of each would prove to be too unwieldy for a short paper. Therefore he may prefer to group these types further as subheadings under more general headings that will classify all autobiographies according to what they reveal about the authors' experiences; he could thus show that any autobiography could be appropriately entitled "What I Saw," "What I Felt," or "What I Did," and he could illustrate each type by representative examples. Then he would list these main headings in a logical order (see **31b** and **32e**):

    I. Autobiographies about "What I Did"
   II. Autobiographies about "What I Saw"
  III. Autobiographies about "What I Felt"

After more thought, the writer may limit his subject further by omitting some of the items listed in the first column—e.g., journals like Pepys's *Diary,* collections of letters, and disguised autobiographies. The logical arrangement of the remaining items as miscellaneous details (with further additions during the writing of the paper) under the three main headings gives the outline as it appears under **32c** below. The writer's purpose thus is to *inform* (exposition), and he decides to develop his central idea chiefly by the method of classification—see **31d(4)**—with exemplification as a subordinate method—see **31d(2)**. All the other methods of development described in Section **31** are equally adaptable to the development of the whole essay. (See also the examples under **32a**.)

Only one other decision in planning the composition remains: whether or not to include introductory and concluding paragraphs. See **32g(2)**. If these paragraphs are desirable or deemed necessary, the writer should add to his plan an explanation of each. In a topic or a sentence outline, these statements need not be numbered. See **32c**.

Once the writer has thought his subject through, he may wish to select a more appropriate or more interesting title. He may also change the wording of his tentative central idea.

32c
Use an outline of the type specified by your instructor.

The types of outlines most commonly used are (1) the topic outline, (2) the sentence outline, and (3) the paragraph outline. Topic outlines and sentence outlines have the same parts and the same groupings; they differ only in the fullness of expression. In the paragraph outline no effort is made to classify the material into major headings and subheadings: the topic of each paragraph is simply listed in the order in which it is to come. Paragraph outlines are especially helpful in writing short papers. Topic or sentence outlines may be adapted to papers of any length.

Topic Outline:

THE FACE IN THE MIRROR

CENTRAL IDEA   Since the three types of autobiographies mirror their authors' experiences, any autobiography can be appropriately entitled "What I Did," "What I Saw," or "What I Felt."

INTRODUCTION   An interesting autobiography—one of three possible kinds—inside of every person if he would tell the whole story of his life

  I. Autobiographies about "What I Did"
     A. Books by self-made men
     B. *The Second World War* by Churchill

 II. Autobiographies about "What I Saw"
     A. Books like *Kon-Tiki*
     B. *Travels in Arabia Deserta* by Doughty
     C. Some descriptions of wars
        1. *Recollections of Rifleman Harris*
        2. Documents concerning the Civil War

III. Autobiographies about "What I Felt"
     A. Books about failure, disaster, regeneration
     B. Descriptions of the process of growing up
        1. Edward Gibbon's autobiography
        2. Self-studies of Mill, Spencer, and Adams
     C. Records of religious struggles and spiritual victories
        1. *Confessions* of St. Augustine
        2. Journals of John Bunyan
        3. Writings of George Fox
     D. Many reports of contemporary events
        1. Reminiscences of Cellini, Rousseau, and Boswell
        2. Works of Yeats and Gide

CONCLUSION   Difficulty in classifying autobiographies because the most interesting give something of all three kinds of experience

Sentence Outline:

THE FACE IN THE MIRROR

CENTRAL IDEA   Since the three types of autobiographies mirror their authors' experiences, any autobiography can be appropriately entitled "What I Saw," "What I Did," or "What I Felt."

INTRODUCTION   An interesting autobiography—one of three possible kinds—is inside of every person if he would tell the whole
story of his life.

 I. The first group of autobiographies could be issued under the
    title "What I Did."
    A. Self-made men like Franklin and Cobbett have written
       books of this type.
    B. Churchill told about what he did in *The Second World
       War.*

 II. The second group of autobiographies might be called "What
     I Saw."
     A. Books like *Kon-Tiki* place emphasis upon the authors'
        observations.
     B. *Travels in Arabia Deserta* by Doughty is probably the
        greatest autobiography of this type.
     C. Some documents about war describe what the authors saw.
        1. *Recollections of Rifleman Harris* gives scenes from the
           Napoleonic Wars.
        2. Other books describe scenes of the Civil War.

 III. The third group of autobiographies could be entitled "What
      I Felt."
      A. Among these are books about failure, disaster, and regen-
         eration.
      B. Other books of inner adventure describe the process of
         growing up.
         1. One example is Gibbon's autobiography.
         2. More famous examples are the self-studies of Mill,
            Spencer, and Adams.
      C. Some autobiographies mirror the inner struggles and spir-
         itual victories of religious authors.
         1. One example is St. Augustine's *Confessions.*
         2. Another example is John Bunyan's journals.
         3. Still another example is George Fox's writings.
      D. Many autobiographies show how contemporary events
         affect the personalities of authors.
         1. Such are the reminiscences of Cellini, Rousseau, and
            Boswell.
         2. Such also are the works of Yeats and Gide.

CONCLUSION   It is difficult to classify types of autobiographies
because the most interesting give us something of all three kinds
of experience.

Paragraph Outline:

THE FACE IN THE MIRROR

CENTRAL IDEA   Since the three types of autobiographies mirror their authors' experiences, any autobiography can be appropriately entitled "What I Saw," "What I Did," or "What I Felt."

1. An interesting autobiography is inside of every person if he would tell the whole story of his life.
2. There are three different ways of telling the story of one's life.
3. The first group of autobiographies could be issued under the title "What I Did."
4. Churchill's *The Second World War* is an autobiographical record describing what the author did.
5. The second type of autobiography might be called "What I Saw."
6. The third kind of autobiography describes "What I Felt."
7. It is difficult to make divisions between types of autobiographies because the most interesting give us something of all three kinds of experience.

32d

Make sure that the outline covers the subject, that it treats of everything promised in the title.

An adequate outline is essential to a successful composition. The major headings (I, II, III, etc.) must be sufficient in number and in scope to satisfy the expectation aroused by the title. And each of these major headings must, in turn, be covered by its subheads just as the title is covered by the major headings. These subheads, however, should not be unduly detailed.

TITLES NOT ADEQUATELY COVERED BY MAJOR HEADINGS

Characteristics of Ideal Parents
  I. A father's sense of humor
 II. His generosity
III. His understanding

The Grading System
  I. What a *B* means
 II. What a *C* means

TITLES ADEQUATELY COVERED

Characteristics of Ideal Parents
  I. Their sense of humor
  II. Their generosity
  III. Their understanding

The Grading System
  I. Differences between an *A* and a *B*
  II. Differences between a *C* and a *D*
  III. The meaning of *F*

It would also be proper to leave the main headings unchanged and to alter the titles to agree, thus: "Characteristics of an Ideal Father" and "The Meaning of *B* and *C* in the Grading System."

In reality, making an outline is a kind of process of thinking through the paper. Ordinarily if your outline does not fit the rules for an outline, then there may be something awry with the paper itself—a missing element, a misstated title, or an inadequate purpose. Thus an outline can help you give focus to your paper and possibly show the need for further limitation.

32e
Make sure that the parts of the outline are logically arranged.

Logical arrangement is second in importance only to adequacy. If the outline is disorganized and ineffective, the paper that follows it will also be disorganized and ineffective. (See also **31b.**)

(1) Group related ideas.

Although you may begin your outline by hastily jotting down as many ideas on the topic as possible, without regard to order, you should later bring related ideas together, grouping them under major headings. Compare the first list of ideas on "The Face in the Mirror" (page 372) with the groupings in the finished outline (**32c**).

(2) Arrange the parts in a natural, logical order.

The problem of arrangement within the paper as a whole is much the same as that within each separate paragraph. (See pages 328–32.) The nature of the subject will suggest an appropriate arrangement, such as time order, space order, or order of climax.

Order of climax:
Subject: End of the drought

I. Rains soak the countryside.
II. Farmers rejoice.
III. Headlines all over the nation announce end of the drought.
IV. Rains steal attention from the most significant world affairs.

Time order:
Subject: Process of riveting

I. Preparation of rivets
II. Passing of red-hot rivets
III. Securing the rivets in place

▶ EXERCISE 2   First make a list of three, four, or five main points closely related to one of the following subjects; then arrange the items in a natural, logical order. (In parentheses are suggestions for appropriate arrangements.)

1. Ways to start an argument (order of climax)
2. An amusing practical joke (time order)
3. A walk across the campus (space order—see page 330)
4. A successful experiment (time order)
5. The joys of being a freshman in college (order of climax)

(3) Do not allow headings to overlap.

Overlapping often occurs when a writer attempts a division according to more than one principle.

TYPES OF ARRANGEMENT MIXED

Advertising on Television

I. Since the advent of color   Time
II. Its effect on sales   Result
III. Pain relievers   Group

TYPES OF ARRANGEMENT UNMIXED

Advertising on Television

Time	*Result*	*Group*
I. Before color	I. Creates demand	I. Detergents
II. After color	II. Influences sales	II. Household appliances
	III. Affects economy	III. Pain relievers

(4) Do not coordinate any heading that should be subordinated. Do not subordinate any heading that should be coordinated.

ILLOGICAL   Wonder Products in TV Advertisements

       I. Detergents
         A. Household appliances
      II. Washing machines
    III. Remedies for headaches
         A. Pain relievers
         B. Cures for upset stomachs

LOGICAL   Wonder Products in TV Advertisements

       I. Detergents
      II. Household appliances
         A. Washing machines
         B. Refrigerators
    III. Pain relievers
         A. For headaches
         B. For upset stomachs

(5) Do not allow single headings or subheadings to stand anywhere in the outline.

Headings and subheads stand for divisions, and a division denotes at least two parts. Therefore, each outline, to be logical, should have at least two main headings, I and II. If it has a subheading marked A, it should also have a B; if it has a 1, it should also have a 2.

INCOMPLETE   II. Household appliances
             A. Washing machines

Unless another subheading is added, the second main heading should be revised to read simply "Washing machines." The next heading in the outline would then name a different type of product.

32f

Check the outline for the formal details of (1) notation and indention and (2) parallel structure.

(1) In the outline use consistently one system of notation, and indent headings to indicate degrees of subordination.

Any intelligible system of notation is acceptable. The one used for the complete sentence outline and the topic outline in **32c** is in very common use and may well be adopted. This system, it will be noted, is as follows:

I.	[Used for major headings]
A.	[Used for subheadings of the first degree]
B.	
1.	[Used for subheadings of the second degree]
2.	

Seldom will a short outline (or even a longer one) need subordination beyond the first or second degree. If it does, it may use *a*, *b*, *c*, etc., for the third degree and (*1*), (*2*), (*3*), etc., for the fourth degree.

The indention, as well as the notation, should indicate the degree of subordination. Major headings (I, II, III, etc.) should be indented equally, subheadings of the first degree (*A*, *B*, *C*, etc.) should be indented more, and subheads of the second degree (*1*, *2*, *3*, etc.) should be indented still more. If a heading or subheading runs beyond the end of the line, it is given "hanging indention," as in the sentence outline above (**32c**).

(2) Give parallel structure to parallel parts of the outline to make clearer the coordination of the parts. (See the full discussion of parallel structure under Section **26**.)

PARALLEL STRUCTURE

     I. Autobiographies about "What I Did"
       [Noun—prepositional phrase]
      A. Books by self-made men
         [Noun—prepositional phrase]
      B. *The Second World War* by Churchill
         [Noun (a title)—prepositional phrase]
    II. Autobiographies about "What I Saw"
       [Noun—prepositional phrase]

The major headings (I, II, III, etc.) should be expressed in parallel structure, as should each group of subheads. But it is unnecessary to strive for parallel structure between different groups of subheads; for example, between *A, B, C* under I and *A, B, C* under II. (Parallel structure is no problem in the complete sentence outline, for parallelism is insured by the requirement of complete sentences.)

▶ EXERCISE 3 Make an outline (of the type specified by your instructor) on one of the subjects you used for Exercise 1. Then check your outline with the principles set forth in **32d–f.**

32g

Write the paper from the outline.

Once you have checked your outline to make sure that it covers the subject (see **32d**), is logically arranged (**32e**), and has proper notation, indention, and parallel structure (**32f**), you are ready to write the paper. You simply write a series of effective paragraphs, with good transitions between them (see **31b[6]**), to cover all items in the outline, taking up each item in the order in which it comes in the outline. The actual writing of the paper may very well suggest a better arrangement for some of the details.

(1) **The paragraphs in relation to the outline.** Although the paragraphs must develop the headings (including the sub-

headings) of the outline in the exact order in which they come in the outline, there is no rule regarding the number of these headings a paragraph may cover. In a general way, however, the writer is limited by the need to make each paragraph a unit and to keep it from being unduly long or short. Let us notice, for example, how the seven paragraphs of "The Face in the Mirror" (see Exercise 4 below) are related to the topic outline (see page 374):

Paragraphs	*Relation to outline*
1 and 2	Introduction
3	I and the subheading A
4	Subheading B (special treatment requires more words than for A)
5	II and all subheadings
6	III and all subheadings
7	Conclusion

Since each paragraph in the body of a composition (see paragraphs 3 through 6 above) should be easily identified with a main heading or subheading in the outline, the writer may wish to revise his outline to make it agree with his organization into paragraphs.

▶ EXERCISE 4 Carefully read the following essay so that you can intelligently participate in a class discussion of the (1) selection and limitation of the subject, (2) purpose of the writer, (3) choice of the title, (4) development of the central idea, (5) arrangement of main points, (6) transitions between ideas, and (7) relationship of the division into paragraphs to the topic outline on page 374.

THE FACE IN THE MIRROR[1]

(1)   Every man and every woman has one book inside him or her. Some have more, but everybody has at least one—a volume of autobiography. We have all been talked almost to death by bores who attached themselves to us in a club car or a ship's smoking

[1] Abridged from *Talents and Geniuses,* copyright 1957 by Gibert Highet. Reprinted by permission of Oxford University Press, Inc.

room and insisted on giving us a play-by-play account of their marital troubles or their complete medical history. I once met one who carried a set of his own x-rays. Yet even these people might be interesting if they could tell the whole truth. They are boring not because they talk about themselves but because they talk about only one aspect of themselves, that phase of their lives which fascinates and worries them personally. If they were really to tell us everything, we should listen with amazement.

(2)   Apparently there are three kinds of autobiography: three different ways of telling the story of one's life. (We can leave out journals like Pepys's *Diary*, which was not meant to be published, and collections of letters and disguised autobiographies, which so many modern novels are.)

(3)   The first group could all be issued under the same title. They could all be called "What I Did." They are essentially success stories. In them, a man who has achieved something of wide importance explains how he did it, what were the obstacles in his way, how they were overcome, and what was the effect on the world. Self-made men often write such books—or have such books written for them. There is a splendid one by Ben Franklin and an equally good one by his English opposite number, William Cobbett: these are optimistic works, a good tonic for anyone who despairs of solving his own problems.

(4)   Sir Winston Churchill's six-volume work *The Second World War* is really an autobiographical record. He himself says it is "the story as I knew and experienced it as Prime Minister and Minister of Defence of Great Britain." Therefore it cannot be called anything like a complete history of the war. For example, Churchill tells the story of one of the crucial events of the war, one of the crucial events of this century—the reduction of Japan to impotence and surrender by intensive bombardment culminating in what he calls the "casting" of two atomic bombs—in only eight pages, while a greater amount of wordage is devoted to a reprint of the broadcast which he made to British listeners on VE day.

(5)   So much for the first type of autobiography: "What I Did." The second type might be called "What I Saw." Here the emphasis is not on the achievements of the narrator but rather on the strange sights he saw and the strange experiences through which he lived. Most good books of exploration are like this. Both the book *Kon-Tiki* and the film were absorbingly interesting, not because the author was an unusual man but because he could describe to us some unique adventures. We shall never cross New Guinea on foot

or spend a whole year alone with two companions on the Arctic ice or climb Mount Everest; therefore we are delighted when a man who has done such a thing can tell us about it clearly—and modestly. The greatest of all such books in the English language is probably Doughty's *Travels in Arabia Deserta*. Some good adventure autobiographies have been written by ordinary soldiers and sailors. Many of our finest descriptions of the Napoleonic wars come from such books as the *Recollections of Rifleman Harris*, and there are similar documents from the American Civil War.

(6) Then there is a third kind of autobiography. It does not describe "What I Did" or "What I Saw" but "What I Felt," "What I Endured." These are the books of inner adventure. In them there is achievement, yes, but it is a struggle and a victory within the spirit. In them there are dangerous explorations and the discovery of unknown worlds, but the explorer is making his way through the jungles of the soul. Such are the books of failure, disaster, and regeneration which are now so popular: for example, Lillian Roth's *I'll Cry Tomorrow*, which tells how a woman wrecked her life with drink and then rebuilt it. Such also are the books which describe one of the most dangerous of all adventures: the process of growing up. My own favorite among them is Edward Gibbon's autobiography, partly because it is unconsciously funny. More famous perhaps are the self-studies of John Stuart Mill, Herbert Spencer, and Henry Adams—all of which seem to me excruciatingly pompous and dull. The famous records of religious suffering and conversion could all be subtitled "What I Felt": the *Confessions* of St. Augustine, the journals of John Bunyan and of the first Quaker, George Fox. And many of the most famous autobiographers have concentrated on reporting the events which happened during their lifetime, not as objective facts but simply as occurrences which impinged upon their own personalities: in books like the reminiscences of Benvenuto Cellini, of Rousseau, of Boswell, Yeats, and André Gide, we see the world as in an elaborate distorting mirror.

(7) "What I Did," "What I Saw," "What I Felt"—really, it is difficult to make a sharp division between these types of autobiographical writing. The emphasis in one book is more toward reporting of external happenings, in another toward self-analysis, but a man can scarcely describe what he did without also letting us know what he felt and saw. Even the most egoistic of men, like St. Augustine and James Boswell, do from time to time give us valuable information about their outer as well as their inner

worlds. The most interesting of these books give us something of all three kinds of experience. For a time, while we read them, it is possible to enjoy one of the rarest artistic pleasures—complete escape: escape into another sphere of action and perception. From that escape we return—with what relief!—to the real center of the universe, which is our own self.

▶ **EXERCISE 5** After making an outline, write a paper on one of the following topics (or any other topic assigned by your instructor): (1) types of detective stories, (2) kinds of bores, (3) the heroes of TV Westerns, (4) what language habits reveal about a speaker, (5) what dogs (or any other pets) reveal about their owners, (6) the best reasons for going to college.

(2) Effective beginnings and endings.

Although formal introductions and conclusions are often not necessary for short papers, every composition should have an effective beginning and ending.

BEGINNINGS   There are two ways to begin a composition effectively. One way is to begin with a sentence which not only arouses the reader's interest but also starts the development of the topic by discussing the first main point in the outline. The second way is to begin with a formal introduction (often only one paragraph). This arouses the reader's interest and introduces the central idea of the paper but does not start the development of the topic. Sometimes the limitations of the subject are defined in a formal introduction. See the first two paragraphs of "The Face in the Mirror" in Exercise 4, pages 382–83. The choice of the type of beginning depends upon the nature of the topic and the length of the composition.

Whichever method you use, remember that an effective beginning gains the reader's interest. One of the easiest and best ways to gain interest is to use specific facts and details instead of dull generalizations. See **20a(2)** and **31d.** Compare the effectiveness of the introductions on the next page.

Topic: A football game in the Rose Bowl

GENERAL

When football teams play an important bowl game, lots of fans are very enthusiastic supporters of the home-town team. I especially noticed this fact when I recently saw a game in the Rose Bowl.

SPECIFIC

There are two American cities that genuflect to no one in their uncontrollable—one could even say undying—affection for the home-town football team. When citizens of those two cities, Seattle and Minneapolis, assembled for a contest between their Washington Huskies and their Minnesota Gophers on the green grass of Pasadena, sensible natives took shelter. The less sensible— 97,000 of them—were at the Arroyo Seco, where the Rose Bowl sits, and everyone but the ushers appeared to be related to a player on one or the other team. In its long history, the Rose Bowl had never been shaken by such passion from the stands.[2]

Another way to arouse interest is to refer to some common experience (such as shyness on a first date, an encounter with an eccentric door-to-door salesman, a clumsy slip of the tongue on an important occasion, the joy of winning a game or a special honor) which the reader will probably associate with himself; see the introduction to "Carousel— A New Experience" on page 387. A third way to interest the reader is to start with a striking fact. Still another method is to begin with an interesting incident or anecdote that is closely related to the topic:

Title: The Elusive Dr. Szilard

At a party in a university community a few weeks ago the guests amused themselves by drawing up a list of men who have played unique roles in recent history. They finally agreed upon five who had done things which could not have been accomplished, in their times, by anybody else. The first four are familiar to everybody—Lincoln, Gandhi, Hitler, and Churchill. But the fifth might puzzle even many well-informed people. It was Leo Szilard.[3]

[2] From "They Ran All the Way: The Wildest Rose," reprinted from *Sports Illustrated*, January 9, 1961. By permission of the publishers.

[3] From "The Elusive Dr. Szilard" by Alice Kimball, reprinted from *Harper's Magazine*, July, 1960. By permission of *Harper's Magazine*.

An effective beginning introduces a subject and is therefore directly related to it. As you read the following paragraph (written by a student), notice the repetition of the key words of the title: *Carousel, new, experience.* In the last sentence the controlling idea of the composition is given. Such an introduction is closely related to the topic and contributes to the unity of the whole composition.

Title: Carousel—A New Experience

All of us enjoy wearing a new pair of shoes, eating a dish we have not had before, seeing a movie with an unusual plot, or touring in a new section of the country; in other words, we like experiences which are novel, different. I happen to be one of those people who enjoy discovering an unfamiliar poem by a famous poet, reading a good book, or attending a choral or band concert. I like new and different cultural outlets, and a few weeks ago my English assignment brought me face to face with just such an experience: Carousel, theater-in-the-round. The play which I attended was an Irish drama by Paul Vincent Carroll, entitled *Shadow and Substance,* and I should like to use it as the vehicle in my description of Carousel itself—the interior of the theater, the actors, the techniques used.

Caution: Do not write aimless, dull introductions. If you have difficulty writing an interesting and pertinent introductory paragraph which contributes to the effectiveness of your whole composition, then begin with an immediate discussion of your first main point.

Title: Characteristics of a Nonconformist

One of the distinguishing characteristics of a nonconformist is his lack of respect for established authority. For example, ...

▶ EXERCISE 6 Evaluate the effectiveness of the following beginnings of student papers.

1. *Title:* A Description of My Home Town

It is early morning. A light drizzle falls upon the gray cobblestones, and you see two lace-shawled women hurrying to the Cathedral. The trolley-cars begin to clatter down the broad island of Canal Street, and the city begins to awake. This is a day in my city. This is New Orleans.

Soon the sun peeks through the misty heavens, and the city begins to erupt into a myriad of noises. . . .

2. *Title:* Justice in *The Unvanquished*

Justice is a word with many applications and definitions. This point is well illustrated in *The Unvanquished*, a novel of Civil War times by William Faulkner. Justice, as practiced by Faulkner's characters, takes on many forms; indeed, the meaning of the word is warped to suit any occasion which may arise. Applications of justice may range all the way from mouth soaping to murder; many different situations call for different forms of justice.

Loosh, the old Negro slave, felt that he was justified in tearing down Bayard's and Ringo's model of the city of Vicksburg. . . .

ENDINGS   A composition should end; it should not merely stop. Two ways to end a composition effectively are (1) to stress the final point of the main discussion by using an emphatic last sentence and (2) to write a strong concluding paragraph. Often a concluding paragraph clinches, restates, or stresses the importance of the central idea or thesis of the composition. See the concluding paragraph of "The Face in the Mirror," pages 384–85. When the body of a composition describes an experiment or presents evidence, the conclusion often presents a discovery or a theory. A conclusion may also present a brief summary, a pertinent question, a suggestion or challenge, or a solution to a problem.

SUMMARY   (ending of an article giving reasons for the growing popularity of FM radio programs)

FM, in short, is prospering in direct ratio as it provides adults with a refuge from the blaring Children's Hour of the AM juke boxes and from the vacuity of most TV.

QUESTION   (ending of an essay describing the dangers of modern chemical, biological, and radiological warfare)

The question that cannot be avoided is whether any nation, even in its own defense, has the right to destroy half of the rest of the world.

SUGGESTION   (ending of an article discussing the interest of consumers in deceptive packaging which conceals rises in prices)

Efforts at industry self-government directed toward higher ethical standards are, of course, laudable and welcome. But consumers probably would do well to continue to hope, and to urge, that all existing Governmental agencies which exercise regulatory powers in this area—including the FTC, the FDA, certain divisions of the Department of Agriculture, and the Treasury's alcohol-control agency—will, in the future, act with more vigor and with a greater awareness of consumer needs.[4]

SOLUTION TO A PROBLEM   (ending of an essay explaining the problem of American doctors who are barred from hospitals)

What will help to solve the complicated and disturbing problem, he [John G. Steinle, management consultant to hospitals] says, is a greater public awareness of the role of the hospital as a community institution and a willingness on the part of the public to become involved in the management of its community affairs. Such a force of informed public opinion can right more wrongs than any laws devised.[5]

Caution: Do not devote too much space to introductions and conclusions. A short paper often has only one paragraph for a beginning or an ending; frequently one sentence for each is adequate. Remember that the bulk of your composition should be the development of the central idea, the discussion of the main headings and the subheadings in the outline.

▶ EXERCISE 7   In a magazine recommended by your instructor, find and copy a good conclusion to an article. Be prepared to explain why the conclusion is effective and how it is related to the central idea of the article.

[4] From *Consumer Reports*, January, 1961. By permission of Consumers Union, Mount Vernon, New York, a non-profit organization.
[5] From "Why Hospitals Lock Out Doctors," reprinted from *Look*, January 17, 1961. By permission of *Look*.

▶ EXERCISE 8 Giving special attention to the beginning and ending, write a composition based on the outline you prepared for Exercise 3.

▶ EXERCISE 9 Revise the composition you wrote for Exercise 5, using the Check List for Revision (8d[1]).

▶ EXERCISE 10 Be prepared for a class discussion of the following outline and composition, which were written by a college freshman. Be prepared to support your comments by referring to parts of this section (32a–g).

MAYVILLE

CENTRAL IDEA   Visiting such familiar landmarks as Dr. Weaver's drugstore, the old fire hall, and Mel Tanner's service station proved to me that Mayville was still the same quiet, sleepy little town I had left.

INTRODUCTION   Mayville as seen from a train window
    I. Weaver's Drugs
       A. Characteristics sixteen years ago
       B. Characteristics at time of visit
    II. Mayville Fire Hall
    III. Tanner's Gulf Service
       A. Building and property
       B. Action going on at station

CONCLUSION   The small, quiet town, almost extinct

The trip from Lenox City had been a long and tiring one. As I peered through the blackened train window, Mayville came into view. From a distance it seemed even smaller than it actually is: it appeared only as a few boxes scattered beside the thin black line that is the railroad track. Then the conductor cried, "Mayville, all out for Mayville!" As the train huffed and lurched to a halt in front of the station, I took my single bag and stepped out onto the wooden platform in front of the train station; then, draping my coat over my arm, I walked toward town.

There were few cars on the Mayville streets and no noise or clamor to break the stillness of the air. (It was the same quiet, sleepy, little town I had left sixteen years before.) On the right stood

Dr. Weaver's corner drugstore, its white plaster face cracked with wrinkles of age. The drugstore was always a place to go after school for a milkshake or a Coke. It would be so crowded with school children that Dr. Weaver could hardly get around to take orders and to speak to his young friends. When the children left, the drugstore fell into a deep silence broken only by the clinking of glasses as Dr. Weaver cleaned off the counter and the two small tables by the window. The drugstore was just as it had been then. The black tile floor was as spotless as ever, and the black counter-top shone like a mirror, reflecting the stacks of clean glasses on the shelf above. The wooden stools in front of the counter were worn from many pairs of blue jeans, and the brass rail was scuffed by countless shoes. The door hinges creaked as I left, just as I knew they would.

Across the street from the drugstore stood the Mayville Fire Hall. The old red brick building stood tall and erect as if indifferent to age, and the two doors facing the street were open. The antiquated fire engine had seen very little action and was covered with dust. On the pale green plaster wall hung buckets, axes, and hoses, all waiting in readiness. Everyone must have been out to lunch, for beside the fire engine stood a small table on which lay an unfinished checker game. The glass in the side window that Billy Joe Jacobs and I had broken when we were about twelve had not been replaced, and Chief Hansen's office door still lacked a doorknob. Brushing aside the cobwebs, I walked on out the back door.

Across the corner was Mel Tanner's Gulf Station, where I worked for three summers pumping gas and being an all-around junior grease monkey. High on the high building were orange metal letters spelling Tanner's Gulf Service. But the V in "service" had blown away during a storm one summer (before I ever worked there) and had never been replaced. Two stark gas pumps stood alone, projecting from the sea of concrete in front of the station. The often malfunctioning cold drink machine was creased and scarred from the kicks of disgruntled or persistent customers. Mel, unexpectedly aged, was leaning against the wall in a chair and smoking his pipe. A few cans of oil and one or two headlamps were stacked haphazardly on the metal shelves behind him, and a new set of tires for the old Ford service truck lay on the green concrete floor in front of his desk. Monte was in the back washing Mrs. Gillian's old Mercury and singing happily to himself. The grease-covered service rack was empty, and the tools from the open box were scattered on the wooden counter. Jumbled inside a rusted oil drum were discarded oil filter boxes, used paper towels, and a chamois, now beyond further use.

Saying good-by to Mel and Monte, I walked to the hotel and rented a room. The few restful days I spent in Mayville seemed more an escape than a vacation. With the world in a constant rush and everyone struggling to industrialize and urbanize all of the Mayville's in the world, it occurred to me that before many years the peace and quiet will vanish with the death of the small town. And there will no longer be any asylum for a homesick and tired assistant vice-president.   —BAYARD TARPLEY

Library Paper

33

Learn how to prepare a library paper.

A library paper (sometimes called a research or term paper) is usually a formal, well-documented composition based for the most part on outside readings. These readings may be from various books in the library or from a collection of essays on a specific subject, a collection commonly called a *sourcebook*. The usual steps in writing a library paper are as follows:

1. Select and limit a subject (**33a**).
2. Prepare a bibliography (**33b**).
3. Develop an outline (**33c**).
4. Take notes on readings (**33d**).
5. Write a properly documented paper (**33e**).

33a

Select and limit a subject.

If you do not know how to select an appropriate subject and to limit it properly, review **32a,** pages 366–71. How much you limit a subject for a library paper depends not only upon the assigned length but also upon the materials available in your library or sourcebook.

GENERAL   drama of the nineteenth century
LIMITED   the plays of Henrik Ibsen
MORE LIMITED   characterization in Ibsen's *A Doll's House*
EVEN MORE LIMITED   Ibsen's attitude toward women as seen in the character of Nora in *A Doll's House*

REPORT OR THESIS   The type of library paper you write
will depend upon your purpose. Suppose, for example,
that you have chosen the subject "The Meaning of Dreams."
If you develop your subject by an organized presentation
of the opinions of others, such as Jung and Adler, you will
be writing a *report* paper. You may, however, wish to prove
or disprove an opinion or theory. If you wish to convince
your reader that dreams are significantly related to conscious behavior, that they are not merely mirrors of subconscious fears or wishes, you will be writing a *thesis*
paper. Although either purpose should enable you to write
an effective paper, the purpose you select will influence
your collecting of facts and should therefore be determined
as soon as possible.

▶ EXERCISE 1   List three general fields in which you have
some interest. Then by process of limitation derive three
topics (1) which are suitable for library papers of one to
three thousand words each and (2) in which you have a
special interest. The subject headings and the cross references in the card catalog or the *Readers' Guide* (see **33b**
below) may suggest subjects and possible limitations of
them. Determine, if possible, whether each topic lends
itself to development as a *report* or a *thesis*.

33b
Prepare a bibliography in acceptable form.

The bibliography lists sources of information—such as
books, pamphlets, and articles—from which you will draw
the material for your paper. Use (1) the card catalog,
(2) indexes to periodicals, and (3) reference books (as explained on the following pages) to make a preliminary
bibliography by writing down the most promising titles
you can find. Copy each title on a separate card (usually
3 × 5 inches) in the form shown on page 403. You should
keep these cards in alphabetical order until you complete
your paper, adding useful titles as you find them and dis-
carding those that prove useless. The final bibliography to

be copied at the end of your paper will most often include only those works that help in the writing—usually those cited in the footnotes.

(1) Use the card catalog.

The card catalog is the index to the whole library. It lists all books and all bound magazines, whether they are housed in the stacks, on the open shelves of the reference room, or in any other part of the building. In many libraries one general card catalog lists all books owned by the university and shows whether the book is in the general library or in a special collection in another building.

Usually the card catalog consists of cards arranged alphabetically in drawers. These may be "author" cards, "title" cards, or "subject" cards; for in most libraries each book is listed, alphabetically, once according to its author, again according to its title, and again according to its subject or subjects. These three cards (usually printed) are identical except that the title card has the title typewritten in black and the subject card has the subject typewritten in red.

SAMPLE CATALOG CARDS

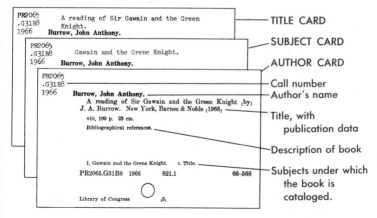

PR2065
.G31B8
1966   A reading of Sir Gawain and the Green
          Knight.
          Burrow, John Anthony. ————————————— TITLE CARD

PR2065
.G31B8
1966   Gawain and the Grene Knight. ————————————— SUBJECT CARD
          Burrow, John Anthony.

PR2065
.G31B8 ——————————————— AUTHOR CARD
1966   —— Call number
          Burrow, John Anthony. ———————— Author's name
            A reading of Sir Gawain and the Green Knight [by]
          J. A. Burrow. New York, Barnes & Noble [1966]
            viii, 199 p. 23 cm. ———————————— Title, with
                                               publication data
            Bibliographical references. ——————————

                                              ————— Description of book

            1. Gawain and the Grene Knight.   I. Title. ——
          PR2065.G31B8 1966   821.1   66–568   ——— Subjects under which
                                                                  the book is
          Library of Congress   ○   [3]   cataloged.

(2) Use indexes to periodicals.

When preparing your bibliography, remember that the periodical indexes do for articles what the card catalog does for books in the library. You will probably find the *Readers' Guide* (an index to over one hundred magazines) the most useful. You may have occasion, however, to use others of the following indexes to periodicals.

INDEXES TO PERIODICALS

GENERAL

Poole's Index. 1802–1906. (Subject index only)
Nineteenth Century Readers' Guide. 1890–99. (Author, subject)
Readers' Guide. 1900—. (Author, title, subject)
Book Review Digest. 1905—. (Author, title, subject)
International Index. 1907–65. Succeeded by *Social Sciences and Humanities Index.* 1965—. (Author, subject)
New York Times Index. 1913—. (A useful guide for finding the dates of important events which can then be looked up in all other newspapers)

SPECIAL

Agricultural Index. 1916–64. Succeeded by *Biological and Agricultural Index.* 1964—. (Subject)
Art Index. 1929—. (Author, subject)
Bibliographic Index. 1937—. (Subject)
Biography Index. 1946—. (Subject)
Book Review Index. 1965—.
Catholic Periodical Index. 1930—. (Subject)
Education Index. 1929—. (Author, subject)
Engineering Index. 1884—. (Subject)
Index Medicus. 1879–1926; *Quarterly Cumulative Index Medicus.* 1927—. (Author, subject)
Index to Book Reviews in the Humanities. 1960—.
Index to Legal Periodicals. 1908—. (Author, subject)
Industrial Arts Index. 1913–57. Succeeded by *Applied Science and Technology Index.* 1958—; *Business Periodicals Index.* 1958—. (Subject)
Music Index. 1949—. (Subject)
Public Affairs Information Service. 1915—. (Subject)

Technical Book Review Index. 1917–29; 1935—.

> [See also the various abstracts, such as *Biological Abstracts,* 1926—, *Chemical Abstracts,* 1907—, and *Psychological Abstracts,* 1927—.]

(3) Use reference books.

Dictionaries, encyclopedias, atlases, and other books especially helpful for reference are usually kept on the open shelves of the reference room, where students may use them directly without the trouble of having them brought from the stacks. Each of these books is listed in the card catalog, and the call number will often aid in finding the book. The student should learn the general location of the chief classes of reference books in order that he may turn to them without loss of time. For a detailed list of such books, with a short description of each, he should consult Constance M. Winchell's *Guide to Reference Books* (Seventh Edition, supplements 1950–52). Since many reference books, especially some of the encyclopedias, are kept up to date by frequent revisions, the student should cite the last copyright date of the edition he is using. A few of the more important reference books are listed below (with abbreviated entries).

GENERAL DICTIONARIES (UNABRIDGED)

Century Dictionary and Cyclopedia. 12 vols. 1911. 3 vols. 1927–33.
Dictionary of American English. 4 vols. 1936–44.
New Standard Dictionary. 1947, 1952.
Oxford English Dictionary. 12 vols. and supplement. 1933. Originally issued as *A New English Dictionary.* 10 vols. and supplement. 1888–1933.
Webster's New International Dictionary, Second ed., 1934.
Webster's Third New International Dictionary, 1961.

SPECIAL DICTIONARIES

Allen, F. S. *Allen's Synonyms and Antonyms.* 1938.
Evans, Bergen and Cornelia. *A Dictionary of Contemporary American Usage.* 1957.

Fowler, H. W. *Dictionary of Modern American Usage.* Second ed., revised by Sir Ernest Gowers. 1965.

Horwill, H. W. *Dictionary of Modern American Usage.* Second ed., 1944.

Lewis, Norman. *The New Roget's Thesaurus.* 1961.

Nicholson, Margaret. *A Dictionary of American-English Usage.* 1957. (Based on Fowler)

Partridge, Eric. *Dictionary of Slang and Unconventional English.* Fifth ed., 1961.

Roget's International Thesaurus. Third ed., 1962.

Webster's Dictionary of Synonyms. 1942.

Wright, Joseph. *English Dialect Dictionary.* 6 vols. 1961.

GENERAL ENCYCLOPEDIAS

Collier's Encyclopedia. 20 vols.

Columbia Encyclopedia. 1950, 1953.

Encyclopedia Americana. 30 vols.

Encyclopœdia Britannica. 24 vols.

SPECIAL ENCYCLOPEDIAS

Adams, J. T. *Dictionary of American History.* 6 vols. 1942.

Bailey, L. H. *Cyclopedia of American Agriculture.* 4 vols. 1907–09.

Catholic Encyclopedia. 17 vols. 1907–22. New edition, 1936—.

Encyclopaedia of the Social Sciences. 15 vols. 1930–35.

Encyclopedia of World Art. 1959—.

Grove's Dictionary of Music and Musicians. 9 vols. 1954. Supplement, 1961.

Harris, Chester W. *Encyclopedia of Educational Research.* 1960.

Hastings, James. *Encyclopaedia of Religion and Ethics.* 13 vols. 1908–27.

———. *Interpreter's Dictionary of the Bible.* 4 vols. 1962.

Jewish Encyclopedia. 12 vols. 1925.

McGraw-Hill Encyclopedia of Science and Technology. 15 vols. 1966.

McLaughlin, A. C., and A. B. Hart. *Cyclopedia of American Government.* 3 vols. 1914. Reprint, 1949.

Monroe, Paul. *Cyclopedia of Education.* 5 vols. 1911–13.

Munn, Glenn G. *Encyclopedia of Banking and Finance.* Sixth ed., 1962.

New Schaff-Herzog Encyclopedia of Religious Knowledge. 13 vols. 1908–12.

New Standard Encyclopedia of Art. 2 vols. in 1. 1939.
Thompson, O. *International Cyclopedia of Music and Musicians.*
    Ninth ed., 1964.
Thorpe's Dictionary of Applied Chemistry. 12 vols. 1937–56.
Universal Jewish Encyclopedia. 10 vols. 1939–43.
Van Nostrand's Scientific Encyclopedia. 1958.
Worldmark Encyclopedia of the Nations. 5 vols. 1963.

ATLASES AND GAZETTEERS

Collier's New World Atlas and Gazetteer. 1953.
Columbia Lippincott Gazetteer of the World. 1952.
Encyclopædia Britannica World Atlas. 1962.
Hammond's Ambassador World Atlas. 1954.
Rand-McNally Commercial Atlas. 1962. Revised annually.
Times (London) *Atlas of the World.* 5 vols. 1955—.
Webster's Geographical Dictionary. Revised ed., 1962.

YEARBOOKS—CURRENT EVENTS

Americana Annual. 1923—.
Annual Register. 1758—.
Britannica Book of the Year. 1938—.
Economic Almanac. 1940—.
Facts on File. 1940—.
Information Please Almanac. 1947—.
New International Year Book. 1907—.
Statesman's Year-Book. 1864—.
Statistical Abstract of the United States. 1878—.
Whitaker's Almanack. 1869—.
World Almanac. 1868—.

BIOGRAPHY

Current Biography. 1940—.
Dictionary of American Biography. 20 vols. and index. 1928–43.
    Supplements to date.
Dictionary of National Biography. (British.) 22 vols. 1908–09.
    Indexes and supplements to date.
International Who's Who. 1935—.
Kunitz, S. J., and Howard Haycraft. *American Authors, 1600–
    1900.* 1938.
———. *British Authors of the Nineteenth Century.* 1936.

————. *Twentieth Century Authors.* 1942. Supplement, 1955.
————. *British Authors before 1800.* 1952.
Webster's Biographical Dictionary. 1943, 1956.
Who's Who. 1848—.
Who's Who in America. 1899—.
Who Was Who in America. 3 vols. 1897–1960.

LITERATURE—MYTHOLOGY

Barnhart, Clarence L. *The New Century Handbook of English Literature.* 1956.
Bartlett's Familiar Quotations. 1955.
Bateson, F. W. *Cambridge Bibliography of English Literature.* 5 vols. 1941–57.
Benét, William Rose. *The Reader's Encyclopedia.* Second ed., 1965.
Brewer's Dictionary of Phrase and Fable. 1953.
Cambridge History of American Literature. 4 vols. 1917–21.
Cambridge History of English Literature. 15 vols. 1907–27.
English Association. *Year's Work in English Studies.* 1920—.
Fiction Catalog. 1941. Seventh ed., 1960.
Frazer, Sir J. G. *The Golden Bough.* 12 vols. 1907–15.
Gayley, C. M. *Classic Myths in English Literature and in Art.* 1939.
Granger, Edith. *Index to Poetry and Recitations.* Fifth ed., 1962.
Harper's Dictionary of Classical Literature and Antiquities. 1897.
Hart, James D. *Oxford Companion to American Literature.* Fourth ed., 1965.
Harvey, Sir Paul. *Oxford Companion to Classical Literature.* 1937.
————. *Oxford Companion to English Literature.* 1946.
Modern Humanities Research Association. *Annual Bibliography of English Language and Literature.* 1920—.
Mythology of All Races, 13 vols. 1916–32.
Oxford Classical Dictionary. 1949.
Sears, Minnie Earl, and Marian Shaw. *Essay and General Literature Index.* 1900—.
Short Story Index. 1953. Supplements.
Spiller, Robert E., and others. *Literary History of the United States.* 3 vols. 1956. (Helpful bibliographies)
Stevenson, B. E. *Home Book of Quotations.* 1956.
Thrall, Hibbard, and Holman. *A Handbook to Literature.* 1960.

(4) **Use a standard bibliographical form.**

Put each item of your bibliography on a separate card (3 × 5 or 4 × 6 inches in size) so that you can readily drop or add a card and can arrange the list alphabetically without copying. Write in ink and follow exactly and consistently the bibliographical form you are directed to use. The form illustrated by the models below (and by the footnote forms on pages 409–12) is based in general on the revised *Style Sheet* of the Modern Language Association (MLA) but follows several other widely used style manuals in giving the name of the publisher.

MODEL BIBLIOGRAPHICAL ENTRIES

BOOKS

Burrow, John Anthony. *A Reading of Sir Gawain and the Green Knight.* New York: Barnes & Noble, 1966. [Capitalization of the title follows general usage (see **9c**) instead of the special library usage, which capitalizes only first words and proper names. Note that this bracketed comment and the others below are not a part of the bibliographical entries. These entries fall into three units: (1) the author's name; (2) the title; and (3) the place of publication, publisher, and date of publication taken from the latest copyright date as shown on the copyright page.]

Duverger, Maurice. *Political Parties.* Translated from the French by Barbara and Robert North. New York: John Wiley & Sons, Inc., 1954. [A translation]

Hervey, George F., and Jack Hems. *Freshwater Tropical Aquarium Fishes.* London: Batchworth Press, 1952. [Two authors]

Johnson, R. U., and C. C. Buel, editors. *Battles and Leaders of the Civil War.* 4 volumes. New York: The Century Company, 1887–88. [Edited work]

McConnell, F. J., and others. *The Creative Intelligence and Modern Life.* Boulder: The University of Colorado Press, 1928. (University of Colorado Semicentennial Series, 1877–1927. Vol. V.) [A book by more than two authors; also a book in a series]

Prescott, William Hickling. *History of the Reign of Philip the Second, King of Spain.* Edited by John Foster Kirk. 3 volumes. Philadelphia: J. B. Lippincott & Company, 1871. [Author and editor]

Ryan, Cornelius. *The Last Battle.* New York: Simon and Schuster, Inc., 1966.

MAGAZINES AND NEWSPAPERS

King, Larry L. "Requiem for a West Texas Town," *Harper's Magazine,* CCXXXII (January, 1966), 46–53.

"Latest on Getting into College," *U.S. News & World Report,* LX (January 3, 1966), 50–52.

Schonberg, Harold C. "Modern Literalism and Repeats," New York *Times,* March 20, 1966, Section 2, p. 11. [The *p.* or *pp.* (for *page* or *pages*) are not used when the volume number in Roman numerals precedes, as in the two items above.]

"Will the Credit Medicine Be Enough?" *Business Week* (August 13, 1955), pp. 26–28.

ENCYCLOPEDIAS

"Jackson, Andrew." *Encyclopædia Britannica,* 1954, XII, 851–53.

Lee, Edwin A. "Vocational Education." *Encyclopedia Americana,* 1950, XXVIII, 160–61. [A signed article]

BULLETINS AND PAMPHLETS

Standards of Practice for Radio Broadcasters of the United States of America. Washington: The National Association of Radio and Television Broadcasters, 1954.

Velvetbean Caterpillar, The. Dept. of Agriculture, Bureau of Entomology and Plant Quarantine Leaflet No. 348. Washington: Government Printing Office, 1953.

UNPUBLISHED DISSERTATION

Woodall, Guy Ramon. "Robert Walsh, Jr., as an Editor and Literary Critic: 1797–1836." Ph.D. dissertation, University of Tennessee, 1966.

The models given above, with hanging indention, show the proper form for the entries in the final bibliography, which is to be written out and submitted as a part of the library paper. On the separate bibliography cards, the same form may be used; or the author, title, and facts of publication may be written on separate lines.

Watkins, Walter Barker Critz.

Johnson and English Poetry before 1660.

New York: Gordian Press, 1965.

PR 3537
.E6 W3

The form of the bibliographical models given above is commonly used by books and periodicals in languages and social sciences. Scientific periodicals tend to use boldface Arabic numerals for the volume number and to place the date at the end. Indexes to periodicals employ a compact form, but one not commonly used in books or periodicals and consequently not suitable as a model.

Whatever bibliographical form a writer adopts, he should give due heed to the three divisions of each entry: the author's name (if it is given), the title, and the facts of publication. He should take great pains to be consistent, each time using commas, periods, italics (underlining), and quotation marks exactly as they are called for by his model. This model will usually be suggested by the periodical, the organization, or the department for which the paper is being written. If the instructor does not specify a form, the student may adopt the commonly used form described in this handbook.

▶ EXERCISE 2 Prepare a preliminary bibliography on the topic selected for your library paper. Use at least ten of the most promising references (books, bulletins, articles in periodicals or reference books) you can find. (Often you will find helpful bibliographies in the books that you consult, especially at the end of articles in encyclopedias and other reference works.) Arrange your cards in alphabetical order.

33c

Prepare the outline.

After completing a preliminary bibliography and a minimum of general reading on your subject (an encyclopedia article and parts of one or two other works may suffice), make a preliminary outline that will give direction to your investigation. This tentative outline will enable you to discard irrelevant material from your bibliography and to begin spotting valuable passages on which you will want to take notes. There is nothing but frustration in store for anyone who attempts to take notes without first knowing what he is looking for.

Be careful, however, not to become a slave to your preliminary outline. For although the outline will direct your reading, your reading will almost certainly suggest ways in which the outline may be improved. No outline should be regarded as complete until the research paper has been finished. As you take notes, you will probably revise your original outline frequently, adding subheads to it, changing subheads to major headings, perhaps dropping some headings entirely.

Follow the general directions for outlining given in **32b-f,** pages 371–81. Make either a topic outline or a complete sentence outline. A paragraph outline would be less satisfactory for a paper as long as a library paper.

33d
Take notes (after evaluating the sources).

As you take notes on your readings, learn how to find and evaluate useful passages with a minimum of time and effort. Seldom will a whole book, or even a whole article, be of use as subject matter for any given research paper. To get what is needed for your paper, you will find that you must turn to many books and articles, rejecting most of them altogether and using from others only a section here and there. You cannot take the time to read each book carefully. Use the table of contents and the index of the book, and learn to scan the pages rapidly until you find the passages you need.

One important consideration always is the reliability of the source. Does the author seem to know his subject? Does he have an official position that implies competence? Do others speak of him as an authority? Is he prejudiced? Is the work recent enough to give the information needed? Is the edition being used the latest one available? Use your best judgment to determine the most dependable sources for your paper. You may find in the *Book Review Digest* convenient summaries of critical opinion on a book in your bibliography.

The common and best way to take notes is on cards or paper sheets of uniform size, usually 3 × 5 or 4 × 6 inches. (Often the smaller card is used for bibliography and the larger for notes.) Each card should contain a single note with a heading keyed to a significant word in the outline— not to the notation (IA, II, IIIC, etc.), which is especially subject to change. If the paper is to use the customary footnotes, each card must also show the source of the note, the exact page or pages.

A student preparing a library paper on Ibsen's drama might find the following passage and write from it the note given on the next page.

SOURCE

> And I know of no crime against virtue, good order and the revelation of God that he was not accused of. The product of all this pawing and bawling was the Ibsen legend, that fabulous picture of a fabulous monster, half Nietzsche and half Dr. Frank Crane, drenching the world with scandalous platitudes from a watch-tower in the chilblained North. The righteous heard of him with creepy shudders; there was bold talk of denying him the use of the mails; he was the Gog and the Magog, the Heliogabalus, nay, the downright Kaiser, of that distant and pious era.
>
> No such Ibsen, of course, ever really existed. The genuine Ibsen was anything but the Anti-Christ thus conjured up by imprudent partisans and terrified opponents.[1]

[1] H. L. Mencken, Introduction to *Eleven Plays of Henrik Ibsen*, (New York, [1935]), p. vii. Permission by Random House copyright © 1935.

NOTE CARD

> Misunderstanding of Ibsen's purpose
> Ibsen loudly denounced as great sinner—
> criticisms gave rise to the "Ibsen legend,"
> which made of him a " fabulous monster."
> "The righteous heard of him with creepy
> shudders ... he was the Gog and the Magog...
> of that distant and pious era."
> Not true ! The real Ibsen was not wicked.
>
> Mencken, p vii

The above note is an abbreviation or précis. Carefully observe that copied words are inside quotation marks. Notice that the words not enclosed in quotation marks are those of the student, not those in the source.

DIRECT QUOTATIONS

Very seldom should you write a note that is merely a quotation. Too many quotations in the library paper suggest a lack of mastery of the subject. And besides, the more you quote, the less practice you get in composition. A quotation must be a very telling and important one before you are justified in using it in your paper. Occasionally, however, you will discover such a passage. When you do, you should take down the passage verbatim—that is, write every word, every capital letter, every mark of punctuation exactly as in the original. Be sure to enclose the quoted passage in quotation marks. When you quote, quote accurately. When you are not quoting, use your own sentence structure and phraseology, getting entirely away from that of the original.

PLAGIARISM

If you fail to acknowledge borrowed material, then you are plagiarizing. Plagiarism is literary theft. When you copy the words of another, put those words inside quotation marks, and acknowledge the source with a footnote. When you paraphrase another's words, use your own words and your own sentence structure, and be sure to use a footnote giving the source of the idea. A plagiarist often merely changes a few words or simply rearranges the words in the source. As you take notes and as you write your paper, be especially careful to avoid plagiarism.

▶ **EXERCISE 3** Read carefully the paragraph by Harlow Shapley reprinted on pages 335–36. First write, in a single sentence, the central idea of the paragraph. Then write a note half as long as the paragraph. Finally write a note approximately as long as your source. [Avoid entirely the sentence patterns of the source. Choose your words carefully. Give variety to your sentences.]

33e

Using the outline, the bibliography, and the notes, write the library paper.

After you have made the outline as complete as possible and have taken a number of notes on every major section of the outline and every subsection, you are ready to begin writing. Arrange your notes in the order of the outline, and then use them as the basis of your paper, section by section. Naturally you will have to expand some parts, to cut others; and especially will you need to provide transitional sentences and even transitional paragraphs. Write the material in the best way you can—in your own style, in your own words. Follow the suggestions under **32g.**

(1) Footnotes and Footnote Forms. Since you will get your material for the library paper largely from others, you should, of course, give proper credit. To do so, use footnotes numbered consecutively throughout the paper and placed at the bottoms of the pages (or in one list at the end of the paper, if so directed). The number needed will vary with the paper. Every quotation must have its footnote, and so must all the chief facts and opinions drawn from others. Usually from two to six footnotes per page will be needed for proper documentation of the average library paper.

In the model forms that follow, note that the first footnote reference to a source is similar to, but not identical with, the bibliographical entry.

Moorehead, Alan.   The White Nile.   New York: Harper &
      Brothers, 1960.

[Bibliographical entry]

[1]Alan Moorehead, The White Nile (New York, 1960),
p. 351.

[First footnote reference]

The footnote has the normal paragraph indention (not the hanging indention used to make each entry stand out in a bibliography); the author's name comes in normal order with surname last (since the name is not to be alphabetized as in the bibliography); a comma replaces the period between author's name and title, and the facts of publication are put in parentheses without the publisher's name; and the exact page of the source is given.

MODEL FOOTNOTES—FIRST REFERENCES

BOOKS

[1] John Anthony Burrow, *A Reading of Sir Gawain and the Green Knight* (New York, 1966), p. 23.

[2] Maurice Duverger, *Political Parties,* trans. from the French by Barbara and Robert North (New York, 1954), p. 114. [A translation]

[3] George F. Hervey and Jack Hems, *Freshwater Tropical Aquarium Fishes* (London, 1952), p. 44. [Two authors]

[4] R. U. Johnson and C. C. Buel, eds, *Battles and Leaders of the Civil War* (New York, 1887–88), I, 9. [Edited work; also a work in several volumes]

[5] General James Longstreet, "Our March Against Pope," in *Battles and Leaders of the Civil War,* ed. R. U. Johnson and C. C. Buel (New York, 1887–88), II, 516. [Contributing author in an edited work]

[6] F. J. McConnell and others, *The Creative Intelligence and Modern Life,* University of Colorado Semicentennial Series, V (Boulder, Colo., 1928), pp. 29–30. [A book by more than two authors; also a book in a series]

[7] William Hickling Prescott, *History of the Reign of Philip the Second, King of Spain,* ed. John Foster Kirk (Philadelphia, 1871), III, 87.

[8] Cornelius Ryan, *The Last Battle* (New York, 1966), p. 31.

MAGAZINES AND NEWSPAPERS

[9] Larry L. King, "Requiem for a West Texas Town," *Harper's Magazine,* CCXXXII (January, 1966), 47.

[10] "Latest on Getting into College," *U.S. News & World Report,* LX (January 3, 1966), 50–51.

[11] Harold C. Schonberg, "Modern Literalism and Repeats," New York *Times*, March 20, 1966, Section 2, p. 11. [A signed article]

[12] Louisville *Times*, June 4, 1938, p. 16. [An unsigned news story]

[13] "Will the Credit Medicine Be Enough?" *Business Week* (August 13, 1955), pp. 26–27. [An unsigned magazine article]

ENCYCLOPEDIAS

[14] "Jackson, Andrew," *Encyclopædia Britannica*, 1954, XII, 853. [An unsigned encyclopedia article. The title here is given as "Jackson, Andrew" because it is found listed alphabetically under *J* and not under *A* in the encyclopedia.]

[15] Edwin A. Lee, "Vocational Education," *Encyclopedia Americana*, 1950, XXVIII, 160. [A signed encyclopedia article. Note the variant spellings: *Encyclopædia* for the *Britannica; Encyclopedia* for the *Americana.*]

BULLETINS AND PAMPHLETS

[16] *Standards of Practice for Radio Broadcasters of the United States of America* (Washington, 1954), p. 18.

[17] *The Velvetbean Caterpillar*, Department of Agriculture, Bureau of Entomology and Plant Quarantine Leaflet No. 348 (Washington, 1953), p. 3.

UNPUBLISHED DISSERTATION

[18] Guy Ramon Woodall, "Robert Walsh, Jr., as an Editor and Literary Critic: 1797–1836" (Ph.D. dissertation, University of Tennessee, 1966), p. 186.

MODEL FOOTNOTES—SECOND REFERENCES

The second (or later) footnote references below follow the order of the works cited in the Model Footnotes—First References.

BOOKS

[19] Burrow, p. 95.   [20] Duverger, pp. 113–14.

[It is permissible to place extremely short footnotes two, and even three, on a line, so long as there is no appearance of overcrowding.]

²¹ Hervey and Hems, p. 41.   ²² Johnson and Buel, I, 5.

²³ Longstreet, II, 515.   ²⁴ McConnell and others, p. 28.

²⁵ Prescott, III, 125.

²⁶ *Ibid.* [Same work, same volume, and same page as in footnote immediately preceding]

²⁷ *Ibid.,* II, 94–95. [Same work (Prescott's), but a different volume]

²⁸ *Ibid.,* p. 95. [Same work, same volume, but only one page this time]

²⁹ *Ibid.,* III, 125. [Same work, but back to a volume not cited in the *immediately* preceding footnote]

³⁰ Ryan, p. 133.

³¹ Prescott, III, 127. [An *ibid.* here would refer to Ryan's work, not Prescott's.]

³² Ryan, p. 133.

MAGAZINES AND NEWSPAPERS

³³ King, p. 279.   ³⁴ "Latest on Getting into College," p. 51.

³⁵ Schonberg, p. 1.

³⁶ Schonberg, "Modern Literalism and Repeats," p. 11. [This is the form that would have been needed if Schonberg had furnished more than one of the sources included in your bibliography.]

³⁷ Harold C. Schonberg, p. 11. [This is the form that would have to be used if another author also named Schonberg were included in your bibliography.]

³⁸ Louisville *Times,* p. 16. [Proper if only one article from this newspaper is used. If more than one are used, the secondary form is the same as the primary. See footnote 12.]

³⁹ "Will the Credit Medicine Be Enough?" p. 27.

ENCYCLOPEDIAS

⁴⁰ "Jackson, Andrew," pp. 851–52. [This is the proper form if only one article with this title has been used. It is possible that a research paper may use articles with identical titles from several different encyclopedias. In that case, the proper secondary footnote form would be as follows (footnote 41).]

⁴¹ "Jackson, Andrew," *Encyclopædia Britannica,* pp. 851–52. [The year of publication and the volume number are cited in your primary footnote and need not be repeated here.]

⁴² Lee, p. 160.

BULLETINS AND PAMPHLETS

    [43] *Standards of Practice for Radio Broadcasters of the United States of America,* p. 17.
    [44] *The Velvetbean Caterpillar,* p. 3.

UNPUBLISHED DISSERTATION

    [45] Woodall, p. 135.

Abbreviations. Some abbreviations used in footnotes are as follows (those from Latin usually written in italics):

c. or *ca.* (*circa*)	about (*ca.* 1550)
cf. (*confer*)	compare [The English *see* is more common.]
ch., chs.	chapter, chapters
ed.	edited by, edition, editor
f., ff.	and the following page, pages
ibid. (*ibidem*)	in the same place
l., ll.	line, lines
loc. cit. (*loco citato*)	in the place cited
MS., ms., MSS., mss.	manuscript, manuscripts
n.d.	no date given
n.p.	no place (of publication)
op. cit. (*opere citato*)	in the work cited
p., pp.	page, pages
passim	here and there
rev.	revised
tr., trans.	translated by
vol., vols.	volume, volumes

(2) **Final Outline and Paper.** After writing the first draft of your paper, complete with footnotes, read it over carefully, correcting all errors in spelling, mechanics, and grammar, and making sure that the arrangement is logical and that the writing is as clear, concise, and pleasing in style as you can possibly make it. You will probably rewrite some sentences, strike out others, and add still others. Your outline, which has developed steadily throughout the note-taking

and the first draft of the paper, should now be in its final form. It has served primarily, of course, as a guide to the writing of the paper; but it will also serve, if copied in its final stage, as a guide to the contents of the paper.

With your first draft corrected and revised, and with your outline put in its final form, write the final draft of your paper. Use a typewriter if possible; if not, use pen and ink, writing legibly and neatly.

(3) **Final Bibliography.** You assembled a preliminary bibliography early in your research. As you pursued your investigation, you eliminated some items and added others. Not until you have completed your paper can you know the items that should make up your final bibliography. Now, with your writing completed, look through your footnotes. Every book or article appearing even once in a footnote belongs in the bibliography. Your instructor may ask you to include everything that you have examined, whether you have actually used it in your writing or not. In that case your bibliography may have, instead of a dozen items, as many as fifty or a hundred. But, on the whole, the best practice is to include only items which have actually been used. Once you have determined the items that should be included, you can easily arrange the bibliography cards and copy them, either in one alphabetical list or in a list classified according to the instructor's directions.

The completed library paper will consist of three units (or four units if a separate page is used for title, author's name, instructor's name, course number, and date of writing):

1. Outline, serving as the table of contents (numbered with small Roman numerals if it occupies more than one page).
2. Text of the paper, with footnotes.
3. Bibliography, on a separate page or pages numbered with the text (with Arabic numerals).

Students are often asked to submit, along with the completed paper, the materials used in the preparation of the paper: (1) one of the preliminary outlines, (2) the notes, on cards, (3) the rough draft of the paper, with footnotes, and (4) the bibliography, on cards.

▶ EXERCISE 4   On the following pages is a library paper written by a college freshman. The pages facing those of the library paper contain passages from the sources used by the student in preparing the paper, so that you may compare the original material with the student's use of it. Be prepared for a class discussion of this paper—its strengths and weaknesses. Give special attention to both content and form, organization and documentation.

Ibsen's Nora

by Barbara J. Reid

OUTLINE

CENTRAL IDEA   The character of Nora reflects Ibsen's

attitude toward women.

INTRODUCTION   The storm of controversy aroused by

Ibsen's A Doll's House

   I. The early Nora

      A. Her doll-like qualities

      B. Her faulty sense of morality

  II. Nora's awakening

      A. Her latent instincts

      B. Her self-recognition

      C. Her reevaluation of her marriage

 III. Nora as the Ibsen woman

      A. Foreshadows woman of the twentieth century

      B. Indicates needed reforms in the nineteenth

         century

CONCLUSION   Debated issues showing misunderstanding

of Ibsen's purpose

Original Sources

The "problem play," a serious drama concentrated on a particular weakness or evil, presumably remediable if attacked from a
new direction, brought the theatre into the arena of social reform.
Because problem plays are pointed at existing problems which may
in time be alleviated if the action they call for is taken, they sometimes seem dated by the problem, or limited to a sociological
meaning only. The best of them, however, outlive the problem because it was only an external means for exhibiting universal human
nature under tragic forces. Ibsen's plays, which served as powerful
arguments both for realistic drama and realistic thought, have
passed the "time test" and emerged as dateless serious dramas or
tragedies. [From *Introduction to Literature: Plays,* eds. Lynn
Altenbernd and Leslie L. Lewis. Reprinted by permission of The
Macmillan Company.]

The theme of the play, with its insistence on the woman's right
to individual self-development, provoked a storm of discussion, and,
in many quarters, an outpouring of violent abuse. [From Introduction by R. Farquharson Sharp to *A Doll's House: And Two Other
Plays,* by Henrik Ibsen (translated by R. Farquharson Sharp and
Eleanor Marx-Aveling.) By permission of E. P. Dutton & Co. Inc.
and J. M. Dent & Sons, Ltd.]

No work of Ibsen's, not even his beautiful Puritan opera of
Brand, has excited so much controversy as *A Doll's House.* This
was, no doubt, to a very great extent caused by its novel presentment
of the mission of woman in modern society. In the dramas and
romances of modern Scandinavia, and especially those of Ibsen
and Björnson, the function of woman had been clearly defined. She
was to be the helper, the comforter, the inspirer, the guerdon of
man in his struggle towards loftier forms of existence. When man
fell on the upward path, woman's hand was to be stretched to
raise him; when man went wandering away on ill and savage
courses, woman was to wait patiently over her spinning-wheel,
ready to welcome and to pardon the returning prodigal; when the
eyes of man grew weary in watching for the morning-star, its rays
were to flash through the crystal tears of woman. [From *Northern
Studies,* by Edmund Gosse.]

IBSEN'S NORA

Henrik Ibsen's $\underline{A}$ $\underline{Doll's}$ $\underline{House}$ is today regarded by many authorities as a timeless classic.[1] When it appeared in 1879, however, it aroused a heated controversy over the problem that Ibsen presented. $\underline{A}$ $\underline{Doll's}$ $\underline{House}$ has to do with woman's place in the home in the nineteenth century. The main theme, according to one critic, is the play's "insistence on the woman's right to individual self-development."[2] This was revolutionary doctrine in the nineteenth century, because woman's role at that time was to be "the helper, the comforter, the inspirer, the guerdon of man in his struggle towards loftier forms of existence."[3]

---

[1] See, for example, Lynn Altenbernd and Leslie L. Lewis, _Introduction to Literature: Plays_ (New York, 1963), p. 164.

[2] R. Farquharson Sharp, Introduction to _A Doll's House: And Two Other Plays_, by Henrik Ibsen (New York, 1946), p. lx.

[3] Edmund Gosse, _Northern Studies_ (London, 1890), p. 88.

The subject of *A Doll's House*—the awakening to the sense of individual responsibility on the part of a woman who has always been treated as a spoilt child—was of itself sufficient matter for any amount of discussion. Whether Nora acted rightly or wrongly, naturally or unnaturally, in leaving husband, home and children in order to develop her own "individuality"; whether her casting herself adrift was indispensable to her development—all this is hotly debated. [From Introduction by R. Farquharson Sharp to *A Doll's House: And Two Other Plays*, by Henrik Ibsen (translated by R. Farquharson Sharp and Eleanor Marx-Aveling.) By permission of E. P. Dutton & Co. Inc. and J. M. Dent & Sons, Ltd.]

. . . she [Nora] is now a mother, and the wife of a man who shields her carefully from all contact with the world. He refrains from sharing with her his work or his trouble; he fosters all her childish instincts; she is a source of enjoyment to him, a precious toy.

[From *The New Spirit,* by Havelock Ellis.]

Therefore, Ibsen's implication that women ought to walk away from the shadows of men, to find their own place in the sun, caused quite a stir.

In the character of Nora in <u>A Doll's House</u>, Ibsen at first presents a nineteenth-century stereotype wife who is simple, flighty, childish, sweet, and irresponsible; then she gradually becomes aware of her individuality and breaks from the mold.[4] Her doll-like nature is caused by her upbringing. Both her husband, Helmer, and her father have babied her for many years; her opinions and ideas of morality are just echoes of these men in her life. As he refuses to tell her of his work and his difficulties, Helmer protects her from the outside world. Calling her his "little lark" and "little squirrel," he considers Nora as only "a source of enjoyment to him, a precious toy."[5]

---

[4]Sharp, p. ix.

[5]Havelock Ellis, <u>The New Spirit</u> (New York, 1892), p. 161.

... He is a man of aesthetic tastes, and his love for her has something of the delight that one takes in a work of art. Nora's conduct is the natural outcome of her training and experience. She tells lies with facility; she flirts almost recklessly to attain her own ends; when money is concerned, her conceptions of right are so elementary that she forges her father's name. But she acts from the impulses of a loving heart; her motives are always good; she is not conscious of guilt. Her education in life has not led her beyond the stage of the affectionate child with no sense of responsibility. But the higher instincts are latent within her; and they awake when the light of day at length penetrates her doll's house, and she learns the judgment of the world, of which her husband now stands forth as the stern interpreter. [From *The New Spirit*, by Havelock Ellis.]

Poor example
paraphrased too much info

3

According to Havelock Ellis, Nora's behavior can
be traced to her experience and environment. It
bothers her not at all to tell lies. For example,
even when she is swallowing the last bite of the
macaroons (which Helmer has forbidden her to buy),
Nora answers Helmer's questions by saying that she has
not bought macaroons nor is she eating them. To get
what she wants, she also resorts to flirting with her
own husband. When she wants to keep her husband from
going to the mail box, she convinces him that without
his constant help she could not learn the Tarantella
dance before the party--though actually she knows
the dance well. Although she has worthy motives,
she does actually forge her father's signature. Her
motives are always praiseworthy, and like a child who
has no knowledge of wrong and right she has no guilty
conscience.[6]

When Helmer explains to her the immorality involved in her forging the signature of her father,

---

[6]Ibid.

HELMER (*walking about the room*). What a horrible awakening! All these eight years—she who was my joy and pride—a hypocrite, a liar—worse, worse—a criminal! The unutterable ugliness of it all! For shame! For shame! [NORA *is silent and looks steadily at him. He stops in front of her.*] I ought to have suspected that something of the sort would happen. I ought to have foreseen it. All your father's want of principle—be silent!—all your father's want of principle has come out in you. No religion, no morality, no sense of duty—. How I am punished for having winked at what he did! I did it for your sake, and this is how you repay me.

NORA. Yes, that's just it.

HELMER. Now you have destroyed all my happiness. You have ruined all my future. It is horrible to think of! I am in the power of an unscrupulous man; he can do what he likes with me, ask anything he likes of me, give me any orders he pleases—I dare not refuse. And I must sink to such miserable depths because of a thoughtless woman!

NORA. When I am out of the way, you will be free.

.   .   .

HELMER. Nora—!

NORA. You mean that I would never have accepted such a sacrifice on your part? No, of course not. But what would my assurances have been worth against yours? That was the wonderful thing which I hoped for and feared; and it was to prevent that, that I wanted to kill myself.

HELMER. I would gladly work night and day for you, Nora—bear sorrow and want for your sake. But no man would sacrifice his honour for the one he loves.

NORA. It is a thing hundreds of thousands of women have done.

HELMER. Oh, you think and talk like a heedless child.

.   .   .

4

Nora begins to understand how naive she has been and
how unkind and selfish her husband really is. Nora
sees that he is selfishly concerned for his own reputation as she listens to him say these words:

> Now you have destroyed all my happiness. You
> have ruined all my future. It is horrible to
> think of! I am in the power of an unscrupu-
> lous man; he can do what he likes with me, ask
> anything he likes of me, give me any orders he
> pleases--I dare not refuse. And I must sink
> to such miserable depths because of a thought-
> less woman.[7]

He is so concerned with himself that he does not stop
to think what could have made her do such a thing.

The breach between Nora and Helmer widens. In
the course of their quarrel, Helmer says,

> I would gladly work night and day for you,
> Nora--bear sorrow and want for your sake.
> But no man would sacrifice his honour for
> the one he loves.[8]

And Nora, with eyes newly opened, responds, "It is a

_____

[7]Henrik Ibsen, _A Doll's House_, trans. by William
Archer, in _Interpreting Literature_, eds. K. L. Knick-
erbocker and H. Willard Reninger (New York, 1960),
pp. 638-39.

[8]_Ibid._, p. 643

NORA. What do you consider my most sacred duties?

HELMER. Do I need to tell you that? Are they not your duties to your husband and your children?

NORA. I have other duties just as sacred.

HELMER. That you have not. What duties could those be?

NORA. Duties to myself.

HELMER. Before all else, you are a wife and a mother.

NORA. I don't believe that any longer. I believe that before all else I am a reasonable human being, just as you are—or, at all events, that I must try and become one. I know quite well, Torvald, that most people would think you right, and that views of that kind are to be found in books; but I can no longer content myself with what most people say, or with what is found in books. I must think over things for myself and get to understand them.

HELMER. Can you not understand your place in your own home? Have you not a reliable guide in such matters as that—have you no religion? [From *A Doll's House*, by Henrik Ibsen, trans. by William Archer.]

5

thing hundreds of thousands of women have done."[9] She
now fully understands that her marriage has not been a
true marriage, that she has really been living in a doll
house. In fact, Nora has just courageously contradicted
Helmer's statement that her function in life is to be a
wife and mother. With new insight, she has clearly
expressed her opposing view:

> I don't believe that any longer. I believe that
> before all else I am a reasonable human being,
> just as you are--or, at all events, that I must
> try and become one. I know quite well, Torvald,
> that most people would think you right, and that
> views of that kind are to be found in books; but
> I can no longer content myself with what most
> people say, or with what is found in books. I
> must think over things for myself and get to
> understand them.[10]

Nora knows that she must educate herself and must
develop her own personality. She believes that the
only way to do this is to leave her husband until he
learns to understand her, an understanding which to
her would be "the most wonderful thing of all." The

---

[9]_Ibid._

[10]_Ibid._, p. 642.

... Wilder's play differs from Ibsen's in the conviction it creates in the minds of the audience that Nora's desertion is permanent rather than temporary, Ibsen's idea having been that the separation was to last only long enough for both husband and wife to make the adjustments necessary for a true marriage. [From *Milestones of the Drama,* ed. by Helen Louise Cohen. Reprinted by permission of Harcourt, Brace & World, Inc.]

I know no more important lessons for women than those contained in the *Doll's House* and *Ghosts.* They are full of the beautiful truth that Woman is a responsible being, as complete in herself, as capable of exercising self-government as Man. They sound a clarion call to women to throw off the yoke of the Past, to arise, to put aside their worn out ideal and to boldly assume the duties of the present age. In the *Doll's House,* there is shadowed forth the perfect marriage of the future. [From "Ibsen's Attitude Toward Woman," by Annie Nathan Meyer.]

6

play ends as Nora leaves.

What is this "most wonderful thing of all" or
this "miracle of miracles" that Ibsen uses to hint
that the separation of husband and wife will not be
permanent? It is the development of perfect commun-
ion, which both Nora and Helmer may achieve by growing
in individual responsibility, by making the adjustments
needed for a happy marriage.[11] In this way, Ibsen does
"sound a clarion call to women to throw off the yoke
of the Past, to arise, to put aside their worn out
ideal and to boldly assume the duties of the present
age."[12] In a sense, Ibsen was foreseeing women in the
twentieth century.

Because of the widespread misunderstanding of
Ibsen's purposes, the dramatist was loudly denounced
as a great sinner. A kind of "Ibsen legend" arose,
which made the man a "fabulous monster." According to

---

[11]Helen Louise Cohen, _Milestones of the Drama_ (New
York, 1940), p. 271.

[12]Annie Nathan Meyer, "Ibsen's Attitude Toward
Woman," _The Critic_, XVI (March 22, 1890), 148.

See page 406 for the original passage in Mencken and the student's note card on it.

Ibsen himself refused to admit that he had purposed writing a play on the subject of a woman's rights. He did not wish to distinguish in his mind between the rights of men and the rights of women, but liked to think that the liberty of all human beings was uppermost in his mind when he wrote the play. "In our times," said Ibsen in 1882, "every literary work has the mission of extending boundary lines." [From *Milestones of the Drama,* edited by Helen Louise Cohen. Reprinted by permission of Harcourt, Brace & World, Inc.]

... search Ibsen throughout and it will be found that his subject matter is fundamentally the same as that of all great masters of tragedy. It is his novel manner of presentation, his transposition of themes hitherto treated epically, to the narrow, unheroic scale of middle-class family life that blinded critics to his true significance. This tuning down of the heroic, this reversal of the old aesthetic order extorted bitter remonstrances. [From *Egoists: A Book of Supermen,* by James Huneker. Reprinted by permission of Charles Scribner's Sons, Inc.]

7

H. L. Mencken, Ibsen was "the Gog and the Magog . . .
of that distant and pious era."[13] Many angry critics
accused Ibsen of being an advocate of "the emancipated
woman." All of these were false accusations. Ibsen
himself said that he had no patience with women who
abandoned their own world for the man's world. Ibsen
firmly insisted that a woman should not only develop
her own individuality but also use her feminine gifts
as a mother. Actually, Ibsen did not set out to write
a play on the rights of emancipated women; instead he
was insisting upon the rights of all human beings,
both women and men.[14]

Perhaps it was Ibsen's use of the "unheroic scale
of middle-class family life that blinded critics [of
Ibsen's time] to his true significance."[15] They debated the morality of Nora's leaving her husband and

---

[13]Introduction to Eleven Plays of Henrik Ibsen
(New York, [1935]), p. vii.

[14]Cohen, p. 270.

[15]James Huneker, Egoists: A Book of Supermen (New
York, 1932), p. 323.

. . . yet Nora Helmer, when she slammed the door of her doll's home, caused an echo in the heart of every intelligent woman in Christendom. It is not necessary now to ask whether a woman would, or should, desert her children; Nora's departure was only the symbol of her liberty, the gesture of a newly awakened individuality. [From *Egoists: A Book of Supermen,* by James Huneker. Reprinted by permission of Charles Scribner's Sons, Inc.]

His reply to those who accused him of a merely destructive philosophy was that his task, as he conceived it, was to point out the weaknesses of the social fabric, and to leave constructive philosophy to those who were not dramatists. He diagnosed, and left the cure to others. [From Introduction by R. Farquharson Sharp to *A Doll's House: And Two Other Plays,* by Henrik Ibsen (translated by R. Farquharson Sharp and Eleanor Marx-Aveling). By permission of E. P. Dutton & Co. Inc. and J. M. Dent & Sons, Ltd.]

. . . unity lies not in the said but in the saying.

In this saying is Ibsenism. Modern drama, as a historical development, is surely partly created by Ibsenism. And Ibsenism is not so much a system as an attitude: thoughtfulness, seriousness, and especially searching characterization. [From *Contemporary Drama: Fifteen Plays,* eds. E. Bradlee Watson and Benfield Pressey. Reprinted by permission of Charles Scribner's Sons.]

children in order to develop herself. They completely missed Ibsen's message; to him, Nora's leaving was a symbol, a kind of declaration of independence.[16] Ibsen did present, as Sharp has pointed out, "the weaknesses of the social fabric,"[17] but he did this as an artist. He was content to leave the solutions of the problems he presented to the philosophers. Certainly Ibsenism is not a philosophy. As one modern critic has written: "Ibsenism is not so much a system as an attitude: thoughtfulness, seriousness, and especially searching characterization."[18] And the characterization of Nora striving to develop her own personality shows one of Ibsen's most important attitudes: his belief that every woman has a right to be a person.

---

[16]*Ibid.*, p. 331.

[17]Sharp, p. x.

[18]E. Bradlee Watson and Benfield Pressey, *Contemporary Drama*: *Fifteen Plays* (New York, 1959), p. 4.

9

BIBLIOGRAPHY

Altenbernd, Lynn, and Leslie L. Lewis, eds. Intro-
    duction to Literature: Plays. New York: The
    Macmillan Company, 1963.

Cohen, Helen Louise, ed. Milestones of the Drama.
    New York: Harcourt, Brace & World, Inc., 1940.

Ellis, Havelock. The New Spirit. 3rd ed. New York:
    The Walter Scott Publishing Company, Ltd., 1892.

Gosse, Edmund. Northern Studies. London: The Walter
    Scott Publishing Company, Ltd., 1890.

Huneker, James. Egoists: A Book of Supermen. New
    York: Charles Scribner's Sons, 1932.

Ibsen, Henrik. A Doll's House, trans. William Archer,
    in Interpreting Literature, eds. K. L. Knicker-
    bocker and H. Willard Reninger. Rev. ed. New
    York: Holt, Rinehart and Winston, Inc., 1960.

Mencken, H. L. Introduction to Eleven Plays of
    Henrik Ibsen. New York: Random House, [1935].

Meyer, Annie Nathan. "Ibsen's Attitude Toward Woman,"
    The Critic, XVI (March 22, 1890), 147-48.

Sharp, R. Farquharson. Introduction to A Doll's
    House: And Two Other Plays, by Henrik Ibsen.
    New York: E. P. Dutton & Company, Inc., 1946.

Watson, E. Bradlee, and Benfield Pressey, eds. Contem-
    porary Drama: Fifteen Plays. New York: Charles
    Scribner's Sons, 1959.

Letters

34

Letters should follow the forms prescribed by usage.

Many college graduates will find letter-writing a major part of their life's work. All the principles of good writing set forth in this handbook apply to letters and should be used by the student whenever he is called on to write letters.

Business letters are preferably typewritten on one side only of sheets 8½ × 11 inches in size. These sheets are folded either (1) once horizontally and twice in the other direction to fit an envelope about 3½ × 6½ inches in size or (2) twice horizontally to fit an envelope about 4 × 10 inches in size.

Personal letters and social notes are commonly written by hand on note paper—a four-page sheet to be folded once horizontally for insertion in a matching envelope; or on club paper—a sheet about 7¼ × 11 inches, to be folded twice horizontally to fit a matching envelope 3¾ × 7½ inches. Both sides of the sheets may be used.

34a

Business letters should follow prescribed usage with respect to the six essential parts:

(1) Heading.
(2) Inside address.
(3) Salutation (or greeting).

(4) Body of the letter.
(5) Complimentary close.
(6) Signature.

MODEL BUSINESS LETTER

(1) 1288 Catawba Street
Columbia, Missouri 65201
May 3, 1966

(2) Mr. J. W. Rice
Editor, Rushville _News_
122 East Market Street
Rushville, Missouri 64484

(3) Dear Mr. Rice:

Mr. Erskine Freeman, of your City Room, has mentioned to me your
regular practice of employing two student reporters every summer.
I am now majoring in journalism at the University of Missouri,
and I should like, therefore, to apply for one of those positions
for this next summer.

By the end of this college year I shall have completed three
quarters of the university program in journalism. Included in
this work are two courses in reporting and one in copyreading.
Before I began my college work, I had served four years as
sports editor of my high school newspaper, where I learned some
of the fundamentals of page make-up. Last year I was awarded
the Missouri Press Association Scholarship for journalism.

I have permission to refer you to my employer of the last three
summers:

(4)
          Mr. George Armour
          Armour Drug Store
          Rushville, Missouri 64484

and to the professors under whom I have taken courses in journalism:

          Dr. James D. Turner
          Professor of Journalism
          University of Missouri
          Columbia, Missouri 65201

          Dr. John M. Cain
          Assistant Professor of Journalism
          University of Missouri
          Columbia, Missouri 65201

I shall be in Rushville after June 6 and should appreciate an
opportunity to call at your office for an interview at your
convenience.

(5)   Very truly yours,

(6) _Donald Burke_

      Donald Burke

(1) The heading must give the full address of the writer and the date of the letter.

The heading is blocked as in the model.

```
860 Fremont Street          [End punctuation is regularly
Bessemer, Alabama 35020     omitted with the blocked head-
February 3, 1967            ing.]
```

If there is a letterhead (which supplies the address), the date may be written either under the letterhead or flush with the right margin.

(2) The inside address (identical with the address to appear on the envelope) must give the name and the full address of the person to whom the letter is written.

The inside address must be consistent in form with the heading. The inside address is typed flush with the left margin about six spaces lower than the heading.

(3) The salutation (or greeting) should be consistent with the tone of the letter, the first line of the inside address, and the complimentary close.

The salutation is written flush with the left margin two spaces below the inside address and is followed by a colon. The following salutations are used:

FOR MEN	FOR WOMEN
Dear Sir:	Dear Madam:
Dear Mr. Smith:	Dear Mrs. Smith:
Gentlemen:	Ladies:

Note: The masculine salutation is used to address an organization (Gentlemen) or an individual (Dear Sir) whose name the writer does not know.

In some instances a business letter is addressed to a company or a department of a company but marked for the attention of a particular person. In such letters, the "attention line" is placed two lines above the salutation, thus:

<u>Attention</u>: Mr. L. W. Jones

Gentlemen:

For the proper form of salutation in letters to government officials, ecclesiastical dignitaries, etc., consult a good dictionary.

In salutations and addresses, abbreviations are generally disapproved except for *Mr.* (plural, *Messrs.*), *Mrs.* (plural, *Mmes.*), and *Dr.*

MODEL ADDRESSED ENVELOPE

Donald Burke
1288 Catawba Street
Columbia, Missouri 65201

Mr. J. W. Rice
Editor, Rushville <u>News</u>
122 East Market Street
Rushville, Missouri 64484

(4) The body of the letter should follow the principles of good writing.

Typewritten business letters are usually single-spaced, with double spacing between paragraphs. All paragraphs (1) should begin flush with the left-hand margin, as in the model business letter on page 434, or (2) should be indented equally (usually five spaces). The subject matter should be well organized and paragraphed, but the para-

graphs will frequently be shorter than in ordinary writing.
The style should be clear and direct. Indirect, abbreviated,
or outdated phrasing should be avoided.

INDIRECT	I beg to inform you that we have . . . I beg to send . . . Permit us to report that we now supply . . .
BETTER	We have . . . I send . . . We now supply . . .
ABBREVIATED	Hope to have . . . Enclose check for six dollars.
BETTER	We hope to have . . . I enclose a check for six dollars.

Note: If the letter goes over to a second page, the sender's
address (whether on letterhead or a typed heading) should
not be repeated. The name (surname only) of the recipient,
the page number, and the date should be given, arranged
either across the top of the page or at the upper left
margin.

(5) **The complimentary close should be consistent with the
tone of the letter and with the salutation.**

Ordinary business letters addressed to strangers should
close with *Yours truly, Yours very truly,* or *Very truly
yours.* Professional letters, or business letters addressed to
an individual with such an opening as *Dear Mr. White,*
may well close with the more friendly *Yours sincerely,
Sincerely yours, Sincerely, Faithfully yours,* or *Cordially
yours.*

(6) **The signature should be written by hand directly below
the complimentary close.**

If the writer's name does not appear in the letterhead,
it may be typed just below the signature. Ordinarily,
neither professional titles nor degrees should be used with
the signature, but the writer's official capacity may be
indicated:

INAPPROPRIATE	James M. Smith, LL.D.
PERMISSIBLE	James M. Smith
	President

A married woman should sign her own name (*Mary Hughes Black,* not *Mrs. John K. Black*). In business letters her status is indicated by the use of parentheses as follows:

CORRECT   **Mary Hughes Black**
              (Mrs. John K. Black)

CORRECT   **(Mrs.) Mary Hughes Black**

(7) The letter should be folded to fit the envelope.

Below are the steps for the proper folding of a business letter to fit the long standard envelope and for placing it inside the envelope.

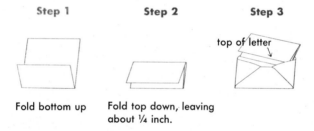

Step 1	Step 2	Step 3
Fold bottom up	Fold top down, leaving about ¼ inch.	top of letter

Fold the standard-sized paper to fit a small business envelope as follows:

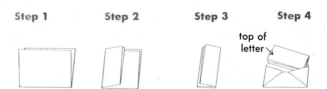

Step 1	Step 2	Step 3	Step 4
Fold bottom up	Fold left side in	Fold right over left, leaving about ¼ inch.	top of letter

34b

Personal letters and informal social notes follow in general the form of business letters.

Friendly letters usually omit the inside address. If it is included, it may be placed either at the beginning flush with the right margin or at the end of the letter flush with the left margin.

The salutation is usually followed by a comma instead of the more formal colon. As in the business letter, the salutation should be in keeping with the complimentary close and with the tone of the letter. A letter beginning with *Dear Mr. Brown* may close with *Sincerely yours, Yours sincerely,* or *Cordially yours.* A more familiar salutation and complimentary close may be justified by the intimacy of the correspondents.

The body of the letter will vary greatly with the occasion and with the personality of the writer. An easy, informal style is best.

34c

Formal social notes—announcements, invitations, answers to invitations—follow very definite conventions.

For the rare occasions when formal notes are required, engraving or handwriting (not typing) is the rule. Formal notes are always written in the third person. They have no inside address, no salutation, no complimentary close, and no signature. The writer's street address and the month and the date may be placed below at the left. Every word (except the street number and the abbreviations *Mr., Mrs.,* and *Dr.*) is spelled out in full. Acceptances and regrets follow the form of the invitation closely, repeating the hour and the date to insure understanding.

▶ EXERCISE 1   Write the following business letters:

1. Request the circulation manager of your newspaper to send your paper to a new address.
2. Ask the manager of a New York hotel to reserve a room for you.
3. Call the attention of your representative in the city government to some needed repairs in a street near your home.
4. Apply for a position that you are competent to fill. Be sure to include the following: (a) a brief description of the job desired—be specific; (b) your qualifications, including age, schooling, and experience; (c) at least three references—people who know you well and are able to evaluate your ability; (d) a request for an interview. See the model business letter on page 434.
5. Explain to your employer why you must resign your position at the end of the year.
6. Recommend to your employer (to fill the position you must resign) a young man or woman with whom you have worked.
7. Request permission of a former employer to use his name as a reference in applying for a new position.

▶ EXERCISE 2   Write the following personal letters:

1. Invite a friend to spend a weekend in your home.
2. Accept an invitation to spend a weekend with a friend.
3. Answer a friend's inquiry about the course in dramatics (or chemical engineering, astronomy, political science, etc.) in your college.
4. Congratulate a friend in another college on his election to some class office (or on any other honor).
5. Introduce a friend to one of your former classmates who lives in a distant city.

Grammatical Terms

35

Consult the following list as needed for explanations of grammatical terms.[1]

Absolute element. A parenthetical word or word group which qualifies a whole clause but which is not linked to it by a conjunction or a relative pronoun.

> *Rain or shine,* the class will have a cookout.
> *Oh,* that door, *I believe,* is locked.
> Fred has not read James Agee's novels, *has he?*

A NOMINATIVE ABSOLUTE is a phrase consisting of a noun or noun substitute followed by a participle (with any complements or modifiers).

> *Jobs being scarce,* competition was keen.

See also **12d(3)**.

Abstract noun. See **Noun.**

Active voice. See **Voice.**

Adjective. A part of speech used to modify (qualify, describe, or limit) a noun or a noun substitute. The adjectives *a, an,* and *the* are often called "noun determiners." See **Articles.**

DESCRIPTIVE ADJECTIVES:

> *cloudy* sky, *good* acting, *greatest* work, *reasonable* prices
> They seem *happier* now. Were your neighbors very *friendly?*

LIMITING ADJECTIVES:

DEMONSTRATIVE	*this* one, *that* map, *these* rods, *those* keys
INDEFINITE	*some* milk, *more* effort, *many* others, *few* pets

---

[1] See the index for grammatical terms not in this list and for further treatment of those listed.

INTERROGATIVE	*Whose* cap is it? *What* ticket? *Which* one?
NUMERICAL	*one* pear, *three* plums, *third* base, *tenth* year
POSSESSIVE	*my* opinion, *its* nest, *their* homes, *our* right
RELATIVE	The boy *whose* dog had died remained silent.

PROPER ADJECTIVES (capitalized) may be either descriptive or limiting, or both: *American* traditions, *Indian* territory, *English* classes.

Note: Nouns may function as adjectives: a *college* student.

See also Section **4, Adjectives and Adverbs.**

Adjective clause. A subordinate clause used as an adjective.

> Velasquez, *whose work affected the French Impressionists,* was a famous Spanish realist. [The adjective clause modifies the noun *Velasquez.*]

Adverb. A part of speech used to modify a word (or word group) other than a noun or pronoun. An adverb may qualify or limit a verb, an adjective, another adverb, a verbal, or even a whole clause. An adverb often indicates time ("are *now* going"), place ("stayed *there*"), manner ("acting *quickly*"), or degree ("*very* eager").

> Mildred owns an *extremely* old clock, which runs *very quietly.* [*Extremely* modifies the adjective *old; quietly* modifies the verb *runs; very* modifies the adverb *quietly.*]
>
> *Naturally,* the villain succeeds at first by *completely* outwitting the hero. [*Naturally* modifies the rest of the sentence, and *completely* modifies the gerund *outwitting.*]

A noun functioning as an adverb is called an *adverbial noun:* "He left *home Monday.*" See also **Conjunctive adverb.**

See also Section **4, Adjectives and Adverbs.**

Adverb clause. A subordinate clause used adverbially. According to meaning, it may be classified as an adverb clause of time, place, manner, cause, purpose, condition, concession, comparison, or result.

> The common mole is valuable *because it eats insects.*
> *Although George Mason is not famous,* his ideas were used in our Bill of Rights.
> Cartoonists make at least eighteen drawings *so that Woody Woodpecker can laugh victoriously.*

Agreement. The correspondence in form of one word with another (for example, a verb with its subject or a pronoun with its antecedent) to indicate person and number. See Section **6, Agreement.**

Antecedent. The name given to a word or group of words to which a pronoun refers.

> This is the *man who* came to the house. [*Man* is the antecedent of the relative pronoun *who*.]

> When *John* and *Mary* came, *they* told us the facts in the case. [*John* and *Mary* are the antecedents of the personal pronoun *they*.]

Appositive. A noun or noun substitute set beside another noun or noun substitute and indentifying or explaining it.

> Dr. Smith, our *dentist,* is visiting England, his native *country*. [*Dentist* is in apposition with *Dr. Smith,* and *country* is in apposition with *England*.]

See also **12d(2).**

Article. The definite article *the* and the indefinite articles *a* and *an* are adjectives. They are often called *determiners* because they indicate that a noun or a noun substitute is to follow.

Auxiliary. A verb helper in a verb phrase: *will* dine, *were* talking, *had* risen, *should be* studying, *ought to* pay. See also Sections **1a** and **7.**

Case. The inflectional form of a noun (*man's*) or pronoun (*he, his, him*) to show such relations as subject (subjective or nominative case—*he*), possession (possessive case—*man's, his*), or object (objective case—*him*). See also **Inflection** and Section **5, Case.**

Clause. A group of words that contains a verb and its subject and is used as a part of a sentence. A clause may be main (independent, principal) or subordinate (dependent).

MAIN (INDEPENDENT, PRINCIPAL) CLAUSE   A main clause can stand by itself as a simple sentence.

> *The moon rose,* and *the stars came out.* [Two main clauses, either of which can stand by itself as a simple sentence]

SUBORDINATE (DEPENDENT) CLAUSE   A subordinate clause cannot stand alone. It is used as a noun, an adjective, or an adverb.

That he will run for office is doubtful. [Noun clause: a subordinate clause used as subject of the sentence]

Collective noun. See **Noun.**

Colloquial. Appropriate for conversation and informal writing rather than for formal writing.

Common noun. See **Noun.**

Comparison. The change in the form of an adjective or adverb to indicate degrees in quality, quantity, or manner. There are three degrees: positive, comparative, and superlative.

Positive	*Comparative*	*Superlative*
good	better	best
high	higher	highest
quickly	more quickly	most quickly

See also **Inflection.**

Complement. A word or words used to complete the sense of the verb, the subject, or the object.

SUBJECT COMPLEMENTS
>The boy is *obedient.* [The predicate adjective *obedient* modifies the subject *boy.*]
>Samuel is a good *child.* [The predicate noun *child* refers to the subject *Samuel.*]

OBJECTS
>William lent *Susan* his *book.* [*Book* is the direct object; *Susan* is the indirect object.]

OBJECT COMPLEMENTS
>He called the man a *hero.* [*Hero* refers to *man,* which is the direct object.]
>Jack painted his garage *blue.* [The adjective *blue* modifies the object *garage.*]

Complete predicate. See **Predicate.**

Complete subject. See **Subject.**

Complex (compound, compound-complex) sentence. See **Sentence.**

Concrete noun. See **Noun.**

Conjugation. A grouping of verb forms to indicate tense, voice, mood, as follows:

CONJUGATION OF THE VERB *TO SEE*
(Principal Parts: *see, saw, seen*)

Active Voice		*Passive Voice*	
Singular	*Plural*	*Singular*	*Plural*

INDICATIVE MOOD

PRESENT TENSE

1. I see	we see	I am seen	we are seen
2. you see	you see	you are seen	you are seen
3. he (she, it) sees	they see	he (she, it) is seen	they are seen

PAST TENSE

1. I saw	we saw	I was seen	we were seen
2. you saw	you saw	you were seen	you were seen
3. he saw	they saw	he was seen	they were seen

FUTURE TENSE

1. I shall see	we shall see	I shall be seen	we shall be seen
2. you will see	you will see	you will be seen	you will be seen
3. he will see	they will see	he will be seen	they will be seen

PRESENT PERFECT TENSE

1. I have seen	we have seen	I have been seen	we have been seen
2. you have seen	you have seen	you have been seen	you have been seen
3. he has seen	they have seen	he has been seen	they have been seen

PAST PERFECT TENSE

1. I had seen	we had seen	I had been seen	we had been seen
2. you had seen	you had seen	you had been seen	you had been seen
3. he had seen	they had seen	he had been seen	they had been seen

FUTURE PERFECT TENSE (seldom used)

1. I shall have seen	we shall have seen	I shall have been seen	we shall have been seen
2. you will have seen	you will have seen	you will have been seen	you will have been seen
3. he will have seen	they will have seen	he will have been seen	they will have been seen

SUBJUNCTIVE MOOD

PRESENT TENSE

Singular that I, you, he see   that I, you, he be seen
Plural that we, you, they see   that we, you, they be seen

PAST TENSE

Singular that I, you, he saw   that I, you, he were seen
Plural that we, you, they saw   that we, you, they were seen

PRESENT PERFECT TENSE

Singular that I, you, he have seen   that I, you, he have been seen
Plural that we, you, they have seen   that we, you, they have been seen

PAST PERFECT TENSE

(Same as the Indicative)

IMPERATIVE MOOD

PRESENT TENSE

see   be seen

Conjunction. A part of speech (often called a *function word*) used to connect words, phrases, or clauses. There are two kinds, coordinating conjunctions and subordinating conjunctions.

COORDINATING CONJUNCTIONS connect words, phrases, and clauses of equal rank: *and, but, or, nor, for,* and sometimes *so* and *yet.*

SUBORDINATING CONJUNCTIONS connect subordinate clauses with main clauses: *if, although, since, in order that, as, because, unless, after, before, until, when, whenever, where, while, wherever,* etc.

Conjunctive adverb. An adverb used to connect or relate main clauses: *however, therefore, nevertheless, hence, then, besides, moreover, thus, otherwise, consequently, accordingly,* etc.

Construction. See Syntax.

Coordinate. Of equal rank. For example, two nouns, two infinitives, or two main clauses.

Correlatives. Coordinating conjunctions used in pairs: *both . . . and, either . . . or, neither . . . nor, not only . . . but also.* See **26c.**

Declension. A grouping of pronoun forms. See **Inflection.**

Demonstrative. See **Adjective** and **Pronoun.**

Dependent clause. See **Clause.**

Descriptive adjective. See **Adjective.**

Determiner. A word such as *a, an,* or *the* which signals the approach of a noun.

Diagraming. An arrangement of words on lines to show relationships within the sentence. Various forms are used. Any form is serviceable if it helps the student to understand the sentence. A diagram is only a means to an end, not an end in itself. The following is a traditional form of diagraming.

THE SENTENCE BASE

SUBJECT—VERB.

The *students* always *cooperated.*

| Students | cooperated |

SUBJECT—VERB—SUBJECT COMPLEMENT.

His *son seems* very *busy.*

| son | seems \ busy |

Was he a skilled *mechanic?*

| he | Was \ mechanic |

SUBJECT—VERB—OBJECT.

One of them *is buying* a *house.*

| One | is buying | house |

SUBJECT—VERB—OBJECT—OBJECT COMPLEMENT.

Should we paint it green?

| we | Should paint | it \ green |

INDIRECT OBJECT

He will not lend *her* a dollar.

| He | will lend | dollar |
\ her

EXPLETIVE

There were no complaints.

There

| complaints | were |

MODIFIERS

Equally important, the suspect *cleverly* evaded *the* questions *of very astute detectives.*

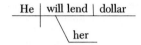

important   [an absolute element]

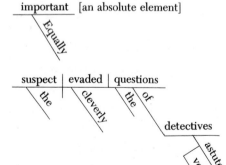

suspect | evaded | questions

detectives

VERBALS

GERUND

Taking pictures is an art.

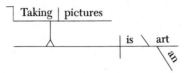

PARTICIPLE

Seeing a rat, she gasped.

INFINITIVES The first thing *to do* is *to call* him.

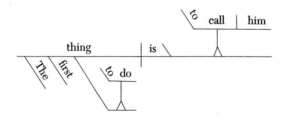

CLAUSES

MAIN The moon rose, and the stars twinkled.

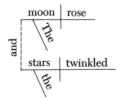

SUBORDINATE

adjective The man *who is honest* should succeed.

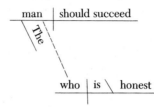

adverb I shall leave the house *after she comes.*

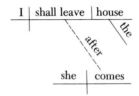

noun *What the newspapers say* may be false.

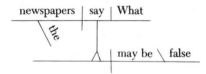

A COMPOUND-COMPLEX SENTENCE

Engines roared overhead, and a bomb fell where we had stood.

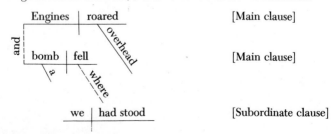

[Main clause]

[Main clause]

[Subordinate clause]

Direct address. A noun or pronoun used parenthetically to direct a speech to a definite person.

>I hope, *Mary,* that you will go. *Mary,* close the door.

Direct object. See **Object.**

Direct quotation. The exact oral or written words of others.

>DIRECT QUOTATION John asked, "Why didn't you join us, Martha?"
>INDIRECT QUOTATION John asked Martha why she had not joined the group.

See also **16a.**

Elliptical elements. Words which are omitted but are clearly understood.

>Mary is prettier than Helen (is pretty).
>Whenever (it is) possible, you should take exercise.

Expletive. *It* or *there* used merely as an introductory word or filler.

>*It* is true that he is not coming.
>*There* were few men present.

Finite verb. A verb or verb phrase that serves as a predicate. Infinitives, participles, and gerunds are **verbals,** not finite verbs.

Form change. See **Inflection.**

Function words. Words (such as prepositions, conjunctions, and articles) which indicate the grammatical relationship of the words connected or signaled.

Gerund. See **Verbals.**

Gerund phrase. See **Phrase.**

Idiom. An expression in good use that is peculiar to a language. (Idioms sometimes violate established rules of grammar but are nevertheless sanctioned by usage.)

>I have known him for *many a year.*
>He *gave himself away* by smiling.

Imperative. See **Mood.**

Indefinite pronoun. See **Pronoun.**

Independent clause (Main clause, principal clause). See **Clause.**

Independent element. See **Absolute element.**

Indicative. See **Mood.**

Indirect object. See **Object.**

Indirect quotation. See **Direct quotation.**

Infinitive. See **Verbals.**

Infinitive phrase. See **Phrase.**

Inflection. A change in the form of a word to show a change in meaning or in grammatical relationship to some other word or group of words. The inflection of nouns and pronouns is called **declension;** the inflection of verbs, **conjugation;** that of adjectives and adverbs, **comparison.**

INFLECTIONS OF VERBS (indicating tense, person, mood)
look, looking, looks, looked
drink, drinking, drinks, drank, drunk
know, knowing, knows, knew, known
be, being, am, is, are, was, were, been

INFLECTIONS OF NOUNS (indicating number, case)
dog, dogs; dog's, dogs'
child, children; child's, children's

INFLECTIONS OF PRONOUNS (indicating case, person, number)

I, me, my, mine   we, us, our, ours
who, whom, whose   someone, someone's
This is old. *These* are old. *That* is older than *those.*

INFLECTIONS OF MODIFIERS (indicating comparison, number)

fast, faster, fastest   bad, worse, worst
attractive, more attractive, most attractive
this letter, *these* letters, *that* letter, *those* letters

Intensive pronoun. See **Pronoun.**

Interjection. A part of speech used for simple exclamations: *Oh! Ouch! Whew!* When used in sentences, interjections are set off by commas. See **Absolute elements.**

Interrogative pronoun. See **Pronoun.**

Intransitive verb. See **Verb**.

Irregular verb (Strong verb). A verb that forms its principal parts in various ways *other than* by the addition of *-ed*, *-d*, or *-t*. See also **Inflection** and Section **7**.

Vowel changes	swim, swam, swum
Addition of -en	beat, beat, beaten
No change	set, set, set

Limiting adjective. See **Adjective**.

Linking verb. A verb which relates the subject to the subject complement. Words commonly used as linking verbs are *become, seem, appear, feel, taste, smell,* and parts of the verb *be*.

The tires *look* good.	The surface *feels* rough.
Did she *become* a nurse?	What *could* that *be?*

Main clause (Independent clause, principal clause). See **Clause**.

Mode. See **Mood**.

Modifier. Any word, phrase, or clause functioning as an adjective or an adverb.

Modify. To describe or qualify the meaning of a word or group of words.

> A *very old* man hobbled *slowly along the road.* [A and *old* modify *man; very* modifies *old; slowly* and *along the road* modify *hobbled; the* modifies *road.*]

Mood (Mode). The form of the verb that is used to indicate the manner in which the action or state is conceived. English has indicative, imperative, and subjunctive moods. See Section **7**.

The INDICATIVE MOOD states a fact or asks a question.

You *have* a good mind.	*Have* you any ideas?
Mother *is* here.	*Is* Mother here?

The IMPERATIVE MOOD gives a command, makes a request, or gives directions.

Be careful.	*Watch* your step, please.
Take the next street on the right.	

The SUBJUNCTIVE MOOD is used in stating conditions contrary to fact and in certain idiomatic expressions. See **7c**.

I wish Mother *were* here.
If I *had* my way, you would not go.

Nominative. See **Case**.

Nominative absolute. See **Absolute element**.

Nominative of address. See **Direct address**.

Nonrestrictive modifier. A nonessential modifier. A parenthetical phrase or clause which does not identify the person or thing modified. See **12d**.

The airplane, *now being manufactured in large numbers,* is of immense commercial value. [Phrase]
The airplane, *which is now being manufactured in large numbers,* is of immense commercial value. [Clause]

See also **Restrictive modifier**.

Noun. A part of speech (the name of a person, place, thing, quality, or action: *Mary, America, apples, courage, departure*) that usually changes form to make the possessive case and the plural, as in *man, man's, men*. See also **Inflection**.

Types of nouns

COMMON   a *man,* the *cities,* some *trout* [General classes]
PROPER   *Mr. Ford,* in *Boston,* the *Forum* [Capitalized specifics]
COLLECTIVE   a *flock,* the *jury,* my *family* [Groups—singular in form but singular or plural in meaning]
CONCRETE   an *apple,* the *radio,* his *face,* two *trees* [Tangibles]
ABSTRACT   *ambition, jealousy, pity, hatred* [Qualities, concepts]

Functions of nouns

SUBJECT OF VERB OR VERBAL *Dogs* barked. I want *Ed* to be here.
OBJECT OF VERB, VERBAL, OR PREPOSITION Someone opened the *door* to let the *dog* into the *house.*
SUBJECT COMPLEMENT (PREDICATE NOUN)   She is a *nurse.*
APPOSITIVE   Moses, a *prophet,* saw the promised land.
DIRECT ADDRESS   What do you think, *Angela?*
OBJECT COMPLEMENT   They named him *Jonathan.*

Noun clause. A subordinate clause used as a noun.

> *Whoever comes* will be welcome. [Subject]
> I hope *that he will recover.* [Direct object]
> This is *what you need.* [Subject complement]
> Spend it for *whatever seems best.* [Object of preposition]

Noun substitute. A pronoun or any group of words (especially a gerund phrase, an infinitive phrase, or a noun clause) functioning as a noun. See also **Substantive.**

Number. The change in the form of a word (e.g., noun, pronoun, etc.) to designate one (*singular*) or more than one (*plural*). See also **Inflection** and Section **6.**

Object. A noun or noun substitute governed by a transitive active verb, by a verbal, or by a preposition.

DIRECT OBJECT   Any noun or noun substitute that answers the question *What?* or *Whom?* after a transitive active verb. A direct object frequently receives, or is in some way affected by, the action of the verb.

> William raked *leaves.*   *What* did he say?
> The Andersons do not know *where we live.*

A direct object may be converted to a subject with a passive verb. See **Voice.**

OBJECT OF A VERBAL   Any noun or its equivalent that follows and completes the meaning of a verbal.

> Washing a *car* takes time. He likes to wear a *tie.*

INDIRECT OBJECT   Any noun or noun substitute that states *to whom* or *for whom* (or *to what* or *for what*) something is done. An indirect object ordinarily precedes a direct object.

> He bought *her* a watch.
> I gave the *painting* a second coat of varnish.

It is usually possible to substitute for the indirect object a prepositional phrase with *to* or *for.*

> He bought a watch *for her.*

OBJECT OF PREPOSITION   Any noun or noun substitute which a preposition relates to another word or word group.

Cedars grow tall in these *hills*. [Object of *in*]
What am I responsible for? [Object of *for*]

Object complement. See **Complement.**

Objective. See **Case.**

Participial phrase. See **Phrase.**

Participle. See **Verbals.**

Parts of speech. The eight classes into which most grammarians group words according to their form changes, their positions, their meaning, and their uses in the sentence: *verb, noun, pronoun, adjective, adverb, conjunction, preposition,* and *interjection.* Each of these is discussed separately in this section. It is important to note that *part of speech* is determined by function. The same word is often used as several different parts of speech. See **1c.**

Passive voice. See **Voice.**

Person. Changes in the form of verbs and pronouns which indicate whether a person is speaking (first person), is spoken to (second person), or is spoken about (third person).

FIRST PERSON   *I* see the boy.
SECOND PERSON   Can *you* see the boy?
THIRD PERSON   *He* sees the boy.

Personal pronoun. See **Pronoun.**

Phrase. A group of related words not having a subject and a predicate and functioning as a single part of speech.

VERB   Don *will be calling* soon.
PREPOSITIONAL   A mower is *in the garage.* [Adverb]
   The man *at the door* smiled. [Adjective]
PARTICIPIAL   *Rearing its head,* the snake hissed.
GERUND   *Building a patio* can be fun.
INFINITIVE   Mrs. Raines went *to buy groceries.* [Adverb]

See also **1d.**

Predicate. The part of the sentence comprising what is said about the subject. The **Complete predicate** consists of the verb (the **Simple predicate**) along with its complements and modifiers.

He *runs* through the house. [*Runs* is the simple predicate; *runs through the house* is the complete predicate.]

Predicate adjective, predicate complement, predicate nominative, predicate noun, predicate objective. See **Complement.**

Preposition. A part of speech (often called a *function word*) that is used to show the relation of a noun or noun-equivalent (the *object of the preposition*) to some other word in the sentence.

The telephone is *in* the hall. [The preposition *in* shows the relationship of its object *hall* to the verb *is*.]
Across, after, at, before, between, by, for, from, in, of, on, over, to, under, with, up, and *near* are commonly used as prepositions.

See also **1c.**

Prepositional phrase. See **Phrase.**

Principal clause (Main clause, independent clause). See **Clause.**

Principal parts. The forms of any verb from which the various tenses are derived: (1) present stem (infinitive), (2) past tense, and (3) past participle.

see	saw	seen
take	took	taken
love	loved	loved

See also Section **7.**

Progressive verb. A form of the verb (ending in *-ing* and accompanied by a part of the auxiliary *be*) used to express continuous action or state of being.

Sally *was singing* a cowboy ballad.
I *have been playing* tennis all afternoon.

See also Section. **7.**

Pronoun. A part of speech (one of a special group of words) used as a noun substitute.

PERSONAL	*You* and *I* will see *him.*
INTERROGATIVE	*Who* is he? *Which* do you prefer? *What* is it?
RELATIVE	The boy *who* served us is the one *that* I tipped.
DEMONSTRATIVE	*This* is better than *that.*

INDEFINITE	*Each* of you should help *someone.*
RECIPROCAL	Help *each other.* They like *one another.*
REFLEXIVE	Carl blames *himself.* Did you hurt *yourself?*
INTENSIVE	We need a vacation *ourselves.* I *myself* saw it.

See also **Inflection** and Sections **5** and **7.**

Proper adjective. An adjective formed from a proper noun, as *Spanish* from *Spain.*

Proper noun. See **Noun.**

Quotation. See **Direct quotation.**

Reciprocal pronoun. See **Pronoun.**

Reflexive pronoun. See **Pronoun.**

Regular verb (Weak verb). Any verb that forms its principal parts by adding *-ed, -d,* or *-t* to the infinitive: *love, loved, loved; weep, wept, wept.*

Relative pronoun. See **Pronoun.**

Restrictive modifier. An essential modifier. A phrase or clause which identifies the word modified and which therefore cannot be omitted without changing the essential meaning of the sentence.

    Any girl *who talks incessantly* is a bore.

See also **Nonrestrictive modifier.**

Sentence. An independent unit of expression. A grammatically complete sentence (with the exception of the imperative) has at least one subject and one predicate. (For the grammatically incomplete sentence, see page 26.) Sentences are classified structurally as (1) simple, (2) compound, (3) complex, or (4) compound-complex. See **1e.**

SIMPLE	She may be a famous actress someday. [One main clause]
COMPOUND	He lost the game, but he had done his best. [Two main clauses]
COMPLEX	When the whistle blew, the parade began. [One subordinate clause and one main clause]
COMPOUND-COMPLEX	The work stops when it rains, but the tools are kept in readiness. [Two main clauses and one subordinate clause]

See the ten patterns of simple sentences on pages 7–8.

See also **Diagraming**.

Simple predicate. See **Predicate**.

Simple sentence. See **Sentence**.

Simple subject. See **Subject**.

Strong verb. See **Irregular verb**.

Subject. A noun or a noun substitute about which something is asserted or asked. One of the two basic grammatical divisions of a sentence, the subject usually precedes the predicate and answers the question *Who?* or *What?* in front of the predicate. (Imperative sentences do not have stated subjects.) The subject and the words associated with it make up the **Complete subject**.

> The *dog* at the front of the house barked at the car. [*Dog* is the **Simple subject**; *the dog at the front of the house* is the complete subject.]

Subjective. See **Case**.

Subject complement. See **Complement**.

Subjunctive. See **Mood**.

Subordinate clause. A dependent clause. See **Clause**.

Substantive. Any word or group of words used as a noun. Substantives may be nouns, pronouns, phrases (especially gerund or infinitive phrases), or noun clauses. See **Noun substitute**.

Syntax (Construction). Sentence structure. The grammatical functions of words, phrases, clauses.

Tense. The time of occurrence indicated by the form of the verb. See **Inflection** and Section **7**.

Transitive. See **Verb**.

Verb. A predicator used to make a statement, ask a question, or to give a command or direction. Inflections indicate tense (and, in the present tense, a third-person singular subject) and mood. See **Inflection, Voice,** and Section **7**.

TRANSITIVE VERB   A verb that requires an object to complete its meaning. Transitive verbs can usually be changed from active to passive voice. See **Object** and **Voice**.

> The general *laid* a wreath on the tomb.

INTRANSITIVE VERB   A verb, such as *go* or *sit*, that does not have an object to complete its meaning, is intransitive. Linking verbs, which take subject complements, are intransitive.

> I *was* in New York last Christmas.
> She *has been waiting* patiently for hours.

The same verb may be transitive in one sentence and intransitive in another.

TRANSITIVE   Lydia *reads* novels. [Object: *novels*]
INTRANSITIVE   Lydia *reads* well. [No object]

Verb equivalent (Verb-adverb combination) A word group equal in meaning to a single-word verb.

> The parade *held up* [stopped] traffic.
> Please *turn on* [start] the motor.

Verb phrase. See Phrase.

Verbals. Verb forms used as nouns, adjectives, or adverbs. The three verbals are gerunds, participles, and infinitives. Like verbs, verbals may take objects, complements, and modifiers. Infinitives may have subjects.

GERUND   Verb form used as a noun and always ending in *-ing*.

> ***Watching*** *the new color television* kept our guests entertained. [Subject of *kept*]
> By ***swimming*** *rapidly*, he escaped. [Object of preposition *by*]

PARTICIPLE   Verb form used as an adjective. Endings of participles vary—for instance, *-ing, -ed, -t, -en*.

> ***Swimming*** *rapidly*, he soon reached the dock. [*Swimming* modifies *he*.]
> ***Confused*** *by improperly* ***marked*** *streets*, they lost their way. [*Confused* modifies *they*; *marked* modifies *streets*.]

INFINITIVE   Verb form used chiefly as a noun, less frequently as an adjective or an adverb. The infinitive is usually made up of *to* plus a verb form but after such verbs as *let, make,* and *dare* the *to* may be omitted.

> Hal wanted *to open the present.* [Object of *wanted*]
> The noise made *the baby cry.* [*Baby* is subject of the infinitive *cry;* the infinitive phrase is object of *made.*]
> I have work *to do.* [*To do* is adjective modifying *work.*]
> *To tell the truth,* I never eat breakfast. [The infinitive phrase modifies the rest of the sentence and is therefore used as an adverb.]

Voice. Only verbs have voice. A verb having a direct object is in the active voice. When the direct object is converted to a subject, as is done in the sentences below, the verb is in the passive voice. A passive verb is always a verb phrase containing a part of the verb *be* as an auxiliary plus a past participle. The subject of an active verb acts. The subject of a passive verb does not act.

ACTIVE VOICE	PASSIVE VOICE
Priscilla *chose* John.	John *was chosen* by Priscilla.
Ed *must learn* that.	That *must be learned.*

Weak verb. See **Regular verb.**

Index

[Numbers in **boldface** refer to rules; other numbers refer to pages. A colon is used after each boldface number to indicate that the following pages refer to the rule or the part of the rule concerned. An *ex* indicates that appropriate drill exercises are included. The **boldface** rule is given in detail—**9a(4)** or **20a(3)**, for example—in order to pinpoint a needed correction, but a less detailed reference (**9** or **9a**) will usually be sufficient for the student.]

a

A, an, **19i:** 204

A half a, for *a half* or *half a,* **19i:** 213

Abbreviations, **11:** 103–06 *ex*
capitalization of, **9a(4):** 92
contractions, with apostrophe, **15c:** 144
first names, spelled out, **11e:** 104
from Latin, in italics, **33e(1):** 412
in footnotes, **11e:** 105, **33e(1):** 412
misused in letters, **34a:** 437
names of organizations, permissible abbreviations of, **11:** 105
names of states, months, days of week, **11b:** 104
parts of proper names, **11c:** 104
period after, **17a:** 155
titles, **11a:** 103
verified in dictionary, **11:** 105
volume, chapter, page, **11d:** 104
when permissible, **11:** 105
with dates or numerals, when permissible, **11:** 105

Absolute element, defined, 441

Absolute phrase
commas with, **12d(3):** 126

defined, 441

Abstract and general words, **20a(3):** 228–31 *ex*

Abstract noun, defined, 454

Accent, shown in the dictionary, 187

Accept, except **19i:** 204

Accidentally, incidentally, **19i:** 205

Accordingly, as a conjunctive adverb, **14a:** 135

Accusative case. *See* Objective case.

Acknowledgment of borrowed material, in footnotes, 406–07 *ex*

Active voice
defined, 461
for emphasis, **29d:** 305–06 *ex*

Ad, for *advertisement,* **19i:** 205

Address of a letter, **34a:** 433–36
consistency, **34a(2):** 435
inside address, **34a(2):** 435
model addressed envelope, **34:** 436
one of six essential parts, **34a:** 433
shown in model letter, **34a:** 434

C

Inflection (*Cont.*)
 of nouns and pronouns, 47
 of verbs, 66–69, 445–46
 See also Form changes.
Informal, or colloquial. *See* Levels of usage.
Ingenious, ingenuous, **19i:** 215
Initial words, capitalization of, **9e:** 94
Insertions, in manuscript, **8d(1):** 86
Inside address, of letter, **34a(2):** 435
Inside of, for *within,* **19i:** 215
Instead, as a conjunctive adverb, **14a:** 135
Intensive pronouns, 49, **19i:** 217, 457–58
Inter-, prefix, 188
Interjections
 commas with, **12d(3):** 126
 defined, 13, 452
 exclamation point with, **17c:** 157–59 *ex*
Interpolation in quotation, in brackets, **17g:** 164–65 *ex*
Interrogative pronouns, defined, 457
Interrogative sentence, for variety, **30e:** 317 *ex*
Interrupters, set off by commas, **12d:** 119–26 *ex*
Interrupters, set off by dashes, **17e(3):** 163
Into, in, **19i:** 214
Intransitive verb, defined, 460
Inversion, for emphasis, **29f:** 307 *ex*
Invitations, formal, **34c:** 439
Invite, for *invitation,* **19i:** 215
Irregardless, for *regardless,* **19i:** 215
Irregular (strong) verb, defined, 453

Is when, is where, **23c(2):** 259–60 *ex*
It, expletive, followed by singular verb, **6a(4):** 56
Italics, **10:** 98–102 *ex*
 for emphasis, to be used rarely, **10e:** 101–02 *ex*
 for foreign words and their abbreviations, **10b:** 99–100 *ex*
 for Latin abbreviations, 412
 for names of ships, **10c:** 100
 for titles of publications, **10a:** 98–99 *ex*
 for titles of works of art, **10c:** 100
 for words, etc., spoken of as such, **10d:** 100
 indication of, by underlining, 98
 overuse of, for emphasis, **10e:** 101–02 *ex*
It is me, **5f:** 52–53 *ex*
It's, its, **15b:** 144, **19i:** 215

j

Jargon, **19c:** 196–97
Joint possesssion, **15a(4):** 143–44 *ex*
Just, for *truly, very,* **19i:** 215
Just, position of, **25a(1):** 271 *ex*

k

Kind, sort, with *that* or *this,* **19i:** 215
Kind of, sort of, for *rather,* **19i:** 215
Kind of a, sort of a, **19i:** 215

l

Lady, for *woman,* **19i:** 212
Language, development of our, 188–91 *ex*
Larger elements, **31–34:** 321–440 *ex*
Later, latter, **19i:** 216

r

Raise, rise, **19i:** 219–20

Reading for library paper, **33b:** 394–400

Real, for *very,* **19i:** 219

Reason is because, **19i:** 219

Reciprocal pronouns, defined, 457–58

Reckon, for *think,* **19i:** 219

Record of errors, **8e:** 90

Redundancy. *See* Wordiness.

Reference books, **33b(3):** 397–400

atlases and gazetteers, 399

biography, 399–400

general dictionaries, 397

general encyclopedias, 398

Guide to, 397

literature and mythology, 400

special dictionaries, 397–98

special encyclopedias, 398–99

yearbooks, for current events, 399

Reference of pronouns, **28:** 292–97 *ex*

agreement with antecedent, **6b:** 61–65 *ex*

ambiguous (two possible antecedents), **28a:** 292–93

broad (antecedent not expressed), **28c:** 294–95

indefinite *it, you, they,* **28c(3):** 295

remote (antecedent too far away or in subordinate position), **28b:** 293–94

repetition causing confusion, **28d:** 295–97 *ex*

to a general idea, **28c(1):** 294

to title of a theme, **28b:** 293–94

Reference words, for paragraph coherence, **31b(4):** 334–35 *ex*

Reflexive pronouns, 49, **19i:** 217, 457–58

Regular (weak) verb, defined, 458

Related ideas, expressed in parallel structure, **26:** 278–85 *ex*

Relative pronouns, defined, 457

Remote reference of pronouns, **28b:** 293–94

Repetition

careless, **21c:** 244–47 *ex*

for clearer parallelism, **26b:** 282–83 *ex*

for emphasis, **29e:** 306–07 *ex*

for paragraph coherence, **31b(3):** 333–34 *ex,* **31b(5):** 335–36 *ex*

Report type of library paper, **33a:** 394 *ex*

Reputable use. *See* Good use.

Research paper. *See* Library paper.

Respectfully, respectively, **19i:** 219

Restrictive and nonrestrictive modifiers

defined, 454, 458

use of the comma with, **12d(1):** 119–22 *ex*

Reverend, correct use of, **19i:** 219

Revision of student papers, **8d:** 85–89

See also Manuscript revision.

Right along, for *continuously,* **19i:** 219

Rise, raise, **19i:** 219–20

Root, distinguished from prefix in spelling, **18c:** 172

Rough draft, of library paper, **33e(2):** 412–13

Rules for spelling, **18:** 172–75 *ex*

Run-together sentences, **3:** 34–39 *ex*

s

-s and *-es,* plurals in, **18d(4):** 174–75 *ex*

Said, for *this* or *that,* **19i:** 220

Salutation, of letter, **34a(3):** 435–36